REGULATING KNOWLEDGE IN AN ENTANGLED WORLD

Regulating Knowledge in an Entangled World uses case studies from the sixteenth to the eighteenth centuries to study knowledge transfer in early modern knowledge societies.

In the early modern period the scale, intensity, and reach of exchange exploded. This volume develops a historicised understanding of knowledge transfer to shed new light on these fundamental changes. By looking at the preconditions of knowledge transfer, it shifts the focus from the objects circulating to the interactions by which they circulate and the way actors cement their relations. The novelty of this approach shows how rules and regulations were enablers of knowledge circulation, rather than impediments. The chapters identify changing patterns of knowledge transfer in cases such as sixteenth-century Venice, the Spanish Empire in the Americas, continental Habsburg, early seventeenth-century Dutch at sea, and the Offices of the Catholic Church. Through the perspective of 'regulating', this volume advances the historiography of knowledge circulation by forging a new combination of histories of circulation and of institutions.

By bringing together historians from intellectual history, economic history, book history, the history of science, religion, art, and material culture, this volume is useful for students and scholars interested in early modern knowledge societies and changing patterns of knowledge transfer.

Fokko Jan Dijksterhuis is Associate Professor of History of Science and Technology at the University of Twente and Louise Thijssen-Schoute Professor of Early Modern History of Knowledge at Free University, Amsterdam. He studies early modern knowledge cultures, in particular relating to the mathematical sciences. He co-edited *Locations of Knowledge in Dutch Contexts* (2019) and *Rethinking Stevin Rethinking* (2021).

Knowledge Societies in History

Series Editors: Sven Dupré, Utrecht University and University of Amsterdam, Netherlands, and Wijnand Mijnhardt, Utrecht University, Netherlands.

The expertise of the history of knowledge is essential in tackling the issues and concerns surrounding present-day global knowledge society. Books in this series historicize and critically engage with the concept of knowledge society, with conceptual and methodological contributions enabling the historian to analyse and compare the origins, formation, and development of knowledge societies.

In this series:

Knowledge and the Early Modern City
A History of Entanglements
Edited by Bert De Munck & Antonella Romano

Histories of Knowledge in Postwar Scandinavia
Actors, Arenas, and Aspirations
Edited by Johan Östling, Niklas Olsen and David Larsson Heidenblad

Early Modern Knowledge Societies as Affective Economies
Edited by Inger Leemans and Anne Goldgar

Threatened Knowledge
Practices of Knowing and Ignoring from the Middle Ages
to the Twentieth Century
Edited by Renate Dürr

Regulating Knowledge in an Entangled World
Edited by Fokko Jan Dijksterhuis

For more information about this series, please visit: https://www.routledge.com/Knowledge-Societies-in-History/book-series/KSHIS

REGULATING KNOWLEDGE IN AN ENTANGLED WORLD

Edited by Fokko Jan Dijksterhuis

LONDON AND NEW YORK

Cover image: Page 141 from 'Il Decameron... Ricorretto in Roma...', 1573 (print) © British Library Board. All Rights Reserved / Bridgeman Images

First published 2023
by Routledge
4 Park Square, Milton Park, Abingdon, Oxon OX14 4RN

and by Routledge
605 Third Avenue, New York, NY 10158

Routledge is an imprint of the Taylor & Francis Group, an informa business

© 2023 selection and editorial matter, Fokko Jan Dijksterhuis; individual chapters, the contributors

The right of Fokko Jan Dijksterhuis to be identified as the author of the editorial material, and of the authors for their individual chapters, has been asserted in accordance with sections 77 and 78 of the Copyright, Designs and Patents Act 1988.

All rights reserved. No part of this book may be reprinted or reproduced or utilised in any form or by any electronic, mechanical, or other means, now known or hereafter invented, including photocopying and recording, or in any information storage or retrieval system, without permission in writing from the publishers.

Trademark notice: Product or corporate names may be trademarks or registered trademarks, and are used only for identification and explanation without intent to infringe.

British Library Cataloguing-in-Publication Data
A catalogue record for this book is available from the British Library

Library of Congress Cataloging-in-Publication Data
Names: Dijksterhuis, Fokko Jan, editor.
Title: Regulating knowledge in an entangled world / edited by Fokko Jan Dijksterhuis.
Description: Abingdon, Oxon ; New York, NY : Routledge, 2023. | Series: Knowledge societies in history | Includes bibliographical references and index.
Identifiers: LCCN 2022023010 (print) | LCCN 2022023011 (ebook) | ISBN 9780367234522 (hbk) | ISBN 9780367233242 (pbk) | ISBN 9780429279928 (ebk)
Subjects: LCSH: Censorship—Europe—History—Case studies. | Knowledge management—Europe—History—Case studies. | Information society—Europe—History—Case studies. | Information behavior—Europe—History—Case studies.
Classification: LCC Z658.E85 R44 2023 (print) | LCC Z658.E85 (ebook) | DDC 363.31094—dc23/eng/20220805
LC record available at https://lccn.loc.gov/2022023010
LC ebook record available at https://lccn.loc.gov/2022023011

ISBN: 978-0-367-23452-2 (hbk)
ISBN: 978-0-367-23324-2 (pbk)
ISBN: 978-0-429-27992-8 (ebk)

DOI: 10.4324/9780429279928

Typeset in Bembo
by codeMantra

CONTENTS

List of figures   *vii*
List of tables   *ix*
List of contributors   *xi*
Acknowledgements   *xiii*

Introduction: Regulating Knowledge: Rules as Enablers   1
Fokko Jan Dijksterhuis

PART 1
Labelling   21

1 Guidelines for Reading: Medieval *censura* and
 Roman Censorship   23
 Irene van Renswoude

2 Regulating *Dangerous Knowledge*: John Lockman's
 (1698–1771) Enlightened Readings of Jesuit Letters   44
 Renate Dürr

PART 2
Validating   69

3 Validating Linguistic Knowledge of Amerindian Languages   71
 Werner Thomas

4 Regulating the Form: How Manuscript Newsletters
  Influenced the Standards for Dutch Printed Newspapers
  (c. 1580–1630) 92
  Renate Pieper

5 Lost in Regulation: The Hybrid Stage of Trade Knowledge 107
  Ida Nijenhuis

PART 3
Instructing 127

6 Instructing Trade and War: Regulating Knowledge and
  People on Faraway Dutch Voyages ca. 1600 129
  Djoeke van Netten

7 Regulating the Transfer of Secret Knowledge in
  Renaissance Venice: A Form of Early Modern Management 149
  Ioanna Iordanou

PART 4
Disciplining 167

8 Risking Private Ventures: The Instructive Failure of a
  Well-Traveled Artist, Cornelis de Bruyn 169
  Harold J. Cook

9 On Censors and Booksellers: Curial Elites and the
  Regulation of Roman Book Trade in the
  Seventeenth Century 193
  Andreea Badea

10 Regulating the Exchange of Knowledge: Invoking the
   'Republic of Letters' as a Speech Act 211
   Dirk van Miert

Index *241*

FIGURES

8.1 Three views of Palmyra. Top, from *Philosophical Transactions*, 19 (1695), p. 129; middle, Hofsted van Essen's oil on wood panel, Allard Pierson Museum, Amsterdam; bottom, Cornelis de Bruyn, *Reizen I*, p. 335, with base of fallen column (item G) highlighted 172
8.2 Herbert de Jager's portrayal of Persepolis in *Philosophical Transactions*, 18 (1694), p. 117. Gate of All Nations depicted on right 175
8.3 Cornelis de Bruyn, first view of Persepolis from *Reizen II* 178
8.4 Cornelis de Bruyn, two monuments on either side of Gate of All Nations, *Reizen II*, plates 122 and 123 181
8.5 Jean Chardin, two monuments on either side of Gate of All Nations, *Voyages*, vol. 3, plate LVI 182
8.6 Kaempfer, two monuments on either side of Gate of All Nations, *Amoenitatum Exoticarum*, Fasciculus II, p. 337 183
8.7 De Bruyn, bas-relief, *Reizen II*, plate 142 184

TABLES

10.1 Search terms and hits 215

CONTRIBUTORS

Andreea Badea is Researcher in Early Modern History at Goethe University, Frankfurt am Main. She has published on the history of knowledge, historiography, early modern bureaucracy, and on Confessionalism and religious dissent. She co-edited *Catholic Missionaries in Early Modern Asia* (2019) and *Making Truth in Early Modern Catholicism* (2021).

Harold J. Cook is John F. Nickoll Professor of History at Brown University and author of *Matters of Exchange: Commerce, Medicine and Science in the Dutch Golden Age* (2007). Among his chief research interests are processes of translation v. impersonal and commensurable sameness.

Fokko Jan Dijksterhuis is Associate Professor of History of Science and Technology at the University of Twente and Louise Thijssen-Schoute Professor of Early Modern History of Knowledge at Free University, Amsterdam. He studies early modern knowledge cultures, in particular relating to the mathematical sciences. He co-edited *Locations of Knowledge in Dutch Contexts* (2019) and *Rethinking Stevin Rethinking* (2021).

Renate Dürr is Professor of Early Modern History at the University of Tübingen. Her research focuses on Jesuit missions within the context of global history and the history of knowledge. Together with Ulrike Strasser (San Diego), she is currently writing a monograph on 'De-centering the Enlightenment: Global Knowledge, Emotions, and Jesuit Practices in a German *Cultural Encyclopedia*'.

Ioanna Iordanou is Reader in Human Resource Management at Oxford Brookes Business School (UK) and an Honorary Research Fellow at the Centre for the Study of the Renaissance (University of Warwick, UK). She is the author of *Venice's Secret Service: Organizing Intelligence in the Renaissance* (2019), which was shortlisted for the Royal Historical Society's Gladstone Prize 2020. She's an organisational historian, studying the development of organisational entities and managerial practices in the early modern period.

Dirk van Miert is Director of the *Huygens Institute for the History and Culture of the Netherlands* (Royal Netherlands Academy of Arts and Sciences) and Associate Professor of Early Modern Cultural History at Utrecht University. He was co-editor of *The Correspondence of Joseph Justus Scaliger* (2012) and author of *The Emancipation of Biblical Criticism in the Dutch Republic, 1590–1670* (2018). He is PI of the ERC Consolidator project *SKILLNET: Sharing Knowledge in Learned and Literary NETworks: The Republic of Letters as a Pan-European Knowledge Society* (2017–2022).

Djoeke van Netten is Senior Lecturer of Early Modern History at the University of Amsterdam. Her research is at the crossroads of the history of knowledge, maritime history, and the history of print. She publishes on Blaeu and other publishers, secrecy, astronomy, cartography, and navigation.

Ida Nijenhuis has published internationally on the contribution of early modern Dutch authors to transnational debates on commerce, agriculture, and republicanism. She co-edited *Information and Power in History. Towards a Global Approach* (Routledge, 2020) and is presently working on a monograph on the history of Dutch commercial republicanism.

Renate Pieper is Professor of Economic and Social History at Graz University (Austria). Her work is focused on economic and cultural history of the Spanish Empire and its connection to the Casa de Austria. She is co-editor of *Mining, Money and Markets in the Early Modern Atlantic: Digital Approaches and New Perspectives* (2019).

Irene van Renswoude is Professor of Medieval Manuscripts and Cultural History at the Department of Book History of Amsterdam University, and Researcher at the Department of Knowledge and Art Practices of research institute Huygens ING. She has published on the rhetoric of free speech, cultures of debate, and the art of reasoning, and is currently working on anonymous knowledge and practices of censorship in medieval manuscripts.

Werner Thomas is Professor of Spanish and Spanish American History at KU Leuven. He publishes on Protestantism in Spain and the relations between the Netherlands and the Spanish Empire. His research projects include the circulation of Flemish prints in the Spanish Empire, translation in the Netherlands, and early modern descriptions of America's indigenous languages.

ACKNOWLEDGEMENTS

This book is produced in the broader context of the project *Creating a Knowledge Society in a Globalizing World (1450–1800)*, resulting from a collaboration between the Descartes Centre for the History and Philosophy of the Sciences and the Humanities (University of Utrecht), the Max Planck Institute for the History of Science, and the Netherlands Institute for Advanced Study in the Humanities and Social Sciences (NIAS – KNAW). We thank the initiators and principal investigators of the project Sven Dupré (University of Utrecht and University of Amsterdam) and Wijnand Mijnhardt (University of Utrecht) for giving us the opportunity to start a working group on 'Transfer of Knowledge' and for their intellectual and practical support in the subsequent process. We have also very much enjoyed working and discussing our plans with the PI's of the other working groups of *Creating a Knowledge Society in a Globalizing World*: Bert De Munck, Inger Leemans, Thijs Weststeijn, and Marieke Hendriksen.

The historiographical concept of the project and the arrangement of the individual contributions have developed in close collaboration of the author team. The historiographical approach to 'knowledge transfer' was sketched in a preparatory meeting in the summer of 2017. The team elaborated the concept of the volume during an intensive research stay at the Netherlands Institute for Advanced Study (NIAS) of the Royal Academy of the Netherlands (KNAW) in the spring of 2018. The concept and the outline of the volume was finalised in a reading session a year later. Also part of the team were Harro Maas (Lausanne) and Iris van der Linden (Amsterdam). We thank them for their participation and inspiration. We sincerely thank the staff of the NIAS for hosting our theme group, in particular director Jan Willem Duyvendak. The NIAS provided an extremely stimulating research environment that has fostered the team work enormously. We hope that this volume will reflect the enthusiasm and engagement with which we have worked on this project.

Fokko Jan Dijksterhuis. February 2022

INTRODUCTION

Regulating Knowledge: Rules as Enablers

Fokko Jan Dijksterhuis

Transfer of knowledge is considered vital to knowledge societies. Transfer makes knowledge into what it is: if it is not shared it is not knowledge. With the new media of the twenty-first century, impediments to sharing knowledge seem to have vanished. The internet provides unlimited access to information that can be produced and presented by everyone. Yet, the massive amount of readily available knowledge has created its own problems of sifting wheat from chaff. It is increasingly difficult to single out the reliable and valuable in the overload of information. Fake news and trolling seem to spread much more easily than truth, facts and reason; traditional institutions of trust are systematically undermined. Zooming out a bit, it is institutions that were established with the rise of modern society that have become adrift, like science and mass media.[1]

Our early twenty-first-century situation is not unlike the challenges of the early modern period. In those days too, knowledge institutions were under pressure. The fragmentation of religion and the rise of new conceptions of knowledge unsettled understandings of truth; the printing revolution and the emancipation of *idiotae*[2] created an overload of information; new knowledge from exotic places challenged existing frameworks of learning. There was a rapidly growing body of knowledge and it was increasingly accessible, but it was also becoming ever more difficult to find out what to believe and who to trust.[3] This is not to say that uncertainty about the quality of knowledge did not exist in the Middle Ages – or in modern society for that matter. Yet, the social and cultural transformations of the early modern period were particularly disruptive for established structures of truth and trust. The Reformation undermined religious dogma and ecclesiastical authority, and the learning of the schools came under heavy criticism. How did people cope with these challenges in early modern knowledge societies? How was meaningful transfer of knowledge made possible?

This volume addresses questions like these by looking at the preconditions of knowledge transfer. It shifts the focus from the objects circulating to the interactions by which they circulate and the way actors cement their relations. The idea is that written and unwritten rules are crucial in this and thus that regulation is vital for the transfer of knowledge.

Between 1450 and 1800, the scale, intensity, and reach of exchange exploded; more information moved between more people and more places. Global expansion generated new flows of products and ideas and induced societal shifts in Europe. Cultural, institutional, and economic transitions opened up and reconfigured structures of exchange and a basis for modern patterns was created. This volume is part of a book series Knowledge Societies in History that resulted from the international collaboration project 'Creating a Knowledge Society in a Globalizing World 1450–1800'. The project viewed early modern knowledge history through the lens of knowledge societies. The concept of knowledge society is grounded in studies of the modern period and earlier periods are often viewed from this perspective. The series aims at developing a historicized understanding of knowledge societies and this volume does so for knowledge transfer.[4]

This volume shares the series' broad, inclusive view of knowledge practices as it has been developed in recent historiography of science, technology, and the arts. Besides explicit, written, and codified knowledge, we look at tacit, artifactual, and practical ways of knowing, emphasizing the ways in which people employ and interpret knowledge. One universal problem concerns the application of the modern concept of 'knowledge transfer' to early modern contexts. Historiography on knowledge transfer is dominated by standard notions of dissemination of codified, textual knowledge through education and publishing, often privileging 'science'. To study early modern knowledge transfers, we not only have to redefine our understanding of 'knowledge' – as the field of history of knowledge aspires to – but also of 'transfer' and its dynamics. Indeed, we aspire to develop a historicized understanding of the features and dynamics of early modern knowledge transfers as well as the fundamental changes taking place.[5]

In addition to the challenge of historicizing 'knowledge transfer', a second, more general, challenge arises: What makes knowledge move and enables the transfer between different locations? Knowledge does not move by itself and access is not mere availability: knowledge needs to be wrapped and labelled to become meaningful and exchangeable. Knowledge is exchanged between people and this involves relations and trust. This process goes beyond the mere individual reception of knowledge; it also concerns social and cultural infrastructure. Relations are cemented by conventions and understandings. Written and unwritten rules are thus vital to knowledge exchange. Rules are often seen as impediments to transfer and access, but in our view they are *enablers* of knowledge exchange. The novelty of our enterprise lies in the focus on the ways transfer was regulated in the early modern period, investigating the patterns and structures that enabled transfer.

This volume's take on the question of how transfer of knowledge worked in the early modern period has been developed by the whole team of contributors.

We have worked closely together to develop the historiographical concept of the project and the individual contributions. After an exploratory preparation meeting, the team developed the concept of the volume during an intensive research stay at the Netherlands Institute for Advanced Study (NIAS) of the Royal Academy of the Netherlands (KNAW) in 2018. The concept was finalized in a reading session a year later, in which the draft contributions and their connections were discussed. The volume is thus the result of a carefully planned research project, which aimed to innovate the field of knowledge history studies by bringing together a novel combination of expertise from various disciplines. By bringing together historians from intellectual and economic history, book history, history of science, religion, art, and material culture, this volume offers a historically and geographically broad view of early modern knowledge societies and changing patterns of knowledge transfer. Cases range from such diverse settings as sixteenth-century Venice, the Spanish empire in the Americas, continental Habsburg, early seventeenth-century Dutch at sea, the Offices of the Catholic Church, and the Republic of Letters in its diverse manifestations. Within these settings, we investigate how actors arranged relationships to share valuable knowledge.

Transfer, Circulation

Knowledge transfer is a complex historiographical theme that emphasizes the ways knowledge is mediated by processes of exchange. Knowledge travels in all sorts of ways, through direct encounters, over distance, over time, across geographical, social, cultural borders. Be it in workshops, salons, coffee houses; on missions, journeys, *peregrinationes*; through networks of commerce and correspondence; transfer of knowledge takes place in concrete interactions between people and communities. Transfer is transmission as well as transformation: in transfer, knowledge is produced, acquires value and meaning. Transfer is often seen as essential to knowledge production: only in reception, ideas and practices become knowledge.[6]

The integrative perspective on cognitive and artifactual aspects of knowledge practices that is characteristic of the history of knowledge field is also visible in analytical frameworks for knowledge transfer. From the 1960s, diffusion theory articulated the dynamics of knowledge transfer in particular for technological innovation. It problematized the dissemination of novel knowledge by mapping the dynamics of social networks. Although in a superficial reading diffusion is often dismissed in history of knowledge, as a conceptual framework it has been applied fruitfully in STS and history of technology. As early as 1986, Karel Davids incorporated such notions in his analysis of the development of navigational techniques in the Dutch Republic. In a classical article on the diffusion of technical knowledge in the Middle Ages and the early modern period, Liliane Hilaire-Pérez developed the concept of 'circulation' to articulate the mediation of knowledge in transfers. She argues that circulation consists of constant adaptations and translations driven by actors that include merchants and consumers besides producers. Territorial ties and connected markets are crucial to technological diffusion, with a key role played by journeymen and apprenticeships. From the perspective of history of technology that has emphasized objects and practices, Hilaire-Pérez argues for taking into account cognitive and linguistic aspects of technological knowledge as well.[7]

In the meantime, from the perspective of history of science, the concept of circulation draws attention to the tangible aspects of knowledge transfer – media, objects, encounters. Here the concept has been developed to understand the ways in which locally produced knowledge acquires translocal value and meaning. It emphasizes how knowledge, rather than being exchanged ready-for-use, is processed and given shape in circulation. In an influential article, Kapil Raj positions the concept of circulation in the turn to global history, pointing out a tension between the local character of knowledge production and interlocal mobilization of knowledge. In order to develop an understanding of knowledge circulation, he proposes to focus on the transformational effect of local knowledge practices rather than looking for epistemic features that enable mobilizing knowledge. Building upon the work of Raj, Wiebke Keim develops a systematic discussion of circulation of knowledge in a global history context, in particular regarding European and non-European interaction in social sciences. She points out that knowledge is always locally situated. The production of knowledge is socially and culturally heterogeneous and globally embedded, mediated by the process of circulation. The perspective of circulation, in other words, emphasizes the ways knowledge takes shape in geographical, social, and epistemic transfers. It can be used to develop the history of knowledge as a social and cultural history, in which communication and exchange are essential to knowledge-making.[8]

The concept of circulation remains historiographically fluid, and this volume too uses it in a flexible and pragmatic way.[9] Building upon existing scholarship, the concept of circulation provides as a useful means to study knowledge transfer. Rather than trying to develop a sharp definition of 'circulation' or 'knowledge transfer', this volume aims at highlighting the structures and processes that facilitate knowledge circulation. The relevance of such conditions has been pointed out, but they remain understudied. Drawing on Raj and Anna Tsing, Keim points out that circulation is spatially and socially rooted and that the preconditions of exchange need to be taken into account. She adds that the study of knowledge circulation must provide 'a buffer against the liberal dream of unlimited open spaces of circulation beyond all borders and boundaries. Circulation always happens within given spaces and according to certain enabling mechanisms'.[10] The work of Mary Morgan et al. on the dissemination of reliable knowledge explicates such mechanisms in the form of requirements for facts to travel well. Besides a functional social and epistemic infrastructure, they argue, to travel fruitfully and with integrity, knowledge has to be labelled and packaged, acquiring proper attributes. Such labelling and packaging takes place in relationships and interactions between historical actors.[11]

By shifting the focus from the objects circulating to the interactions by which they circulate, this volume zooms in on the actors and the way they cement their relations. This is where the term 'entangled' in the title of this volume refers to. We approach knowledge transfer from the relations and interactions between actors. We use the term 'entangled' in a rather loose sense though. In global history 'entanglement' – 'Verflechtung', 'histoire croisée' – pertains to social history and efforts to transcend the traditional focus on the nation-state. In problematizing 'transfer', we connect with this historiography without presuming to engage with such conceptual debates. The term 'entangled' is often used for the increasingly interconnected world of the early modern period, but we use it in a more basic sense of a 'Verschränkung' between actors or objects. Rather than the messengers or the message, we intend to focus on the relationships, assuming this to be the basis for building trust in a network.[12]

Rules as Enablers

In studying the conditions and dynamics of knowledge circulation, we add to the literature by zooming in on the ways relationships and interactions are regulated. The novelty of our approach is to see rules and regulations as enablers of knowledge circulation rather than only as impediments. Exchange of knowledge requires trust between actors, especially when it is perceived as novel or uncertain, and rules can help cementing relations. Hilaire-Pérez, for example, explains how privileges made transfer for technical knowledge possible by creating protected spaces of exchange. Sebastian Felten and Christine von Oertzen have shown how bureaucracies enable knowledge circulation by mediating between fixating regulations and scope for action. This dynamics is also visible in Badea's contribution on the inquisition in this volume.[13]

History of knowledge approaches knowledge as a process and knowing as a cultural practice. Even at the level of 'information', Lars Behrisch argues, it is not so much the objects of knowledge that are relevant for inquiry but the processes of informing and mediating. We apply such a praxeological understanding of knowledge also to rules and regulations. Emphasizing the emergent character of rules, implicit and explicit agreements to configure actions and meanings, we lay focus on regulat*ing* rather than regulat*ions*. This is particularly relevant for early modern societies, where rules were the outcomes of regulating practices to align interests and find opportunities rather than deliberate policies. Starting point of our investigations are the practices of actors managing and assessing exchanges instead of the (implicit) rules applied.[14]

By emphasizing practices of regulation and the emergent character of rules, this volume ties in with the perspective of new institutionalism. Neo-institutional theories emphasize dynamic and evolutionary aspects of social, political, and economic change and highlight the ways rules and norms undergird social systems. Such perspectives have been adopted, for example, to uncover regulatory practices and institutionalization processes in sociotechnical regimes. In more Foucauldian terms, Badea speaks of a *Dispositif* as the stratum where discourse and interaction can unfold and acquire meaning in order to point out that practices of censorship vary over different sociocultural settings. Historical institutionalism has applied neo-institutional frameworks to emphasize internal and external competition and adaptation in early modern state formation or international trade. By forging a new combination of histories of circulation and institutions, we intend to bring recent historiography of knowledge circulation a step further.[15]

Our perspective on rules as enablers of knowledge transfer draws upon the work of Irene van Renswoude on the notion and practices of *censura*. Van Renswoude investigated the meaning of the term – literally: assessment, examination – and the practices connected to it in her studies of textual culture of Late Antiquity and early Middle Ages, transposing it here as a general analytical concept to the early modern period. The practice of *censura* could for example exist by adding marginal notes in manuscripts (and later books) to explain to the reader how to read certain passages and warn of dangerous ideas. This medieval notion indicates an open practice of aiding reading and we extend it towards engagement with knowledge in general. It shows how assessment makes knowledge accessible and useable: how does the right information get to the right people, in the right place; how does knowledge get a proper form and how does someone know whether it is useful and reliable? The notion of *censura* shows how labelling, valuing, and protecting enables and stimulates exchange knowledge in ways that Morgan et al. have also identified. Moreover, it was a practice that was performative rather than based on codified rules. In this way, the notion of *censura* reflects our praxeological approach to regulating.[16]

In addition to the analytical use of *censura*, it can be used to unpack the historiographical understanding of censorship. It was rooted in ecclesiastical contexts and the case of the Holy Office shows that it continued to be. Censorship has acquired a rather reductionist modern connotation of top-down restrictions that is often applied anachronistically to the early modern period. As the chapters of Van Renswoude and Badea in particular show, regulative practices of indexing and censoring were open and multi-layered rather than monolithic. Besides prohibition, censorship also included the management of permissions and exceptions in the form of reading licenses. The continuity between medieval *censurae* and modern censoring is an instance of the ways in which practices of assessing evolved into institutionalized strictures. In this sense, it may form a bridge between medieval and early modern knowledge assessment and the open moderating practices of twenty-first-century information platforms. The notion of *censura* thus enhances awareness of the special nature of regulating as we address it, not merely focussing on its restrictive and prohibitive qualities, but emphasizing its open, practical, and constructive features.[17]

Outline of This Volume

The chapters in this volume are arranged in four sections according to different modes of regulating: labelling, validating, instructing, disciplining. The first section highlights the *labelling* of knowledge that enables access to proper as well as disputable writings. Irene van Renswoude shows how the medieval practice of *censura* informed sixteenth-century revisions of the Index to open up censorial flexibility. She discusses a set of notes by one of the committee members, Antonio Agustín, addressing the question how to deal with books that contained aberrant views. Agustín reflected upon early medieval *censura* to delineate guidelines for assessment that enabled the critical reading of suspect texts. It shows how *censura* enabled knowledge transfer rather than being a counterproductive tool that obstructed the flow of knowledge. In her chapter on John Lockman's translation and edition of Jesuit travelogues, Renate Dürr shows that similar practices of assessing knowledge were still in use in the eighteenth century. In the view of Lockman and many contemporaries, Jesuit reports contained valuable information, but had to be read with caution because of the notoriously manipulative character of Jesuits. Dürr shows how a body knowledge that was considered dangerous could be made accessible by careful mediation. Lockman guided the reader, and in the process reflected extensively on how to deal with such *dangerous knowledge*. He developed the idea of an 'antidote' as the remedy against poisonous vipers, consisting of elaborate footnotes discussing specific words, events, or interpretations. In this way, Lockman demonstrated for the reader the critical reading that was needed when engaging with a text. Labelling appears as a way of contextualizing knowledge, to make clear where it comes from and how it can be used and understood. It helps avoiding confusion over meaning, even if knowledge comes from supposedly suspicious sources like Reformed theologians or Jesuit travelogues. Appropriate labelling, in the words of Morgan et al., enables safe transfer between people and places, making knowledge accessible and closing certain contents off from impertinent eyes.

Section two addresses various ways of *validating* knowledge, presenting knowledge in a format that guarantees the reliability and exchangeability of the contents. Regulating here applies to the form rather than the contents of knowledge. Werner Thomas analyses the *censura* that was applied in the process of producing linguistic knowledge of Amerindian languages by means of catechisms, grammars, and dictionaries. Censorship guaranteed the doctrinal correctness of catechisms, a principal linguistic tool, but also played a constructive role in developing means of translation and controlling the quality of the accuracy of linguistic knowledge contained in grammars and dictionaries. Renate Pieper analyses the ways the first *Courante* of Amsterdam appropriated the schemes of the already well-established handwritten gazettes from Habsburg Europe in their reporting of overseas merchandize. Within a very short period of time, print culture effected significant changes, further regulating the external format, the contents, and the language of the news, guiding the reader towards Amsterdam

8 Fokko Jan Dijksterhuis

as the central node in the information flow. Rather than guarding or guiding, this chapter emphasizes the promotion of valuable knowledge. Ida Nijenhuis discusses the early modern genre of *ars mercatoria*, arguing its significance for the budding political economy of the eighteenth century. The guides on the art of trading show what was understood by commercial knowledge at a certain point of time, but also who was the 'owner' of this type of information. These mercantile manuals contained instrumental information for merchants but also anticipated trade theories and thus functioned both as a guide and as a treatise, as prescriptions and critical reflections that move beyond the mere codification of regulations.

Discussing practices of *instructing*, the third section shifts the focus to processes of exchange and the regulating of behaviour. Djoeke van Netten analyses the instructions for the officers of the V.O.C. travels of exploration in the early seventeenth century, aimed at securing commercial interests. These written rules were attempts at exercising power over time and distance. The instructions served in a dual sense of regulating knowledge transfer – what had to be done with the knowledge acquired during the voyage – as well as transferring knowledge of regulations themselves – how to act and who to inform. The instructions were speech acts of reading out and swearing oaths, thus establishing the confines and order on board (and showing features of the governance language of the state). The case indicates that an important feature of knowledge transfer is the management of secrets; in order to share valuable knowledge, it needs to be kept carefully and only disclosed to designated people. Ioanna Iordanou turns to sixteenth-century Venice, the state that boasts one of the world's earliest centrally organized state intelligence organizations. She analyses formal regulations that determined and dictated the transfer of official knowledge that had to be protected and concealed through methods of encryption, primarily cryptography. Moreover, she aims to show how methods of encryption acted as enablers of the transfer of knowledge that had to be concealed. Iordanou shows how these regulations transcended the realm of mere instructions to assume a managerial overtone, even an outright managerial function. The management of secrets was formative to the Venetian state. In this sense, the process of regulating secrecy and its maintenance was more important than the secrets and its contents.[18] Such a process is similar to the functioning of censorship in the Catholic Church, as discussed by Badea. The term *instructing* may suggest that the regulating is more explicit, but in the chapters of this section it transpires that regulation is a multi-layered affair of instructing and performing.

The final section moves to the level of regulating systems and the communities that are solidified by socially constructed patterns of regulative discourse and behaviour. Regulating is a way of *disciplining*, labelling the bearer of knowledge and assessing behaviour. At this level of systems, rules become object of action and discussion. Cook discusses the case of Cornelis de Bruyn's early eighteenth-century knowledge-gathering expeditions through Russia and Persia and shows how his appeal to values of truthfulness effectively side-lined him.

The case revolves around the question of how the trustworthiness of accounts from unknown places was established. It shows how features of knowledge (pictures, in this case) function as ways of assessing. De Bruyn's success depended upon the patricians of the Dutch Republic who generally sought proofing of accuracy. When his depictions of Persepolis were questioned by his own patrons, his only recourse was to publish a public defence that pointed out the accuracy and completeness. But arguing his correctness in every detail turned out to be impolitic in the learned world of the Republic of Letters. In this case, rules are also explicated but in a sense of appealing to norms and values that are implicitly applied. It confirms Mary Morgan's idea that it is not so much epistemic features that make knowledge acceptable, but the packaging and reputation of the messenger. Andreea Badea presents a seemingly obvious case of top-down regulating in the form of the Inquisition and the Congregation of the Index. Highlighting the primacy of the censors and the heterogeneity of catholic doctrine, the practices of censoring are shown to be quite subtle and much more constructive than would be expected. Rather than being merely repressive, it shows how censorship gave guidance to readers and created trust. The offices had to watch over a system within which heterodox knowledge was required to flow and thus properly channelled. In the final chapter, Dirk van Miert discusses the concept and history of the Republic of Letters and the ways patterns of exchange transform over time and rules can precipitate. From the rather informal 'imagined community' of the Erasmian Respublica Literaria of the sixteenth century, the Republic of Letters became a more self-aware community with explicit strategies of gaining authorial recognition by creating scholarly *personae*. At a systems level, it is not so much the rules themselves that count and have to be maintained, but the system in which rules are linked together, function, and are performed. The processes of regulating the transfer of secrets, doctrines, and information are more important than the contents of those secrets and doctrines. Even when regulating practices precipitate in codified regulations and institutions, rules require use and maintenance to be effective. Rules acquire meaning and effect in practice; there is always a trade-off between rules and capacity to act. Even the seemingly strict Inquisition was performative, as Badea shows. Regulating is an ongoing process of constant renewal and maintenance of relationships and arrangements.

In addition to the different modes of regulating highlighted in the four sections – labelling, validating, instructing, and disciplining – the chapters combined point out further aspects and effects of regulating knowledge transfer. By controlling what and who have access to knowledge, rules create safe spaces in which people can communicate freely. The Holy Office, the Venetian state, and Lockman's antidotes, all show how discreet handling of knowledge creates an environment where the reliability of persons and information can be secured. A secret can be trusted when it is certain it has not fallen into wrong hands. Whether institutionalized (Iordanou, Badea) or unwritten (Van Miert, Dürr), management of relations and behaviour creates spaces for knowledge exchange. In a paternalizing sense, *censura* protects people from dangerous knowledge.

In this regard, censoring has pastoral features of guiding and protecting people and communities. Badea emphasizes the pastoral task of the Roman authorities, instead of seeing censorship as a mere instrument of power.

Explication of rules serves its own means for regulating by establishing relations between actors and lay down their behaviour. By saying how to read and correspond, people can also be called to account. This works both ways, as instructions regulate the behaviour of the instructors as well. Like instructions, manuals seem explicit ways of regulating, but their nature and working are also multi-layered. On the one hand, they describe and prescribe objects and handling, and on the other, they are tools for employing knowledge and maintaining relations. Nijenhuis adds that manuals not only inform practitioners in the field, but also stakeholders. Standardizing is a way of explicating rules; by habit or codification, it establishes the form of objects and processes. The form in which knowledge is presented guarantees the reliability and exchangeability of the contents, as do modern practices of quality control like peer review and industrial standards. Explication of rules and the system of rules gives a new dimension to regulating practices and the knowledge involved, creating a sphere that can be managed, as Iordanou, Thomas, and Nijenhuis show in various ways. Transfer of knowledge becomes understood as a reality that is reflected upon, can be managed, and employed; descriptions becoming prescriptive.

Final Remarks

Recapitulating, the goal of this volume is to problematize 'transfer' and to explore ways to study knowledge transfer in early modern knowledge societies. Through the perspective of 'regulating', we aspire to bring the historiography of knowledge circulation a step further by forging a new combination of histories of circulation and of institutions. We have drawn on the concept of *censura* as an analytical reference for understanding critical assessment of knowledge as an enabler of transfer. Anticipating the actual chapters, in these final remarks we want to briefly outline how this volume contributes to the historiography of early modern knowledge societies.

The new knowledge practices and conceptions that emerged in the early modern period – novelty, discovery, news – raised questions regarding the legitimation of knowledge.[19] Transfer is a means of legitimizing knowledge, giving shape to what is known and what is understood by 'knowledge'. Examples of regulating practices that generated epistemic requirements are the linguistic tools discussed by Thomas and the ideal of 'Republic of Letters' discussed by Van Miert. Thomas shows how a doctrinal desire for evangelization enhanced the demand for accuracy in dictionaries and grammars. Van Miert shows how values of communicativeness were grounded in a community of exchange and reciprocity, in which participation consisted of the very act of writing letters. Towards the eighteenth century, explicit reflections developed upon what the 'Republic of Letters' entails – or ought to entail. The early modern Republic of

Letters thus is a paradigmatic example of the way knowledge transfer produced new knowledge practices.

This volume indicates how new knowledge practices are linked to new players and arrangements in the early modern knowledge societies. New institutional structures carry disciplining effects on epistemic behaviour. The cases of Venice and the VOC are enlightening in this regard, developing regulating roles that the state would start to undertake later. In the church, including the new protestant ones, disciplining remained, of course, a prominent feature in the training of clerics but also through catechisms and manuals. Guilds had been disciplining bodies, but their role was swiftly decreasing, only to be succeeded by professional training and association in the nineteenth century.[20] In the domain of learning, the Republic of Letters functioned as a disciplining network, singling out who has a right to speak and the proper way of speaking. Towards the eighteenth century, such correspondence networks institutionalized into journals and societies, reconfiguring scholarly discipline and disciplines and setting new norms for exchange and communication.[21]

The concept of *censura* illustrates the multi-layered ways in which new knowledge practices and configurations emerged. Historically, *censura* was rooted in ecclesiastical contexts, but in the early modern period practices developed alongside these in other settings and other forms. New practices of censoring emerged in the context of the Republic of Letters and the book market, reconfiguring notions of *censura* that also affected established practices. Pieper details the way papers set a standard for information supply in the setting of commerce, while Dürr highlights emerging reviewing practices. Peer review as we know it today was not yet institutionalized, and systems of assessment rather were open, wiki like. Dürr's shows how Lockman explicated his censoring in order to explain how to read texts critically. Alongside the evolving practices of *censura* in the Holy Office, other bodies took on censoring practices, like the VOC and learned societies. States performed censoring activities – like the granting of privileges – but not in the way and to the extent modern states would do. Rather than being a mere preamble of modern censorship, early modern practices of *censura* gave shape to a wide array of communication and information arrangements. As Badea writes:

> ... it is imperative to keep in mind that [discourses on free participation in knowledge] sprang, to a great extent, from contemporary measures to *control* the consumption and production of knowledge through the regulation of the printing and publishing business and through various forms of censorship.

Instead of a linear history, the early modern transformation of knowledge circulation was a ramified aggregate of developments.

The topics of the final two chapters seem to be dipoles in terms of openness and circulation. Still, as Badea and Van Miert stress, the Inquisition and the

Republic of Letters were fundamentally entwined and facilitated each other. The seeming exemplarity of open learned exchange required quite some regulating, while the apparently restrictive Inquisition was aimed at maintaining knowledge flow. The reading licenses of the Congregation of the Index can be compared to the management of secrets discussed by Iordanou. In terms of regulating knowledge transfer, the Inquisition and the Republic of Letters did the same: enabling. Juxtaposing the Inquisition and the Republic of Letters is intended as an eye-opener regarding standard conceptions of openness and regulations.

Notes

1. Vosoughi, 'Spread'; O'Connor, 'Modeling'; Oreskes, *Merchants of Doubt*.
2. Non-academics, illiterate in Latin.
3. Blair, *Too Much to Know*; Behrisch, 'Zu vielen Informationen!'.
4. On the intensification of exchange: Behringer, *Im Zeichen der Merkus*; Behringer, 'Communications Revolutions'; Pettegree, *Bookshop*. On the concept of knowledge society: Kohlrausch, *Building Europe*; Jäger, 'Wissensgesellschaft'; Mokyr, *Culture of Growth*. Earlier volumes in the project: Munck, *Knowledge and the Early Modern City*; Leemans, *Early Modern Knowledge Societies*.
5. Instances of a focus on education and publishing, see Burke, *Social History 1*; Burke, *Social History II*; Burke, *What Is*; Mokyr, *Gifts*. Vogel, 'Von der Wissenschafts – zur Wissensgeschichte' provides a critical historiographical reflection on the concept of knowledge society.
6. On epistemic aspects of knowledge transfer: Fleck, *Entstehung*; Longino, *Science as Social Knowledge*; Herfeld, 'Knowledge Transfer'; and a general overview in Oreskes, *Why Trust Science?*. Early modern mediation aspects: Cook, *Translating Knowledge*; Dupre, *Silent Messengers*; Stockhorst, *Cultural Transfer*; Van Miert, 'What Was the Republic of Letters?'. On the geography of knowledge: Livingstone, *Putting Science in Its Place*; Nyhart, 'Historiography'; Burghartz, *Sites of Mediation*.
7. Diffusion theory is developed in subsequent editions of Rogers, *Diffusion* (1995, originally 1962). Responses in history of knowledge: Keim, 'Conceptualizing Circulation'; Östling, 'Circulation'. Lux and Cook, 'Closed Circles' uses network analysis for the case of seventeenth-century medicine and the new philosophies; for recent examples: Herfeld, 'Diffusion'; Stehr, 'Global Distribution'. Davids, *Zeewezen en Wetenschap* and also Davids, *Rise and Decline*. Hilaire-Pérez, 'Dissemination'; Hilaire-Pérez, *L'Europe*. See also Margóczy's contribution to the first volume of the Knowledge Societies in History series, Margóczy, 'Technology Transfer'.
8. The concept of circulation has been developed in history of science in particular in Secord, 'Knowledge in Transit'; Cook, *Matters of Exchange*; Cook, *Translating Knowledge*; Dupré, *Silent Messengers*. See also Sarasin, 'Zirkulationen'; Raj, *Relocating Modern Science*; Raj, 'Beyond Postcolonialism'; Raj, 'Introduction'; Keim, 'Conceptualizing Circulation'; Schmidt 'Knowledge Products'.
9. See the reflection of Bergvik and Holmberg in Östling, *Circulation of Knowledge*: 'When 'circulation' is employed to describe every kind of movement an object undertakes, differences and varieties are blurred, and insights of a more precise nature are lost. …' In several review articles, the Lund Centre for the History of Knowledge argue how the circulation perspective provides a way to further develop the history of knowledge field. Acknowledging that the concept of circulation still remains underdefined, these map relevant questions, yet without providing much analytical hold. Östling, *Forms of Knowledge*; Östling, *Histories of Knowledge*; Östling, 'Fulfilling'; Östling, 'Circulation'.

10 Keim, 'Conceptualizing Circulation'; also referring to Tsing, 'Global Situation': 'A focus on circulation shows .. movement of people, things, ideas, .. institutions, but it .. not .. how this movement depends on defining tracks .. grounds or scales and units of agency'.
11 Morgan, 'Travelling Facts'; Werner, 'Vergleich, Transfer, Verflechtung'.
12 The concept of entanglement goes back to early twentieth-century quantum mechanics. Originally called 'Verschränkung' (Schrödinger, 'Gegenwärtigen Situation'), it was later translated back to 'Verflechtung'. Gherardi, 'Practice Theory', explains how 'entanglement' can be linked to practices and mediation processes, emphasizing how knowers and 'things' emerge through and as part of their entangled intra-relating. De Munck, *Knowledge and the Early Modern City*, emphasizes how knowledge claims are justified in the entanglement economic, political, and cultural settings of knowledge production. On 'entanglement' in global history, see, for example: Werner, 'Vergleich, Transfer, Verflechtung'. For other uses, see Choi, *Knowledge Entanglements*; Hock, *Entangled Knowledge*.
13 Hilaire-Pérez, 'Dissemination'; Felten, 'Bureaucracy'. Rogers already gave clues towards the importance of trust, as innovations are almost always perceived as uncertain or even risky. See also Iordanou in this volume on the way the management of secrecy in the Venetian state created an infrastructure that allowed sensitive knowledge to travel.
14 Behrisch, 'Zu vielen Informationen!'. Praxeological understandings in history of knowledge are elaborated in Brendecke, *Praktiken*; Brendecke *Information* (introduction), but also Dürr in this volume; Damme, 'When Practices, Places and Materiality Matter'; Gherardi, 'Practice Theory'; Zedelmaier, *Praktiken*. For an introduction, see Füssel, *Wissensgeschichte*. On emergent aspects of rules, see Gelderblom, *Cities of Commerce*.
15 Scott, *Institutions*; Scott, 'Approaching Adulthood'. Recent applications: Geels, 'Micro-Foundations'; Fuenfschilling, 'Structuration'; Badea in this volume. In early modern historiography: Ertman, *Birth*; Gelderblom, *Cities of Commerce*.
16 Van Renswoude, 'Censorship'; Van Renswoude, 'Signs'; Van Renswoude, 'Responses'.
17 On moderating practices of information platforms, see Karlsson, 'Is There No One Moderating'.
18 See also Margóczy, 'Technology Transfer' for the case of Amsterdam and its mayors.
19 Shapin, *Social History*; Dear, *Discipline and Experience*; Daston, *Objectivity*; Cook, *Matters of Exchange* to mention only the usual suspects.
20 Epstein and Prak, *Guilds* (in particular the introduction); Munck, 'Disassembling the City'; 'Artisans as Knowledge Workers'; De Munck, *Knowledge and the Early Modern City*.
21 On the Republic of Letters: Bots, *Commercium Literarium*; Van Miert, Hotson, and Wallnig, 'What Was the Republic of Letters?'; Ogilvie, 'Correspondence Networks'; Boscani Leoni, 'Men of Exchange'.

Bibliography

Ash, Eric H. ed. 'Expertise and the Early Modern State.' *Osiris* 25 (2010): 1–24.

Blair, Ann. *Too Much to Know. Managing Scholarly Information before the Modern Age*. New Haven, CT and London: Yale University Press, 2010.

Behringer, Wolfgang. *Im Zeichen des Merkur: Reichspost und Kommunikationsrevolution in der Frühen Neuzeit*. Göttingen: Vandenhoeck & Ruprecht, 2003.

Behringer, Wolfgang. 'Communications Revolutions: A Historiographical Concept.' *German History* 24, no. 3 (2003): 333–374.

Behrisch, Lars. 'Zu viele Informationen! Die Aggregierung des Wissens in der Frühen Neuzeit.' In Brendecke, Arndt; Friedrich, Markus; Friedrich, Susanne eds. *Information in der Frühen Neuzeit. Status, Bestände, Strategien.* Berlin: Lit, 2008, pp. 455–473.

Blair, Ann. *Too Much to Know. Managing Scholarly Information before the Modern Age.* New Haven, CT: Yale University Press, 2010.

Boscani Leoni, Simona. 'Men of Exchange: Creation and Circulation of Knowledge in the Swiss Republics of the Eighteenth Century.' In Holenstein, André; Steinke, Hubert; Stuber, Martin eds. *Scholars in Action. The Practice of Knowledge and the Figure of the Savant in the 18th Century.* Leiden: Brill, 2013, pp. 507–533.

Bots, Hans; Waquet, Françoise eds. *Commercium Litterarium. La communication dans la République des Lettres/Forms of Communication in the Republic of Letters 1600–1750.* Amsterdam: APA, 1994.

Brendecke, Arndt; Friedrich, Markus; Friedrich, Susanne eds. *Information in der Frühen Neuzeit. Status, Bestände, Strategien.* Berlin: Lit, 2008.

Brendecke, Arndt ed. *Praktiken der Frühen Neuzeit. Akteure, Handlungen, Artefakte.* Köln: Böhlau, 2015.

Burghartz, Susanna; Burkart, Lucas; Göttler, Christine eds. *Sites of Mediation: Connected Histories of Places, Processes, and Objects in Europe and Beyond, 1450–1650.* Leiden: Brill, 2016.

Burke, Peter. *A Social History of Knowledge. From Gutenberg to Diderot.* Cambridge: Polity Press, 2000.

Burke, Peter. *A Social History of Knowledge. From the Encyclopaedia to Wikipedia.* Cambridge: Polity Press, 2012.

Burke, Peter. *What Is the History of Knowledge?* Cambridge: Polity Press, 2016.

Choi, Chong Ju; Millar, Carla; Wong, Caroline eds. *Knowledge Entanglements: An International and Multidisciplinary Approach.* Basingstoke: Palgrave Macmillan, 2005.

Cook, Harold J. *Matters of Exchange. Commerce, Medicine, and Science in the Dutch Golden Age.* New Haven, CT and London: Yale University Press, 2007.

Cook, Harold J.; Dupré, Sven eds. *Translating Knowledge in the Early Modern Low Countries.* Zürich: LIT Verlag, 2012.

Cools, Hans; Keblusek, Marika; Noldus, Badeloch eds. *Your Humble Servant. Agents in Early Modern Europe.* Hilversum: Verloren, 2006.

Damme, Stéphane van. 'When Practices, Places and Materiality Matter: A French Trajectory in the History of Knowledge.' *Journal for the History of Knowledge* 1, no. 1:4 (2020): 1–8.

Daston, Lorraine; Galison, Peter. *Objectivity.* Princeton, NJ: Princeton University Press, 2007.

Daston, Lorraine; Lunbeck, Elizabeth eds. *Histories of Scientific Observation.* Chicago, IL: University of Chicago Press, 2011.

Davids, Karel. *Zeewezen en Wetenschap : De Wetenschap en de Ontwikkeling van de Navigatietechniek in Nederland tussen 1585 en 1815.* Amsterdam: De Bataafsche Leeuw, 1986.

Davids, Karel. *The Rise and Decline of Dutch Technological Leadership: Technology, Economy and Culture in the Netherlands, 1350–1800.* Leiden: Brill, 2008.

Dear, Peter. *Discipline and Experience. The Mathematical Way in the Scientific Revolution.* Chicago, IL: University of Chicago Press, 1994.

Dupré, Sven; Lüthy, Christoph eds. *Silent Messengers. The Circulation of Material Objects of Knowledge in the Early Modern Low Countries.* Berlin: LIT Verlag, 2011.

Eamon, William. *Science and the Secrets of Nature. Books of Secrets in Medieval and Early Modern Culture.* Princeton, NJ: Princeton University Press, 1994.

Epstein, S.R.; Prak, Maarten eds. *Guilds, Innovation, and the European Economy, 1400–1800.* Cambridge: Cambridge University Press, 2008.
Ertman, Thomas. *Birth of the Leviathan. Building States and Regimes in Medieval and Early Modern Europe.* Cambridge: Cambridge University Press, 1997.
Fauser, Markus. *Das Gespräch im 18. Jahrhundert. Rhetorik und Geselligkeit in Deutschland.* Stuttgart: M und P. Verlag für Wissenschaft und Forschung, 1991.
Felten, Sebastian; Oertzen, Christine von. 'Bureaucracy as Knowledge', *Journal for the History of Knowledge* 1, no. 1:8 (2020): 1–16.
Fleck, Ludwig. *Entstehung und Entwicklung einer wissenschaftlichen Tatsache. Einführung in die Lehre vom Denkstil und Denkkollectiv.* Frankfurt am Main: Suhrkamp, 1980.
Fuenfschilling, Lea; Truffer, Bernard. 'The Structuration of Socio-Technical Regimes – Conceptual Foundations from Institutional Theory.' *Research Policy* 43 (2014): 772–791.
Füssel, Marian. 'Wissensgeschichten der Frühen Neuzeit: Begriffe – Themen – Problem.' In Füssel, Marian ed. *Wissensgeschichte.* Stuttgart: Franz Steiner, 2019, pp. 7–39.
Geels, Frank. 'Micro-Foundations of the Multi-Level Perspective on Socio-Technical Transitions: Developing a Multi-Dimensional Model of Agency through Crossovers between Social Constructivism, Evolutionary Economics and Neoinstitutional Theory.' *Technological Forecasting & Social Change* 152 (2020): 1–17.
Gelderblom, Oscar. *Cities of Commerce: The Institutional Foundations of International Trade in the Low Countries, 1250–1650.* Princeton, NJ: Princeton University Press, 2013.
Gherardi, Silvia. 'Has Practice Theory Run Out of Steam?' *Revue d'anthropologie des connaissances* 11, no. 2 (2017): bk–bu.
Göttler, Christine. 'The City as Constcamer: The Place of the Exotic in Early Seventeenth-Century Antwerp.' In Schrader, Stephanie ed. *Looking East: Rubens's Encounter with Asia.* Los Angeles, CA: Getty Museum, 2013.
Hacking, Ian. 'Styles of Scientific Thinking Or Reasoning: A New Analytical Tool for Historians and Philosophers of the Sciences.' In Gavroglu, K.; Christianidis, J.; Nicolaidis, E. eds. *Trends in the Historiography of Science.* Dordrecht: Springer, 1994, pp. 31–48.
Harkness, Deborah E. *The Jewel House: Elizabethan London and the Scientific Revolution.* New Haven, CT: Yale University Press, 2007.
Herfeld, Catherine; Lisciandra, Chiara. 'Knowledge Transfer and Its Contexts.' *Studies in History and Philosophy of Science Part A* 77 (2019): 1–10.
Herfeld, Catherine; Doehne, Malte. 'The Diffusion of Scientific Innovations: A Role Typology.' *Studies in History and Philosophy of Science Part A* 77 (2019): 64–80.
Hess, Charlotte; Ostrom, Elinor. *Understanding Knowledge as a Commons. From Theory to Practice.* Cambridge: MIT Press, 2007.
Hilaire-Pérez, Liliane; Verna, Catherine. 'Dissemination of Technical Knowledge in the Middle Ages and the Early Modern Era: New Approaches and Methodological Issues.' *Technology and Culture* 47, no. 3 (2006): 536–565.
Hilaire-Pérez, Liliane; Simon, Fabien; Thébaud-Sorger, Marie. *L'Europe des Sciecnes et des Techniques xve-xviiie siècle.* Rennes: Presses Universitaires de Rennes, 2016.
Hock, Klaus; Mackenthun, Gesa eds. *Entangled Knowledge. Scientific Discourses and Cultural Difference.* Münster: Waxmann, 2012.
Howlett, Peter; Morgan, Mary S. eds. *How Well Do Facts Travel?: The Dissemination of Reliable Knowledge.* Cambridge: Cambridge University Press, 2010.
Huigens, Siegried; Jong, Jan L. de; Kolfin, Elmer eds. *The Dutch Trading Companies as Knowledge Networks.* Leiden: Brill, 2010.

Jäger, Wieland. 'Wissensgesellschaft.' In Schützeichel, Rainer ed. *Handbuch Wissenssoziologie und Wissensforschung*. Konstanz: UVK, 2007, pp. 662–669.
Karlsson, Maria. "Is There No One Moderating Wikipedia?????' Impartiality, Revisionism, and Knowledge about the Armenian Genocide on Wikipedia.' In Östling, Johan; Heidenblad, David Larsson; Nilsson Hammar, Anna eds. *Forms of Knowledge: Developing the History of Knowledge*. Lund: Nordic Academic Press, 2020, pp. 87–104.
Keim, Wiebke. 'Conceptualizing Circulation of Knowledge in the Social Sciences.' In Keim, Wiebke; Çelik, Ercüment; Wöhrer, Veronika eds. *Global Knowledge in the Social Sciences. Made in Circulation*. Farnham: Ashgate, 2014, pp. 87–113.
Knorr-Cetina, Karin. *Epistemic Cultures: How the Sciences Make Knowledge*. Cambridge: Harvard University Press, 2003.
Kohlrausch, Martin; Trischler, Helmuth. *Building Europe on Expertise. Innovators, Organizers, Networkers*. Basingstoke: Palgrave Macmillan, 2014.
Kusukawa, Sachiko; Maclean, Ian eds. *Transmitting Knowledge. Words, Images, and Instruments in Early Modern Europe*. Oxford: Oxford University Press, 2006.
Leemans, Inger; Goldgar, Anne eds. *Early Modern Knowledge Societies as Affective Economies*. Abingdon: Routledge, 2020.
Livingstone, David. *Putting Science in Its Place. Geographies of Scientific Knowledge*. Chicago, IL: University of Chicago Press, 2003.
Livingstone, David; Withers, Charles eds. *Geographies of Nineteenth-Century Science*. Chicago, IL: University of Chicago Press, 2011.
Long, Pamela. *Artisan/Practitioners and the Rise of the New Sciences, 1400–1600*. Corvallis: Oregon State University Press, 2011.
Long, Pamela. 'Trading Zones in Early Modern Europe.' *Isis* 106, no. 4 (2015): 840–847.
Longino, Helen. *Science as Social Knowledge: Values and Objectivity in Scientific Inquiry*. Princeton, NJ: Princeton University Press, 1990.
Lux, David; Cook, Harold J. 'Closed Circles Or Open Networks?: Communicating at a Distance during the Scientific Revolution.' *History of Science* 36, no. 2 (1998): 179–211.
Maas, Harro. 'Letts Calculate: Moral Accounting in the Victorian Period.' *History of Political Economy* 48 (2016): 16–43.
Margócsy, Dániel. *Commercial Visions. Science, Trade, and Visual Culture in the Dutch Golden Age*. Chicago, IL: Chicago University Press, 2014.
Margócsy, Dániel. 'Technology Transfer, Ship Design and Urban Policy in the Age of Nicolaes Witsen.' In Munck, Bert de; Romano, Antonella. *Knowledge and the Early Modern City. A History of Entanglements*. Abingdon: Routledge, 2020, pp. 149–170.
Miert, Dirk van ed. *Communicating Observations. Epistography and Epistemology in the Age of the Scientific Revolution, 1500–1675*. London: The Warburg Institute, 2013.
Miert, Dirk van. 'What Was the Republic of Letters. A Brief Introduction to a Long History (1417–2008).' *Groniek* 204/205 (2014): 269–287.
Miert, Dirk van; Hotson, Howard; Wallnig, Thomas. 'What Was the Republic of Letters?' In Hotson, Howard; Wallnig, Thomas eds. *Reassembling the Republic of Letters in the Digital Age*. Göttingen: Göttingen University Press, 2019, pp. 23–40.
Mijnhardt, Wijnand. 'Urbanization, Culture and the Dutch Origins of the European Enlightenment.' *Bijdragen en Mededelingen betreffende de Geschiedenis der Nederlanden* 125 (2010): 137–173.
Mokyr, Joel. *The Gifts of Athena: Historical Origins of the Knowledge Economy*. Princeton, NJ: Princeton University Press, 2003.

Mokyr, Joel. *A Culture of Growth: The Origins of the Modern Economy.* Princeton, NJ: Princeton University Press, 2017.

Moor, Tine de. 'What Do We Have in Common? A Comparative Framework for Old and New Literature on the Commons.' *International Review of Social History* 57 (2012): 269–290.

Moor, Tine de. 'The Silent Revolution: A New Perspective on the Emergence of Commons, Guilds, and Other Forms of Corporate Collective Action in Western Europe.' *International Review of Social History* 53 (2008): 179–212.

Morgan, Mary S. 'Travelling Facts.' In Howlette, Peter; Morgan, Mary S. eds. *How Well Do Facts Travel? The Dissemination of Reliable Knowledge.* Cambridge: Cambridge University Press, 2011, pp. 3–39.

Mulsow, Martin. *Prekäres Wissen: eine andere Ideengeschichte der frühen Neuzeit.* Frankfurt am Main: Suhrkamp, 2012.

Munck, Bert de. 'Disassembling the City: A Historical and an Epistemological View on the Agency of Cities.' *Journal of Urban History* 43, no. 5 (2017): 811–829.

Munck, Bert de. 'Artisans as Knowledge Workers: Craft and Creativity in a Long Term Perspective.' *Geoforum* 99 (2019): 227–237.

Munck, Bert de; Romano, Antonella. *Knowledge and the Early Modern City. A History of Entanglements.* Abingdon: Routledge, 2020.

Naylor, Simon. 'Introduction: Historical Geographies of Science – Places, Contexts, Cartographies.' *British Journal for the History of Science* 38 (2005): 1–12.

Nyhart, Lynn. 'Historiography of the History of Science.' In Lightman, Bernard ed. *A Companion to the History of Science.* Chichester: Wiley, 2016, pp. 7–22.

O'Connor, Cailin; Weatherall, James Owen. 'Modeling How False Beliefs Spread.' In Hannon, Michael; Ridder, Jeroen de. *The Routledge Handbook of Political Epistemology.* Abingdon: Routledge, 2021, pp. 203–213.

Ogilvie, Brian. 'Correspondence Networks.' In Lightman, Bernard ed. *A Companion to the History of Science.* Chichester: Wiley, 2016, pp. 358–371.

Ophir, Adi; Shapin, Steven. 'The Place of Knowledge: A Methodological Survey.' *Science in Context* 4, no. 1 (1991): 3–21.

Oreskes, Naomi; Conway, Erik M. *Merchants of Doubt. How a Handful of Scientists Obscured the Truth on Issues from Tobacco Smoke to Global Warming.* New York: Bloomsbury, 2010.

Oreskes, Naomi. *Why Trust Science?* Princeton, NJ: Princeton University Press, 2019.

Östling, Johan. 'Circulation, Arenas, and the Quest for Public Knowledge: Historiographical Currents and Analytical Frameworks.' *History and Theory* 58 (2020): 111–126.

Östling, Johan; Heidenblad, David Larsson. 'Fulfilling the Promise of the History of Knowledge: Key Approaches for the 2020s.' *Journal for the History of Knowledge* 1, no. 1:3 (2020): 1–6.

Östling, Johan; Heidenblad, David Larsson; Nilsson Hammar, Anna eds. *Forms of Knowledge: Developing the History of Knowledge.* Lund: Nordic Academic Press, 2020.

Östling, Johan; Heidenblad, David Larsson; Sandmo, Erling; Nilsson Hammar, Anna; Nordberg, Kari. 'The History of Knowledge and the Circulation of Knowledge: An Introduction.' In Östling, Johan; Sandmo, Erling; Larsson Heidenblad, David; Nilsson Hammar, Anna; Nordberg, Kari eds. *Circulation of Knowledge: Explorations in the History of Knowledge.* Lund: Nordic Academic Press, 2018, pp. 9–33.

Östling, Johan; Olsen, Niklas; Heidenblad, David Larsson eds. *Histories of Knowledge in Postwar Scandinavia: Actors, Arenas, and Aspirations.* Abingdon: Routledge, 2020.

Pettegree, Andrew; Weduwen, Arthur der. *The Bookshop of the World. Making and Trading Books in the Dutch Golden Age.* Yale: Yale University Press, 2019.
Popplow, Marcus. 'Why Draw Pictures of Machines? The Social Context of Early Modern Machine Drawings.' In Lefèvre, Wolfgang ed. *Picturing Machines 1400–1700.* Cambridge: MIT Press, 2004, pp. 13–48.
Raj, Kapil. *Relocating Modern Science. Circulation and the Construction of Knowledge in South Asia and Europe, 1650–1900.* New York: Houndmills, 2007.
Raj, Kapil. 'Introduction: Circulation and Locality in Early Modern Science.' *British Journal for the History of Science* 43, no. 4 (2010): 513–517.
Raj, Kapil. 'Beyond Postcolonialism ... and Postpositivism: Circulation and the Global History of Science.' *Isis* 104, no. 2 (2013): 337–347.
Renswoude, Irene van (with Christoph Baumgartner). 'Censorship, Free Speech and Religion.' In Hedges, Paul ed. *Controversies in Contemporary Religions, vol. 2: Debates in the Public Square.* Oxford: Oxford University Press, 2014, pp. 123–152.
Renswoude, Irene van. 'The censor's rod. Textual criticism, judgment and canon formation in late Antiquity and the early Middle Ages.' In Teeuwen, M.J.; Renswoude, I. van eds. *The Annotated Book in the Early Middle Ages: Practices of Reading and Writing.* Turnhout: Brepols, 2017, pp. 587–627.
Renswoude, Irene van. 'Responses to the First Index of Banned Books (c. 500 to c. 1100).' In Dürr, Renate ed. *Threatened Knowledge. Practices of Knowing and Ignoring from the Middle Ages to the Twentieth Century.* London: Routledge, 2021, pp. 25–51.
Rexroth, Frank. 'Praktiken der Grenzziehung in Gelehrtenmilieus der Vormoderne. Einige einleitende Bemerkungen.' In Mulsow, Martin; Rexroth, Frank eds. *Was als wissenschaftlich gelten darf. Praktiken der Grenzziehung in Gelehrtenmilieus der Vormoderne.* Frankfurt am Main: Campus, 2014, pp. 11–38.
Roberts, Lissa; Schaffer, Simon; Dear, Peter eds. *The Mindful Hand. Inquiry and Invention from the late Renaissance to Early Industrialization.* Amsterdam: Edita, 2007.
Roberts, Lissa. 'The Circulation of Knowledge in Early Modern Europe: Embodiment, Mobility, Learning and Knowing.' *History of Technology* 31 (2013): 47–68.
Rogers, Everett. *Diffusion of Innovations.* New York: Free Press, 2003.
Rothman, E.; Brokering Empire, Nathalie. *Trans-Imperial Subjects between Venice and Istanbul.* Ithaca: Cornell University Press, 2011.
Sarasin, Philipp; Kilcher, Andreas. 'Editorial – Zirkulationen.' *Nach Feierabend. Zürcher Jahrbuch für Wissensgeschichte* 7 (2011): 7–11.
Schäfer, Dagmar; Popplow, Marcus. 'Technology and Innovation within Expanding Webs of Exchange.' In Kedar, B.Z.; Wiesner-Hanks, M.E. eds. *The Cambridge World History. Vol. 5. Expanding Webs of Exchange and Conflict, 500 Ce – 1500 Ce.* Cambridge: Cambridge University Press, 2015, pp. 309–338.
Shapin, Steven. *A Social History of Truth. Civility and Science in Seventeenth-Century England.* Chicago, IL: University of Chicago Press, 1994.
Schmidt, Benjamin. *Inventing Exoticism. Geography, Globalism, and Europe's Early Modern World.* Philadelphia: University of Pennsylvania Press, 2015.
Schmidt, Benjamin. 'Knowledge Products and Their Transmediations: Dutch Geography and the Transformation of the World.' In Friedrich, Susanne; Brendecke, Arndt; Ehrenpreis, Stefan eds. *Transformations of Knowledge in Dutch Expansion.* Berlin: De Gruyter, 2015, pp. 121–158.
Schrödinger, Erwin. 'Die gegenwärtigen Situation in der Quantenmechanik.' *Die Naturwissenschaften* 23–48; 49; 50 (1935): 807–812; 823–828; 844–849.

Scott, W. Richard. *Institutions and Organizations. Foundations for Organizational Science.* Thousand Oaks, CA: Sage, 1995.
Scott, W. Richard. 'Approaching Adulthood: The Maturing of Institutional Theory.' *Theory and Society* 37 (2008): 427–442.
Secord, James. 'Knowledge in Transit.' *Isis* 95, no. 4 (2004): 654–672.
Smith, Pamela H; Schmidt, Benjamin eds. *Making Knowledge in Early Modern Europe. Practices, Objects, and Texts, 1400–1800.* Chicago, IL: University of Chicago Press, 2007.
Stehr, Nico; Ufer, Ulrich. 'On the Global Distribution and Dissemination of Knowledge.' *International Social Science Journal* 60–195 (2009): 7–24.
Stockhorst, Stefanie ed. *Cultural Transfer through Translation. The Circulation of Enlightened Thought in Europe by Means of Translation.* Amsterdam: Rodopi, 2010.
Tsing, Anna. 'The Global Situation.' *Cultural Anthropology* 15, no. 3 (2000): 327–360.
Turnbull, David. 'The Ad Hoc Collective Work of Building Gothic Cathedrals with Templates, String, and Geometry.' *Science, Technology & Human Values* 18, no. 3 (1993): 315–340.
Vogel, Jakob. 'Von der Wissenschafts- zur Wissensgeschichte. Für eine Historisierung der "Wissensgesellschaft".' *Geschichte und Gesellschaft* 30, no. 4 (2004): 639–660.
Vosoughi, S. 'The Spread of True and False News Online.' *Science* 6380 (2018): 1146–1150.
Wennerlind, Carl. *Casualties of Credit.* Cambridge: Harvard University Press, 2011.
Werner, Michael; Zimmermann, Bénédicte. 'Vergleich, Transfer, Verflechtung. Der Ansatz der Histoire croisée und die Herausforderung des Transnationalen.' *Geschichte und Gesellschaft* 28, no. 4 (2002): 607–636.
Wintergrün, D.; Renn, J.; Lalli, R.; Laubichler, M.; Valleriani, M. *Netzwerke als Wissensspeicher.* Berlin: Max-Planck-Institut für Wissenschaftsgeschichte, 2015.
Withers, Charles. 'Place and the "Spatial Turn" in Geography and in History.' *Journal of the History of Ideas* 70, no. 4 (2009): 637–658.
Zedelmaier, Helmut; Mulsow, Martin. *Die Praktiken Der Gelehrsamkeit in Der Frühen Neuzeit.* Tübingen: M. Niemeyer, 2001.

PART 1
Labelling

1
GUIDELINES FOR READING
Medieval *censura* and Roman Censorship

Irene van Renswoude

In 1562, the humanist scholar and jurist Antonio Agustín (1517–1586) took part in a committee appointed by the council of Trent to revise the Index of Forbidden Books.[1] It was generally felt that the first Index, published in 1559 under the direction of Pope Paul IV, was too excessive in its restrictions. In a set of autographical notes preserved in manuscript Kopenhagen, Arnamagnæan 813, Agustín addressed the issue of what to do with books that contained heretical or suspicious views, but were for the main part useful.[2] Should one throw away what was good just because parts were bad? In Agustín's opinion, the present Index adopted a too strict attitude on the matter. Quoting the late antique Pope Leo I (d. 461), he argued that changing times and circumstances called for moderation.[3] The advice that Agustín offered on how to revise and relax the Index of Forbidden Books shows that the process of determining what should be outright rejected and what could be permitted (under certain conditions) was far from straightforward. In his notes, we find considerations concerning books or parts of books that had been condemned in the recent or more remote past, which, to his mind, should be treated more leniently:

> Now I come to those books that are for the main part useful, but are condemned because of scholia or because of one or the other rejected opinion. In that category are the books corrected by Erasmus or Rhenanus. I readily allow that suspicious scholia are being removed, but I would leave those that concern learning and interpretation of ancient authors. For it is nothing new that something useful can be gained from heretical or suspicious books. How much has been said against Origen by catholic men? Yet they take evidence from that same Origen. How worthy a man was Tertullian? But Gelasius calls his books apocryphal at the council of the 70 bishops.

DOI: 10.4324/9780429279928-3

Yet he (Gelasius) does not say that those (books) that pertain to teaching, of Arnobius, Lactantius, Clemens of Alexandria and Eusebius of Caesarea, whose history (is deemed apocryphal) because of one single record of events, should be rejected altogether. What should I say about Tychonius, from whom the blessed Augustine took so much? "We read some of them", the blessed Ambrose said, "so that we do not neglect them". [....] To prevent a too excessive licence, or refutation for that matter, from harming less cautious readers, let it rather please us that assessments (*censurae*) were written by learned men without which no one could use these books.[4]

Antonio Agustín's recommendations were incorporated in the Tridentine Index, printed in Rome in 1564. They were taken over in the general rules for censorship preceding the Tridentine Index, notably in rules 3, 8 and 9. What is particularly striking in Agustín's notes is his comment on the *censurae* of the fathers of the church. Thanks to the written assessments of learned men, such as Pope Gelasius, Augustine and Ambrose, he observed, readers could now read books that, although not fully orthodox, contained useful information and were advantageous for teaching. In Agustín's opinion, books (and glosses) that pertained to learning and teaching should be exempted from rigorous censorship and be treated more leniently, just as the venerable fathers of the church had done when they wrote their *censurae*.

In this chapter, I shall investigate the reading guidelines that emerged in late Antiquity and the early Middle Ages to regulate the reading of books that did not conform to prevailing orthodox and moral standards. I will focus in particular on practices of assessment that Agustín referred to as *censurae*, which, to his mind, had ensured the preservation and transmission of useful knowledge contained in heterodox books. Such an investigation is relevant for the purpose of the present volume on regulation of knowledge in the early modern period, since Agustín's reflections on the *censura* of the early church shaped the rules of reading and interpretation of the Tridentine Index and the censorship procedures in its wake. As a humanist and a legal scholar, Antonio Agustín had a vast knowledge of classical and patristic sources and medieval canon law. Investigating the sources that informed Agustín's recommendations for the Tridentine Index allows us to explore continuities between late antique reading regulations, medieval *censura* and early modern censorship.

Censorship and Control

Censorship, as we define it today, did not exist in the manuscript culture of late antique and early medieval Latin Europe. It has been argued that censorship was, in fact, impossible in the age before print. The unstable nature of manuscript transmission made it difficult for authorities to steer the production, dissemination and reception of books. As Kathryn Kerby-Fulton remarked, 'manuscript culture was not much amenable even to authorial control, let alone authoritarian control'.[5] Once authors had submitted their work to be copied and allowed it to go into the public sphere (*edere in publicum*), it was out of their hands.[6] Occasionally, curses were added at the end of a book to keep scribes from changing a single syllable on pain of hellfire and damnation, but no threat of divine punishment could prevent that texts were altered with every round of copying.[7] Yet, despite the absence of efficient or systematic means of control, there were attempts to guide the production and reception of books. Already in late antiquity, procedures were established that would in the course of time be termed *censura praevia* and *censura posterior*, that is, assessment before and after publication.[8] Authors could send their work to a patron or an ecclesiastical authority to have their work examined before distribution. When Augustine (d. 430) composed a rebuttal of the teachings of the 'Pelagians', he first submitted it to Pope Boniface I for examination and asked him to make emendations in case anything would displease him.[9] Problematic passages, offensive wording or plain errors could thus be detected beforehand, and if necessary, emended. The voluntary submission of one's books to a higher authority for correction and emendation served multiple purposes, such as gaining patronage, ensuring a favourable reception, or reaching consensus before publication. It also provided evidence of the authors' commitment to orthodoxy. Whatever errors might be found in their writings, their willingness to submit their work to an authority before publication showed they were no obstinate deviant thinkers who refused to be corrected.

Those who were worried about the possible heterodox content of a book that already circulated – usually a book that was produced outside their immediate circle and control – could bring the contested publication to the attention of ecclesiastical authorities. Books that had come under suspicion were examined during councils and read out in public. Hilary of Poitiers (d. 368) mentions written assessments, drawn up at the Council of Constantinople in 336, where the assembled bishops judged a book of Marcellus of Ancyra (d. 374) to be heretical. According to Hilary, the assessments were kept in the archives of the church to provide 'a memory and a warning' for future generations.[10] Requests for an examination of contested books did, however, not always result in a condemnation. When the writings of Faustus de Riez (d. 495) became a topic of debate after his death, the North African Bishop Possessor (fl. c. 520) appealed to Pope Hormisdas (d. 523) to assess Faustus' writings. Personally, Possessor had nothing against Faustus, but he hoped the pope would settle the dispute on Faustus' orthodoxy once and for all.[11] Pope Hormisdas replied, much to the chagrin of Faustus' opponents, that he saw no reason to forbid the reading of Faustus' works. Although he acknowledged that Faustus' teaching was problematic and his writings should not be reckoned among the authoritative writings of the church, he recommended to preserve what was good in Faustus' books and reject what was contrary to the teaching of the fathers. His recommendation went with a reminder of Apostle Paul's advice to 'test all things and keep what is good'.[12]

An author had the option to offer his work to the scrutiny of his superiors, but he could also ask his peers for their approval and corrections. This procedure stands midway between *censura praevia* and what we would now call peer review. It was an established practice in literary circles in late antiquity, which continued in the early Middle Ages in what could be termed communities of reading. In the 790s, the scholar Alcuin of York (d. 804) submitted a doctrinal treatise to a group of bishops and abbots and asked for their *iudicium*, their judgement. He would rather not have his writings, he wrote, 'go out unto public ears unless they have been examined with the assessment (*censura*) of your authority, and confirmed in a reading of the fraternal community'.[13] The practice of submitting one's work to the critical reading and evaluation of one's peers as well as the word choice (*censura*) drew on literary conventions established by classical and late antique poets and authors. In many prologues, we find references to the criticism of colleagues and patrons to whom authors gladly but anxiously submitted the fruits of their labour.[14] The Roman poet Ausonius (d. 395) asked his friend and fellow poet Pacatus Drepanius to carefully read and judge the lines of his poem. He pressed upon him to correct his work without mercy:

> Read through these lines, Drepanius, heedfully judging whether you think they should be pardoned or examined. With you as judge I shall be content, whether you think the verse I send worth reading or concealing. For my first aim. Pacatus, is to earn your favour: to defend my modesty shall be my second thought. I can bear a stern reader's criticism (*censura*) [...] Set down your critical marks (*obeli*) – brands which distinguish the foremost bards: I will consider them marks of fame, not blame; and will call those passages corrected rather than condemned, which the polishing file of a learned man shall mark against me.[15]

Ausonius audaciously stated that he did not fear his stern reader's criticism (*censura*) because he realized it would improve the quality of his work. The critical marks (*obeli*), which Ausonius asked Drepanius to add to lines that were in need of correction, would in the following centuries also be used as reading aids to guide a reader safely through heterodox books. I shall turn to their new function later.

The word *censura* had a variety of meanings. It could refer to investigation, judgement or to the duties of the censor: a Roman magistrate responsible for maintaining the census, overseeing finances and supervising morals and conduct.[16] In the Middle Ages, the word *censura* was increasingly employed to denote public authority and ecclesiastical or secular disciplinary justice.[17] When used in reference to book assessment, *censura* meant 'judgement', 'evaluation' or 'assessment'. Its meaning was closer to (literary) criticism than to the modern-day understanding of censorship. The term *censura* was not necessarily used to denote negative feedback. When a book was evaluated by superiors or peers, their *censura* could go both ways. It could result in a dismissive assessment but also in a positive evaluation or simply in a set of recommendations for improvement. When the monk Ratramnus of Corbie (d. 868) submitted his doctrinal treatise to the *censura* of his superiors, he received corrections and suggestions for improvement from the archbishop of Reims, Hincmar (d. 882).[18] Hincmar added notes in the margin of the manuscript to indicate where he thought the wording needed to be changed.[19] This is a telling example of *censura* on request, which did not lead to preventing or restricting publication, but to what was felt to be an improvement of the book. Its aim was to ensure a smooth reception, in this case from Pope Nicholas I (d. 867), to whom the book would be sent after having been checked and proofread. As this case demonstrates, *censura* need not be restrictive but could also be productive, at least in intention. Yet, corrections coming from an ecclesiastical superior must have been constraining per se, since it is hard to imagine that Ratramnus had any other choice but to change his work according to the archbishop's directives.

In late antiquity and the early Middle Ages, *censura* did not necessarily have a negative connotation comparable to the modern notion of censorship. Nowadays, censorship refers to blocking content from being either read, heard or seen, but in this period *censura* aimed at quality control.[20] Procedures of *censura praevia* and *censura posterior* were intended to improve and guide the form and content of an author's work and bring it in line with accepted mores as well as safeguard the spiritual well-being and moral behaviour of readers. Moreover, *censura* aimed at ensuring a favourable reception and transmission of a book by taking away criticism beforehand and reaching consensus through a ritualized procedure of submission to the examination of one's superiors and peers and a demonstrative willingness on the part of the author to be open to corrections.

Although it was fairly common practice in late antiquity and the early Middle Ages to have a work checked and approved beforehand, this was no standardized, obligatory part of the publication process. Moreover, the convention of sending a book to a pope, bishop or peer for examination and emendation was not consistently called *censura*. Next to *censura*, we find *examinatio, correctio, iudicium* and *sententia* and their correlates in reference to the assessment of books. Although the word *censura* occurred regularly in letters and prologues of this period, it was no standardized term that covered every form of book assessment. By the time Antonio Agustín drew up his report for the Index in the 1560s, *censura* had become an established term that was applied in retrospect to all forms of assessment in the late antique and early medieval period. Before the twelfth century, however, the vocabulary of reading regulation and quality control of books was much more varied. This variety in terminology may be taken as evidence of the absence of a coherent or widely shared discourse on censorship. As Sita Steckel aptly phrased it, 'the unsystematic, apparently merely situational distribution of references to *examinatio* or *censura* implies that there was no real ecclesiastical censorship of books in this period'.[21] What constitutes 'real' censorship, however, is a matter of debate. Book burning, for example, which was a rare phenomenon in the early Middle Ages and should rather be regarded as a powerful symbolic act of rejection than an effective means of control, was nonetheless a form of actual censorship, in that it prevented readers from accessing these particular manuscript copies of a rejected text.[22] The same logic applies to condemnations of books by popes, bishops and councils: they were irregular events without standardized protocol; nevertheless, such condemnations did amount to concrete (albeit ineffective) acts of censorship.[23] Yet I do agree with Steckel that there was no *systematic* censorship of books in late antiquity and the early Middle Ages. Notions on how to assess books and protect readers from harm, however, did exist. It is to these notions I shall now turn.

Assessment of Books: How to Read the Heretics

Let us take a closer look at some late antique and early medieval practices of assessment and start with the patristic authors that Antonio Agustín turned to in support of his plea for more leniency towards heterodox books. In the passage from his autograph notes, with which I opened this chapter, Agustín argued that learned men, such as Augustine, Ambrose and Gelasius, wrote *censurae* to enable the reading of unorthodox books. In their writings, he found evidence that suggested to him that they adopted a flexible attitude towards books that were pagan, heretical or not fully orthodox, but that were useful for teaching and learning nonetheless. In the following, we will see that Agustín's quotations from patristic texts are occasionally at variance with the form in which these texts have come down to us in manuscripts and editions. I should like to make clear in advance that it is not my intention to demonstrate that Agustín misquoted or misinterpreted his sources. Rather, I am interested in how the interpretation of late antique texts that were fundamental for the rhetoric of revising the Index in the 1560s shifted in the course of the centuries. For it is precisely this shift of interpretation that reflects changing attitudes towards heterodox books and the regulation of reading that is central to this chapter.

Prime among Agustín's *viri docti*, learned men, was his namesake, Augustine (d. 430), philosopher and bishop of the North African diocese Hippo Regius. In 397, Augustine published the first three books of his compendium for the Christian student of literature and learning, *On Christian Teaching*. In 426, he added a fourth book, in which he offered a Christian adaptation of classical rhetoric. Augustine's *On Christian Teaching* did much for the acceptance of pagan learning. In the words of Gerald Press, the work 'legitimized and even recommended a partial adoption of the "pagan" arts and sciences and outlined something like an educational curriculum for Christians in opposition to those within the church who considered all intellectual culture spiritually dangerous or unnecessary'.[24] In the third book of his compendium, Augustine devoted considerable attention to a book written by an author who was considered to be a heretic: Tychonius (fl. ca. 370/390). He wrote an extensive assessment report of Tychonius' *Book of Rules*, in which he discussed both the strong and the weak points of Tychonius' work, much like we would now expect from an academic book review. After due consideration, Augustine reaches the conclusion that Tychonius' *Book of Rules*, with its seven rules for interpretation, is a recommended read for 'the studious'. He considers the book to be of great assistance in understanding Scripture, although, he adds, 'no more may be expected from it than it really contains'.[25] Augustine warns readers that the book must be read with caution (*caute sane legendus est*), seeing that the author advocates the heresy of the Donatists.[26] It would appear that Augustine's cautious recommendation worked towards acceptance of Tychonius' *Book of Rules*. About 150 years later, in another manual for the Christian student, Tychonius' book was included without further notes of warning among the recommended handbooks for correct interpretation, alongside Augustine's own *On Christian Teaching*.[27]

The next person Antonio Agustín put forward as assessor par excellence, who, he said, had written assessments reports (*censurae*) that made it possible to read books that were unorthodox but useful, was Bishop Ambrose of Milan (d. 397). At the beginning of this chapter, I rendered a passage from Agustín's autograph notes, but abbreviated Agustín's quotation from Ambrose. I will now give the quotation in full:

> "We read some of them [i.e. heterodox books]", the blessed Ambrose said, "so that we do not neglect them, we read them so that we may not be ignorant of them, we read them not in order to retain them, but to refute them."[28]

There is something odd about this quotation. It occurs in Ambrose's *Commentary on the Gospel of Luke* in the context of a discussion of apocryphal gospels. However, in the modern edition of Ambrose's commentary, Ambrose does not say 'we read some of them, so that we do not *neglect* them', but 'we read some of them, *not* so that they may be *read*', which has a whole different meaning.[29] Where did Agustín come across the variant form of this quotation? In the *Decretum Gratiani*, the twelfth-century canon law collection with which Agustín was well acquainted, the quotation occurs in a section where several statements of ecclesiastical authors were gathered to address the question of what was permitted to read.[30] Did Agustín perhaps find the variant form of the quotation in the manuscripts that he used for his emendations to the edition of the *Decretum Gratiani*?[31] Interestingly, the alternative version of the saying of Ambrose that we find in Agustín's notes, which has 'neglect' instead of 'read', also occurs in the treatise *Why we should read the books of the heretics* by Jan Hus (d. 1415). Hus cites Ambrose saying 'we read some of them so we *do not neglect them*' in support of his plea not to burn the books of Wycliff.[32] Instead of destroying books that are considered heretical, Hus argues, one should read them 'as long as they contain some truth'. Hus draws on several church fathers, among whom was Ambrose, who, he maintained, argued along similar lines. Without implying that Agustín read Jan Hus' treatise and borrowed the quotation directly from him, this example shows that an alternative version of Ambrose's saying was in existence from at least the early fifteenth century onwards, and second that Agustín was not the first to use it as an argument to advocate a more lenient attitude towards books that were, in the eyes of current guardians of correct doctrine, not fully orthodox.[33]

The last part of Agustín's quotation from Ambrose ('we read [these books] not to retain, but to refute them') appears to contradict Agustín's notion that Ambrose had written assessment reports that enabled readers to read heterodox books. Ambrose does not refer, at least not here, to reading as a means to assess books beforehand so that others could safely read them, but rather as a means to reject such books and do away with them. Church fathers such as Ambrose hardly ever spoke out for the preservation of unorthodox books.[34] They regarded book burning, curses, forgery and counter-forgery as legitimate means in the fight against heresy.[35] Apart from a few isolated quotations, patristic authors rarely provided arguments on how to read (if at all) banned literature. Support can rather be found in the writings of other ecclesiastical authors, such as Gennadius Scholasticus, also known as Gennadius of Marseille (d. 496).

Gennadius published a reading guide *On illustrious men*, in which he not only discussed orthodox authors and their books, but also heretical authors or authors who at some point in their career fell into heresy. Gennadius does not dismiss their entire corpus out of hand, but advises readers to pay attention to when a specific book was written. A book written before an author's lapse into heresy should be weighed and interpreted differently than a book written after said lapse. In Gennadius' opinion, even the heresiarch Pelagius wrote works of value for students and scholars before he was proclaimed a heretic.[36] A point of interest is that Gennadius considered Pelagius' pre-heretical books to be profitable for students and scholars in particular, which means he had an educational purpose in mind when he presented the writings of a heterodox author as recommended reading. Gennadius' nuanced judgement of Pelagius' oeuvre should, however, not be taken to indicate that he was a remarkably tolerant man or a secret adherent of Pelagius' doctrine, for he wrote three books against Pelagius. Yet, Gennadius did aim to preserve what was useful and valuable. His balanced assessments were sometimes copied in medieval manuscripts as an introduction or a header to a heterodox text, serving as an introduction to the author and on some occasions even as a reading permit to read heterodox books.[37]

Cassiodorus (d. c. 585), former statesman and founder of the monastery Vivarium, is another scholar who explicitly reflected on how to deal with heterodox books. He offered insight into his practices of assessment and into the considerations that informed them. Cassiodorus professes to a view that is close to Gennadius' and in fact to Agustín's own position, namely that it is a waste to dismiss a book or entire corpus of an author just because parts of it are heretical. Cassiodorus' *Institutes of Divine and Secular Learning* discussed the books of the widely admired textual scholar Origen (d. 253/254). Origen's doctrinal views had come under attack already in the third century and were eventually condemned at the Council of Constantinople in 533. Cassiodorus, who wrote his *Institutes* not long after the condemnation, notes about Origen:

> It is said of him 'where he writes well, no one writes better; where he writes badly no one writes worse.' So we must read him cautiously and judiciously

to draw the healthful juices from him, while avoiding the poisons of his perverted faith that are dangerous to our way of life [...] Later writers say that [Origen] should be shunned completely because he subtly deceives the innocent. But if, with God's help, we take proper precaution, his poison can do no harm.[38]

Cassiodorus was of the opinion there was little danger in reading the learned heterodox authors of the past as long as one took proper precautions. What kind of precautions he had in mind can best be explained by means of another unorthodox author he discussed in his manual of learning, namely the earlier mentioned Tychonius (fl. ca. 370/390), whose *Books of Rules* Augustine had declared safe to read. Cassiodorus followed Augustine's lead and included Tychonius' *Book of Rules* in his manual among the recommended handbooks for correct interpretation.[39] Another text written by Tychonius, however, namely his commentary on the Apocalypse, he considered much more problematic. In his opinion, the commentary was 'contaminated with the foul teachings of his (Tychonius') poisonous belief'.[40] But since the commentary also contained 'some unobjectionable material', Cassiodorus decided to include it in his manual after all, among the books recommended for study. To prevent readers from getting confused, he provided a manuscript copy of Tychonius' commentary, which he carefully annotated with a set of symbols. Cassiodorus writes:

> Where appropriate I have affixed the *chresimon* ('useful') on the approved statements and on all the unacceptable statements I found in reading through it, I have fixed the mark of disapproval, the *achriston* ('useless'). I urge you to do likewise on suspect commentators so that the reader will not be bewildered by the admixture of unacceptable teachings.[41]

Cassiodorus presented his annotated copy of Tychonius' commentary as a model for transmitting and preserving heterodox books, which he encouraged others to follow ('I urge you to do likewise'). The symbols he referred to, *chresimon* (the chi-rho sign) and *achreston* (a sign also called *obelus*), went back to a set of critical signs that had been used in Antiquity for textual criticism and correction.[42] Roman poet Ausonius, discussed earlier, referred to such critical signs when he asked his friend Drepanius to add the symbol of the *obelus*, the mark of rejection, to lines that were in need of correction.[43] The *obelus* generally took the shape of a dotted or plain straight line ($\div$) and was put in the margin next to offensive, spurious or faulty lines. While the original purpose of the *obelus* and other critical signs was to judge the form of texts or mark a passage that required examination, Cassiodorus used them to judge the *content* of books.[44] This was not entirely a new development. The Roman rhetorician Quintilian (d. ca. 100) already referred to the *obelus* as a *censoria virgula* – a censor's rod used by literary experts to expel books from the canon just as censors expelled unworthy members from the senate.[45] What was new in Cassiodorus' programme of annotating heterodox texts was to use these critical signs as reading aids to guide readers through dangerous content. The symbols of approval and disapproval, which Cassiodorus recommended to apply to suspect commentaries, informed readers which parts of a text could be trusted and which parts were dangerous.[46] The critical signs provided tools for guided interpretation and a safe conduit to read heterodox books as well as an alternative to banning such books completely.

Knowledge of how to apply these signs was widely available in the early Middle Ages. Sign treatises circulated that listed all known critical symbols, with brief explanations on how to use them for annotation. One such sign treatise was drawn up by Bishop Isidore of Seville (d. 636). In his encyclopaedia of classical and contemporary knowledge, he listed them under the heading *notae sententiarum* – signs of judgement.

Antonio Agustín was familiar with these critical signs. When he was preparing an edition of Isidore's encyclopaedia, he came across Isidore's list of *notae sententiarum* and made drawings of the symbols he encountered in manuscripts.[47] Agustín's notes and drawings show an interest in the shape of these critical signs and in their potential as tools for guided reading of heterodox texts.

Let us now turn to the next authority mentioned in Agustín's notes, Pope Gelasius, and to the book list that was attributed to him, which has become known, rightly or wrongly, as the first Roman Index of Forbidden books.

A Medieval Index of Banned Books

In his autograph notes, Agustín speaks of 'books that were deemed apocryphal by Gelasius at the council of the seventy bishops'.[48] The document he refers to is a list of recommended and rejected books, also known as the *Decretum Gelasianum* or, in full, *Decretum Gelasianum de libris recipiendis et non recipiendis*.[49] It was attributed to Pope Gelasius I (d. 496) and a council of seventy learned bishops gathered in Rome. The *Decretum Gelasianum* has, however, little to do with the late antique pope Gelasius. It is a pseudonymous literary production that originated in sixth-century Gaul. The document should therefore be regarded as a regional medieval index rather than a first Roman index rooted in antiquity.[50] The *Decretum Gelasianum* consists of five parts and only the last two parts form the book list proper. The list starts with 'books to be accepted' followed by 'books not to be accepted', the latter consisting of apocryphal and heretical books. The learned heterodox authors that Agustín mentioned in his notes, Tertullian, Arnobius, Lactantius, Clemens of Alexandria and Eusebius of Caesarea, can be found in the apocryphal section. Here, we also find the earlier mentioned Tychonius. Origen is also on the list, but he is placed in the ambiguous section of authors who are neither fully approved nor fully rejected.[51]

According to Agustín, Pope Gelasius never said that the books of Tertullian, Lactantius, Clemens of Alexandria and Eusebius of Caesarea should be rejected altogether, even though he judged them to be apocryphal.[52] Agustín had intimate knowledge of the pseudo-Gelasian decretals. He referred regularly to this decree in his study on the late antique and early medieval sources of ecclesiastical law. In this study, Agustín offered his judgement (*iudicium*) and assessment (*censura*) on the reliability of information found in canonical collections before the twelfth century.[53]

Seeing that Agustín was well acquainted with the stipulations of the *Decretum Gelasianum de libris recipiendis et non recipiendis*, it is rather puzzling that he stated that the books of Tertullian, Clemens, Lactantius and other authors, which were labelled apocryphal, were not altogether rejected. Because, if one reads the *Decretum Gelasianum* in the versions that have come down to us, this is exactly what Pope Gelasius (or rather the anonymous compiler from Gaul) is doing: their books are rejected, full stop. The final statement of the *Decretum Gelasianum* proclaims that all apocryphal and heretical books 'should be rejected and eliminated' and 'damned in the indestructible shackles of anathema forever'.[54] So, how did Agustín arrive at the interpretation that Pope Gelasius did not fully reject these apocryphal books? As stated at the outset, it is not my intention to demonstrate that Agustín misquoted or misinterpreted his sources. The purpose of this chapter is rather to investigate how the interpretation of late antique and early medieval texts and decrees, which played such an important role in Agustín's recommendations for the revision of the Index of Forbidden Books, shifted over time.

Loopholes

Perhaps Agustín's interpretation of pseudo-Gelasius' judgement can be explained by the fact that the word 'apocryphal' underwent a change of meaning in the course of the centuries. In antiquity, the term 'apocryphal' (Latin *apocryphus*, from the Greek ἀπόκρυφος) meant 'secret' or 'hidden' and was used for texts of unknown origin.

Texts that circulated without the name of an author or under a false name were considered unreliable. No matter how valuable the information was that the text contained, it could not be considered trustworthy without the name of a reliable author to guarantee its truth-value. In the course of time, the term no longer referred solely to anonymous or pseudonymous texts, but to all books that were deemed unreliable for a variety of reasons. If an author was believed to have erred on one or several points, his or her writings were subsumed under the apocrypha.[55] Thus the writings of authors such as Tertullian, Lactantius, Clemens and Eusebius ended up among the apocryphal writings, even though their names were known and the source of their writings could hardly be called 'hidden'. The label 'apocryphal' came to be applied to widely different categories of books and authors, ranging from mildly unorthodox to downright heretical. In the sixth century, when the pseudo-Gelasian decree was composed, the widened applicability of the term did not tamper the severity of the restrictions regarding apocrypha, but it did open the door for more liberal interpretations in the centuries to come.

Agustín was not the first to interpret the stipulations of the *Decretum Gelasianum* somewhat freely. Soon after the pseudo-Gelasian decree was put together and started to spread, medieval readers and commentators negotiated its terms and found loopholes in its restrictions.[56] Abbot Aldhelm of Malmesbury (d. 709), arguing from the very principles that informed the judgement of pseudo-Gelasius, held that apocrypha should only be rejected if they were found to contradict Scripture, or if the author of the work was unknown or had been condemned by a council. Aldhelm, who became bishop of Winchester in 705, did acknowledge that 'the *censura* of canonical truth and the teachings of the orthodox fathers in decretal writings' had sanctioned the complete destruction of apocrypha, but he was not prepared, as Augustine Casiday put it, to write off all apocryphal writings simply because the pseudo-Gelasian decree said to do so. He relied on his own judgement.[57]

With his interpretation of the restrictions of the pseudo-Gelasian decree, Agustín touched on an issue that others also came to find increasingly problematic: the wording of the decree was very unclear from a juridical point of view.[58] Although pseudo-Gelasius unequivocally rejected apocryphal and heretical books and anathematized them, technically speaking he never said one should not read them. The Latin verb of prohibition used here is 'non recipere' or rather the gerundive 'non recipiendus' ('not to be accepted'). Theoretically, one could argue that the injunction not to accept certain books does not necessarily imply a prohibition to read them. This was exactly what Robert Bellarmine (1542–1621), censor for the Index, argued when he signalled that the *Decretum Gelasianum* had no relevance for the Index's general guidelines for censorship, since Gelasius provided no authority for prohibition. Bellarmine pointed out that:

> Gelasius did not prohibit to read the books he condemned, but distinguished the good from the bad ones and the authentic from the apocryphal ones, so that all would understand in which books they should put their trust and which books should be set aside.[59]

It takes the frame of mind of a jurist to argue that condemnation does not equal prohibition, but technically speaking it is correct.

Censurae of Learned Men

Agustín referred in his autograph notes to the assessments of heterodox books by learned men such as Ambrose, Augustine and Gelasius and called their assessments *censurae*. As we have seen in the introduction to this chapter, the term *censura* was already used in late antiquity and the early Middle Ages to denote the evaluation of new books. Yet, it was no umbrella term that covered all instances of quality control, supervision of orthodoxy or regulation of reading. In the *Decretum Gelasianum*, for example, the term *censura* is not employed to indicate the judgement that declared certain books acceptable and others unacceptable. In the sixteenth century, however, pseudo-Gelasius' assessment of books was in retrospect called *censura*. Erasmus, in a dedicatory letter introducing his edition of the works of the martyr Cyprian, published in 1520, referred to pseudo-Gelasius' evaluation of the author as 'Cyprian, to whom the *censura* of the Roman see allotted prime place'.[60] In Erasmus' vocabulary, the term *censura* could evidently still refer to a positive assessment after due consideration. Antonio Agustín uses the term in a similar sense in his study of the sources of canon law before the twelfth century, published after his death in 1611. His *censura* at the end of each discussion of a source is often very critical, but also highlights its positive aspects.[61] The way Agustín employs *censura*, in his study on canon law as well as in his recommendations for the Index, could be translated as 'expert opinion' or 'review', resulting in either a positive or negative assessment or in a balanced critical evaluation. In that sense, his use of the term was not that far removed from the meaning of *censura* in late antiquity and the early Middle Ages in those cases where the word was employed to denote book assessment. As Lucia Bianchin has shown, only in the seventeenth century the polysemous term *censura* grew away from its core meaning 'opinion' and came to refer to a set of techniques to control and regulate society.[62] By that time, *censura* had become a catch-all word that was projected onto all types of reading regulation in the past. It was inserted in printed editions of early medieval texts, even when the word did not occur in the manuscripts transmitting these texts.[63]

Conclusion

As this chapter has shown, late antique and early medieval reading regulations informed Antonio Agustín's recommendations for the revised Index. They tailored the rhetoric of his appeal to relax the stringent rules of the previous Index of Forbidden Books. His interpretations of patristic and medieval sources on the assessment of books reveal a tension or shift between practices of regulation of the past (occasionally denoted as *censura*) and the understanding of *censura* in his own day and age.

The assessments of patristic and medieval authors may also have provided Agustín with a (extra) licence to read banned books. The catalogue of his private library reveals that Agustín owned a number of books that had been placed on the 'first index of banned books', the sixth-century *Decretum Gelasianum*, as well as on the latest index, the Tridentine Index, which he had helped to revise.[64] The first rule of the Tridentine Index declared that 'all books which have been condemned either by the supreme pontiffs or by ecumenical councils before the year 1515 and are not contained in this list shall be considered condemned in the same manner as they were formerly condemned'.[65] This stipulation apparently did not keep Agustín from collecting such books. After all, the rules and prohibitions of the Index did not fully apply to him, being an expert assessor and adviser for the revision of that very Index.[66] For how could he offer his advice and *censura* on the scholia of Erasmus and Rhenanus or on late antique books that pertained to teaching and learning and establish that 'useful things can be gained from heretical or suspicious books' if he did not read and examine them himself?[67]

Agustín's recommendations were taken on board in the Tridentine Index, published under Pius IV in 1564. Some formulations of Agustín's notes were incorporated almost verbatim in the general rules for censorship that preceded the lists of books in the Index.[68] Especially in rule eight that permitted (under certain conditions) 'books whose chief contents are good but in which some things have incidentally been inserted', we recognize the concerns Agustín expressed in his autograph notes.[69] The book lists of Tridentine Index formed the basis of all later indexes, while its general rules continued to serve as a guide for future censors. Yet, where the wording of the rules was based on that of older authorities, such as pseudo-Gelasius' *Decretum*, the phrasing of these older regulations did not quite fit the normative framework of the Index, as we have seen with Bellarmine's recommendations for revision.

The flexibility and relative imprecision of late antique and early medieval reading regulations, which allowed room for different interpretations, were perhaps not an easy match for early modern Roman censorship, although they did serve as a source of inspiration and authority. Perhaps the mechanisms of regulation that prevailed in a manuscript culture, in which texts had a fluid nature and asked for flexible responses, were not well suited to the age of print, when a more narrow interpretation of censorship slowly came into being that is our frame of reference today. Yet when Antonio Agustín formulated his recommendations for the Tridentine Index, *censura* had not yet acquired a meaning equivalent to modern notions of prohibitive censorship. It was still a flexible tool that regulated reading and provided scholars and assessors with the licence to read heterodox books, assess them and collect them for their private libraries – for teaching and learning, evidently.

Notes

1 I would like to thank Renate Dürr, Andreea Badea and Sebastiaan van Daalen for their careful reading of this chapter and the members of the NIAS group 'Regulating knowledge' for inspiring discussions and valuable suggestions.
2 The autograph notes have been published by Juan F. Alcina Rovira in the appendix to 'Antonio Agustín y el índice de libros prohibidos', pp. 12–14.
3 Ibid., p. 12: '… Indicis moderationem fieri necesse arbitror esse. Nam beatus Leo scribit, multa sunt qua…pro necessitate temporum, aut pro consideratione aetatum oportet temperari'.
4 'Venio nunc ad eos libros, qui magna ex parte sunt utiles, sed propter scholia, vel propter unam atque alteram opinionem improbatam damnatur. In quo ordine sunt libri ab Erasmo vel a Rhenano emendati. Scholia suspecta ut tollantur, facile concedo. Sed quae pertinent ad eruditionem et interpretationem veteris scriptoris relinquerem. Neque novum est hoc, ut ex libris haereticorum aut suspectorum utilitas percipiatur. Quam multa contra Origenem (sic) dicta sunt a catholicis viris? Sed ex eodem Origine testimonia sumunt. Quantus vir Tertullianus fuit? Sed eius libros apocryphos appellat Gelasius in concilio LXX episcoporum. Ut Arnobii, Lactantii, Clementis Alexandrini et Eusebii Caesariensis, cuius historiam propter rerum singularem notitiam, quae ad instructionem pertinet usquequaque non dicit esse renuendam. Quid de Tychonio dicam, ex quo permulta sumit Divus Augustinus? Legimus aliqua, inquit Beatus Ambrosius, ne negligamus [legimus, ne ignoremus, legimus, non ut teneamus,

sed ut repudiemus.] Ne vero nimia licentia, vel dissolutio potius, noceat minus cautis lectoribus, valde placeret, ut censurae a doctis viris scriberentur, sine quibus nemo his libris uteretur'. Ms. Kopenhagen, Arnamagnaean 813, ff. 301–304, ed. Alcina Rovira, appendix to 'Antonio Agustín y el índice de libros prohibidos', pp. 12–14. In the translation, I have left out the part in square brackets. I will discuss the omitted section further on in this chapter.
5 Kerby-Fulton, *Suspicious Books*, p. 17.
6 Meyvaert, 'Medieval Notions of Publication', pp. 81, 82.
7 Drogon, *Anathema! Medieval Scribes and the History of Book Curses*. More politely formulated requests not to change the form and content of the texts are listed in Mülke, *Der Autor und sein Text. Die Verfälschung des Originals*.
8 Godman, *The Silent Masters*, pp. 11, 25–27; Flahiff, 'Ecclesiastical Censorship of Books', p. 1.
9 Augustine, *Contra duas epistolas Pelagianorum* I, 3, ed. PL 44, col. 551: 'Haec ergo ... ad tuam potissimum dirigere sanctitatem, non tam discenda quam examinanda, et ubi forsitan aliquid displicuerit, emendanda constitui'.
10 Hilary of Poitiers, *Fragmenta ex opera historico*, ed. PL 10, col. 661A: 'Propter memoriam posterorum cautelamque [....] in archivo ecclesiae considerunt'. The book that was condemned was Marcellus' *Against Asterius*. The edition refers to the written assessments as 'censura' in the heading added to the chapter (In archivo Ecclesiae asservatur doctrinae ipsius censura). This word, however, does not occur in Hilary's text. It only occurs in the chapter's heading added by the editor.
11 Bishop Possessor, Letter to Pope Hormisdas (520 AD), ed. Thiel, ep. 115, p. 695; Pereira, 'Faustus of Riez's *De Gratia Dei*'.
12 Pope Hormisdas, Letter to Bishop Possessor (520), par. 11–12, ed. Glorie, p. 118:

> Hi uero, quos uos de <libris> Fausti cuiusdam Galli antistitis consuluisse litteris indicastis, id sibi responsum habeant: neque illum neque quemquam, quos in auctoritatem patrum non recipit examen, catholicae fidei aut ecclesiasticae disciplinae ambiguitate<m> posse gignere, aut religiosis praeiudicium comparare. Fixa sunt a patribus, quae fideles sectari debeant instituta; siue interpretatio, seu praedicatio, seu uerbum pro populi aedificatione compositum: si cum fide recta et doctrina sana concordat, admittitur; si discordat, aboletur. [...] Quod si ita non esset, numquam doctor ille gentium acquieuisset annuntiare fidelibus: omnia probate, quod bonum est tenete.

13 Alcuin, *Adversus Elipandum*, ed. Migne, PL 101, cols. 231–270, at. Col. 232C: '... nec in publicas aures easdem meae devotionis litterulas procedere velim, nisi prius auctoritatis censura examinentur, et fraternae congregationis lectione confirmentur'. Alcuin, Ep. 120, ed. Dümmler, p. 175: Alcuin's letter is discussed in Sita Steckel, 'Between Censorship and Patronage', pp. 104, 105.
14 Janson, *Latin Prose Prefaces*.
15 Ausonius, *Ludus septem sapientium/The masque of the seven sages*, p. 310:

> Ignoscenda istaec an cognoscenda rearis/ adtento, Drepani, perlege iudicio/ aequanimus fiam te iudice, sive legenda/sive tegenda putes carminia, quae dedimus/nam primum est meruisse tuum, Pacate, favorem/ proxima defensi cura pudoris erit/possum defense cura pudoris erit/[...] pone obelos igitur primorum stigmata vatum/ palmas, non culpas esse putabo meas./ et correcta magis quam condemnata vocabo/ adponet docti quam quae mihi lima viri.

16 *Thesaurus linguae latinae* vol. 3, lemma 'censura', cols. 803–806.
17 Niermeyer, *Mediae latinitatis lexicon minus*, lemma 'censura', p. 167.
18 Ratramnus submitted his treatise to 'the *censura* of your correction' (*vestrae correctionis censuram*) at the end of the fourth book of his *Contra Greacorum oppositum*, ed. PL 121, col. 346: 'Quae si placuerint, Deo gratias agimus; sin vero displicuerint, vestrae correctionis censuram praestolamur'.

19 See Hincmar's letter, ed. Lambot, 'L'homélie du Pseudo-Jérome', p. 270: 'Nunc autem transcucurri eum sub oculis et sicut petisti, in quibus locis mihi aliter visum fuit, adnotare curavi, ponens viritim signa in marginalibus paginarum et secundum eadem signa haec scedula quae mihi visa sunt tuae dilectioni scripsi. Quae sit ita et tibi visa fuerint, retractabis'.
20 In common parlance, censorship refers to blocking content from being read, heard or seen. For a more nuanced and historical definition of censorship, see the *Historical Dictionary of Journalism* ('Censorship consists of any form of control over, or access to, the dissemination of information or ideas') or the *New Dictionary of the History of Ideas*, p. 290: 'Censorship comprises many methods of preventing the publication or dissemination of speech, printed matter, art, theatre, music, electronic media, or other forms of expression'. For *censura* as quality control, see the contribution of Werner Thomas in this volume. Add definition of censorship from the Oxford handbook of journalism and the Dictionary of Intellectual ideas.
21 Steckel, 'Between Censorship and Patronage', p. 107.
22 On book burning in late antiquity and the Middle Ages, see Speyer, *Buchvernichtung und Zensur*; Werner, *Den Irrtum liquidieren*; Murray, 'The Burning of Heretical Books'; Rohmann, *Christianity, Book-Burning and Censorship*.
23 A book condemnation did not necessarily spell the end of an author's career or obstruct the dissemination of their writings, but it affected their reputation and social standing, at least temporarily. See, for example, the career of the ninth-century author Amalarius of Metz, van Daalen, *Amalarius of Metz*.
24 Press, '"Doctrina" in Augustine's *De doctrina Christiana*', p. 98
25 Augustine, *De doctrina christiana* III, 30, ed. Martin: 'non de illo speretur tantum quantum non habet'. See the full quotation below.
26 Ibid.:

> Quod ideo dicendum putavi, ut liber ipse et legatur a studiosis, quia plurimum adiuvat ad scripturas intellegendas, et non de illo speretur tantum, quantum non habet. Caute sane legendus est non solum propter quaedam, in quibus ut homo erravit, sed maxime propter illa, quae sicut donatista hereticus loquitur.

27 Cassiodorus, *Institutiones divinarum et saecularium litterarum (Institutes of Divine and Secular Learning)* I, 10, 1, ed. Mynors, p. 34. Cassiodorus' manual shall be discussed further on in this chapter.
28 'Legimus aliqua, inquit Beatus Ambrosius, ne negligamus, legimus, ne ignoremus, legimus, non ut teneamus, sed ut repudiemus'. For the full Latin passage, see note 4.
29 Ambrose, *Expositio secundum Lucam*, I, 2, ed. Schenkl, p. 10, 11: 'fertur etiam aliud euangelium, quod scribitur secundum Thoman. novi aliud scriptum secundum Matthian. legimus aliqua, ne legantur; legimus, ne ignoremus; legimus, non ut teneamus, sed ut repudiemus et ut sciamus qualia sint in quibus magnifici isti cor exaltant suum';

> Another Gospel is found written according to Thomas. I know of another one written according to Matthias. We read some of them not so that they may be read; we have read them so that we may not be ignorant of them; we have read them not in order to retain them, but to reject them and to know in what kind of things these proud [men] have lifted their hearts.

30 *Decretum Gratiani*, Distinctio 37, chapter 9, Seculares litterae legendae sunt, ut non ignorentur: 'legimus aliqua, ne legantur; legimus, ne ignoramus'. https://geschichte.digitale-sammlungen.de/decretum-gratiani/kapitel/dc_chapter_0_390 (consulted 27 July 2022).
31 Antonio Agustín, *De emendatione Gratiani dialogorum libri duo* (Tarragona, 1587).
32 Jan Hus, *De libris hereticorum legendis*, ed. Eršil, p. 23: 'Legimus aliqua, ne negligamus, legimus, ne ignoremus, legimus, non ut teneamus, sed ut repudiemus'; Fudge, *Jan Hus, Religious Reform and Social Revolution*, p. 101; Werner, *Den Irrtum liquidieren*, pp. 371–372.

Guidelines for Reading 39

33 It is, however, not unthinkable that Agustín read Jan Hus' treatise, even though Hus was considered a heretic par excellence. Agustín owned a collection of sermons from Jan Hus, collected by Johan Dobneck (Iohannes Cochlaeus). Rovira and Recasens, eds., *La biblioteca de Antonio Agustín*, p. 263, item 341 (4): Iohannes Cochlaeus, *De immensa Dei misericordia erga Germanos ex collatione sermonum Ioannis Hus* (Lipsiae: in officina Nicolai Wolrab, 1538).
34 Werner, *Den Irrtum liquidieren*, pp. 371–372, Speyer, *Buchvernichtung und Zensur des Geistes*, p. 166.
35 Speyer, *Buchvernichtung und Zensur des Geistes*, p. 166.
36 Gennadius, *De viris illustribus* (or *De scriptoribus ecclesiasticis*) 42, ed. PL 58, col. 1083A: 'Pelagius haeresiarcha, antequam proderetur haereticus, scripsit studiosis viris necessarios tres de fide trinitatis libros [...] Post haereticus publicatus scripsit haeresi suae faventia'.
37 See for example ms. Reims, Bibliothèque municipale, 1351, tenth century, from the cathedral chapter of Reims, containing Rufinus' translation of Eusebius, *Historia ecclesiastica* (marked as dubious by the decree ascribed to Pope Gelasius, see note 4 and 49), f. 1r–2r and ms. Paris, Bibliothèque nationale de France, latin 2166, ninth century, from the monastery of Corbie, containing Faustus de Riez, *De gratia*, condemned in 529, flyleaf, verso, where the reader is encouraged to make up their own mind and see whether they agree with Gennadius' assessment: 'Videat quis quem preferat et cuius magis auctoritatem sequi debeat et utrum ita faustus sentiat sicut gennadius testatur'; 'Let he [the reader] consider who he prefers, and whose authority should rather be followed and whether Faustus thinks as Gennadius testifies'.
38 Cassiodorus, *Institutiones* I, 1, 8, ed. Mynors, p. 14: *De quo conclusive dictum est*:

> Ubi bene, nemo melius: ubi male, nemo peius', et ideo caute sapienterque legendus est, ut sic inde sucos saluberrimos assumamus, ne pariter eius venena perfidiae vitae nostrae contraria sorbeamus. [...] posteriores autem in toto dicunt eum esse fugiendum, propterea quia subtiliter decipit innocentes; sed si adiutorio Domini adhibeatur cautela, nequeunt eius nocere venenosa.
> Translation Halporn, p. 114

39 Cassiodorus, *Institutiones* I, 10, 1, ed. Mynors, p. 34.
40 Ibid. I, 9, 3, ed. Mynors, p. 33: 'Ticonius etiam Donatista in eodem volumine quaedam non respuenda subiunxit, quaedam vero venenosi dogmatis sui fecilenta permiscuit'. Translation Halporn, p. 132.
41 Ibid. I, 9, 3, ed. Mynors, p. 33: 'cui tantum in bonis dictis chresimon, in malis achriston quantum transiens valui reperire, ut arbitror, competenter affixi. quod et vobis similiter in suspectis expositoribus facere suademus, ne lectoris animus fortasse turbetur nefandi dogmatis permixtione confusus'. Translation Halporn, p. 132.
42 van Renswoude and Steinová, 'The Annotated Gottschalk'; Steinová, *Notam superponere studui*, pp. 117–122.
43 See note 15.
44 Manuscripts that originated from Cassiodorus' monastery Vivarium show that scribes and readers of this community employed the critical sign of the *obelus* for 'dogmatic correction'. Mark Vessey, Introduction to Halporn, *Cassiodorus, Institutions*, p. 47, n. 139. As Vessey indicates, the origin and provenance of these manuscripts are not entirely certain.
45 Quintilian, *Institutio oratoria* I, 4, 1. See van Renswoude, 'The Censor's Rod', p. 588.
46 Cassiodorus advised the readers of his manual to treat the books of Origen in the same way. As long as a mark of rejection was put in the margin next to Origen's 'perverted doctrines' to indicate where he is dangerous, Cassiodorus held, Origen would not be able to succeed in deceiving readers. Cassiodorus, *Institutiones* I, 1, 8, ed. Mynors, p. 14: 'quapropter in operibus eiusdem Origenis, quantum transiens invenire praevalui, loca quae contra regulas Patrum dicta sunt achresimi

repudiatione signavi, ut decipere non praevaleat qui tali signo in pravis sensibus cavendus esse monstratur'.
47 Agustín's edition of Isidore's *Etymologiae* was never finished, but his notes and drawings were used in a later edition, republished in Migne, Patrologia Latina 82. References to Agustín's drawings of the signs can be found in the footnotes to columns 96–98, for example: 'Obelus superne adpunctus. Placet A. Augustine sic pingi, ut est in pandectis Florent'.
48 See note 4: 'Sed eius libros apocryphos appellat Gelasius in concilio LXX episcoporum'.
49 *Decretum Gelasianum*, ed. Von Dobschütz, pp. 21–60.
50 Van Renswoude, 'What Not to Read', pp. 28–30. Parts of the decree, however, predate the sixth century and do have a Roman origin, in that these segments go back to decrees of popes Damasus (d. 384) and Hormisdas (d. 523).
51 As is Eusebius of Caesarea, who occurs twice in the booklist: once in the ambiguous section (together with Origen and Rufinus of Aquileia) and once in the apocryphal section. *Decretum Gelasianum*, ed. Von Dobschütz, p. 46 and again on p. 55.
52 See note 4: 'Ut Arnobii, Lactantii, Clementis Alexandrini et Eusebii Caesariensis, cuius historiam propter rerum singularem notitiam, quae ad instructionem pertinet usquequaque non dicit esse renuendam'.
53 The study, entitled *De quibusdam veteris canonum ecclesiasticorum collectoribus iudicium ac censura*, was published after Agustín's death in 1611 in Rome. It was included in the second volume of the eight-volume edition of the collected works of Antonio Agustín, with a prologue by Étienne Baluze.
54 *Decretum Gelasianum*, ed. Von Dobschütz, p. 60: '… non solum repudiata verum ab omni Romana catholica et apostolica ecclesia eliminata atque cum suis auctoribus auctorumque sequacibus sub anathematis insolubili vinculo in aeternum confitemur esse damnata'.
55 Rose, *Ritual Memory*, pp. 23–78; Van Renswoude, 'What Not to Read'.
56 Van Renswoude, 'What Not to Read'.
57 Casiday, 'St. Aldhelm on Apocrypha', pp. 156, 157. On the '*censura* of canonical truth', see Aldhelm, *De uirginitate* 24, p. 256: '….quam canonicae ueritatis censura promulgat, credere et cetera apocriforum deleramenta […] penitus abdicare et procul eliminare orthodoxorum patrum scita scriptis decretalibus sanxerunt'.
58 Stéphane Gioanni speaks of an 'évolution juridique' and suggests that the strongly worded final paragraph of the *Decretum Gelasianum* (cited in note 54) was added at a later stage to strengthen the normative framework of the decree. Gioanni, 'Les listes d'auteurs', pp. 31, 38.
59 Robert Bellarmine, *Indice, Protocolli* B, fol. 296r, edited in Godman, *The Saint as Censor*, Part II: 'Censura librorum et propositionum Bellarminiana', II, 2, a, p. 238: 'Non enim Gelasius prohibuit eos libri legi, quos damnavit, sed distinxit bonos a malis et authenticos ab apocryphis, ut omnes intelligerent, quibus libris fides habenda, quibus deroganda esset'. Bellarmine pointed out that the first rule of the Index did not pertain to the books condemned by Gelasius: 'Non agit haec regula de libris a Gelasio damnatis'.
60 'Cyprianus, cui primum locum tribuit sedis Apostolicae censura', Erasmus, Letter to Lorenzo Pucci, epist. 1000 11, l. 181–185, ed. Allen and Allen, p. 29. Erasmus refers here to pseudo-Gelasius' decree (via the Decretum Gratianum in which the decree was incorporated) where Cyprian is indeed listed among the authors whose works are highly recommended; see *Decretum Gelasianum* 4, 2, ed. Von Dobschütz, p. 36.
61 See, for example, the *censura* at the end of chapters 21, 23 and 27 in Antonio Agustín, *De quibusdam veteris canonum ecclesiasticorum collectoribus iudicium ac censura* (the 1611 edition has no page numbers). Since the study was only published after Agustín's death, it is not entirely certain whether Agustín himself introduced each critical assessment at the end of each chapter with *censura* or whether that term was added by the editor in 1611. See also note 63. Even the title of the work might not be his.
62 Bianchin, *Dove non arriva la legge*, p. 7.

63 See, for example, Gilbert Manguin's edition of a ninth-century treatise, *De tenenda scripturae veritate*, ascribed to Remigius of Lyon. In the edition, published in 1650, the heading 'censura' has been added more than thirty times to provide structure to Ps-Remigius' argument. In none of the manuscripts of this ninth-century treatise, however, the word *censura* can be found. Also modern scholars tend to apply the term *censura* as a descriptive label to medieval practices of assessment, even when that term does not occur in the sources.
64 Alcina Rovira and Recasens eds., *La biblioteca de Antonio Agustín*.
65 *Index librorum prohibitorum* (1564), p. 13: 'Libri omnes, quos ante annum MDXV aut summi Pontifices, aut Concilia oecumenica damnarunt, & in hoc Indice non sunt, eodem modi damnati esse censeantur, sicut olim damanti fuerunt'.
66 See the chapter of Andreea Badea in this volume.
67 '.... ut ex libris haereticorum aut suspectorum utilitas percipiatur'. See note 4.
68 See Alcina Rovira's comparison between the wording of the rules in the Tridentine Index and Agustín's autograph notes. Alcina Rovira, 'Antonio Agustín y el índice de libros prohibidos'.
69 *Index librorum prohibitorum* (1564), p. 17: 'Libri, quorum principale argumentum bonum est, in quibus tamen obiter aliqua inserta sunt [quae ad haeresim, seu impietatem, divinationem, seu superstitionem spectant]'; 'books whose chief contents are good but in which some things have incidentally been inserted, [regarding heresy, impiety, divination or superstition]'.

Bibliography

Primary Sources

Alcuin. *Adversus Elipandum*. Ed. Migne, Jacques-Paul, Patrologia latina 101. Paris: Garnier, 1863, pp. 231–270.

Aldhelm. *De uirginitate*. Ed. Ehwald, R., Monumenta Germaniae Historica, Auctores antiquissimi 15. Berlin: Weidman, 1919, pp. 226–323.

Ambrose. *Expositio secundum Lucam*. Ed. Schenkl, C., *Sancti Ambrosii Opera. Pars Quarta. Expositio Evangelii secundum Lucam*, Corpus Scriptorum Ecclesiasticorum Latinorum 32, 4. Praag and Vienna: Tempsky; Leipzig: Freytag, 1902.

Antonio Agustín. *De emendatione Gratiani dialogorum libri duo*. Tarragona: Mey, 1587.

Antonio Agustín. *De quibusdam veteris canonum ecclesiasticorum collectoribus iudicium ac censura*, in *Antonii Augustini archiepiscopi Tarraconensis Opera omnia*. 8 vols. Lucca: typis Josephi Rocchii, 1765–74, vol. 2, pp. 219–43.

Antonio Agustín. Autograph notes, Ms. Kopenhagen, Arnamagnaean 813, ff. 301–304. Ed. Alcina Rovira, Juan F., 'Antonio Agustín y el índice de libros prohibidos del concilio de Trento (Roma 1564).' *Calamus renascens* 3 (2002), pp. 7–14, appendix pp. 12–14.

Augustine. *Contra duas epistolas Pelagianorum*. Ed. Migne, Jacques-Paul, Patrologia latina 44. Paris: Garnier, 1865, pp. 549–638.

Augustine. *De doctrina christiana*. Ed. Martin, J., Corpus Christianorum Series Latina 32. Turnhout: Brepols, 1962, pp. 1–167.

Ausonius. *Ludus septem sapientium/The masque of the seven sages*, in *Ausonius*, with an English translation by Hugh G. Evelyn White. 2 vols. London and New York: Loeb Classical Library, 1919–1921, I, 13, pp. 311–330.

Bellarmine, Robert. *Censura librorum et propositionum Bellarminiana*. Ed. Godman, Peter, *The Saint as Censor: Robert Bellarmine between Inquisition and Index*. Leiden, Boston, MA and Köln: Brill, 2000, pp. 235–310.

Cassiodorus. *Institutiones divinarum et saecularium litterarum*. Ed. Mynors, R.A.B., *Cassiodori Senatoris Institutiones*. Oxford: Clarendon Press, 1963. Trans. Halporn, J.W., *Cassiodorus:*

Institutions of Divine and Secular Learning and on the Soul, Translated Texts for Historians 42. Liverpool: Liverpool University Press, 2004.

Decretum Gelasianum. Ed. von Dobschütz, Ernst, *Das Decretum Gelasianum de libris recipiendis et non recipiendis im Kritischen Text herausgegeben und untersucht*, Texte und Untersuchungen 38. Leipzig: J. P. Hinrichs, 1912, pp. 21–60.

Erasmus. Letters. Eds. Allen, P.S.; Allen, H.M., *Opus epistolarum Des. Erasmi Roterodami*. Vol. 4. Oxford: Oxford University Press, 1922, pp. 1519–1521.

Gennadius. *De viris illustribus* (or: *De scriptoribus ecclesiasticis*). Ed. Migne, Jacques-Paul, Patrologia latina 58. Paris: Garnier, 1847, pp. 1061–1120.

Hilary of Poitiers. *Fragmenta ex opera historico*. Eds. Migne, J.P.; Migne, Jacques-Paul, Patrologia latina 10. Paris: Garnier, 1845, pp. 627–723.

Hormisdas. *Letter to Bishop Possessor*. Ed. Glorie, F., CCSL 85A, Turnhout: Brepols, 1978.

Hus, Jan. *De libris hereticorum legendis*, in id., *Polemica*. Ed. Eršil, J., *Magistri Iohannis Hus Opera omnia* 22. Praha: Academia, nakl. Československé akademie věd, 1966, pp. 19–37.

Index librorum prohibitorum cum regulis confectis per Patres a Tridentina Synodo delectos, auctoritate sanctiss. D. N. Pii IIII, Pont. Max. comprobatus. Roma: Paulus Manutius, 1564.

Possessor. *Letter to Pope Hormisdas*. Ed. Thiel, A., *Epistolae Romanorum Pontificum* I. Braunsberg: Peter, 1868.

Secondary Literature

Alcina Rovira, Juan Francisco; Recasens, Joan Salvadó eds. *La biblioteca de Antonio Agustín: Los impresos de un humanista de la Contrareforma*. Palmyrenus, Colección de Textos y Estudios Humanísticos. Alcañiz: Instituto de Estudios Humanísticos; Madrid: Consejo Superior de Investigaciones Científicas, 2007.

Alcina Rovira, Juan Francisco. 'Antonio Agustín y el índice de libros prohibidos del concilio de Trento (Roma 1564).' *Calamus renascens* 3 (2002): 7–14.

Bianchin, Lucia. *Dove non arriva la legge. Dottrine della censura nella prima età moderna*, Annali dell'Istituto storico italo-germanico in Trento, Monografie 41. Bologna: Il Mulino, 2005.

Casiday, Augustine M. C., 'St Aldhelm on apocrypha', *Journal of Theological Studies*, NS, 55,1 (2004): 147-156.

Daalen, Sebastiaan van. 'The Reception of Amalarius of Metz' Liber Officialis in Medieval Manuscripts.' MA thesis, University of Amsterdam, 2021.

Drogin, Marc. *Anathema! Medieval Scribes and the History of Book Curses*. Totowa, NJ: Allanheld, Osmun; Montclair, NJ: A. Schram, 1983.

Flahiff, G.B. 'Ecclesiastical Censorship of Books in the Twelfth century.' *Mediaeval Studies* 4 (1942): 1–22.

Flores Sellés, Candido, 'Escritos inéditos de A. Agustín (1517–16586), referents al Concilio de Trento.' *Revista Española de Derecho Canónico* 34 (1978): 109–130.

Fudge, Thomas. *Jan Hus, Religious Reform and Social Revolution in Bohemia*, International library of historical studies 73. London and New York: I. B. Tauris, 2010.

Gioanni, Stéphane. 'Les listes d'auteurs « à recevoir » et « à ne pas recevoir » dans la formation du canon patristique: le Decretum Gelasianum et les origines de la "censure" ecclésiastique.' In Depreux, Ph.; Bougard, F.; Le Jan, R. eds. *Compétition et sacré au haute Moyen Âge: entre mediation et exclusion*. Turnhout: Brepols, 2015, pp. 17–38.

Godman, Peter. *The Silent Masters: Latin Literature and Its Censors in the High Middle Ages*. Princeton, NJ: Princeton University Press, 2000.

Godman, Peter. *The Saint as Censor: Robert Bellarmine between Inquisition and Index*. Leiden, Boston, MA and Köln: Brill, 2000.

Janson, Tore. *Latin Prose Prefaces: Studies in Literary Conventions*, Studia Latina Stockholmensia 13. Stockholm: Almqvist & Wiksell, 1964.

Kerby-Fulton, Kathryn. *Suspicious Books. Censorship and Tolerance of Revelatory Writing in Late Medieval England*. Notre Dame: University of Notre Dame Press, 2006.

Lambot, C. 'L'homélie du Pseudo-Jérôme sur l'assomption et l'évangile de la nativité de Marie d'après une lettre inédite d'Hincmar.' *Revue bénédictine* 46 (1934): 265–282.

Meyvaert, Paul. 'Medieval Notions of Publication: The "Unpublished" Opus Caroli regis contra synodum and the Council of Frankfort (794).' *The Journal of Medieval Latin* 12 (2002): 78–89.

Mülke, Markus. *Der Autor und sein Text. Die Verfälschung des Originals im Urteil antiker Autoren*, Untersuchungen zur antiken Literatur und Geschichte 93. Berlin and New York: de Gruyter, 2008.

Murray, Alexander. 'The Burning of Heretical Books.' In Roach, A.P.; Simpson, James R. eds. *Heresy and the Making of European Culture. Medieval and Modern Perspectives*. Farnham: Routledge, 2013, pp. 77–88.

Niermeyer, J.F. *Mediae latinitatis lexicon minus*. Leiden: Brill, 1976.

Pereira, Matthew J. 'Augustine, Pelagius and the Southern Gallic Tradition: Faustus of Riez's De Gratia Dei.' In Y. Hwang, Alexander; Matz, Brian J.; Casiday, Augustine eds. *Grace for Grace. The Debates after Augustine and Pelagius*. Washington, DC: The Catholic University of America Press, 2014, pp. 180–207.

Press, Gerald A. "'Doctrina' in Augustine's De doctrina Christiana.' *Philosophy & Rhetoric* 17, no. 2 (1984): 98–120.

Renswoude, Irene van. 'The Censor's Rod. Textual Criticism, Judgment and Canon Formation in Late Antiquity and the Early Middle Ages.' In Teeuwen, M.J.; Renswoude, Irene van eds. *The Annotated Book in the Early Middle Ages. Practices of Reading and Writing*, Utrecht studies in medieval literacy 37. Turnhout: Brepols, 2017, pp. 555–595.

Renswoude, Irene van. 'What (Not) to Read in Times of Crisis. The First Index of Banned Books.' In Dürr, Renate ed. *Threatened Knowledge. Practices of Knowing and Ignoring from the Middle Ages to the Twentieth Century*. Abingdon: Routledge, 2021, pp. 25–51.

Renswoude, Irene van; Steinová, Evina. 'The Annotated Gottschalk: Symbolic Annotation and Control of Heterodoxy in the Carolingian Age.' In Chambert-Protat, P.; Delmulle, J.; Pezé, W.; Thompson, J.C. eds. *La controverse carolingienne sur la prédestination: Histoire, textes, manuscrits*, Haut Moyen Âge 32. Turnhout: Brepols, 2019, pp. 249–278.

Rohmann, Dirk. *Christianity, Book-Burning and Censorship in Late Antiquity*. Berlin and Boston, MA: de Gruyter, 2016.

Rose, Els. *Ritual Memory: The Apocryphal Acts and Liturgical Commemoration in the Early Medieval West* (c. 500–1215), Mittellateinische Studien und Texte 40. Leiden: Brill, 2009.

Speyer, Wolfgang. *Buchvernichtung und Zensur des Geistes bei Heiden, Juden und Christen*. Stuttgart: A. Hiersemann, 1981.

Steckel, Sita. 'Between Censorship and Patronage: Interaction between Bishops and Scholars in Carolingian Book Dedications.' In Danielson, S.; Gatti, E. eds. *Envisioning the Bishop: Images and the Episcopacy in the Middle Ages*, Medieval Church Studies 29. Turnhout: Brepols, 2014, pp. 103–126.

Steinová, Evina. *Notam superponere studui. The Use of Annotation Symbols in the Early Middle Ages*, Bibliologia 52. Turnhout: Brepols, 2019.

Werner, Thomas. *Den Irrtum liquidieren. Bücherverbrennungen im Mittelalter*. Göttingen: Vandenhoeck & Ruprecht, 2007.

2
REGULATING *DANGEROUS KNOWLEDGE*

John Lockman's (1698–1771) Enlightened Readings of Jesuit Letters

Renate Dürr[1]

In the history of science, knowledge has often been defined by scholars as "justified true belief".[2] In times of fake news and uncertainties all over the world, it is no coincidence that scholars have also begun to think about the other side of knowledge: knowledge as "contested belief" for instance or "precarious knowledge", which is sometimes summarised as the "history of ignorance".[3] All these approaches underline that knowledge production depends on specific actors and the interests and beliefs they hold. As such, these approaches have also been very helpful to address the limits of knowledge production; its fragility and the precariousness of knowledge, which always runs the risk of being lost, forgotten, or destroyed. All the same, the underlying model of knowledge for the actors as well as for scholars researching them is that it is either accepted *or* contested. "Precarious knowledge" is true to those who believe in it and false to everyone else. In this chapter, I would like to think about yet another type of knowledge, which could be called *dangerous knowledge*. Unlike the concept of "precarious knowledge", this knowledge is simultaneously accepted *and* contested by the same people. This knowledge is *dangerous* precisely because it is knowledge one depends on without being able to prove said knowledge right or wrong. The underlying problem can perhaps be compared to the daily challenge of a secret service agent who knows that they can never really trust their sources.[4] In an article on spy networks in Elizabethan England, Michael Kempe, for instance, calls this knowledge "suspicious knowledge".[5] John Lockman (1698–1771), who is at the centre of this chapter, at some point named Jesuit knowledge "occult knowledge."[6] Knowledge that is considered *dangerous knowledge*, therefore, needs to be verified; and since many of the insights Jesuits brought to Europe couldn't be checked personally, Lockman, for instance, developed a multilayered way of assessment which are understood in this chapter as moments of *regulation* and *censura*.[7]

DOI: 10.4324/9780429279928-4

In the early modern period, all knowledge derived from long-distance communication was knowledge that one could not check personally. This was the case for accounts about faraway places in the world as much as for the results of experiments conducted by members of various learned societies. In the end, as the history of science has shown time and again, all scientific endeavours had to deal with this challenge.[8] In response, early modern intellectuals developed a nuanced set of elements to replace the direct testimony of eyewitnesses. Among the most important of these was establishing the reputation of the author and following specific narrative strategies when presenting new results or information. But how to deal with this knowledge when it was provided by an untrustworthy agent? What if the information, in some way, explicitly contradicted commonly held truths – for instance, by inserting miracle stories into their accounts? In eighteenth-century Europe, many scholars dealing with Jesuit accounts from all over the world found themselves facing this problem. Obviously, not all of them had a problem with Jesuit knowledge. The German polymath Gottfried Wilhelm Leibniz (1646–1716), for one, wrote long lists of questions he hoped Jesuits would be able to answer.[9] Others, however, were convinced that Jesuit knowledge was problematic. Throughout the eighteenth century, a growing number of enlightened scholars agreed that one had to be careful with the knowledge propagated by Jesuits. To many enlightened scholars, the Jesuits had become the most untrustworthy people in the world – evil and manipulative.[10] The reproach of manipulation implied that Jesuit knowledge was not just "raw information" about regions in the world nobody else had yet reached, but that it was already "cooked knowledge" which would always also transport a Jesuit world view – a world view one should avoid falling for.[11]

Sometimes, enlightened scholars would simply cherry-pick what they needed and leave out the rest of the account. The epistemological idea behind this way of reading was that 'facts' supposedly could not be affected by opinion. For some of the authors of Diderot's *Encyclopédie*, what was trustworthy in an untrustworthy report was what they thought untouched by the Jesuits: descriptions of nature or accounts of the culture before the arrival of the missionaries. To give but one example, the article in the *Encyclopédie* on the *Mojos*, a tribe located in present-day Bolivia, shows how the author did use the report presented in the Jesuit collection *Lettres édifiantes et curieuses*, but only copied small parts verbatim, leaving out most of the account.[12] The result of this approach is that the author denied the *Mojos* a history of their own, regardless of whether this was the intention or not. Even a century after the start of these Jesuit missions, he exclusively connected the culture of the *Mojos* with their customs, rites, and beliefs of the era before their conversion to Christianity, thus effectively portraying their culture as unchanging.[13] Unlike John Lockman, whose ways of *censura* I will discuss in this chapter, the author of the *Encyclopédie* was convinced that he could differentiate facts from stories or what was right or wrong within any given account.

This chapter focuses on John Lockman's translation of the first ten volumes of the *Lettres édifiantes et curieuses*, which he published in 1743 under the innocuous title *Travels of the Jesuits, into Various Parts of the World: Compiled from Their Letters*.[14] Although he had planned to publish five volumes, he only finished the first two. Together, they contain 48 letters, treatises, or prefaces from the *Lettres édifiantes et curieuses* and five other travelogues Lockman found interesting, although they were not written by Jesuits and were not been published in the original French collection.[15] He omitted seventeen texts, always making sure to tell the reader when he did so and why – mostly because he thought them too similar to a previous text.[16] Despite his strong anti-Jesuit attitude, Lockman was convinced of the importance of presenting the entire account as a way of doing justice to the author. Time and again, he stressed, he would avoid just publishing extracts, unlike "Several eminent Authors, of different Nations, [who] have had Recourse to the *Lettres édifiantes et curieuses*, as a Storehouse […]".[17] Instead, he mostly translated the long treatises fully and carefully without cherry-picking those passages that drew his ire. In so doing, he was acutely aware that the danger of being manipulated by the Jesuits also grew.[18]

In the preface to the first volume of translations, Lockman reflected at length on the way he dealt with this *dangerous knowledge* at his disposal. Reading the Jesuits, he explained, necessitated a very active and highly emotional way of gauging truth in stories. In what follows, I will try to reconstruct the way he would read such Jesuit reports and how he assessed the *dangerous knowledge* they contained.[19] In so doing, I will analyse Lockman's reading practices and the way he attested to the reliability (or lack thereof) of a text. In other words, my focus will be on reading and translating as an emotional process. This means first that this article is part of a series of long and lively discussions on the "history of reading".[20] It also aims to show that the study of scientific practice should include reflections on the role of emotions in the production and transfer of knowledge, which, in turn, plays a significant part in the way histories of knowledge are being shaped in the present.[21] For this article, I will begin by reconstructing the process of reading and assessing information as visible in the annotations to Lockman's translations. Then, I will study two very different examples of *dangerous knowledge* visible in his work. Nonetheless, the letters from the remote region of the Mojos will provide an example for the type of knowledge one could hardly check for accuracy.[22] The Jesuits, after all, were the first European people travelling these frontier areas in the Andes and practically remained the sole purveyors of information on the region for decades. The second example is a famous 60-page letter by Jean Venant Bouchet (1655–1732) on religions on the Indian subcontinent, originally published in 1711.[23] This letter was intended to be part of an ongoing discussion on whether or not Indian religions had discernable Jewish and Christian roots. It did not even attempt to hide its apologetic intentions. Based on these examples, I will finally draw some broader conclusions on regulating *dangerous knowledge* as a mode of *censura* during the European Enlightenment.

Lockman's Antidote: Emotions and the "tête-à-tête" of Opinions

Although John Lockman has been nearly forgotten in historical research, he was well known and well regarded among the Enlightenment scholars of the eighteenth century.[24] To give only a few examples: together with Thomas Birch, he took it upon himself to promote the English edition of Pierre Bayle's *Dictionnaire historique et critique* published in 1734 – an edition for which he had also translated many articles.[25] Apart from that, he translated more than twenty books from French into English, amongst them several works by Voltaire and some volumes of the *Cérémonies et Coutumes Religieuses* by Bernard and Picart.[26] John Lockman was also famous for his cooperation with William Boyce and Händel, for whom he wrote the text of some oratorios and particularly for his poems and ballads.[27] Finally, in 1750, he became secretary to the *Free British Fishery Society*, a typical Enlightenment project aimed at promoting economical relief for the poor while simultaneously strengthening British maritime power.[28] In spite of all his accomplishments, Lockman never went to university. He also hardly ever left London. All that he knew, therefore, came from books he had read.

Even for a man of his time, Lockman's aversion to the Jesuits was strong. In the course of a fierce libel case, for instance, he called Lemuel Dole Nelme, his colleague at the *Free British Fishery Society*, a *Jesuit* on nearly every single page.[29] This was not for any overtly religious reason: both parties had accused one another of misappropriating 50 pounds from the society. Nelme blamed Lockman and Lockman defended himself by calling the society's accountant "little", "dapper", "double-tongued" Jesuit, who was telling "monstrous Untruth", culminating in Lockman's description of his opponent as "a low, venal, dirty Reptile" and a "viper".[30] Here, as so often, Lockman used the viper metaphor as an invective against the Jesuits, even if Nelme was a fish merchant at the London Exchange Alley and certainly not a Jesuit of all people.[31] Another telling example of this is Lockman's martyrology, written only shortly after the *Travels of the Jesuits* albeit published much later.[32] In this world view, the Jesuits were the worst evil in the world and an embodiment of the anti-Christ because of the way they concealed their true intentions. "Thrice happy Great-Britain, which has long since purged itself of those noxious vipers!", Lockman exclaims at the end of one of his chapters.[33]

As Lockman knew, one needs an antidote against the poison of the vipers. He explained this in his long preface to the *Travels of the Jesuits*:

> But as Matters stand, no one, I presume, will wonder that an English Protestant, who endeavours to give an accurate Version of their [the Jesuits', R.D.] Missions, without disguising a single Circumstance; should as a Lover of Truth, of Mankind, and of his native country, present an Antidote along with it.[34]

To Lockman, this antidote consisted of lengthy commentaries – digressions of five pages or more – with which Lockman attempted to place words, interpretations, or results in a new, more acceptable light. In so doing, Lockman inserted himself into a specific enlightened way of debating and scepticism which he might have come across while translating articles from Pierre Bayle's *Dictionnaire historique et critique* and Bernard/Picart's *Cérémonie et coutumes religigieuses*.[35] Furthermore, the way Lockman administered his cures also allows historians to peek over his shoulder to watch him work.

According to Lockman, the effects of his antidote would occur in two "phases".[36] First, it was important to give free rein to one's own emotions. Apparently, Lockman trusted his own emotional outbursts. As he explains, he always did his utmost to treat these Jesuit texts in a fair and balanced manner, but at times found it impossible to restrain his "indignation". In those cases, he needed to express his feelings in writing:

> [...] 'tis only on certain Occasions which raised such an Indignation in me as I could not possibly conceal. Having a natural Aversion to Hypocrisy in every Shape, and a strong Inclination to speak my Thoughts at all Times when I presume it necessary; I could not forbear venturing them on Paper, whenever I supposed an Imposition glaring, or even suspicious.[37]

In other words, Lockman trusted the emotions he felt while engaging with the text. It is possible that Lockman here harkened back to an ancient rhetorical model, according to which, in the words of Irene van Renswoude, "emotions, and in particular the emotion 'indignation', was considered a tool of assessment to distinguish true from false arguments".[38] It was thought that emotions could not be manipulated and that their unprompted, unplanned rise might indicate an underlying truth. In this way, they might have acted like Lockman's "natural aversions", which showed him when Jesuit texts were wrong if not manipulative. After all, also in the eighteenth century, Catholics and Protestant were still influenced by a common Christian interpretation of the Aristotelian theory of affects, which emphasised that God made his works known through feelings – albeit primarily fear and joy.[39] To Lockman, emphasising the spontaneous nature of his writings thus served to counteract the calculated manipulation in the Jesuit texts. Time and again, Lockman wrote that a thought or argument simply occurred to him because a "fictitious these [...] puts me in Mind of a Relation publishe'd in one of our News-Papers some Years since".[40] All the same, the cross-references underpinning such commentaries demonstrate that such footnotes were not written down impulsively, but that they were put in the service of an equally carefully orchestrated counterargument.[41]

In the preface to his translation, Lockman confessed that his indignation sometimes got so overwhelming that he was all but forced to take recourse to irony.[42] Nevertheless, he would usually engage with this *dangerous knowledge* by seeking out philosophical counterarguments. This second phase of administering antidote was what Lockman referred to as a *tête-à-tête* of opinions.[43] This concept invokes the idea of a meeting of minds in a familiar setting. Emotions play an important role here as well. Lockman himself described the satisfaction he would feel when drafting his commentaries:

> Desirous of instructing myself, and delighted with the Articles I was compiling, my Pen slid along sensibly, and frequently took in more than I at first designed, as Men who set out for a pleasurable Airing, are often invited to wander much farther than they at first intended to go. Again, some of these Notes will, perhaps, betray the Familiarity of a tête-à-tête, and appear not writ with the Regard which ought always to be shown the Public. I must crave their Indulgence on this Occasion. Wrapt in my Subject, I sometimes imagined I was writing only for myself, or for an intimate Friend [...].[44]

By presenting it in this way, the encounter with the *dangerous knowledge* of the Jesuits was turned into an enjoyable educational programme, which proved irresistible to Lockman. Once again, he conjures an image of a spontaneous exchange of ideas, during which, as shown by this passage, the expression of emotions served to alleviate mistrust and raise confidence in one's own position. This rhetorical conceit has three important consequences. First, it replaces the previously suspicious stance on Jesuit self-representation, including their alleged lies and manipulations, with the "familiarity" of a conversation among friends or even lovers. There is no shouting during a *tête-à-tête*. Nobody calls each other names and plenty of room is given to contrary opinions. Second, the juxtaposition between Jesuit and anti-Jesuit positions not only gives the discourse an air of objectivity, but also makes it an exercise in self-reflection. Lockman had thus far described himself as an aloof translator, eager to see justice done to the texts and their authors, but here he suddenly becomes an author himself: "my pen", "instructing myself", "writing for myself", "wrapt in my Subject". This however implies that the hitherto "objective", external position actually reflects Lockman's own personal struggle, a struggle to establish a truth that was so important to him that he understood it as a political programme.[45] Third, Lockman emphasises once again that *dangerous knowledge* may be rendered harmless if one opts to neither believe it straight away, nor to dismiss it outright, but instead to debate it with an open mind. The *tête-à-tête* of opinions is thus more than a mere metaphor. It is a tool to envisage real and imagined conversations that were meant to be so realistic that Lockman even went so far as to preface a comment in a footnote with the cautious: "If I might be allowed to add a Word or two [...]".[46]

By reading this exchange of opinions or viewpoints, readers become eyewitnesses, and consequently, they would serve as the arbiters, presented with the task to authenticate the knowledge generated through debate. In certain passages, Lockman even went so far as to include his audience in the performative process of the debate: "The Reader may remember what was quoted from Bernier, on this Head, a little above".[47] A similar effect is created by the many dates and times added into the commentary. Time and again, Lockman would note exactly when he had translated and commented on a certain text: "I write this in 1741", he wrote at a certain point – and note how he renders this in the present tense.[48] Another time, Lockman would specifically mention that he finally had maps "now before me".[49] This immediacy, finally, also allows us to watch as Lockman discovered his mistakes and corrected them. For instance, while working on reports about Ethiopia, he mentions on page 341 that he had not been aware of two important travel accounts while he was composing his commentaries on pages 236, 244, and 337.[50] Only four pages separated the old, erroneous knowledge from these new insights.[51] Lockman saw this not as a reason to revisit what he had previously written, but to underline once again that the reader was in a direct and open dialogue with the texts presented. And this dialogue was spurred forward by new encounters and new insights: "I did not meet with them [the two travelogues, R.D.] till after the Sheets [...] were gone to Press [...]".[52]

To Lockman, encountering a book was like meeting an acquaintance. Both could be consulted whenever he was unsure about something, such as when a "Gentleman of my Acquaintance, who resided some Years at Canton" confirmed to Lockman that the information the Jesuits provided about the size of cities in China was more or less correct.[53] With an "English Gentleman, who was a considerable Time in the Spanish West-Indies", he spoke about the treatment of indigenous peoples by the Spanish, learning among others "that the Spaniards treat the Americans, with much greater Lenity, then our Countrymen [...]".[54] The assertion that people in Ethiopia were brown-skinned instead of black, which Lockman apparently found hard to believe, was indeed contradicted by "all Travellers I have met with" – leading to the question of exactly how many of those travellers had really gone to Ethiopia.[55] The pattern that emerges is that Lockman, whenever he was in doubt, left his desk to question and debate the experts he knew. He never failed to mention that these acquaintances were well-travelled "English Gentlemen", signalling that their social status, the mores they represented, and especially their role as eyewitnesses lent an extra layer of credibility to the accounts of the Jesuits.

As a rule, Lockman's footnotes were meant to spare his readers the long searches for necessary background information, so they tended to consist of lengthy excerpts from relevant books.[56] Nonetheless, Lockman quoted works that explicitly dealt with the Jesuits, their activities and their self-promotion. To that end, the key witnesses were usually Jansenists and their writings, such as Antoine Arnauld's *La morale pratique des Jésuites*, Pascal's *Lettres provinciales*, or an English translation of a treatise, issued in Paris, about the Chinese Rites controversies, with the telling title *The New Gospel of the Jesuits, Compared with the Old One of Jesus Christ*.[57] Another important source for Lockman was travelogues and geographical treatises – the more recent, the better. This purported direct usage of books and the safe knowledge they contained showed that Lockman saw value in using the very newest publications he could find, so as to better assess the dangerous knowledge of the Jesuits. In that sense, the complete absence of geographical literature from Antiquity is all the more striking. Throughout Lockman's translations, I have only been able to find one reference to a classical work, namely the then-current English translation of Horace's *Odes and Satyres*.[58] Generally, however, Lockman uses travel accounts published in the 1720s and 1730s – hot off the press, by the standards of the time. Among these, recent works featured books published in London, such as his own translation of *The Religious Ceremonies of All Nations* by Bernard Picart and Jean-Frédéric Bernard published in 1731; a translation of medieval Arabic travelogues on Asia edited by Abbé Renaudot and published in 1733; John Atkins' *A Voyage to Guinea, Brazil and the West Indies* published in 1735; and Thomas Salmon's *Modern History or the Present State of Nations* from 1739. Additional recent works used by Lockman include Benoît de Maillet's *Description de l'Égypte* published in Paris in 1735 or the *Histoire du Christianisme d'Ethiopie et d'Armenie* by Matyrin Veyssière La Croze published in 1739. To these recent publications were added a number of Jesuit descriptions of China, most notably the one by Jean-Baptiste Du Halde, *Description Geographique, Historique, Chronologique, Politique, et Physique de l'Empire de la Chine et de la Tartarie*, which appeared as a four-volume series in Paris in 1735.[59]

Using these travelogues, Lockman checked the Jesuit reports for accuracy regarding their statements on cities, landscapes, or the everyday life of the local populace. Nevertheless, the first step to this process was always to verify the routes taken by the missionaries as precisely as possible. Most pre-eminently, Lockman used an atlas by Herman Moll, which had also appeared quite recently and which covered the entire known world.[60] He looked up every single location mentioned, which gave him enormous satisfaction whenever he was successful.[61] It was a lot of work, as the indigenous place names were rendered in a curious French notation in the *Lettres édifiantes et curieuses*, which made it difficult to compare them with the English maps at his disposal. In order to do so, Lockman would therefore attempt to reconstruct the French "sounds" using English spelling.[62] Should this not yield the desired result, Lockman would give the French spelling in a footnote as well.[63] In the process, he documented not only his attention to even the smallest of details while translating, but also emphasised once again the newsworthiness of the information, some of which had not even made it to the most recent atlases. Lockman employed a similar strategy for concepts he did not know and which had not yet found their way into French dictionaries, for example, when he translated the word "Damiers" with "Boobies, (which are birds)", adding: "I have not found this Word in Any of my Dictionaries; but I believe the Interpretation I have given of it is right".[64]

Given that the Jesuits would often report on regions about which even the newest maps contained only scanty information, one of Lockman's challenges was to make plausible the distances as well as the latitudes and longitudes logged so as to retain some indication about the locations described.[65] For instance, he had to deal with an island to the North of Madagascar, "not specified in Moll's Maps, nor mentioned in any Travels I have met with".[66] Sometimes he too lost track of things, such as when a letter about a naval voyage to China mentions that the company rested on an island called "Polaure". Lockman almost took "this to be Pooleron", but didn't "find it to agree very well with the Course our Jesuit was steering".[67] In other cases, he would simply explain to his readers that "I don't meet with this Name [...] in our Maps", drawing attention to the parallels that existed between his imaginary travels and the way he, as a translator, checked the information given in the maps at his disposal.[68] This was an important addition to the imagined conversations with books and acquaintances in his commentaries: imagining a journey was given a central place in the assessment of *dangerous knowledge*.

But what could Lockman do when neither a comparison with other books nor a conversation with other travellers or even a reconciliation with known maps helped put this knowledge in the picture? In some cases, Lockman would take recourse to his own experiences. Even if he lived almost his whole life in London, Lockman did spend some time in France in the year 1741.[69] During this time, he showed himself to be an inquisitive investigator, who described church decorations,[70] commented on intra-Catholic quarrels,[71] and observed the tenacity of mendicants with wide-eyed wonder.[72] Despite his anti-Catholic attitude, he opened himself up to new experiences: he dined with Jesuits and Benedictines,[73] wrote about "a friend of mine (a roman Catholic)",[74] and attended Catholic Mass several times:

> Being at Mass, one Sunday, at the great Carthusians in Paris, some of the Fathers or Brothers, did not only strike their Heads against the Ground; but lay a considerable Time upon their Bellies, in two Lines; a Sight that is not a little odd to an Englishman.[75]

Through these experiences in Paris, Lockman was able to contextualise descriptions of Catholic practices in China – in the process making those same practices in Paris seem more exotic. In some cases, he used his own knowledge to explicitly authenticate reports which he could not otherwise confirm, such as when he reflected on Chinese commercial practice by comparing it with its French counterpart. "Seeing (when at Paris) the Keys of the River Seine there, [...] I considered the Kingdom of France in much the same Light (in Miniature) as this Father does China [...]".[76] Sometimes, he even took explicit recourse to the scientific panacea of casting himself as an eyewitness: when comparing the European practice of bloodletting to the ascetic practices to combat fevers in India, he would, for example write that "I myself have been often an Eye-witness" to this.[77]

What we see here, then, is the extent to which reading about experiences in exotic locations became inextricably bound up with one's own background. It was not just that the process of reading itself became an emotional experience *per se*, because the narratives written by the missionaries already contained many different emotions. Oftentimes, we read exciting accounts about the boundary experiences they found themselves in on their travels: shipwrecks from which they narrowly escaped with their lives, dealing with endless tropical rains, or living through wars and persecutions. The adventures of these missionaries thus also created a sense of fear and excitement, but also of accomplishment; a sense of desolation, but also of faith in God. Reading, to Lockman, helped to relive all these experiences, including the emotions that accompanied one on their journey. As he candidly writes in the dedication of his second book:

> [...]
> Led by the FATHERS, o'er th'Atlantic fly,
> Whilst circling Months shew only Waves and Sky:
> Amaz'd, see Lightnings flash; hear Thunders roul;
> See Ocean gape as to th'Antartic Pole:
> View distant Shipwrecks; hear th'expiring Groan;
> Then land in Regions, barbarous and unknown.
> [...].[78]

Debating *Dangerous Knowledge*: The Perspective of the Other

Thanks to all these comments added and the commentaries to these comments, the *Travels of the Jesuits* took the form of a dialogue as well. The layout already shows how Lockman considered all his options and attempted to render the *dangerous knowledge* harmless using the power of contextualisation. Many pages show how the "antidote" simply overwhelms the potential poison of the Jesuit vipers through its sheer volume. In what follows, I will offer an interpretation of two such imaginary debates: first, the way Lockman engaged with three interconnected letters about the Mojos region, and second, the debate about Jewish or Christian roots of the religions in India. The first of these cases concerns a region about which Europeans knew practically nothing, meaning that Lockman was not able to confirm his information by using other reports. Here, Lockman's fear of being manipulated by the Jesuits shaped his commentaries; he, therefore, focused on the Society of Jesus especially. The latter case, about religious practices in India, had become a central building block for the conceptualisation of the divine during the Enlightenment, which made it a debated issue indeed – and Lockman knew he would enhance one side with his footnotes at the expense of the other.

The comments to the letters about the Mojos make clear that Lockman's vocal advocacy for immediacy does not mean he always wrote down his comments spontaneously. Instead, the comments show careful planning and have their own internal logic.[79] The comments to the first translated letter on the Mojos put the Jesuits themselves in the centre of the *tête-à-tête* of opinions.[80] Consequently, Lockman specifies that the descriptions of cannibalism by Stanislaus Arlet will be the subject of a later footnote.[81] The longest comment to this letter was prompted by the statement that Jesuits had come to the Mojos to teach Christianity and serve the Lord.[82] As "antidote" to this appraisal, Lockman cites two anecdotes from Antoine Arnauld's *Morale Pratique* written in 1669, which are supposed to have happened more or less in the same geographic area.[83] In the first of these, the Jesuits were accused of not properly continuing the education of the populace after their conversion. It is even suggested that this neglect led to a rebellion against the Jesuits. The second story is about envy amongst the Jesuits themselves. This is illustrated using the example of the Jesuit Mendiola, who was accused of having left the order to marry an indigenous woman.[84] In a subsequent note, also taken from the *Morale pratique*, Lockman explains that the Jesuits would always do their best to ingratiate themselves with local populations and even went so far as to forge letters to facilitate that process.[85] Comments such as these fit perfectly with the ideas presented in Lockman's martyrology, mentioned at the start of this article: as far as Lockman was concerned, Jesuits were untrustworthy, self-centred, and manipulative.

The second translated letter on the Mojos, written by Father Nyel in 1705 also gave Lockman the occasion to engage with the Jesuits themselves.[86] This time, the focus is on their theology and the longest comment is about the idea that Jesuits liked to take confession often.[87] Quoting a lengthy passage from the *Lettres Provinciales* by Blaise Pascal, Lockman treats his readers to a conversation between a Jansenist and a Jesuit, during which the latter – according to Pascal – shamelessly declared that Jesuits always find a way to absolve anyone of their sins.[88] They got away with this, the text goes on, because they would explain away the circumstances surrounding a sin or a crime in such minute detail that every transgression ends up seeming relatively insignificant. This leads Lockman, on the one hand, to take a strong position against such practices: "If the Jesuits who went to propagate the *Christian* Religion among the *Moxos*, allowed of the Maxims above ascribed to the Society, their Arrival must have been a Curse to that People, instead of a Blessing [...]".[89] On the other hand, the "if" in that sentence demonstrates that Lockman was not quite sure of Pascal's interpretation. Perhaps this can be explained with the main argument about Jesuit confessional practice that is made in the letter. It is emphasised that the Jesuits did not require penance from the sinners, but only personal self-reflection.[90] Given that Lockman, himself an Anglican Protestant, cites these passages from the *Lettres Provinciales*, the anti-Jesuit sentiments contained within might have ultimately missed their mark, because Anglicans did not practice the private confession or penance alluded to by Pascal. This of course raises the question why Lockman chose this topic out of all the possibilities to criticise Jesuit theology, but he himself clarifies this right at the beginning of his comment, when he writes by distancing himself from Jansenist argumentation: "The Ennemies of the Jesuits accuse them of sometimes dispensing this Sacrament" (i.e. confession, R.D.), adding in brackets: "as it is called by the Romanists".[91]

Yet another point of criticism is addressed when Lockman comments on the abbreviated description of the life and death of the Jesuit missionary Cyprian Baraza, which was the third translated text with information on the Mojos region and culture in Lockman's compilation.[92] Lockman here decidedly succumbs to several types of cultural relativism at once. For example, he compared the never-ending rains and the mosquitoes that plague the Llanos de Mojos with similarly horrible weather conditions – and similarly uneducated inhabitants – in Lincolnshire or Somersetshire.[93] The body paint and decorations of the Mojos, conversely, reminded Lockman of the make-up worn by certain women in Paris.[94] All this culminates in a discussion of prejudices held by travellers and specifically by Jesuits, vis-à-vis peoples like the Mojos: "I believe Travellers, and especially the Jesuits, often represent these un-enlightened Nations as much more ignorant than they are in reality [...]".[95] Using a plethora of quotations from the *Essais* by Michel de Montaigne published in the 1580s, Lockman argues that people have a tendency to describe other cultures in negative terms for the simple reason that they were different from their own culture. He then goes on to compare European law to that encountered elsewhere, and also contrasts the conceptions of power and rulership in the various regions in a way that is decidedly Eurosceptic.[96] Echoing Montaigne, Lockman thus expresses his dislike of the Jesuit idea that "[they] shou'd first make 'em Men, before they [the Mojos, R.D.] cou'd be *Christians*".[97] All these comments lead Lockman towards the previously announced engagement with the supposed cannibalism of the Mojos: an argument prompted by the assertion of the original report that the Mojos "have made themselves formidable to all other Nations, by their native Fierceness, and the barbarous Custom they have of eating Man's Flesh".[98] In an emotional reaction to this claim, Lockman quotes long passages from a travelogue by John Atkins (1685–1757), a ship's doctor and personal acquaintance of Lockman.[99] According to Atkins, the idea that cannibalism was so often ascribed to people in many newly discovered regions mostly reflected the fears and ignorance of many Europeans while also lending a sense of adventure to their voyage into the unknown – which could, in turn, be useful to make their travels and safe return appear all the more wondrous or to legitimise future conquests and expropriations.[100] This rendered all supposed eyewitness accounts inherently useless, along with more "empirical" evidence: bones which supposedly indicated the existence of cannibalism more often than not belonged to monkeys or apes.[101] All things considered, Lockman emphasised, following Atkins, the practice of anthropophagy was so contrary to human nature that it was all but impossible to assume it really existed – except maybe during famines or to combat the threat of starvation on the European (!) ships as they travelled across the globe.[102] Juxtaposing these Jesuit letters with anti-Jesuit representations of similar phenomena thus moved from a critique of the Jesuits, their morals and their theology, to a reflection on the way one should treat different cultures in general. The problem did not lie exclusively with Jesuit errors in judgement, but with those committed by all Europeans: a conclusion that was the direct result of Lockman's process of dialogic learning.

Lockman needed all the "antidote" he could get to deal with possible manipulations in the letters from the Mojos region, simply because the Jesuits were nearly the only ones able to report from this region. Jesuit treatises in my second example of this article, meanwhile, were deceptive for wholly different reasons. This example concerns the way arguments were constructed during a debate that was central to the early Enlightenment period: the question of whether or not polytheistic practices of faith should be understood as religious. Scholars nowadays recognise how this debate within European scholars has affected and limited Western understanding about Buddhism, (Neo-)Confucianism, or Hinduism, even going as far as to claim that concepts like "Hinduism" were in many ways a nineteenth-century invention.[103] It should thus be remembered that the Jesuit treatise on Hindu practices in question and all its translations are part of an "Orientalist" discourse as proposed by Edward Said – including those instances where questions or answers by Brahman philosophers are quoted.[104] In any case, the French Jesuit Jean Venant Bouchet started his enquiries by stating that his "design" was "to prove, that the Indians borrowed their Religion from the Books of Moses and the Prophets".[105] With that one statement, Bouchet placed himself on the side of those who interpreted the practices of the people in India as religious practices and also on the side of those who would emphasise similarities between Hindu and Judaeo-Christian practices.

What was at stake in Europe was not only the presence of and competition between European powers in Asia, or the contest between Franciscan and Jesuit missionaries, or even the rivalry between the Catholic and Protestant missions in India, but also the question of what constituted the essence of "religion" more generally. After all, if one defines polytheistic "idolatry" as religion, it becomes possible to compare the practices and fundaments of various such religions. Recognising this, in turn, became one of the foundational ideas of the deistic and natural theological approach to religion during the European Enlightenment. Specifically, early Enlightenment thinkers assumed that the idea of a single creator God combined with a central set of commonly accepted morals and virtues connected all the world's religions.[106] A second assumption was that all extant religions were degenerated versions of a single primeval religion – with the various forms of religion indicating various degrees of degeneracy.[107]

It was a theme close to the Jesuits' own interests. The question of whether Confucian, Buddhist, or Hindu practices could be interpreted as being "religious" directly affected their missionary methods.[108] Accommodation to local customs was fundamental to Jesuit proselytising methods in India and China, to the extent that they ended up provoking the Chinese and Malabar Rites controversies within the Catholic Church, which ended with the Jesuits conceding defeat.[109] Starting in the late sixteenth century, most Jesuits operating in Asia were of the opinion that the traditional rites they encountered – such as ancestor worship – were compatible with the Christian faith and could be continued after baptism, provided they did not contain any explicit religious connotations. Around the year 1600, they would therefore stress the essentially "Atheist" nature of (Neo-)Confucianism and Hinduism in China and India. Several decades later, many Jesuits rejected these ideas. Their accommodation strategy increasingly began to be based on the search for potentially Christian elements in Hindu and Buddhist practices and imagery. During the seventeenth and eighteenth centuries, the Jesuits thus did not have a clear, unambiguous answer to the question of whether

Indian polytheistic rituals could be described as a religion or not. Nevertheless, all their positions should be read as arguments in the rites' controversies. This, in turn, means they were highly biased in themselves. Against this background, it stands to reason that the treatises composed by Jesuits about religious practice in China and India were thus read with great caution by European scholars.

Letters from India and China feature prominently in the *Lettres édifiantes et curieuses*, especially in the first ten volumes translated by Lockman. Among these are several letters and reports by the French Jesuit Jean Venant Bouchet, to whom we will now turn.[110] Some of Bouchet's treatises about India had gone through various editions and translations in Europe, including his letter to Pierre-Daniel Huet (1630–1721), the erstwhile bishop of Avranches. It was first published in 1711, in the ninth volume of the *Lettres édifiantes et curieuses* and translated into English almost immediately.[111] Some years later, it was added to Frédéric Bernard's compilation *Cérémonies et Coutumes Religieuses*.[112] In 1726, it was translated into German for the *Neue Welt-Bott*.[113] Finally, John Lockman was responsible for two further translations, first as part of the English translations of the *Cérémonies et Coutumes Religieuses*, which appeared in 1734, and subsequently for his translation of the *Lettres édifiantes et curieuses* from 1743.[114] In most cases, the treatise was printed without abbreviations. Even self-professed deists like Frédéric Bernard agreed with some of the fundamental propositions formulated by Bouchet. Whereas other reports from India, written by a number of protestant observers, received additional comments, Bouchet's treatise remained untouched, and indeed was the final text before Bernard's own summary of religion in India.[115] John Lockman, however, composed an extensive commentary, which increased the length of Bouchet's text by about a third. Before studying Lockman's comments to Bouchet's treatise, it's necessary to briefly summarise the ideas of this influential text.

Initially, Jean Venant Bouchet was a vocal opponent of Hindu "idolatry". For instance, in letters written shortly after his arrival in India, he proudly described how he had provoked conflicts with Brahmins.[116] Commenting on writings about the destruction of pagodas or "idols", Lockman, in turn, wrote: "Some Persons would say, what Business had the Jesuit [i.e. Bouchet, R.D.] to leave his Native Country, and sail to another so many thousand Miles distant from it, there to disturb the Natives in their Possessions?"[117] As the years progressed, however, Bouchet's opinion started to change, partly in response to his own experiences with Indian religious practices and partly because of his encounters with the bigoted members of the papal investigative commission who visited India during the so-called *Malabar Rites Controversy*. Bouchet subsequently took the name of an Indian renunciant, adopted an ascetic lifestyle, and diligently practiced the Lotus position.[118] He even went so far as to reconcile the belief in reincarnation with Christian ideas about the afterlife, although even he had his limits. For instance, Bouchet refused to accept the idea that animals possessed a soul, thereby quoting René Descartes – of all people – when he tried to convince a Brahman of the absurdity of this idea. The Brahman responded indignantly, prompting Bouchet to grumble in turn that "I realized that one ought not even in jest propose to Indians the systems of the modern philosophers".[119]

Bouchet's deliberations in his letter to the well-known intellectual Pierre-Daniel Huet started from the statement that most Indians "are not so absurd as to give into Atheism".[120] Instead, he assumed that "they entertain a tolerably just Idea of the Deity, tho' depraved and vitiated by the Worship of Idols".[121] Thus, the approach taken by Bouchet is first of all a historical one, based on the idea that he was dealing with a degenerate version of a monotheistic past. The majority of his subsequent treatise is aimed at finding traces of an underlying "ancient truth" in the religious practices he encountered in India.[122] In order to prove this, Bouchet goes in search of common ground between Hinduism and Christianity.

Bouchet starts his argumentation by positing that the Indians actually were monotheistic. They distinguished between one single God and three forces or sub-deities, of which *Bruma* represented creation; *Wistnou*, preservation; and *Routeren*, destruction. Following from these assumptions, Bouchet goes on to find numerous parallels between Indian traditions and the stories of the Old Testament. For instance, he found that in the Indian creation myth, the first man is also created from clay and mention is made of Paradise as the Garden of Eden. There are Indian tales about a Deluge, including a figure that, according to Bouchet, appeared similar to Noah. Abraham, by a similar logic, has a clear parallel in Brahma, as shown already by the similarity in their names and those of their respective wives Sarah and Sarasvadi (especially since *Vadi* simply means "wife/woman"). Bouchet was aware of the limits of his comparisons: "I very possibly [...] may have expatiated too much on the Conformity between the Doctrine of the Indians and that of the Israelites", he writes once, before immediately continuing to describe further similarities – this time between Indian religions and Christianity.[123] Among these are an equivalent to the Trinity represented by the three "sub-deities", the practice of confessional practices, as well as the fact that (the Christian) God has become incarnate several times, which has a parallel in the belief in reincarnation, albeit in a limited fashion.[124]

Lockman was unable to leave Bouchet's letter uncommented as Frédéric Bernard had done. The reason for that probably was the appearance of Thomas Salmon's multi-volume *Modern History Or the Present State of Nation* in 1739.[125] In Chapter 11 of the first volume, Salmon summarised Bouchet's treatise and eventually dismissed it because "none of our own people, or the Portuguese, or the Dutch" would "ever have made this observation of the history of the Bramins" – even if he later qualifies this by stating that "Thus much is true, the Indians do acknowledge one supreme God".[126] Lockman quotes Salmon's comments about Bouchet in full, and adds for his part that Protestants, too, hailing from different nations across Europe, had made observations similar to those of Bouchet – often even long before the arrival of the Jesuits. Lockman's chief witnesses in this regard were the travelogues by the English chaplain Henry Lord, who travelled to Surat from 1624 to 1629, and the Dutch cleric Abraham Rogerius (1609–1649) – both of whom were also featured in the *Cérémonies et Coutumes Religieuses*.

Moreover, the *Voyages* by the French doctor François Berniers (1625–1688) are quoted extensively, as is the account by the Italian traveller Pietro della Valle (1586–1652). Although Lockman was usually interested in the most recent travel reports, all these texts go back to the seventeenth century; Henry Lord's book even appeared as early as 1630. The main ingredient to this antidote thus consisted quite simply of denying the Jesuits the credit for their "discovery". But Lockman goes one step further when he compares Bouchet's description of Indian religious practices with Dr. Hyde's *Historia Religionis veterum Persarum*, which appeared in 1700 but which, he assumes, must have remained under Salmon's radar.[127] Hyde had shown that the ancient Persian religion already demonstrated lots of commonalities with Judaism. And because India bordered directly on Persia, it was thus just as likely that this was how Jewish influences had reached the subcontinent. In a short summary of the relevant chapters from Hyde's work, Lockman locates exactly the same similarities that Bouchet had found between Judaism and Hinduism as well as the link to the narratives of the Old Testament and the Gospel: "The Gospel (according to Dr. Hyde, and several learned Persians) inform us, that the Birth of Christ was revealed to the Persians".[128] Lockman conceded that these hypotheses were on shaky ground, as it would be difficult to say anything with certainty about such ancient religions, "and that we are frequently obliged to grope our Way, at random, and in the dark". Lockman finds certainty in his emotional response. After all, to him it was really "very pleasant" that two intellectuals of the calibre of Dr. Hyde and Mr. Lord had reached such similar conclusions to the ones drawn by the Jesuit missionary Jean-Venant Bouchet, even if the similarities between Jesuit and non-Jesuit descriptions of Indian religions must have been uncanny to both groups involved.[129] But, the pleasure Lockman felt while discovering these similarities reassured Lockman of their verisimilitude. Thus, once again, emotions functioned like sign posts to what was right or wrong to this Enlightened intellectual.

Conclusion: Regulating *Dangerous Knowledge* as a Mode of Enlightened *Censura*

The idea behind John Lockman's "antidote" is a very emotional one. It invokes images of protection against snakes, of a fight to the death against a strong and dangerous enemy – not least because snakes tend to be hidden and are often noticed too late. Poisonous snakes can ruin even the most idyllic situations, as they are usually encountered during day trips which Lockman himself had described as "pleasurable airings". The choice for this particular vocabulary thus already indicates that reading and translating Jesuit texts was a highly emotional process for the staunchly anti-Jesuit Enlightenment scholar John Lockman. Lockman was convinced that he had to regulate the *dangerous knowledge* he encountered so as to render it harmless. The study on Lockman thus provides an exemplary case of *censura* as a highly emotional way of regulation. Following old traditions, the reflection on emotions played a significant role in the process of assessment.

According to Late Antique rhetorical models, *censura* started with *indignation*, an emotion which served as a road sign of sorts. As Lockman explained clearly in his prologue, his sense of indignation helped him identify the passages he mistrusted. Lockman, in other words, did not hide the emotional stimulus of his responses. Quite the contrary: to him, this was a *conditio sine qua non* for his *tête-à-tête* of opinions, which he considered to be a fair and balanced way of providing a platform for different points-of-view. Indignation gave way to satisfaction and inner peace, initial distrust strengthened the faith in one's own convictions, and doubt became certainty. Put bluntly, *dangerous knowledge* turned into *knowledge*. Emotions, to Lockman, therefore were not an undesirable by-product of the production of knowledge. On the contrary, the production of knowledge required these emotions.

Even if Lockman's own emotions played a central role in steering his assessments, the *tête-à-tête* of opinions was primarily meant for his intended audience – in this case, enlightened public intellectuals in England. Lockman made his readers an integral part of his imaginative reconstructions of his subjects' voyages and his imagined conversations with experts and the books they had written. In doing so, they stood witness to his *censura*. The concept of "imagination" might help clarify the importance of subjectivity within this process of *censura* because it underlines how much the acquisition of knowledge is based on one's own imagination, after all. The recourse to imaginative talks and travels characterised and structured Lockman's entire work, from the page layout to the vocabulary used to introduce his readers to the books, maps, and experts he consulted while assessing the information he translated. These imaginative dialogues were the "antidote" to the alleged poison of the Jesuits. By directly addressing the readers, Lockman included them into the *tête-à-tête* of opinions and required them to also practice changing their own perspectives regularly, as this was a cornerstone of Lockman's commentaries.

First and foremost, Jesuit perspectives were juxtaposed with those of their opponents, such as when Lockman referred to Jansenist writings or engendered understanding for the position of some Buddhists. Second, Lockman subjected anti-Jesuit viewpoints to the same process, as we have seen in his footnotes to reports on the Mojos. Thereby, he nuanced his own opinions by furnishing an opinion to counter a counter-opinion. Third, Lockman used this method to defend Bouchet's treatise on the similarities between Hinduism and Judaism, respective Christianity against the criticism from English Protestants. This is striking, as Bouchet had composed his work as part of the Malabar Rites Controversy, during which Protestants tended to follow the Pope's lead by criticising Jesuit ideas about accommodation to local customs. In fact, the very search for structural similarities between the different religions proved to be a common interest between Enlightenment thinkers and Jesuits to a much greater extent than either would dare to admit.[130] Studying suspicion towards knowledge thereby might become a key to understanding the Enlightenment.

Notes

1 A slightly different version of the following chapter will be published by Michiel van Groesen and Johannes Müller in the collective volume *Far from the Truth. Distance and the Problem of Credibility in the Early Modern World*, London and New York: Routledge, 2023. I would also like to thank Rutger Kramer (Utrecht) for the translation of this chapter.
2 Burke, *What Is the History of Knowledge?*; Mulsow, 'History of Knowledge'.
3 Mulsow, *Prekäres Wissen*; Zwierlein, *The Dark Side of Knowledge*; Kirsch, *Regimes of Ignorance*, Dürr, *Threatened Knowledge*.
4 See Ioanna Iordanou's chapter in this book.
5 Kempe, "Burn after Reading".
6 Lockman, *Travels*, vol. 2, 204, fn.
7 See the introduction by Fokko Jan Dijksterhuis and Irene van Renswoude's chapter.
8 Shapin, *A Social History of Truth*; Daston, *Objectivity*.
9 Clarke, *Oriental Enlightenment*, 46; Hsia, *Sojourners in a Strange Land*, 132.
10 Vogel, *Untergang der Gesellschaft Jesu*; Burson and Wright eds., *The Jesuit Suppression in Global Context*.
11 Burke, *What Is the History of Knowledge*, 6.
12 Diderot and d'Alembert et al., *Encyclopédie*, vol. x, 843–844; Du Halde, *Lettres édifiantes et curieuses*, vol. x, 186–252.
13 For the Jesuit mission in the area of the Mojos, see Block, *Mission Culture on the Upper Amazon*; Paschoud, *Le monde améridien*, 170.
14 Lockman, *Travels*: first edition: 1743; second edition 1763, third 1787; for the *Lettres édifiantes et curieuses*, see Rétif, "Brève histoire"; Paschoud, *Le monde améridien*.
15 Lockman, *Travels*, 1743, vol. 1, 279–308: "A Relation of the Expedition of the Portuguese into Abyssinia [...] extracted from Purchas Pilgrim"; ibid., 308–347: "Continuation of the State of the Christian Religion in Ethiopia; from the French of Mr. la Croze [...]", released 1739; ibid., 408–420: "A Descent made by the Spaniards, in the Island of California in 1683"; Lockman, *Travels*, 1743, vol. 2, 126–140: "A Journey undertaken by the Emperor of China into Eastern Tartary, Anno 1682"; ibid., 140–159: "A Journey undertaken by the Emperor of China into Western Tartary, Anno 1683", which he took from Jean-Baptiste Du Halde's *Description [...] de l'Empire de la Chine*, vol. 4.
16 For a similar attitude within the Republic of Letters, see Dirk van Miert's chapter in this volume.
17 Lockman, *Travels*, vol. 1, 1743, Preface, XIX–XX.
18 If he shortened, he mostly told the reader explicitly, for instance, Lockman, *Travels*, vol. 1, 1743, 447fn; vol. 2, 437fn. Sometimes, he does not tell the reader, for instance, with regard to a letter by P. Martin on Jean Venant Bouchet, ibid., 452–278. See Clooney, *Fr. Bouchet's India*, 30 fn15. Often, though, he explained why he kept the whole narrative, although he disagreed with its content, ibid., 392fn: "I would not have translated this idle Story above, had it not been for what follows"; similarly, 373fn:

> I thought proper to insert this Miracle, as our Jesuit is pleased to term it, as being of a very singular kind. [...] So silly a Story might be palm'd to good Purpose, upon a Parcel of ignorant Heathens; but to imagine that the European of Sense and Education would give the least Credit to it, must be as absurd as the Incident itself;

Similarly, vol. 1, 444fn and vol. 2, 410fn, 412fn, 422fn.
19 For a similar approach, see Harold Cook in this volume.
20 Darnton, 'What Is the History of Books?'; Chartier, *The Cultural Uses of Print*; Jardine and Grafton, 'Studied for Action'; Hackel, *Reading Material*; Dobranski, *Readers and Authorship*; Blair, *Too Much to Know*; Schurink, 'Manuscript Commonplace Books'.

21 Shapin, *A Social History of Truth*; Frevert, 'Vertrauen'; Burke, *A Social History of Knowledge*, vol. 1; Scheer, "Are Emotions a Kind of Practice?"; Mulsow, *Prekäres Wissen*; Id., 'History of Knowledge'.
22 Lockman, *Travels*, vol. 1, 1743, 93–101; vol. 2, 160–197, 437–468.
23 "Lettre du Père Bouchet [...] A Monseigneur l'ancien Evesque d'Avranches"; Lockman, *Travels*, vol. 2, 1743, 240–277.
24 For Lockman, see *Dictionary of National Biography*, vol. 12, Oxford: Oxford University Press, 1917, 53–54; Sambrook, "John Lockman", 258; Lee, "The Unexamined Premise", 246–249; Tarantino, *Protestant Approach*, 190–192.
25 British Library, Add MS 4254, fol. 101r; Add MS 4312.
26 *The Religious Ceremonies and Customs of the Several Nations of the World [...]*, London, 1731–1739.
27 For Lockman's role in promoting modernity and the British Empire, see Ogborn, *Spaces of Modernity*, 143.
28 British Library, Add MS 15154 Add 15155; Add MS 15159; Add MS 15160; Harris, "American Idols", 115.
29 Lockman, *Answer*, 4, 5, 8, 10, 13, 15, 16, 17, 18, 24, 25.
30 Lockman, *Answer*, 6, 17, 24.
31 He is mostly known for his essay on the origin of languages, Nelme, *Origin and Elements of Language and Letters*; reprinted: Alston ed., *English Linguistics*, No. 354.
32 Lockman, *History*, London 1760; 2nd ed. Dublin, 1763; Tarantino, "A Protestant Approach".
33 Lockman, *History*, 1763, 326; see also: Dürr, "Shepherd's Boy".
34 Lockman, *Travels*, vol. 1, 1743, Preface, XIII–XIV.
35 Grafton, *Footnote*, 194–221; Rubiés, "Christian Apologetics", 124; Subrahmanyam, *Europe's India*, 114.
36 Lockman, *Travels*, vol. 1, 1743, Preface, XIII–XIV.
37 Lockman, *Travels*, vol. 1, 1743, Preface, XIV–XV.
38 Renswoude, "Crass Insults", 184.
39 Dürr, "Laienprophetien", 21–24; Newmark, *Passion*; Bähr, *Furcht*.
40 Lockman, *Travels*, vol. 1, 1743, 251fn; similarly: vol. 2, 59fn.
41 Dürr, "The Shepherd's Boy". For instance, Lockman explains in vol. 1 he would talk more on cannibalism in another commen; Lockman, *Travels*, vol. 1, 1743, 94fn.
42 Lockman, *Travels*, vol. 1, 1743, Preface, XVII; for example, "Excellent this! As tho' the Spaniards had a right to kill the Natives, in Case they opposed their settling among them", Lockman, *Travels*, vol. 1, 413fn.
43 Lockman, *Travels*, vol. 1, 1743, Preface, XVIII.
44 Lockman, *Travels*, vol. 1, 1743, Preface, XVIII.
45 Lockman, *Travels*, vol. 1, 1743; Dedication to Arthur Onslow; see also Dürr, "The Shepherd's Boy".
46 Lockman, *Travels*, vol. 1, 1743, 307fn.
47 Lockman, *Travels*, vol. 2, 1743, 273fn.
48 Lockman, *Travels*, vol. 1, 1743, 378fn.
49 Lockman, *Travels*, vol. 2, 1743, 61fn.
50 Lockman, *Travels*, vol. 1, 1743, 341–342fn.
51 This passage shows that books were often printed piece by piece in the early modern period; see Grafton, "Rhetoric".
52 Lockman, *Travels*, vol. 1, 1743, 341–342:

> I did not meet with them till after the Sheets [...] were gone to Press, otherwise I should have altered a few of the Notes, particularly that, pag. 236, and 337, relating to the Nile, from Father Lobo, and that pag. 244, where 'tis observed that the Abyssinians acknowledge but two Sacraments.

53 Lockman, *Travels*, vol. 1, 1743, 55fn; similarly: 151fn.
54 Lockman, *Travels*, vol. 2, 1743, 168fn.
55 Lockman, *Travels*, vol. 1, 1743, 230fn.

56 Lockman, *Travels*, vol. 1, 1743, Preface, XVIII.
57 Arnaud, *La morale pratique des Jesuites*; Pascal, *Lettres écrites*; *The New Gospel of the Jesuits*.
58 Lockman, *Travels*, vol. 2, 1743, 212fn; Horace, *The Odes and Satyres*.
59 Lockman, *Travels*, vol. 2, 1743, 329–336fn. See also 306:

> As Father du Halde seems to give in his copious Work of China, the best Account I have met with concerning the Chineze Language, I shall here extract from it such Particulars, as appeared to me most worthy of notice.

60 Lockman doesn't specify which of these two editions he used: Herman Moll, The World Described or A Mew and Correct Sett of Maps [...]. [1730]; or Id., Atlas Minor, or a new and curious Set of Sixty two Maps [...]. London, [1732].
61 Lockman, *Travels*, vol. 1, 1743, Preface, VII:

> To this I would add (had it not been a Satisfaction which infinitely overpaid the Trouble I might be at on this Occasion) my setting the several Maps before me; and accompanying, as it were, the Fathers perpetually in their Peregrinations, both by Sea and Land.

62 Lockman, *Travels*, vol. 1, 1743, Preface, VII.
63 Lockman, *Travels*, vol. 1, 1743, 57fn, similarly 248fn, 261fn, 263fn, 272fn; vol. 2, 20fn, 220fn.
64 Lockman, *Travels*, vol. 1, 1743, 113fn, similarly 116fn, 203fn, 209fn.
65 Lockman, *Travels*, vol. 1, 1743, 51fn, 174fn, 192fn, 202fn, 205fn; vol. 2, 44fn, 161fn, 174fn.
66 Lockman, *Travels*, vol. 1, 1743, 160fn, similarly 162fn; vol. 2, 7fn.
67 Lockman, *Travels*, vol. 1, 1743, 117fn, similarly 194fn, 207fn, 228fn.
68 Lockman, *Travels*, vol. 1, 1743, 266fn, similarly vol. 2, 192fn.
69 Lockman, *Travels*, vol. 1, 1743, 372fn; vol. 2, 127fn.
70 Lockman, *Travels*, vol. 1, 1743, 470fn.
71 Lockman, *Travels*, vol. 2, 1743, 108fn, 182fn.
72 Lockman, *Travels*, vol. 2, 1743, 333fn.
73 Lockman, *Travels*, vol. 2, 1743, 182fn, 495fn.
74 Lockman, *Travels*, vol. 2, 1743, 365fn.
75 Lockman, *Travels*, vol. 2, 1743, 327fn.
76 Lockman, *Travels*, vol. 2, 1743, 303fn.
77 Lockman, *Travels*, vol. 2, 1743, 362fn.
78 Lockman, *Travels*, vol. 2, 1743, Dedication "To a Great Lady", 1–4, here 2.
79 For more details, see Dürr, "The Shepherd's Boy".
80 Lockman, *Travels*, vol. 1, 1743, 93–101.
81 Lockman, *Travels*, vol. 1, 1743, 94fn.
82 Lockman, *Travels*, vol. 1, 1743, 95–97fn.
83 Arnauld, *La morale pratique des Jésuites*.
84 Lockman, *Travels*, vol. 1, 1743, 96.
85 Lockman, *Travels*, vol. 1, 1743, 97. Ibid., 101.
86 Lockman, *Travels*, vol. 2, 1743, 160–197.
87 Lockman, *Travels*, vol. 2, 1743, 162–166fn.
88 Pascal, *Lettres écrites par Louis de Montalte*, Lettre X.
89 Lockman, *Travels*, vol. 2, 1743, 165fn (italics in the original).
90 Lockman, *Travels*, vol. 2, 1743, 162fn.
91 Lockman, *Travels*, vol. 2, 1743, 162fn.
92 Lockman, *Travels*, vol. 2, 1743, 437–468.
93 Lockman, *Travels*, vol. 2, 1743, 438fn, ibid., 441–442fn.
94 Lockman, *Travels*, vol. 2, 1743, 445fn.
95 Lockman, *Travels*, vol. 2, 1743, 441fn.
96 Lockman, *Travels*, vol. 2, 1743, 442fn.

97 Lockman, *Travels*, vol. 2, 1743, 451 (italics in the original).
98 Lockman, *Travels*, vol. 2, 1743, 458.
99 Atkins, *Voyage*; Lockman, *Travels*, vol. 2, 1743, 458–461fn, here: 461.
100 Lockman, *Travels*, vol. 2, 1743, 459fn.
101 Lockman, *Travels*, vol. 2, 1743, 461fn.
102 Lockman, *Travels*, vol. 2, 1743, 461fn.
103 For the European discussion on Indian religions, see Sweetman, *Mapping Hinduism*; Rubiés, *Travel*, chapter 9, 308–348; Id., "Christian Apologetics"; Subrahmanyam, *Europe's India*.
104 Said, *Orientalism*; see also the prudent approach by Subrahmanyam, *Europe's India*, XV–XVI.
105 Lockman, *Travels*, vol. 2, 1743, 241.
106 Wilson and Reill, Art. "Deism", 146–148; Weststeijn, "Spinoza sinicus"; Mulsow, "Joseph-François Lafitau"; Bulman and Ingram eds., *God in the Enlightenment*.
107 Champion, *Pillars*; Rubiés, "Christian Apologetics".
108 Dürr, "Akkomodation und Wissenstransfer".
109 Županov, *Rites Controversies*.
110 For Bouchet's life, see Clooney, *Fr. Bouchet's India*, 1–4.
111 Du Halde, *Lettres édifiantes et curieuses*, vol. 9, 1711, 1–60; *Travels of Several Learned Missioners*, 1–26.
112 Bernard and Picart, *Cérémonies*, vol. 6, 100–108.
113 Stöcklein, *Der Neue Welt-Bott*, vol. 1, n. 118, 84–90.
114 Bernard and Picart, *Religious Ceremonies and Customs*, vol. 3, 157–186; for the similarities of the two translations, see Clines, "Indian Job", 403 fn16.
115 See on the reports on India in the *Cérémonies et Coutumes Religieuses*: Hunt, Jacob, and Mijnhardt, *The Book That Changed Europe*; Ginzburg, "Provincializing the World"; Rubiés, "Christian Apologetics"; Subrahmanyam, *Europe's India*, 103–143.
116 Clooney, *Fr. Bouchet's India*, 1–8.
117 Lockman, *Travels*, vol. 1, 1743, 452–478, here 477fn; see also Clooney, *Fr. Bouchet's India*, 32–33.
118 Clooney, *Fr. Bouchet's India*, 2.
119 Quotation in Clooney, *Fr. Bouchet's India*, 63.
120 Lockman, *Travels*, vol. 2, 1743, 242; summaries of the letter can be found in Clooney, *Fr. Bouchet's India*, 46–54; Hunt, Jacob, and Mijnhardt, *The Book That Changed Europe*, 227–229; Sweetman, *Mapping Hinduism*, 138–139.
121 Lockman, *Travels*, vol. 2, 1743, 243.
122 Lockman, *Travels*, vol. 2, 1743, 247: "This Idea […] shows at least that their Forefathers woprshipped but one God".
123 Lockman, *Travels*, vol. 2, 1743, 272.
124 Clooney, 'Jesuit Intellectual Practice', 40.
125 Salmon, *Modern History*, 3 vols., London, 1739; I used the third edition of 1744, vol. 1, chapter XI on India.
126 Salmon, *Modern History*, 273.
127 Hyde, *Historia Religionis*; Lockman, *Travels*, vol. 2, 1743, 259–260fn.
128 Lockman, *Travels*, vol. 2, 1743, 260fn.
129 Weststeijn, "Spinoza sinicus", 553–556.
130 See also Rubiés, *Jesuits and the Enlightenment*.

Bibliography

Primary Sources

Anonym. *The New Gospel of the Jesuits, Compared with the Old One of Jesus Christ*. London, 1708.

Anonym. *The Travels of Several Learned Missioners of the Society of Jesus, into Divers Parts of the Archipelago, India, China, and America [...]*. Translated from French Original published in the Year 1713. London, 1714.

Arnauld, Antoine. *La morale pratique des Jésuites, Représentée en plusieurs histoires arrives dans toutes les parties du monde [...]*. Cologne, 1669.

Atkins, John. *A Voyage to Guinea, Brazil and the West Indies*. London, 1735.

Bernard, Frédéric; Picart, Bernard. *Cérémonies et Coutumes Religieuses des tous les peoples du monde*. 9 vols. Amsterdam, 1723–1743.

Bernard, Frédéric; Picart, Bernard. *Religious Ceremonies and Customs of the Several Nations of the Known World [...]*. 7 vols. London, 1731–1739.

Diderot, Denis; d'Alembert, Jean-Baptist le Rond. *Encyclopédie ou Dictionnaire raisonné des sciences, des arts et des métiers [...]*. 17 vols. Paris, 1751–1772.

Le Gobien, Charles; Du Halde, Jean-Baptiste; Patouillet, Louis; Maréchal, N. *Lettres édifiantes et curieuses écrites des missions étrangères [...]*. 34 vols. Paris, 1703–1776.

Du Halde, Jean-Baptiste. *Description [...] de l'Empire de la Chine*. 4 vols. Paris, 1736.

Hyde, Thomas. *Historia Religionis veterum Persarum*. Oxford, 1700.

Horace. *The Odes and Satyres of Horace, That Have Been Done into English By the Most Eminent Hands [...]*. London, 1715.

Lockman, John. *Travels of the Jesuits, into Various Parts of the World: Compiled from Their Letters*. London, 1743; 2nd ed., 1763; 3rd ed., 1787.

Lockman, John. *A Proper Answer to a Vile, Anonymous Libel. Written by L.D.N. [Corrected K.?] Chiefly against John Lockman, Secretary to the Society of the Free British Fishery [...]*. London, 1753.

Lockman, John. *A History of the Cruel Sufferings of the Protestants, and Others, by Popish Persecutions, IN Various Countries: Together with a View of the Reformations from the Church of Rome. Interspersed with the Barbarities of the Inquisition. By Question and Answer. [...]*. London, 1760; 2nd ed. Dublin, 1763.

Pascal, Blaise. *Lettres écrites par Louis de Montalte à un Provincial de ses amis et aux R.R. Pères Jésuites*. Cologne, 1657.

Salmon, Thomas. *Modern History, Or the Present State of All Nations ... Illustrated with Cuts and Maps [...] by Herman Moll*. 3 vols., 3rd ed. London, 1744.

Stöcklein, Joseph (ed.). *Der Neue Welt=Bott mit allerhand Nachrichten deren Missionarien Soc. Iesu [...]*. 5 vols. Augsburg/Graz/Wien, 1726–1760.

Secondary Literature

Alston, R.C. ed. *English Linguistics, 1500–1800: A Collection of Facsimile Reprints, No. 354*. Menston: Scolar Press, 1972.

Bähr, Andreas. *Furcht und Furchtlosigkeit. Göttliche Gewalt und Selbstkonstitution im 17. Jahrhundert*. Göttingen: V&R Unipress, 2013.

Blair, Ann. *Too Much to Know: Managing Scholarly Information before the Modern Age*. New Haven, CT and London: Yale University Press, 2010.

Block, David. *Mission Culture on the Upper Amazon: Native Tradition, Jesuit Enterprise, and Secular Policy in Moxos, 1660–1880*. Lincoln and London: University of Nebraska Press, 1994.

Brayman Hackel, Heidi. *Reading Material in Early Modern England. Print, Gender, and Literacy*. Cambridge: Cambridge University Press, 2005.

Bulman, William; Ingram, Robert G. eds. *God in the Enlightenment*. Oxford: Oxford University Press, 2016.

Burke, Peter. *A Social History of Knowledge. Vol. 1 From Gutenberg to Diderot*. Cambridge: Polity, 2000.
Burke, Peter. *What Is the History of Knowledge?* Cambridge and Malden, MA: Polity, 2016.
Burson, Jeffrey D; Wright, Jonathan eds. *The Jesuit Suppression in Global Context. Causes, Events and Consequences*. Cambridge: Cambridge University Press, 2015.
Champion, J.A.I. *The Pillars of Priestcraft Shaken: The Church of England and Its Enemies, 1660–1730*. Cambridge: Cambridge University Press, 2014.
Chartier, Roger. *The Cultural Uses of Print in Early Modern France*. Trans. Cochrane, Lydia G. Princeton, NJ: Princeton University Press, 1987.
Clarke, J.J. *Oriental Enlightenment. The encounter between Asian and Western Thought*. London and New York: Routledge, 1997.
Clines, D.J.A. 'In Search of the Indian Job.' *Vetus Testamentum* 33 (1983): 398–418.
Clooney, Francis X. *Fr. Bouchet's India. An 18th Century Jesuit's Encounter with Hinduism*. Chennai: Satya Nilayam Publications, 2005.
Clooney, Francis X. 'Jesuit Intellectual Practice in Early Modernity. The Pan-Asian Argument against Rebirth.' In Banchoff, Thomas F.; Casanova, José eds. *The Jesuits and Globalization: Historical Legacies and Contemporary Challenges*. Georgetown: Georgetown University Press, 2016, pp. 49–68.
Darnton, Robert. 'What Is the History of Books?' *Daedalus* 111 (1982): 65–83.
Daston, Lorraine; Galison, Peter. *Objectivity*, 3rd ed. New York: Zone Books, 2015.
Dobranski, Stephen. *Readers and Authorship in Early Modern England*. Cambridge: Cambridge University Press, 2005.
Dürr, Renate. 'Laienprophetien. Zur Emotionalisierung politischer Phantasien im 17. Jahrhundert.' In Jarzebowski, Claudia; Kwaschik, Anne eds. *Performing Emotions. Zum Verhältnis von Politik und Emotion in der Frühen Neuzeit*. Göttingen: V&R Unipress: 2013, pp. 17–41.
Dürr, Renate. 'Akkomodation und Wissenstransfer.' *Zeitschrift für historische Forschung* 44 (2017): 487–509.
Dürr, Renate. '"The Shepherd's Boy in the Fable" – zum Umgang mit dem gefährlichen Wissen der Jesuiten in der Aufklärung.' In Schmid Heer, Esther; Klein, Nikolaus; Oberholzer, Paul eds. *Transfer, Begegnung, Skandalon? Neue Perspektiven auf die Jesuitenmissionen in Spanisch-Amerika*. Stuttgart: Kohlhammer, 2019, pp. 171–194.
Dürr, Renate ed. *Threatened Knowledge. Practices of Knowing and Ignoring from the Middle Ages to the Twentieth Century*. London and New York: Routledge, 2022.
Frevert, Ute. 'Vertrauen. Historische Annäherungen an eine Gefühlshaltung.' In Benthien, Claudia, Fleig, Anne; Kasten, Ingrid eds.*Emotionalität. Zur Geschichte der Gefühle*. Köln et al.: Böhlau, 2000, pp. 178–197.
Ginzburg, Carlo. 'Provincializing the World: Europeans, Indians, Jews (1704).' *Postcolonial Studies* 14 (2011): 135–150.
Grafton, Anthony. *The Footnote: A Curious History*. London: Faber and Faber, 1997.
Grafton, Anthony. 'Rhetoric and divination in Erasmus's edition of Jerome: ancient and modern ways to save dangerous, vulnerable texts'. In Renate Dürr ed. *Threatened Knowledge. Practices of Knowing and Ignoring from the Middle Ages to the Twentieth Century*. London and New York: Routledge, 2022, pp. 181–211.
Harris, Bob. "American Idols': Empire, War and the Middling Ranks in Mid-Eighteenth-Century Britain.' *Past and Present* 150 (1996); 111–141.
Hunt, Lynn; Jacob, Margaret C.; Mijnhardt, Wijnand. *The Book That Changed Europe. Picart et Bernard's "Religious Ceremonies of the World"*. Cambridge, MA: Belknap Press of Harvard University Press, 2010.

Hsia, Florence C. *Sojourners in a Strange Land. Jesuits and Their Scientific Missions in Late Imperial China*. Chicago and London: Chicago University Press, 2009.

Jardine, Lisa; Grafton, Anthony. '"Studied for Action": How Gabriel Harvey Read His Livy.' *Past and Present* 129 (1990): 30–78.

Kempe, Michael. 'Burn after Reading: verschlüsseltes Wissen und Spionagenetzwerke im elisabethanischen England.' *Historische Zeitschrift* 296 (2013): 354–379.

Kirsch, Thomas G.; Dilley, Roy eds. *Regimes of Ignorance. Anthropological Perspectives on the Production and Reproduction of Non-Knowledge*. New York and Oxford: Berghahn, 2015.

Lach, Donald; Kley, Jan van. *Asia in the Making of Europe: A Century of Advance*. Vol. 3. Chicago, IL: The University of Chicago Press, 1993.

Lee, Patrick J. 'The Unexamined Premise: Voltaire, John Lockman, and the Myth of the English Letters.' *Studies in Voltaire and the Eighteenth century* 52 (2001): 240–270.

Mulsow, Martin. 'Joseph-François Lafitau und die Entdeckung der Religionsvergleiche.' In Effinger, Maria; Logemann, Cornelia and Pfisterer, Ulrich eds. *Götterbilder und Götzendiener in der Frühen Neuzeit*. Heidelberg: Winter, pp. 37–47.

Mulsow, Martin. *Prekäres Wissen: eine andere Ideengeschichte der Frühen Neuzeit*. Berlin: Suhrkamp, 2012.

Mulsow, Martin. 'History of Knowledge.' In Burke, Peter; Tamm, Marek eds. *Debating New Approaches in History*. London and New York: Bloomsbury Academic, 2019, pp. 159–173.

Newmark, Catherine. *Passion – Affekt – Gefühl. Philosophische Theorien der Emotionen zwischen Aristoteles und Kant*. Hamburg: Meiner, 2008.

Ogborn, Miles. *Spaces of Modernity. London's Geographies, 1680–1780*. New York and London: The Guilford Press, 1998.

Paschoud, Adrien. *Le monde amérindien au miroir des "Lettres édifiantes et curieuses"*. Oxford: Voltaire Foundation, 2008.

Renswoude, Irene van. 'Crass Insults: Ad Hominem Attacks and Rhetorical Conventions.' In Heil, Ute ed. *Das Christentum im frühen Europa: Diskurse – Tendenzen – Entscheidungen, Millennium Studies 75*. Berlin: de Gruyter, 2019, pp. 171–194.

Rétif, André. 'Brève histoire des "Lettres édifiantes et curieuses".' *Neue Zeitschrift für Missionswissenschaft* 7 (1951): 37–50.

Rubiés, Joan-Pau. *Travel and Ethnology in the Renaissance. South India through European Eyes, 1250–1625*. Cambridge: Cambridge University Press, 2000.

Rubiés, Joan-Pau. 'From Christian Apologetics to Deism. Libertine Readings of Hinduism.' In Bulman, William J.; Ingram, Robert G. eds. *God in the Enlightenment*. Oxford: Oxford University Press, 2016, pp. 107–135.

Rubíes, Joan-Pau. 'Jesuits and the Enlightenment.' In Županov, Ines G. ed. *The Oxford Handbook of the Jesuits*. Oxford: Oxford University Press, 2019, pp. 855–890.

Said, Edward. *Orientalism*. New York: Pantheon Books, 1978.

Sambrook, James. Art. 'John Lockman.' In *Oxford Dictionary of National Biography*. Vol. 34. Oxford: Oxford University Press, 2004, p. 258. https://www.oxforddnb.com/view/10.1093/ref:odnb/9780198614128.001.0001/odnb-9780198614128-e-16912 (retrieved 27 July 2022)

Scheer, Monique. 'Are Emotions a Kind of Practice (And Is That What Makes Them Have a History)? A Bourdieuan Approach to Understanding Emotion.' *History and Theory* 51 (2012): 193–220.

Schurink, Fred. 'Manuscript Commonplace Books, Literature, and Reading in Early Modern England.' *Huntington Library Quarterly* 73 (2010): 453–469.

Shapin, Simon. *A Social History of Truth. Civility and Science in Seventeenth-Century England.* Chicago, IL: University of Chicago Press, 1994.
Subrahmanyam, Sanjay. *Europe's India. Words, People, Empires, 1500–1800.* Cambridge, MA: Harvard University Press, 2017.
Sweetman, Will. *Mapping Hinduism."Hinduism" and the Study of Indian Religions, 1600–1776.* Halle: Verlag der Franckeschen Stiftungen zu Halle, 2003.
Tarantino, Giovanni. 'A Protestant Approach to Colonization as Envisaged in John Lockman's Marytrology (1760).' In Broomhall, Susan; Finn, Sarah eds. *Violence and Emotions in Early Modern Europe.* London. New York: 2016, pp. 185–201.
Vogel, Christine. *Der Untergang der Gesellschaft Jesu als europäisches Medienereignis (1758–1773). Publizistische Debatten im Spannungsfeld von Aufklärung und Gegenaufklärung.* Mainz: von Zabern, 2006.
Weststeijn, Thijs. 'Spinoza sinicus: An Asian Paragraph in the History of the Radical Enlightenment.' *Journal of the History of Ideas* 68 (2007): 537–556.
Wilson, Ellen Judy; Reill, Peter Hanns. Art. 'Deism.' In Kors, Alan Charles ed. *Encyclopedia of the Enlightenment.* Vol. 3. Oxford: Oxford University Press, 2004, pp. 146–148.
Županov, Ines G. ed. *The Rites Controversies in the Early Modern Period.* Leiden: Brill, 2018.
Zwierlein, Cornel ed. *The Dark Side of Knowledge. Histories of Ignorance, 1400 to 1800.* Leiden and Boston, MA: Brill, 2016.

PART 2
Validating

3
VALIDATING LINGUISTIC KNOWLEDGE OF AMERINDIAN LANGUAGES

Werner Thomas[1]

In the sixteenth century, Spanish missionary men rapidly produced large quantities of linguistic tools regarding the indigenous languages of America. By doing so, they codified knowledge of formerly unknown languages even before the process of codifying the majority of European vernaculars had begun. The first grammars of Nahuatl (1547), Purepecha (1559), and Quechua (1560) were published only twenty-five years after the conquest of the Mexica and Inca empires respectively. They actually predated their counterparts for Polish (1568), Dutch (1584), English (1586), Danish (1668), and Russian (1696), and appeared only a few decades after the grammars of French (1530), Czech (1533), German (1534), Portuguese (1536), and Hungarian (1539).[2] The speed with which these languages were studied is even more striking when one takes into consideration that all grammars of European languages except for one (French) were composed by native speakers, which was obviously never the case as far as the Amerindian languages were concerned. Moreover, these languages bore no resemblance whatsoever to any of the European languages. The development of this kind of knowledge could therefore not benefit from existing expertise in Europe, while no similar linguistic tools produced by native speakers were available to European settlers.

The codification of Amerindian languages provides an excellent test case for studying how knowledge of formerly unexplored or unstudied early modern phenomena came into being. How was, in this case, linguistic knowledge of languages completely unknown to the people studying them accumulated, codified, and disseminated in order to allow future generations to use it? Even more importantly, how was this knowledge validated and how was validation regulated?

This chapter discusses the process of knowledge production that resulted from the creation of linguistic tools regarding the indigenous languages in Spanish

DOI: 10.4324/9780429279928-6

America. It does so by selecting 16 grammars, 16 dictionaries, and 12 catechisms printed between 1555 and 1640, and in particular by analyzing the paratexts that document this process and that were usually included in the editions of these tools.[3] These paratexts consist of approbations and licenses of the religious and secular authorities, royal provisions, printing privileges, reports of the censors, dedications, prologues to the reader, and guidelines for the use of the tool itself. Together, they offer a fairly complete picture of the production process and especially of the role of regulation within that process.

The codification and validation of linguistic knowledge took place within the framework of empire building in Spanish America. In contrast to the first decades of the Portuguese colonization of Brazil and to the English and the Dutch colonial enterprises in the Caribbean and North America, the Spanish government not only created trading posts in the New World, but also decided to integrate the native inhabitants into Spanish colonial society and, more importantly, Christianity. Conquering the minds of the native population through evangelization – Robert Ricard's *conquête spirituelle*[4] – therefore became a distinctive feature of the Spanish overseas empire.[5]

Acquiring Linguistic Knowledge

Once the conquest of the New World by the Spanish explorers was achieved, language was probably the most important obstacle to the creation of a colonial empire.[6] On an administrative level, the problem was solved by depending on the former leaders of local communities and on interpreters. They acted as intermediaries between the Spanish authorities and the taxpaying population in a way that direct contact between the Spanish population and the natives was in most cases unnecessary. Many local societies, especially in the countryside, continued functioning semi-autonomously and hardly had any contact with Spanish officials.[7]

However, when it came to teaching Christianity to the local population, the formation of an indigenous clergy was quickly abandoned. The Spanish crown believed that Amerindians would never understand the subtleties of Catholicism, while local authorities were convinced that they were incorrigible heretics whose detailed knowledge of Christian doctrine would allow them to propagate their heresies even more efficiently. As a result, the College of the Holy Cross (*Colegio de Santa Cruz*) in Tlatelolco (Mexico-Tenochtitlan), created in 1536 by the Franciscans in order to train young indigenous men – in general the sons of the former *caciques* – for priesthood, banned natives from ordination from 1555 onwards.[8] Evangelization thus became the almost exclusive competence of European clergymen, although in due time native instructors were trained to perform some of the missionary work in provinces where few European clergymen resided.[9]

At the beginning of the colonization, the language policy of the Spanish crown was quite clear: Spanish would be the administrative and operational language of the overseas territories of the empire. Ideally, the new subjects of the King of Castile were to be taught Spanish, thereby facilitating their integration into colonial society and into the community of faith. During the first years of the evangelization campaigns and while awaiting the implementation of the official policy, missionary men therefore started producing catechisms in pictographs in order to Christianize the local population.[10] They also made use of native interpreters. However, missionary men from all over the Hispano-American continent very soon realized that Spanish would never become the lingua franca of the Amerindians.[11] In time, the system of native interpreters was considered to be unreliable.[12] Consequently, as early as 1551, the first provincial council of Lima established the obligation to use vernacular languages; the first Mexican council would do the same in 1555.[13] Apart from enhancing the evangelization process, this allowed clergymen to communicate directly with the local population and to maintain control over the transmission of faith. In the following decades, Nahuatl and Quechua, the widely spoken languages of the Mexica and Inca empires that had conquered a great part of Mesoamerica and the Andes respectively since the beginning of the fifteenth century, which were shared by a large number of indigenous tribes, were established as the *lenguas generales* of New Spain and Peru.[14]

Hence, in the decades that followed, missionary men increasingly studied local languages, and some of them, such as the Franciscan friars Bernardino de Sahagún and Andrés de Olmos, became real polyglots that mastered several indigenous languages.[15] At the same time, they started translating the catechism into vernacular languages. Such catechisms generally included a 'Cartilla de la doctrina christiana' (the catechism itself) written in two or sometimes three languages and a 'Diálogo de doctrina christiana' which was the catechism in the form of short questions and answers, again in two or sometimes three languages, which enabled priests to interrogate the natives about their Christian faith. Most catechisms were illustrated with engravings representing important concepts of Catholicism, such as the Trinity, the Annunciation, the Crucifixion, and the Ascension, or with portraits of the Virgin Mary and the local patron saints. Sometimes the catechisms also included a section in Latin, in general containing the four prayers of the Roman Catholic Church, a calendar of saints that listed the Christian feast-days, day by day and month by month, and/or a set of instructions intended for the native instructors who assisted the priests as sacristans during mass and when administering the sacraments.[16]

Such catechisms have always been looked upon as if they were evangelization tools only.[17] However, they were linguistic tools at the same time. Indeed, many of them also included a 'Cartilla para enseñar a leer los niños' (alphabet book), which consisted of several series of the Latin alphabet in different fonts, including Gothic and Roman capitals and lower-case letter forms, and a syllabary of the indigenous language. On the one hand, the *cartilla* was used to teach children and adults to read, although it remains unclear whether they were taught to read in Spanish, a language they did not master, or in their own vernacular, in which there probably existed no printed texts or even manuscripts. Most likely, the *cartilla* was meant for the training of the native sacristans. On the other hand, the syllabary was intended for future missionaries who needed to learn the language of their flock.[18]

In consequence, catechisms aimed at Amerindians were not only a means of transferring religious beliefs from European clergymen to native Christians, but also an instrument that triggered the acquisition, development, and circulation of linguistic knowledge of Amerindian languages. Of course, it was an instrument directly related to the message that had to be transferred, but an instrument of language acquisition as well. While children in Europe studied Latin by reading simple dialogues such as the *Colloquies* of Erasmus, missionary men in America learned native languages by reading catechisms.

In fact, many missionary men that produced catechisms in Amerindian languages subsequently produced 'proper' linguistic tools such as grammars and dictionaries ('vocabularios'). Dictionaries in general contained a list of Spanish words translated into native languages and a second list of native words translated into Spanish. Many of them also included a section of what was called 'phrases', a set of native expressions, mostly metaphors, and their significance in Spanish. The purpose of these dictionaries was indeed to offer a list as complete as possible of all words of a given native language and not just a list of words that were needed to preach or take confession. Religious terms and expressions therefore constituted only a small part of the dictionaries. The second group of proper linguistic tools were the grammars. They were the tailpiece of the whole process. Heavily drawing on European models such as Antonio Nebrija's *Institutiones latinae*, but with specific sections explaining phenomena that did not occur in Latin, ancient Greek, or European languages, they discussed word categories and syntax and they also contained a part on orthography, pronunciation, and local variations of the standard versions of the *lenguas generales*.

In general, catechisms were produced before dictionaries and grammars and not the other way around.[19] The Franciscan friar Alonso de Molina, for example, first published a catechism in Spanish and Nahuatl in 1547.[20] He then issued his bilingual vocabulary of Nahuatl, which he expanded in 1571.[21] The expanded version was printed at the same time as his grammar of Nahuatl.[22] In the meantime, in 1565, he had also written a manual of confessors.[23] While his motives to conduct this linguistic program were clearly inspired by the need to communicate directly with the natives about the Catholic doctrine, in the prologue to his vocabulary he also showed a significant interest in the language itself, stating that his intention was 'to bring this language to perfection and discover her secrets'.[24]

As a result of this process, the output of linguistic tools produced between 1500 and 1800 by missionary men and other colonizers on the languages of Spanish America was impressive. As of today, our research team at KU Leuven has been able to identify 413 grammars and language descriptions in manuscript and print, 503 vocabularies and wordlists, 107 wordlists that were included in ethnographical and historical works, and 326 catechisms in one or more indigenous languages. Altogether, the linguistic tools make up a provisional corpus of 1,346 items (1,242, if one excludes the wordlists in nonlinguistic works).[25]

The scientific importance of these by-products of evangelization can hardly be overestimated. They allow the study of pre-Columbian Amerindian languages, many of which are nowadays extinct. The linguistic tools are then the sole remnants of these languages. Fray Bartolomé Roldán's catechism in Spanish and Chuchona, the language of the Chochos or Chuchones, a tribe living in Central Mexico, is, for example, the only text that survived in that language, which itself has disappeared in the course of time.[26] And even if these linguistic tools remained unedited, which happened quite a few times, they sometimes exerted a strong influence on later models. Andrés de Olmos produced *Doctrinas*, vocabularies, and grammars of Nahuatl, Totonaca, and Huasteca, none of which was ever published before 1800.[27] However, his grammar, written in 1547 and the first of its kind on an indigenous language of America, served as an example to almost all missionary men who composed similar works in the decades and centuries to come. The impressive number of linguistic tools codified in manuscript or print therefore contributed to the production, accumulation, and circulation of linguistic knowledge of the languages of the Americas in the overseas territories as well as in Europe and would lead to a major reflection on the world's language systems in the eighteenth century.

Regulating Linguistic Knowledge

Evangelization being the driving force behind the development of linguistic knowledge of the Amerindian languages, two important consequences can be attributed to the fact that religious motives formed the underlying reason why Europeans were studying these languages. First, linguistic knowledge was considered to be not theoretical, but practical, and, above all, useful knowledge. Second, linguistic knowledge was supposed to be or even needed to be accurate knowledge. Usefulness and accuracy were key concepts that pop up in almost all paratexts preceding the actual linguistic tools.

First of all, let us consider the aspect of useful knowledge. Time and again the authors of linguistic tools stressed that what they had produced was useful to colonial society: 'útil y provechoso' ('useful and beneficial') or 'necesario y de muy gran utilidad' ('necessary and very useful') are the words that were most frequently used, and they became a standard formulation in the approbations and licenses of the religious and secular authorities that were included in late sixteenth-century editions.[28] With 'útil y provechoso', the authorities referred to a bidirectional transfer of knowledge. Both the missionary men and the natives would benefit from the production of these tools. Missionary men would more easily be able to speak and understand the language of the people they were to instruct, thereby accelerating the dissemination of Christianity, while natives would not only receive the message of Christ more efficiently, but would also acquire knowledge of Spanish, which would speed up their integration in colonial society.[29] Many of the censors included similar judgments in their approval. Being apparently ready-made formulations, the terms 'útil' and 'provechoso' or 'necesario' and 'de muy gran utilidad' nevertheless point to the necessity of the authorities to stress the usefulness of these tools in order to justify their production. It is clear that without this applicability in everyday life, the authorities would have been less likely to grant permission for them to be printed.

The second characteristic, 'accurate' knowledge, was considered to be even more important by the producers of linguistic knowledge as well as by the authorities granting permission to disseminate it. The Gospel had to be passed on to the natives correctly. The salvation of hundreds of thousands of souls being at stake, missionaries could not risk making mistakes by teaching the natives the Christian faith incorrectly. They not only needed to understand and speak the language of their converts, but they needed to have a detailed knowledge of the meaning of the words and expressions the natives used. By not mastering the indigenous languages, missionaries were bound to use the wrong words or make the wrong translations of Christian concepts, thereby turning themselves from preachers of the Word of God into false prophets.[30] Moreover, they needed to be able to hear the natives' confession correctly. If a sin was not absolved as a result of miscommunication between confessor and confessant, the responsibility for the confessant's eternal damnation lay also with the confessor.

In this context, accuracy can be understood in two ways. On the one hand, the Christian message was to be translated into native languages without leaving the possibility that it would be misunderstood. Concepts and stories such as the Trinity, the Incarnation of Christ, the Passion of Christ, and many more were to be unambiguously explained in languages that in many cases did not have the words for it, simply because no equivalents existed in any of the pre-Columbian religions.[31] However, accuracy also addressed another problem. Given the advent of Protestantism in Europe, a process that mostly coincided with the conquest and colonization of the American territories, it was equally important that the Christian message transmitted to the natives was the right one, that is, the version of the Catholic Church.[32]

Both the need to be useful and the need to be accurate were important guidelines that inspired authorities when elaborating a system with which to regulate linguistic knowledge of the indigenous languages. While the need for usefulness undoubtedly determined the type of linguistic tools that were developed, the need for accuracy to a large extent influenced the way this was done. As a result, what had started as a spontaneous and informal process of language acquisition that facilitated the transfer of religious knowledge between Europeans and Amerindians was soon transformed into a highly standardized and regulated procedure that ended in the development of tools that enabled the transfer of linguistic knowledge.

The process of developing linguistic knowledge of Amerindian languages started with the elaboration of catechisms, which were, as I explained before, a sort of linguistic tool in themselves. The first translations of the Christian catechism were elaborated by natives, not by missionary men. In general, these natives were the sons of pre-Columbian *caciques* and had been educated by the

Spanish clergy from their earliest youth onward. By teaching them the Gospel, the missionary men hoped to use them as preachers in their own community.[33] As these youngsters were integrated within Spanish colonial society from a very early age, they were perfectly bilingual and were frequently deployed as translators and interpreters. At a certain point, the local missionary men would then provide them with the Spanish version of the catechism and would ask them to translate it into their own language. These translations were subsequently used to convert and instruct the local population and as didactic tools for newcomers to learn the local language. This process was highly unconstrained and no formal regulation was applied. Religious authorities did not check upon the religious content of the document and the translation was presumably not submitted to other specialists in the local language.[34]

By the 1550s, many religious communities in the Americas had access to their own version of the catechism, elaborated by local missionary men and natives. However, religious authorities became increasingly aware of the disadvantages of locally produced handwritten catechisms. Many catechisms were drawn up in the local dialect and could only be used within the community in which they came into being. If missionary men in surrounding villages wanted to make use of them, they needed to be copied by hand, and as a result, there was the risk that they were copied incorrectly. Copying catechisms was, of course, a time-consuming and particularly ineffective process. But most important, no standard text of the catechism was used; instead, every region had its own version of it, and there were important differences between the different provinces. This hampered the transfer of religious knowledge to the natives as well as language acquisition among the missionary men.[35]

Hence, when the Council of Trent established the prototype of the Roman catechism and insisted on the standardization of its translation into the vernacular languages of Europe, colonial authorities decided to increasingly supervise the production of catechisms in Amerindian languages. Henceforth, all indigenous translations were to be founded on the official text in Latin or its Spanish translation. This would avoid that its content differed from one region to another, causing confusion among the natives about what they had to believe. The number of target languages was limited to the *lenguas generales*, although less important languages were not totally excluded. Finally, catechisms were to be printed in order to avoid mistakes when copying texts. Printed catechisms would then enhance the evangelization process, as many more copies of the same text became available at the same moment and could be distributed over the empire within the same timeframe.[36]

Due to the continuing efforts of ecclesiastical authorities to accelerate the process of evangelization, it was soon decided that in order to enhance the missionary men's command of local languages, proper linguistic tools such as grammars and dictionaries needed to be developed. Critics stated that too few of them were able to spontaneously preach about the topics of the catechism because they were not fluent enough in indigenous languages. Instead, they confined themselves to reading out loud the text of their copy. However, more competent preachers had experienced that the natives were more easily convinced by the Christian message if it was proposed to them in spontaneous conversations by way of examples regarding daily life and put into the metaphorical language they were used to.[37] At the same time, confession also seemed to offer great opportunities to discuss one's beliefs and attitudes of life. However, it was almost impossible to start such discussions without a thorough knowledge of the local language.[38]

Dictionaries and grammars would enable missionary men to learn a local language in a few months and to start the learning process even before they reached America. When arguing the usefulness of their tools, several authors indeed referred to the possibility of learning the language during the many boring weeks of the transatlantic voyage.[39] Acquiring an indigenous language would not depend anymore on the presence of native speakers, on the time one was living among them, or on the availability of translated texts. It would be less of a process of trial and error. One would no longer waste time trying to discover the exact translation of a particular word, as the linguistic tools would provide this information independently of any conversation partners.[40] Grammars and dictionaries were considered to be each other's complement. Without the words of the dictionaries, the rules of the grammar could not be put into practice. Without the grammars, it was difficult to understand the structure of a language and the way words were put into sentences. Dictionaries enhanced one's vocabulary, while grammars enhanced one's capacity to talk spontaneously.[41]

Neither grammars nor dictionaries were exclusively focused on religion, but their main purpose, as was the case of the catechisms, was, of course, to spread the Gospel among the natives. Consequently, the production of catechisms, dictionaries, and grammars was subjected to the same process of regulation. The regulation mechanism that was to supervise this process was borrowed from royal and ecclesiastical legislation. It is generally referred to as censorship or *censura*. Since 1502, any book that was to be printed within the territory of the Crown of Castile, to which America belonged, needed a license from the King. From 1554 onwards, the Council of Castile was charged with the task of examining the manuscripts and subjecting them to preventive censorship. In the Americas, authors or printers had to apply for the license to the viceroy. By then, the Catholic Church also introduced a system of censorship; from 1543 onwards, no book was to be printed without the consent of the local bishop.[42]

Censura therefore started to play an important part in the process of developing linguistic knowledge. It guaranteed the accuracy and usefulness of catechisms, dictionaries, and grammars. As these formed tools that were used for the indoctrination of the natives, their content needed to be in line with the teachings of the Catholic Church. Hence, censors of the Church and/or the Inquisition examined every tool before it was printed and verified whether its content was accurate and whether no heterodox beliefs, no attacks on the Catholic Church or the Catholic clergy, or, in general, no inappropriate language were included.

Once the episcopal authorities approved the content of the linguistic tools, they would issue a license and refer the author to the secular authorities. The representatives of the viceroy would not repeat the process of *censura* but would judge the translation's usefulness before granting their permission to print. This judgment is difficult to assess, because no reports of the secular censors survive, if they ever existed at all. However, the fact that royal licenses emphasize this condition points to the existence of a set of criteria that defined what was useful and what was not (romances of chivalry, for example, were not, and their production and distribution in the Americas was prohibited).[43]

In order to guarantee that missionary men made use of the right tools, secular and ecclesiastical authorities also supervised the production process of the prints. Permission to print was given to one specific printer or to a selected number of printers, and printing was to be supervised at all times by the author of the translation, and in Lima even by representatives of the authorities. All licenses were included in the printed version of the linguistic tools, namely the approvals of the religious censors, the revisers of the translation, the bishop, and the viceroy. Once printing had ended, the printer was obliged to present his copy to the authorities and/or the author and compare it to the original text in manuscript that was generally deposited in the archives of the local bishopric. If both texts corresponded, the royal secretary of the Audience or the author himself – depending on which of both was appointed by the viceroy – would sign the printed copies and grant permission to sell. If the printed version did not correspond to the manuscript, a list of errors was to be included in the same edition, rectifying any mistake that the typesetters had committed. Once the linguistic tool was published, preachers and vicars were not allowed to use any other copies of the text but the ones that were signed by the authorities. In Peru, printed copies of the Quechua translation of the catechism and of the official dictionary and grammar of Quechua were deposited in the archives of the most important royal institutions (the *audiencias* and *chancillerías*) and cathedrals, allowing the authorities to compare any printed version that was circulating locally with the original text produced in Lima.[44]

Validating Linguistic Knowledge

The regular censorship procedure guaranteed the doctrinal correctness of the content that needed to be translated. However, accuracy also involved the checking of the translation and, on a more general level, of the linguistic knowledge contained in catechisms, dictionaries, and grammars itself. One of the main problems the authors of such tools were confronted with was that it was very difficult to know whether the words of the indigenous language faithfully reflected the meaning and concepts of the Spanish text (and vice versa, of course).[45] Therefore, when learning an indigenous language in order to use it when translating, preaching, taking confession, or spiritually guiding the natives, missionary men needed to be provided with accurate tools that allowed them to communicate correctly with the people they were instructing, hence the importance of accurate dictionaries and grammars.

The first step to guaranteeing the accuracy of these tools consisted of selecting their authors. Although some friars still produced some of them on their own initiative, provincial superiors of the different religious orders started to appoint specific friars from their order and task them with the elaboration of such tools. These friars all had in common that they had been living, preaching, and teaching among the natives for many years or even decades, and some of them had even been born in the Indies or were raised there. They were therefore known as authorities on the language of the people they worked with.[46] In their introduction, many of them complained about the burden such task laid upon them and stressed that they had only accepted because they did not want to disobey their superiors.[47] Although this might have been a figure of speech, it does not conceal the fact that the production of linguistic tools was increasingly decided upon and organized by the superiors of the religious orders.

As a result, it seems that the elaboration of linguistic tools became much more of a team effort. While friars who themselves took the initiative to compose a grammar or vocabulary in general worked alone or at least made it appear so in their introductions, the ones that were charged by their superiors increasingly counted upon the aid of fellow friars with extensive experience in native languages. The Dominican friar Francisco de Alvarado, when compiling his *Vocabvlario en lengva misteca*, even received help of all his fellow Dominicans that were living among the Mixteca and were 'experts in that language', Mixteca being a language that was spoken by only a few missionary men.[48]

Furthermore, accuracy was enhanced by redefining the role of the native speakers in the elaboration process. Indian interpreters and translators were increasingly looked upon by some part of the clergy as being unreliable. It was argued that communication between Spaniards and natives should not depend on the good or bad intentions of indigenous interpreters. 'Many times, the water is clear and pure, but the aqueducts it passes through make it turbid', Alonso de Molina wrote in his 1555 dictionary.[49] Rather than totally exclude them from the production process of linguistic knowledge, their participation was progressively monitored by the missionary men. They were carefully selected among the natives, their fluency in Spanish, the years of integration in colonial society, their knowledge of the Catholic doctrine, and the sincerity of their conversion to Christianism, expressed in terms of years or decades of Christian life, being the most important criteria. For his *Vocabvlario dela lengva Aymara*, Ludovico Bertonio chose native speakers who had been raised in the Christian doctrine from an early age and who understood very well 'what was expected from a Christian'.[50] Their participation in the production process was clearly considered a token of accuracy, albeit no author ever mentioned the names of his interlocutors. 'I have taken the natives as my interpreter', wrote the Jesuit Antonio Ruiz de Montoya in the introduction to his *Tesoro de la lengva gvarani*.[51] Francisco de Alvarado stated that 'it are the Indians that are the best experts [in this language], and therefore they are, and have been, the authors [of his vocabulary]'.[52] Bertonio assured that 'nothing in this book [his grammar of Aymara] has not been carefully examined by the Indians themselves, and approved by them'.[53] Most authors stressed that the cooperation of native speakers was a guarantee for the quality of the linguistic information, as it prevented that any misunderstandings of the local language by missionary men would affect the final content of the linguistic tools. Moreover, by emphasizing the participation of native speakers in the production process, they resembled the first descriptions of the people, fauna, and flora of America. Authors of botanic treatises, for example, also mentioned the sources of their information – be they natives or sailors – in order to increase the veracity of their work.[54]

Very few missionary men explained how they proceeded when developing linguistic tools. Bertonio, however, was one who did provide such an explanation. He describes how, after carefully selecting his native interlocutors, he provided them with texts such as sermons, treatises, mystery plays, and narrative prose. Being raised by the Jesuits from their childhood onwards and therefore fluent speakers of Spanish, they subsequently translated these texts into Aymara. Bertonio then extracted every word and gave it a meaning. At the same time, he completed the wordlist by introducing everyday words he used in his conversations with the Lupaca of the city of Juli where he was working and by asking his fellow friars to add any words they knew that were not yet in the list or any additional significance of the words that were already in the list. He also took great care to include synonyms that were used by the Lupaca in the provinces surrounding Juli, and especially by the natives working in the silver mines of Potosí. The result was a Spanish-Aymara dictionary that was 474 pages thick and an Aymara-Spanish dictionary that was 394 pages thick.[55] Regarding his grammar, which was built on the principles of European grammars that the natives were probably unaware of, he not only presented its contents to his fellow friars in and around Juli, but during the ten years he worked on it, he also submitted his linguistic interpretations to the natives themselves, asking them whether they recognized the rules he had codified.[56]

In many cases, the contribution of native experts was therefore decisive and monitoring them was one way to avoid miscommunication or even worse, deliberate sabotage of the missionary men's efforts to codify the indigenous languages. However, religious authorities wanted to be sure that the interaction between local friars and their native parishioners resulted in an accurate knowledge of these languages. How could they make sure that no misunderstandings between both sides had taken place and therefore that the grammatical structures of indigenous languages had been correctly interpreted by the missionary men, and that the vocabularies offered correct translations of as many of the possible meanings an indigenous word could have and vice versa, thereby allowing the linguistic tools to be used in all the native communities belonging to the same linguistic group? For this purpose, a second round of checks, consisting of additional precautionary measures and functioning (at least in theory) independently of the producers of the linguistic tools, came into being. It was at this point that *censura* popped up again, albeit this time not as an instrument of prohibition. *Censura* now guaranteed that the linguistic information contained in these tools, which had been produced by non-native speakers with the help of indigenous people, was accurate. In this context, censorship had a primarily positive connotation, as it became a means not only of content control, but also of quality control.

This second procedure was parallel to the regular censorship procedure. Once the author of a catechism, grammar, or dictionary presented his work to the authorities in order to get a license to print, a second set of revisers was appointed together with the first group that had to examine their doctrinal content. These revisers needed to prove that they were proficient in the indigenous language the linguistic tool was written in, and they would generally mention the years they were living among the natives and the tasks they performed in their communities. Fray Alonso de la Vera Cruz, Master in Theology and Professor at the University of Mexico, when examining the *Dialogo de doctrina christiana* of the Franciscan friar Maturino Gilberti, stated that 'I give my opinion because for about twenty years I know the language of Michoacan, and I have interacted with the Indians, preaching, confessing, and administering the other sacraments to them', while his co-reviser Fray Jacobo de Dacia assured that 'for more than sixteen years I preach to them, and take their confession, and I administer the sacraments to them'.[57] In principle, the revisers acted independently of the authors; they had no part in the production of the linguistic tool. In some cases, the revisers belonged to a different religious order or even the secular clergy, thereby guaranteeing an independent opinion.[58] However, in practice it was sometimes unavoidable that revisers were picked from the same religious convent or province, especially when languages other than the *lenguas generales* were involved. Bartolomé Roldán's catechism, for example, was additionally submitted to two other friars of his convent in Tepexic de la Seda, who were also fluent speakers of Chuchona (which they had to argue), and it is hard to believe that Roldán would never have consulted them when writing his translation.[59] By 1584, this examination by experts regarding the language was imposed by royal legislation and had thus become standard procedure.[60]

The role of this second set of censors was not to once again revise the doctrinal content of the catechism, dictionaries, or grammars; the other censors had already taken care of this. Regarding the catechisms, they were supposed to check the translation of the text from Spanish into the local language, that is, to make sure that the vocabulary and wording in the indigenous language faithfully reflected the meaning of the Spanish text. In the case of grammars and dictionaries, they were asked to verify the linguistic qualities of the tools and to certify them as accurate and reliable. Alonso de Molina's grammar of 1571, for example, was revised by the general commissioner of his order in Mexico, Fray Francisco de Ribera, and several other friars that 'understand the given language' ('que entienden la dicha lengua') in order to verify its accuracy, as it was an important tool to learn Nahuatl. At the end of the revision process, Fray Domingo de la Anunciación concluded that the grammar was 'very good, and with the congruency and clarity that is required, and that it will be of great use and beneficial to those that wish to learn this American language if it would be printed'.[61] Friars Pablo Rodrigues and Pascual de la Anunciación, when revising the *Arte en lengua mixteca* of the Dominican Antonio de los Reyes, stated that 'it is well structured, coherent, written expertly and with seriousness'.[62] The censors of Luis de Valdivia's *Arte y gramatica general de la lengua qve corre en todo el Reyno de Chile* assured that the grammar dealt with all 'reglas universales' usually contained in grammars.[63] These censors thus assessed the accuracy and quality of the translation contained in catechisms and dictionaries and in the case of the grammars, the correctness of the grammatical information.

The coping stone of the second evaluation was, as it appears, the participation of native experts, that is, the introduction of a second double-check in the procedure. Indeed, paratexts of grammars, dictionaries, and catechisms sometimes mention Spanish censors that appealed to members of the local communities in order to confirm their judgment. It seems that this part of the evaluation came into being rather spontaneously and that it was the censors themselves that took the initiative to consult the native experts that were assisting them. In their revision report of Francisco de Alvarado's *Vocabvlario en lengva mixteca*, revisers Rodrigues and De la Anunciación explicitly stated that 'we have consulted the meaning of the words with the Indian natives that are the most fluent and experts in the said language'.[64] Fray Juan Ramírez and Fray Cristóbal de Ortega, both censors of the linguistic qualities of Bartolomé Roldán's translation into Chuchona of the catechism, declared in their report that 'the chiefs, who are natives speaking this language, tell us that it [the doctrine] cannot be explained with better terms and in better ways than the way it is written and translated from Spanish into Chuchona'.[65] When Doctor Lorenzo Hurtado de Mendoza, bishop of Rio de Janeiro, was asked to revise Antonio de Montoya's *Tesoro de la lengva gvarani*, he not only consulted several friars working in Paraguay, but also 'a few Indians coming from those provinces, and others coming from my diocese of Brazil, all experts and fluent in our language as well as in theirs'.[66] However, while the approbation issued by the Spanish censors clearly mentioned their names, position, and expertise, no formal approval of any native expert was ever included in the printed version of linguistic tools, and it is almost sure that no such official document was ever issued. The natives' revision was probably considered to be a part of the quality check conducted by the European revisers, which would explain why not all revisers mention their participation.

Linguistic knowledge that was made available to the community of missionary men – and to the general public – through printed grammars, dictionaries, and catechisms was therefore validated by means of a three-part procedure of quality control. The role of experts in this procedure was fundamental and enhanced its transparency. First, carefully selected missionary men produced linguistic tools with the aid of equally carefully selected natives. Then, two independent religious censors revised the doctrinal content of those tools. Finally, two other religious censors assessed their linguistic qualities with the aid of, again, carefully selected native speakers that were different from the first group. Together, all these experts vouched for the accuracy of the tools and for the correctness of the knowledge being transferred.

Conclusion

In a few decades, the informal way of producing catechisms, wordlists, and even rudimentary grammars of Amerindian languages in the Spanish empire was transformed into a highly regulated, institutionalized, and supervised procedure that guaranteed the usefulness as well as the accuracy of those linguistic tools. *Censura* as a regulating process undoubtedly shaped the production of linguistic tools associated with the indigenous languages of America, and to a large extent influenced the codification and validation of linguistic knowledge. However, *censura* not only consisted of the eradication of heterodox ideas, but it also included a high degree of quality control of the linguistic information, whether this took the form of a translation of a religious text, the native equivalents of complicated concepts and everyday words and sentences, or the grammatical structure of an indigenous language. As a result, the linguistic tools of the second generation boasted many more linguistic qualities than the earlier linguistic by-products of evangelization.

Regulating linguistic knowledge therefore not only assured the usefulness of this knowledge, but also its accuracy. It created the perfect conditions not only for the correct transfer of religious (and other) knowledge from one language into another, but even more importantly, for the correct transfer of linguistic knowledge regarding indigenous languages in particular, thereby validating that knowledge. Regulation was a necessary condition for and not an obstacle to the production of linguistic knowledge in the early modern Spanish American world. Instead, by creating obstacles to the free circulation of linguistic knowledge, regulating that circulation increased the quality and the applicability of that knowledge itself.

Notes

1 I would like to thank Zanna Van Loon, Toon Van Hal, and Pierre Swiggers for their comments on earlier versions of this text, my fellow authors of this volume and in particular Andreea Badea for the critical revision of the final version, and Zanna for her help in using the first version of the RELiCTA database.
2 Auroux, 'Introduction', 14–15.
3 For the possibilities paratexts offer to the study of indigenous grammars and dictionaries, see Cancino Cabello, 'Los paratextos', 407–440.
4 Ricard, *The Spiritual Conquest of Mexico* (first edition in French in 1933, first edition in Spanish in 1947). In this chapter, I have used the 1986 Spanish edition (Ricard, *La conquista espiritual*).
5 For a general overview, see Holloway, *A Companion to Latin American History*.
6 See Stavans, 'Language and Colonization', 230–240; Valdeón, *Translation*; Mufwene, *Iberian Imperialism and Language Evolution*.
7 Cf. Lockhart, *The Nahuas after the Conquest*, in particular the chapter on *altepetl*.
8 Ricard, *La conquista espiritual*, 332–355; SilverMoon, *The Imperial College of Tlatelolco*.
9 Early, *The Maya and Catholicism*, 143; Valdeón, *Translation*, 127.
10 Resines Llorente, *Diccionario*.
11 See Harrison, 'The Language', 1–27; Gómez Margo, *Las lenguas*, 37.
12 Heath, *Telling Tongues*, 12.

13 Lerner, 'Spanish Colonization', 286; Zamora Ramírez, 'Friars Translating into Nahuatl', 6.
14 Heath, *Telling Tongues*, 26; Urban, 'The Semiotics', 312. However, it seems that the Spanish administration opted for Cuzco Quechua as the *lengua general* in Peru and not for the coastal variant which was the lingua franca of the Inca empire. Cf. Durston, *Pastoral Quechua*, 37–49.
15 Ricard, *La conquista espiritual*, 109–137. Cf. the royal decree of 1565 ordering all missionary men to learn the language of the natives they were evangelizing, in Solano, *Documentos*, 65.
16 Cf. Resines Llorente, *Catecismos americanos*.
17 Regarding Roldán's *Cartilla y Doctrina christiana*, Luis Resines Llorente confirms: 'El libro se dirige a los indios. Hay que preguntarse si se destina a los adultos o a los niños. [...] Hay otros destinatarios velados, indirectos: Roldán pensaba también que su libro lo utilizaron otros religiosos'. See Resines Llorente, '*Cartilla*', 118.
18 'Para que mejor se entienda la lengua Chuchona'. Roldán, *Cartilla y Doctrina christiana*, f°IIIIv.
19 Valdeón, *Translation*, 128; Klor de Alva, 'Language', 148.
20 Molina, *Doctrina christiana*.
21 Molina, *Aqui comiença vn vocabvlario*; Molina, *Vocabvlario en lengva castellana y mexicana*.
22 Molina, *Arte de la lengua mexicana*.
23 Molina, *Confessionario mayor*.
24 'Para ponerla en perfeccion y descubrir los secretos de ella'. See also Hernández de León-Portilla, 'Fray Alonso de Molina', 73.
25 The database is described in Van Hal, Peetermans, and Van Loon, 'RELiCTA', 293–306. For a summary of the projects, see https://www.kuleuven.be/onderzoek/portaal/#/projecten/3H160032 and https://www.kuleuven.be/onderzoek/portaal/#/projecten/3H150739. For the database itself, see www.relicta.org.
26 Resines Llorente, '*Cartilla y doctrina christiana*', 115, 121.
27 Only the grammar of Nahuatl survives in manuscript and was edited in the nineteenth century. See Manrique Castañeda, 'Fray Andrés de Olmos', 32–34.
28 Cancino Cabello, 'Los paratextos', 416.
29 See, for example, the statement in the colophon of Gilberti's *Arte de la le[n]gua de Michoaca[n]*, f°yii: '[...] con la qual se podran aprouechar della todos los que pretendieren aprender la lengua de Mechuacan: y tambien podra seruir para los Indios de Mechuacan para aprender la lengua Castellana'.
30 Molina, *Aqui comiença vn vocabvlario*, 'Prologo al lector', f°aIIIv.
31 See Dedenbach-Salazar, *La transmisión*.
32 Cf. the problems Maturino Gilberti suffered with the Inquisition of Mexico at the occasion of the publication of his *Dialogo de doctrina christiana* (Ricard, *La conquista espiritual*, 135–137).
33 Father Peter of Ghent, for instance, spent much of his time in Mexico-Tenochtitlan training a group of young natives that were sent in pairs to their villages during the weekend in order to perform religious teaching. Cf. Torre Villar, *Fray Pedro de Gante*, 19–21.
34 Ricard, *La conquista espiritual*, 118–119.
35 Several of these problems are pointed out in the royal provision and the letter of the Council of Lima included among the paratexts of the *Doctrina christiana, y catecismo para instrvccion de los Indios*.
36 Valdeón, *Translation*, 75, 78, 120; Durston, *Pastoral Quechua*, 81–87.
37 Rincón, *Arte mexicana*, 'Al Illustrisimo y reverendisimo señor don Diego Romano' (no pagination): faith can only be acquired by the sense of hearing and the sense of hearing can only be reached through predication.
38 Gilberti, *Arte de la le[n]gua de Michuaca[n]*, 'Siguese el prologo' (no pagination).

39 *Procurador* Diego de Torres described the anonymous catechism in Quechua, printed in Rome in 1603, together with the grammar and dictionary of Quechua, as 'cosa mas conueniente y necessaria, ni en la nauegacion podremos tener mejor ocupacion yo y mis compañeros, que aprender las dichas lenguas, que es el medio mas proximo y de los mas necesarios para nuestro intento'. Cf. *Confessionario para los cvras de Indios*, 'Al illustrissimo y reverendissimo señor, Don Fernando Niño de Guevara' (no pagination).

40 In his introduction ('Al lector') to his *Arte y grammatica*, the Jesuit Ludovico Bertonio stated that:

> si uno de mediana habilidad, estudiare con cuydado lo que en esta arte se contiene, al cabo de un año mas camino tendra andando, que otro de muy buena habilidad en quatro o cinco, si solamente pretende aprender la lengua per uso,
>
> and 'estudiando con cuydado en muy breue tiempo con el diuino fauor verna a sauer mucho desta tan copiosa lengua, especialmente si con el estudio del arte juntare el exercicio del hablar'.

(17 and 343 respectively)

41 Córdova, *Arte en lengva zapoteca*, 'Prologo al lector' (no pagination); *Arte, y Vocabvlario en la lengva general del Perv*, 'Prohemio' (no pagination).

42 Reyes Gómez, *El libro en España y América*, 207–209, 310, 799–804; García Oro and Portela Silva, *La Monarquía y los libros*, 45; Martínez de Bujanda, *Index*, 35.

43 Leonard, *Books of the Brave*, 81–85.

44 Van Loon, 'How Book History', 165–197.

45 See the viewpoints of José de Acosta and Antonio Ruiz de Montoya, who even wrote an *Apología en defensa de la doctrina Cristiana en lengua Guaraní* (which remained unpublished in the early modern period), discussed in Dürr, 'Reflecting on Language', 50–91.

46 See, for example, the case of Fray Alonso de Molina, author of a dictionary and grammar of Nahuatl, who 'en cuya lengua (desde mi tierna hedad hasta ahora) no he cesado de exercitarme predicar y administrar los sanctos sacramentos a los naturales'. Molina, *Arte de la lengua mexicana*, 'Epistola al muy excelente señor, Don Martin Enrriquez visorey desta Nueua España', f°3v.

47 Molina, *Aqui comiença un vocabvlario*, 'Prologo al lector', f°aIIIv; Alvarado, *Vocabulario en lengua misteca*, 'A nuestro padre fray Gabriel de Sancto Joseph' (no pagination).

48 '[…] con el favor y la ayuda de todos los padres desta nacion, peritos en esta lengua'. Alvarado, *Vocabvlario en lengva misteca*, Approbation of Fray Antonio de los Reyes and Fray Pablo Rodrigues (no pagination).

49 'Porque muchas vezes aunque el agua sea limpia y clara, los arcaduces por donde passa la hazen turbia'. Molina, *Aquí comiença vn vocabvlario*, 'Prologo al lector', f°aIIIr. José de Acosta discusses the role of native interpreters in his *De procuranda indorum salute* of 1588. Cf. Dürr, 'Reflecting on Language', 56–64.

50 '[…] han alcançado a entender muy bien todo lo que puede pedirse a un fiel, y catholico Christiano'. Bertonio, *Vocabvlario dela lengva aymara*, 'A los sacerdotes y curas de la nacion aymara', f°A.

51 'He tenido por interpretes a los naturales'. Ruiz de Montoya, *Tesoro de la lengva gvarani*, 'A los padres religiosos' (no pagination).

52 '[…] de tal suerte que son los mismos Indios que son los mejores maestros que para esto era, y an sido los autores'. Alvarado, *Vocabvlario en lengva misteca*, 'Prologo al lector' (no pagination).

53 '[…] y puedo afirmar que no ay en estos preceptos cosa ninguna que no aya sido muy bien examinada con los mismos Indios y aprouada por ellos'. Bertonio, *Arte y grammatica*, 343. In his prologue to the 1612 edition, he stated that 'ellos [the Indians] son los autores a los que en el uso de su lengua debemos seguir' (*Arte de la lengua aymara*, 'Al estudioso lector', 5).

54 Barrera-Osorio, 'Translating Facts', 317–331.
55 Bertonio, *Vocabvlario dela lengva aymara*, 'A los sacerdotes y curas de la nacion aymara'.
56 Bertonio, *Arte y grammatica*, 343; *Arte de la lengua aymara*, 'Al estudioso lector', 5.
57 Gilberti, *Dialogo de doctrina Christiana*, 'Aprobacion de la obra', f°3r: 'y doy este parecer porque a veynte años poco mas o menos que entiendo la lengua de Mechuaca[n] y he tratado con los Indios, predicando, y confessando, y administrando los demas sacramentos' (Fray Alonso de la Vera Cruz); 'y entiendo lo, porque a mas de diez y seis años que los predico y confiesso y administro los otros sacramentos' (Fray Jacobo de Toral).
58 One example would be Gilberti's *Arte de la le[n]gua de Michuaca[n]*, the censors being an Augustinian friar and two members of the secular clergy.
59 Roldán, *Cartilla y Doctrina christiana*, 'Licencia y examen'.
60 Cancino Cabello, 'Los paratextos', 413.
61 'Que me parece que esta muy buena y con la congruydad y claridad que se requiere, y que sera de mucha utilidad y prouecho si se ymprime para todos los que quisieren deprender esta lengua Americana'. Molina, *Arte de la lengua mexicana*, f°aIIIr–v.
62 'Esta puesto en buen orden, y concierto, con graued̄ad, y propiedad, que hasta ahora en esta lengua se ha podido descubrir, donde el autor ha trabajado mucho, con gran solicitud, y cuidado con el qual, de aqui en adelante la dicha lengua, sera ya muy facil, y clara de deprender, y saber'. Reyes, *Arte en lengua mixteca*, Approbation of Pablo Rodrigues and Pascual de la Anunciación, f°4r–v.
63 Valdivia, *Arte y gramatica general*, 'Aprobacion' of Alonso de Toledo, Diego Gatiea, and Miguel Cornejo (no pagination).
64 '[…] y consultado la significacion de los vocablos con los Indios naturales, mas abiles, y expertos en la dicha lengua'. Alvarado, *Vocabvlario en lengua misteca*, Approbation of Fray Antonio de los Reyes and Fray Pablo Rodrigues (no pagination).
65 'y los principales, que son naturales desta lengua dizen, no se poder declarar por mejores terminos y modos, que va declarada, y traduzida de castellano en chuchon'. Roldán, *Cartilla y Doctrina christiana*, Approbation of Fray Juan Ramírez and Fray Cristóbal de Ortega, f°IIIr.
66 '[…] lo conferi todo con otras personas de allà, y con algunos Indios de las dichas Prouincias, y otros de mi Diocesi del Brasil, practicos, y ladinos, assi en nuestra lengua, como en aquella suya'. Ruiz de Montoya, *Tesoro de la lengva gvarani*, 'Aprovacion del mui Doctor D. Lorenço Hurtado de Mendoza', f°v.

Bibliography

Primary sources

All data related to the listed primary sources can be found in the RELiCTA database (www.relicta.org).

Alvarado, Francisco de. *Vocabvlario en lengva misteca, hecho por los Padres dela Orden de Predicadores, que residen enella, y vltima mente recopilado, y acabado por el Padre Fray Francisco de Aluarado, Vicario de Tamaçulapa, de la misma Orden*. Mexico: Pedro Balli, 1593.

Arte y vocabolario de la lengua general del Peru, llamada Quichua, y de la lengua Castellana. Seville: Clemente Hidalgo, 1603.

Arte, y vocabulario en la lengua general del Peru llamada Quichua, y en la lengua Española. El mas copioso y elegante que hasta agora se ha impresso. Lima: Antonio Ricardo, 1586.

Arte, y Vocabvlario en la lengua general del Perv llamada Quichua, y en la lengua Española. El mas copioso y elegante, que hasta agora se ha impresso. Lima: Francisco del Canto, 1614.

Bertonio, Ludovico. *Arte breve dela lengva aymara, para introdvction del Arte grande dela misma lengva*. Rome: Luis Zanetti, 1603.

Bertonio, Ludovico. *Arte y grammatica mvy copiosa dela lengva Aymara.* Rome: Luis Zanetti, 1603.
Bertonio, Ludovico. *Arte dela lengua aymara, con vna silva de phrases de la misma lengua, y su declaracion en Romance.* Juli: Francisco del Canto, 1612.
Bertonio, Ludovico. *Vocabvlario dela lengva aymara.* Juli: Francisco del Canto, 1612.
Catecismo en la lengva española. Y qvichva del Pirv. Rome: Luis Zanetti, 1603.
Catecismo en la lengva española, y aymara del Pirv. Ordenado por autoridad del Concilio Prouincial de Lima, y impresso en la dicha ciudad el año de 1583. Seville: Bartolomé Gómez, 1604.
Confessionario para los cvras de Indios. Con la instrvcion contra svs Ritos. Seville: Clemente Hidalgo, 1603.
Córdova, Juan de. *Arte en lengva zapoteca.* Mexico: Pedro Balli, 1578.
Córdova, Juan de. *Vocabvlario en lengva çapoteca.* Mexico: Pedro Ocharte and Antonio Ricardo, 1578.
Doctrina christiana, y catecismo para instrvccion de los Indios, y de las de mas personas, que han de ser enseñadas en nuestra sancta fé: Con vn confessionario, y otras cosas necessarias para los que doctrinan, que se contienen en la pagina siguiente, compvesto por auctoridad del Concilio Prouincial, que se celebro en la Ciudad de los Reyes, el año de 1583. Lima: Antonio Ricardo, 1584.
Gilberti, Maturino. *Arte de la le[n]gua de Michuaca[n].* Mexico: Juan Pablos, 1558.
Gilberti, Maturino. *Thesoro spirivtal en lengva de Mechuaca[n].* Mexico: Juan Pablos, 1558.
Gilberti, Maturino. *Dialogo de doctrina christiana, enla lengua d'Mechuaca[n].* Mexico: Juan Pablos, 1559.
Gilberti, Maturino. *Vocabulario en lengua de Mechuacan.* Mexico: Juan Pablos, 1559.
Gilberti, Maturino. *Thesoro spiritual de pobres en le[n]gua de Michuaca[n].* Mexico: Antonio de Espinosa, 1575.
Lagunas, Juan Baptista de. *Arte y dictionario: con otras obras, en lengua Michuacana.* Mexico: Pedro Balli, 1574.
Molina, Alonso de. *Doctrina christiana breve tradvzida en lengua mexicana.* Mexico: probably Juan Pablos, 1547.
Molina, Alonso de. *Aqui comiença vn vocabulario enla lengua Castellana y Mexicana.* Mexico: Juan Pablos, 1555.
Molina, Alonso de. *Confessionario mayor, en lengua Mexicana y Castellana.* Mexico: Antonio de Espinosa, 1565.
Molina, Alonso de. *Arte de la lengua Mexicana y Castellana.* Mexico: Pedro Ocharte, 1571 (2nd ed. Mexico: Pedro Balli, 1576).
Molina, Alonso de. *Vocabvlario en lengva castellana y mexicana.* Mexico: Antonio de Espinosa, 1571.
Molina, Alonso de. *Vocabvlario en lengva mexicana y castellana.* Mexico: Antonio de Espinosa, 1571.
Molina, Alonso de. *Doctrina Christiana, en lengva mexicana muy necessaria: en la qual se contienen todos los principales mysterios de nuestra Sancta Fee catholica.* Mexico: Pedro Ocharte, 1578.
Reyes, Antonio de los. *Arte en lengva mixteca.* Mexico: Pedro Balli, 1593.
Rincón, Antonio del. *Arte mexicana.* Mexico: Pedro Balli, 1595 [includes a small Vocabulario].
Roldán, Bartolomé. *Cartilla y Doctrina christiana, breve y compendiosa, para enseñar los niños: y ciertas preguntas tocantes a la dicha Doctrina, por manera de Dialogo, tradu2ida, compuesta, ordenada, y romançada en la lengua Chachona del pueblo de Tepexic de la Seda, por el muy Reuerendo Padre Fray Bartholome Roldan, de la Orden del glorioso Padre Sancto Domingo.* Mexico: Pedro Ocharte, 1580.

Ruiz de Montoya, Antonio. *Tesoro de la lengva gvarani*. Madrid: Juan Sánchez, 1639.
Ruiz de Montoya, Antonio. *Arte, y bocabvlario de la lengva gvarani*. Madrid: Juan Sánchez, 1640.
Ruiz de Montoya, Antonio. *Catecismo de la lengva gvarani*. Madrid: Diego Díaz de la Carrera, 1640.
Santo Tomás, Domingo de. *Grammatica, o Arte de la lengua general de los Indios de los Reynos del Perú*. Valladolid: Francisco Fernández de Córdoba, 1560.
Santo Tomás, Domingo de. *Lexicon, o Vocabularia de la lengua general del Perv*. Valladolid: Francisco Fernández de Córdoba, 1560.
Tercero cathecismo y exposición de la Doctrina Christiana, por sermones. Para qve los cvras y otros ministros prediquen y enseñen a los Yndios y a las demás personas. Lima: Antonio Ricardo, 1585.
Valdivia, Luis de. *Arte y gramatica general de la lengva qve corre en todo el Reyno de Chile, con vn Vocabulario, y Confessonario*. Lima: Francisco del Canto, 1606.
Valdivia, Luis de. *Doctrina Christiana y cathecismo en la lengua Allentiac, que corre en la ciudad de S. Iuan de la Frontera, con vn Confessionario, Arte y Bocabulario breues*. Lima: Francisco del Canto, 1607.
Vocabvlario enla lengva general del Perv llamada Quichua, y en la lengua Española. Nvevamente emendado y añadido de algunas cosas que faltauan por el Padre Maestro Fray Iuan Martinez Cathedratico dela Lengua. Dela orden del Señor Sant Augustin. Lima: Antonio Ricardo, 1604.

Secondary sources

Auroux, Sylvain ed. *Histoire des idées linguistiques. Vol. 2, Le développement de la grammaire occidentale*. Liège: Mardaga, 1992.
Barrera-Osorio, Antonio. 'Translating Facts: From Stories to Observations in the Work of Seventeenth-Century Dutch Translators of Spanish Books.' In Cook; Dupré, *Translating Knowledge*, pp. 317–331.
Cancino Cabello, Nataly. 'Los paratextos de artes y gramáticas misioneras americanas.' *Nueva revista de filología hispánica* LXV/2 (2017): 407–440.
Cook, Harold; Dupré, Sven eds. *Translating Knowledge in the Early Modern Low Countries* (Low Countries Studies on the Circulation of Natural Knowledge, 3). Munster: Lit Verlag, 2012.
Dedenbach-Salazar Sáenz, Sabine ed. *La transmisión de conceptos cristianos a las lenguas amerindias. Estudios sobre textos y contextos de la época colonial*. Sankt Augustin: Academia Verlag, 2016.
Dürr, Renate. 'Reflecting on Language in Christian Mission: The Significance of Communication in the Linguistic Concepts of José de Acosta and Antonio Ruiz de Montoya.' In Flüchter; Wirbser, *Translating Catechisms*, pp. 50–91.
Durston, Alan. *Pastoral Quechua: The History of Christian Translation in Colonial Peru, 1550–1650*. Notre Dame: University of Notre Dame Press, 2007.
Early, John D. *The Maya and Catholicism: An Encounter of World Views*. Gainesville: University Press of Florida, 2006.
Flüchter, Antje; Wirbser, Rouven eds. *Translating Catechisms, Translating Cultures: The Expansion of Catholicism in the Early Modern World*. Leiden and London: Brill, 2017.
Fuertes, Alberto; Torres-Simón, Esther eds. *And Translation Changed the World (And the World Changed Translation)*. Newcastle upon Tyne: Cambridge Scholars Publishing, 2015.

García Oro, José; Portela Silva, María José. *La Monarquía y los libros en el Siglo de Oro*. Madrid: Editorial Alcalá, 2000.
Gómez Margo, Lidice. *Las lenguas en la formación de los pueblos hispanoamericanos*. Lima: Vida y espiritualidad, 1994.
Gray, Edward G.; Fiering, Norman eds. *The Language Encounter in the Americas, 1492–1800: A Collection of Essays*. New York and Oxford: Berghahn Books, 2000.
Harrison, Regina. 'The Language and Rhetoric of Conversion in the Viceroyalty of Peru.' *Poetics Today* 16, no. 1 (1995): 1–27.
Heath, Shirley Brice. *Telling Tongues: Language Policy in Mexico, Colony and Nation*. New York: Teachers College Press, 1972.
Hernández de León-Portilla, Ascención. 'Fray Alonso de Molina y el proyecto indigenista de la orden seráfica.' *Estudios de Historia Novohispana* 36 (2007): 63–81.
Holloway, Thomas H. ed. *A Companion to Latin American History*. Oxford: Wiley-Blackwell, 2008.
Klor de Alva, J. Jorge. 'Language, Politics, and Translation: Colonial Discourse and Classical Nahuatl in New Spain.' In Warren, *The Art of Translation*, pp. 143–162.
Leonard, Irving. *Books of the Brave: Being an Account of Books and of Men in the Spanish Conquest and Settlement of the Sixteenth-Century New World*. Berkeley: University of California Press, 1992.
Lerner, Isaías. 'Spanish Colonization and the Indigenous Languages of America.' In Gray; Fiering, *The Language Encounter in the Americas*, pp. 281–292.
Lockhart, John. *The Nahuas after the Conquest: A Social and Cultural History of the Indians of Central Mexico, Sixteenth through Eighteenth Centuries*. Stanford, CA: Stanford University Press, 1992.
Manrique Castañeda, Leonardo. 'Fray Andrés de Olmos. Notas críticas sobre su obra lingüística.' *Estudios de Cultura Náhuatl* 15 (1982): 27–36.
Martínez de Bujanda, Jesús. *Index de l'Inquisition espagnole*. Geneva: Droz, 1984.
Mufwene, Salikoko S. ed. *Iberian Imperialism and Language Evolution in Latin America*. Chicago, IL: University of Chicago Press, 2014.
Nuccetelli, Susana; Schutte, Ofelia; Bueno, Otávio eds. *A Companion to Latin American Philosophy*. Oxford: Wiley-Blackwell, 2010.
Resines Llorente, Luis. *Catecismos americanos del siglo XVI*. Salamanca: Junta de Castilla y León, 1992.
Resines Llorente, Luis. *Diccionario de los catecismos pictográficos*. Valladolid: Diputación de Valladolid, 2007.
Resines Llorente, Luis. '*Cartilla y doctrina christiana* de Bartolomé Roldán en lengua chuchona.' Paper published on the internet: http://traduccion-dominicos.uva.es/caleruega/pdf/08_RESINES.pdf (retrieved 10 May 2019).
Reyes Gómez, Fermín de los. *El libro en España y América. Legislación y censura (siglos XV-XVIII)*. Madrid: Arco/Libros, 2000.
Ricard, Robert. *The Spiritual Conquest of Mexico: An Essay on the Apostolate and the Evangelizing Methods of the Mendicant Orders in New Spain, 1523–1572*. Translated by Lesley Byrd Simpson. Berkeley: University of California Press, 1966.
Ricard, Robert. *La conquista espiritual de México*. Translated by Ángel María Garibay. Mexico: Fondo de Cultura Económica, 1986.
SilverMoon. 'The Imperial College of Tlatelolco and the Emergence of a New Nahua Intellectual Elite in New Spain (1500–1760).' Unpublished doctoral dissertation, Duke University, 2007.

Solano, Francisco de ed. *Documentos sobre la política lingüística en Hispanoamerica (1492–1800)*. Madrid: CSIC, 1991.

Stavans, Ilan. 'Language and Colonization.' In Nuccetelli; Schutte; Bueno, *A Companion to Latin American Philosophy*, pp. 230–240.

Torre Villar, Ernesto de la. *Fray Pedro de Gante, maestro y civilizador de América*. Mexico: Seminario de cultura mexicana, 1973.

Urban, Greg. 'The Semiotics of State-Indian Linguistic Relationships: Peru, Paraguay, and Brazil.' In Urban; Sherzer, *Nation-States and Indians*, pp. 307–330.

Urban, Greg; Sherzer, Joel eds. *Nation-States and Indians in Latin America*. Austin: University of Texas Press, 1991.

Valdeón, Roberto. *Translation and the Spanish Empire in the Americas*. Amsterdam: John Benjamins, 2014.

Van Hal, Toon; Peetermans, Andy; Van Loon, Zanna. 'RELiCTA: Repertory of Early Modern Linguistic and Catechetical Texts in America, Asia and Africa: Presentation of an Ongoing Database Project.' *Beiträge zu Geschichte der Sprachwissenschaft* 28, no. 2 (2018): 293–306.

Van Loon, Zanna. 'How Book History Can Contribute to Missionary Linguistics: Exploring the Sixteenth-Century Production and Publishing of the First Quechua Vocabulary and Grammar Printed in South America.' *Beitrage zur Geschichte der Sprachwissenschaft* 30, no. 2 (2020): 165–197.

Warren, Rosanna ed. *The Art of Translation: Voices from the Field*. Boston, MA: Northeastern University Press, 1989.

Zamora Ramírez, Elena Irene. 'Friars Translating into Nahuatl between the 16th and 19th Centuries.' In Fuertes; Torres-Simón, *And Translation Changed the World*, pp. 3–15.

4
REGULATING THE FORM

How Manuscript Newsletters Influenced the Standards for Dutch Printed Newspapers (c. 1580–1630)

Renate Pieper

When the first Dutch weekly newspaper, the *Courante uyt Italien, Duytslandt &c.*[1] was published in 1618, it had to contend with the negative image of irregularly printed spectacular broadsheets and pamphlets, and to compete[2] with handwritten manuscript newsletters which were in circulation all over Europe, informing the elites about the latest events.[3] From the second half of the sixteenth century, handwritten weekly gazettes had set the benchmark for the distribution of fast and accurate news throughout Europe. From 1618 onwards, printed newspapers sought to offer the same sort of information for a broader, generally local, public. This was a challenge: up to the Thirty Years War, printing had been used to publish for an extended local and regional public or for the dissemination of standardized texts such as bibles, questionnaires and well-established knowledge. Information, subject to frequent changes from far distant lands or which met the interests of a limited audience, was usually provided by manuscripts.[4] The printing of ever-changing weekly news by the Dutch *Courante* challenged the established boundaries between the role of print and manuscript. This chapter shows how printed newspapers tried to overcome that boundary and compete with manuscript newsletters, first by emulating the form established in handwritten gazettes and then regulating the form further.

Alongside books and letters, newsletters circulated among those European elites who were able to read and could afford to buy them. Princes, noblemen, merchants, bureaucrats, lawyers and other well-to-do members of early modern societies subscribed to newsletters or bought them individually and copied them for friends and relatives. Regular handwritten newsletters first appeared in Italy and emerged north of the Alps in the second half of the sixteenth century. Newsletters coexisted with printed newspapers from the early seventeenth century until the end of the eighteenth century, when manuscripts finally

DOI: 10.4324/9780429279928-7

disappeared.[5] Newsletters had a rather standardized external and internal format and therefore offer a good sample to study the relationship between the two mediums of information—the manuscript and the imprint.

The production of manuscript newsletters was centred in Venice and Rome in southern Europe. North of the Alps, the production and distribution of handwritten newsletters were focused in Antwerp and Cologne. Besides these primary locations, there were smaller centres of compilation in places such as Lyon and Vienna. The network of manuscript newsletters had its centres of distribution in the realms of Catholic rulers, most of them attached to a certain extent to the Habsburgs.[6] Conversely, the first regularly printed newspapers were published in Amsterdam from 1618 and shortly afterwards, besides Antwerp, in Paris and London as well, places opposing the Habsburg policies.[7] The network of manuscript newsletters had a centre in the southern Netherlands, whereas the first printed one was based in the northern Netherlands. As a result, the analysis and comparison of handwritten versus printed newsletters allow us to examine how informal regulations connected the realms across one of the main political boundaries and of different knowledge systems in early modern Europe.

The borders between the northern and southern Netherlands were especially violent during the Eighty Years War (1568–1648) and even more so during the Thirty Years War (1618–1648). This period of intense warfare in Europe and overseas covers the period of stabilization of the system of weekly handwritten newsletters beginning in the 1570s, of which the collection of the "Fuggerzeitungen" from Augsburg is an outstanding example. By comparison, the first regular printed newspaper was the Dutch weekly *Courante uyt Italien, Duytslandt &c.*, published in Amsterdam between 1618 and 1651. This chapter examines the relationship between and the path dependency of Amsterdam-printed newspapers from the 1620s on manuscript newsletters mainly from Antwerp and Cologne from the 1580s and 1590s, and shows the extent to which the format of manuscript newsletters affected the form of printed news in times of growing hostilities.

Both handwritten and printed gazettes needed paper. The flourishing Flemish and Dutch linen industry provided the raw material for paper, and the Netherlands became one of the most important centres for the paper industry in early modern Europe. This linked Flemish and Dutch gazettes and paper production to the Spanish American overseas trade, for which the *laken* industry was a main supplier. Flemish and Dutch merchants settled in Andalusia to participate more or less directly in the risky but rewarding trade with the American mainland, which produced the much-needed silver for European trade with Africa and Asia.[8] Spanish American silver and European trade in general not only indirectly influenced the Flemish and Dutch publishing sector through the demand for linen and paper but also furnished news to be disseminated on paper: a double layering of knowledge transfer from the material to information on the material. The fate of the Spanish American silver fleets as well as that of other ships crossing the oceans, arriving from the West and the East in Europe, and the contents of their cargoes were always interesting news for the readers of the handwritten and printed gazettes from the northern and southern Netherlands in an age of constant warfare. They are the main source for my study on the development of the formats of different communication media which entangled large geographical areas and distinct political parties in north-western Europe around 1600.

Studies of printed newspapers have a long tradition, as regularly printed news is closely associated with the emergence of the public sphere.[9] Recent research stresses the importance of historical networks: for example, Arthur de Weduwen's vast two-volume study examines the places mentioned in the headings of all preserved collections of seventeenth-century Flemish and Dutch newspapers and Paul Ablaster analyses the network which the printer Abraham Verhoeven used to edit the *Nieuwe Tijdinghen*, the first regularly printed newspaper in the southern Netherlands.[10] Both books show the large geographical areas covered by printed newspapers on the general level of their headings. As the news mentioned under the headings also includes references to a range of geographical sites, it is clear that the network referred to by the printed gazettes must have been even more dense and expansive than A. de Weduwen demonstrated. This is evident in Ablaster's detailed analysis for the year 1623.[11] A different perspective is offered by Michiel van Groesen's article comparing the contents of two Amsterdam newspapers published in 1630, the *Courante uyt Italien, Duytslandt &c.* and the *Tijdinghen uyt verscheyde Quartieren*.[12] Analysing the news about the establishment of a Dutch colony in Brazil, his article underlines that the public perception of printed news as more or less reliable or as outright propaganda depended to a large extent on the editor of the newspapers. According to A. de Weduwen, the initial editors of both newspapers had been pamphleteers during the military campaigns of Maurits von Nassau. When the editors established weekly printed newspapers which aimed to compete with handwritten newsletters, they had to reassure their readers and customers of the quality of the news they presented. Since the information changed every week, the format and terminology were the only guarantors of the reliability of the contents. Therefore, the form and language of the newspapers sought to match handwritten newsletters in order to legitimize the newspapers and distance them from pamphlets.

Handwritten newsletters have generally been considered an isolated phenomenon, only available to princes and very well-to-do merchants. However, Mario Infelise and Filippo de Vivo's study of Venetian newsletters found that handwritten gazettes, called *avvisi*, reached a broad readership and further increased their audience by being read aloud, to the extent that handwritten newsletters were subject to censorship.[13] One of the main characteristics of handwritten newsletters was that they used the places and dates of their compilation as headings to structure the news they presented. From the mid-sixteenth century they developed an almost weekly periodicity even outside of Italy. One of the most famous preserved collections of handwritten newsletters north of the Alps is the "Fuggerzeitungen" (1568–1605). Katrin Keller, Paola Molino and Oswald Bauer offered an extensive analysis of its writers, its content and statistics about the places mentioned in the headings of the newsletters.[14] Their contributions make it possible to compare the networks of handwritten newsletters from the late sixteenth century with those of Flemish and Dutch printed newspapers from the early seventeenth century. An analysis of different European newsletters was offered by Cornel Zwierlein and Renate Pieper,[15] who stressed that the characteristic features of newsletters were used at a European level and that the same information was frequently copied and thus circulated all over the continent. The dissemination of news by copying newsletters was carried out by commercial offices for their customers and by private persons for their friends and relatives. The intertwining of business and private networks contributed to the high regard of handwritten newsletters as a trustworthy source of information. By 1600, according to contemporary accounts, manuscript newsletters were faster, more regular and more accurate than spectacular broadsheets. Thus, the editors of the first printed newspapers had to contend with the benchmark set by handwritten newsletters.[16] It is the purpose of this study to show to what extent the higher esteem of manuscripts led printed newspapers to a dependency on the form of handwritten newsletters.

In order to excavate the traces of handwritten newspapers in printed ones, I analyse the similarities and differences in the formatting and phrasing of news about the arrival of fleets and goods from overseas. The treasure fleets linked the southern and northern Netherlands and their *laken* industries with the commerce of news. Printed newspapers flourished in the Netherlands from the beginning of the Thirty Years War.[17] This was only possible because imprints could assure readers of the validity of their information, especially in comparison to their competition—handwritten newsletters.

In order to determine the extent to which handwritten newsletters influenced the form of printed newspapers, we can first examine the place which news from overseas took within European manuscripts and imprints. Second, we can analyse the description of arriving cargoes from East India and the Americas and the language employed in discussing both warfare and commerce. The degree to which manuscript newsletters regulated the standards for printed newspapers offers some evidence regarding the extent to which printed newspapers competed directly with manuscript news in the representation of distant lands.

Regulating the Place of News from Overseas

At first sight, printed newspapers appear to have more or less maintained the structure of handwritten news. A comparison of the studies of K. Keller, P. Molino, O. Bauer and R. Pieper on manuscript news with the analysis of P. Arblaster and A. de Weduwen on imprints reveals no obvious differences in format. The headings in manuscripts and imprints were almost the same. Both media mention the places and dates of their compilation, often indicating the origin of the information in the text below. A more detailed analysis, however, illuminates some striking formal distinctions.

The form of handwritten gazettes was already well established by the end of the fifteenth century. As manuscript newsletters used a letter format and were sent to customers, both in the vicinity and far away, their headings indicated the places and the dates of their compilation but rarely offered a signature or hint about the compilers themselves—*novellanti*, as they were called in Venice.[18] One newsletter would usually compile information collected from several sites. A typical example comes from two "Fuggerzeitungen" from 12 and 17 April 1598: one assembled notices from Antwerp on 12 April and Cologne on 16 April; the other one included notices from Venice on 17 April and Rome on 12 April.[19] The newsletters structured the notices according to the main places of compilation, and each centre of information gathering received a heading of its own. Well-to-do elites like the Fugger merchants in Augsburg obtained newsletters from various cities, especially from Venice and Antwerp, and because the newsletters included information gathered from different places, facts could be double-checked. The headings of the information centres appeared in chronological rather than a geographical order. In the case of Antwerp, the gazetteers generally first copied reports originating in their own city and included those from Cologne and elsewhere afterwards. In Venice, *novellanti* generally first mentioned notices from Rome and then those of their own city, but this arrangement was not strictly observed.

Printed newsletters differed from the form of the manuscript. Amsterdam newspapers started with news from Italy, usually Venice or Rome, and positioned Dutch news at the end. From April 1621, the month when the Twelve Years' Truce between the Dutch Republic and Spain expired, the *Courante* adopted the scheme of its competitor, the *Tijdinghen uyt verscheyde quartieren*, and drew a line at the end of compiled reports from outside, omitting any heading for Dutch news.[20] Printed news from Antwerp, the *Nieuwe Tijdinghen*, even had a front page headline and an illustration, mirroring broadsheets rather than manuscript newsletters.[21] In Amsterdam, the *Courante* and the *Tijdinghen* avoided any resemblance to printed pamphlets. They had no illustration and thus paralleled manuscript newsletters. Nonetheless, Amsterdam's printed newspapers differed from their handwritten predecessors and competitors when they introduced a stricter regulation for the position of news. The result was that printed newspapers offered two advantages to busy and inexperienced readers. First, the imprint made characters far more regular than handwriting could and facilitated easier reading. Second, imprints regulated the position of news assembled in Amsterdam and arranged it at the end beneath the dividing line, making the information relevant to local readers easier to find. Thus, the *Courante* and the *Tijdinghen* largely maintained the form of handwritten newsletters and avoided any outright resemblance to printed pamphlets, but guided their readers with the positioning of news assembled at Amsterdam and considered to be of particular importance for the local public. Despite their appearance, the new regulation of the format led to guided reading, increased the impact of this information and approached the news beyond the line to pamphleteering.

The change in the positioning of news from handwritten to printed gazettes especially applied to information from overseas. The first handwritten gazette which referred to news from the Caribbean circulated in Venice 1496 and was copied by Marino Sanuto in his diary. This Venetian newsletter mentioned information compiled in Milan between 23 June and 9 July 1496, referring to notices from Spain which announced that Christopher Columbus had arrived at Cádiz with a large quantity of gold.[22] This newsletter set the first standards which regulated the form of notices from overseas and especially news about the arrival of exotic cargoes. Hence, an Italian newsletter obtained and diffused the latest information from Spain. To lend credence to its accuracy, the *avviso* mentioned Spain as an intermediary source of information, meaning the "Spanish"[23] court. It also used the exact name of the Spanish harbour, Cádiz, where the ships arrived.

A century later, the form of information was still similar. The Fugger merchants at Augsburg received a handwritten newsletter from Antwerp compiled on 4 April 1598. It reported that a courier had brought notice from Madrid that a fleet from the (West) Indies had arrived at Seville with 7 million of gold[24] and 8,000 arrobas[25] of cochineal.[26] Like the fifteenth-century gazette, in 1598 news from Antwerp indicated the exact place of arrival: the merchants' town of Seville. Although the ships by that time usually arrived at the bay of Cádiz or at San Lúcar de Barrameda, Seville was still the administrative centre for taxation of silver and other commercial wares and the location where correspondents wrote their letters.[27] In 1598, as in the newsletter from 1496, the Spanish court, by now at Madrid, was an important centre for the further distribution of notices from Spanish America.[28] In this case, at the end of the sixteenth century, the hub at Antwerp collected the information and sent it on to readers and gazetteers in Augsburg and many other cities. Both in 1496 and in 1598, notices from overseas had no specific heading of their own in manuscript newsletters, but were lumped into the news distributed by larger information centres such as Milan and Antwerp. Nonetheless, reports related to overseas territories could usually be traced back through at least one intermediate stop in Europe. Thus, during the sixteenth century, cities on the Iberian Peninsula such as Madrid, Lisbon and Cádiz controlled the distribution of manuscript information from abroad, especially concerning the Spanish and Portuguese realms. Information centres such as Venice and Antwerp assembled and spread the reports further, all over Europe. Because the structure of sixteenth-century handwritten newsletters did not depend on the place where information was collected but rather the date of distribution, the result was that news from overseas appeared interspersed throughout a handwritten newsletter.

The printed newspapers published by Abraham Verhoeven in Antwerp in 1623 maintained the clear connection of news from Spanish America with the Iberian Peninsula. Reports from Havana arrived at Antwerp through the intermediaries of Seville and Madrid.[29] On 5 December 1621, the Amsterdam *Courante* was using the same format. On its first page, the *Courante* printed news compiled in Venice on 12 November 1621: notices from Spain confirming that the fleet, with a rich cargo of 5.5 million, had arrived from New Spain.[30] As was often the case in printed newspapers, the monetary unit was omitted, but it is safe to assume that the sum referred to Spanish ducats because the information came from Spain.[31] Thus, in the first years after the truce with Spain had expired, newspapers printed in Antwerp and Amsterdam still observed the format and conventions established by handwritten gazettes for news from overseas.

During the following years, neither the preserved issues of the *Courante* nor the *Tijdinghen* mention any arrivals from Spanish America. Instead, they focus on news about the East Indies. On 4 June 1622, the *Courante* published that merchants in Amsterdam recently bought 10,000 bundles of pepper from the VOC, with an approximate value of 24 tons of gold.[32] From then on, almost every piece of information relating to overseas territories appeared within the news compiled at Amsterdam. This applied to all regions "beyond the line",[33] that is, the Americas, Africa and Asia except the Ottoman Empire. Even notices about the arrival of silver fleets from Spanish America were now placed among the news collected at Amsterdam. On 19 December 1626, the *Courante* published that a small ship from Saint Malo had come in the day before after a seven-day journey. It brought news that the silver fleet had arrived at San Lúcar with 48 ships and 24 million.[34] In 1626, notices about the arrival of American riches no longer reached Amsterdam exclusively through Madrid but circulated, in this case, through the intermediation of France. As reports from overseas now formed part of the notices assembled at Amsterdam, they appeared on the second and last page, in most cases at the very end of a printed newspaper so that readers could find them easily. Thus, after the Twelve Years' Truce, in the Amsterdam *Courante*, news arriving from overseas—beyond the geographical lines—had found a fixed position beyond a newspaper line.

Regulating or fixing, the place of information from overseas within printed gazettes markedly altered the structure of the printed news network in comparison to the traditional network of manuscript newsletters. Handwritten notices related to overseas were distributed through a network where Venice, Rome, Antwerp and Cologne held the highest degrees of network centrality, whereas cities of the Iberian Peninsula maintained a secondary position.[35] This meant that Madrid could publicize its position regarding events in the Atlantic and Pacific through the network of manuscript newsletters, which communicated across the Mediterranean and north-western Europe almost equally. However, gazetteers at the centres of the network in Venice/Rome and Antwerp/Cologne adjusted the interpretations provided by the Spanish court according to the interests of their own regions and customers. As a result, the competing political influences of early modern Europe had to share the network of manuscript newsletters. Readers, therefore, perceived handwritten news as reliable and trustworthy.

The network of Amsterdam newspapers had a completely different structure. According to the layout of the imprints, Amsterdam was the only place assembling and distributing news from overseas to a local and regional public. As a result, Amsterdam held a position of almost absolute centrality. The same applied to the network of printed newspapers in Antwerp studied by P. Arblaster.[36] In these networks, cities of the Iberian Peninsula, and especially the Spanish court at Madrid, still held a secondary position, at least during the 1620s. So, even though news from the New World still reached Europe and Amsterdam through the Spanish Peninsula, the analysis and presentation of news in the printed gazettes depended on the view of the Dutch Republic, a state in permanent warfare against Spain. Consequently, the impartiality attributed to handwritten gazettes because of their layered influences could not be matched by printed newspapers, which directed the attention of their readers by regulating the position of information and which relied on a network completely controlled by Amsterdam. This format guided the reader towards the intended assessment and approaching the character of Amsterdam newspapers to pamphlets.

Analysis of printed newspapers from Amsterdam shows that they used a mechanism of regulation. Guided reading stressed the Amsterdam point of view. At the same time, printed newspapers tried to avoid an outright resemblance with printed propagandistic newssheets and aimed to compete with handwritten gazettes with a low degree of regulation. To appear as "neutral" as handwritten newsletters, printed newspapers made use of established images and wording.

Regulating Contents and Language of News from Overseas

The content of "news" changes by definition. Regulating the external form of newspapers' presentation was intended to provide readers with a framework which would help them to recognize the type and quality of information in front of them. Besides shaping external features, standardization regulated the content and wording of the news. Handwritten newsletters had already experienced a process of formalization by the end of the fifteenth century, so regularly printed newspapers had to adopt at least the same degree of standardization used by handwritten newsletters in order to avoid any resemblance with informal, occasionally printed pamphlets. Since Elizabeth Eisenstein's seminal study, modern scholarship has considered the advent of printed broadsheets as a groundbreaking step towards the constitution of a public sphere, and the appearance of regular printed newspapers strengthens this argument.[37] Contemporaries were more cautious; if they could afford it, they preferred handwritten newsletters to printed newspapers because they perceived the information in imprints as being biased.[38] The difference in perception of handwritten and printed gazettes might have been due to a different intensity of regulation.

The previous analysis of formal external structures already offered an example of increased regulation of the format in printed newspapers compared to manuscript gazettes, but regulation could also apply to the content and the language of the publication. News from overseas was most frequent when ships arrived from distant lands and readers expected reports of the cargo. Large ships coming in from overseas provided interesting news and happened regularly, so news about arrivals could easily be standardized in both manuscript and printed gazettes.

Notices in the handwritten *avvisi* from the fifteenth and sixteenth centuries and the reports in printed gazettes from the early seventeenth century offer no obvious differences in the descriptions of the Spanish American treasure fleets. When the ships landed, the gazettes mentioned first the place of their arrival and then a brief summary of their cargo. The harbours and cities of Cádiz and Seville appeared in the manuscripts, whereas imprints referred to Seville, Spain and San Lúcar. The cargo consisted, according to the manuscripts, of "great quantities of Gold" or "7 millions of gold and cochineal". Printed newspapers announced a "rich cargo of 5.5 millions" or that 48 ships arrived with a cargo "24 millions rich".

In a newsletter compiled at Lyon on 24 October 1596,[39] the information appeared that letters from Madrid written on 10 October 1596 had brought notices about the arrival of fleets from Peru and New Spain. According to this newsletter, the fleets reached Seville without any danger, that is, without encountering privateers or bad weather. The *avviso* continued: "They bring 12 Millions of gold and silver and different other goods valued around 2 Millions."[40] At the end, the newsletter included a brief listing of the cargo. Besides precious metals, the inventory encompassed seven different groups of commodities: dyes consisting of 5,000 arrobas of cochineal, 480 quintals[41] of indigo, and 1,600 quintals of logwood from Campeche. Medicinal plants for the treatment of syphilis and other diseases amounted to 700 quintals of sarsaparilla, 70,000 chests and 300 quintals of different sorts of lignum and guajacum. The list finished with 4,300 quintals of ginger, used at the time for cooking and dyeing. A similar enumeration appeared in the Amsterdam *Courante* from 5 May 1629,[42] announcing the arrival of the silver fleet from Peru with reference to newsletters from Antwerp, themselves based on information coming from Brussels and Madrid. It first mentioned that the silver fleet had arrived on 7 April with 7 million in gold and silver and commercial wares valued at 2 million,[43] adding that 1 million and 200,000 ducats of the whole cargo belonged to the king and the rest to the merchants. It is noteworthy that the printed newsletter of 1629 noted the distinction made by the Spanish tax administration between the precious metals and goods belonging to the Spanish crown and those treasures and commodities owned by private merchants, but omitted the complete list of the cargo. The "Fuggerzeitungen" from Lyon in 1596 and the *Courante*, referring to news from Antwerp in 1629 and printed above the "line", copied the descriptions stemming from Seville almost exactly. Thus in 1629, Amsterdam gazetteers adhered entirely to the form, content and wording of handwritten newsletters, and adopted the official language of the Spanish tax administration.

Detailed descriptions of the Spanish American treasure fleets appeared in similar circumstances in handwritten and printed gazettes. In both cases—that of the handwritten *avviso* from 14 October 1596 and that of the printed *Courante* from 5 May 1629—the information about the arrival of American treasures was extensive, and each case followed privateer actions; the last attacks of Sir Francis

Drake on the Caribbean coast (November 1595–January 1596) and the success of Piet Hein and his capture of the Mexican fleet at Matanzas (6–8 September 1628) respectively. The Spanish administration had to reassure their creditors and merchants that Spain could still guarantee the arrival of its fleets and was a safe place for investment despite privateering and warfare. This was of interest for Dutch merchants too, as quite a number of them traded with Spain covertly through the Spanish Netherlands.

Nonetheless, in May 1629, the *Courante* omitted the listing of cargo. This would have revealed to readers that the fleet from Peru, missed by Piet Heyn, was about 50% richer than the one captured at Matanzas. Half a year earlier, on 18 November 1628, the *Courante* had reported on the incredible riches obtained by Dutch privateers, estimated at 200 tons of gold and silver, 2,400 chests of indigo and cochineal as well as 37,000 Mexican skins.[44] The expression "tons of gold" will once again have meant 200,000 guilders. As these sums of precious metals and of dyes were far too low for an entire fleet, they would have been the cargo of a single ship. Nevertheless, in this case the cargo was listed in the Amsterdam printed newspaper according to the form, the content and very nearly the wording of Spanish documents and may have been copied directly from the tax registers on board in the Caribbean, thus linking both sides of the Atlantic Ocean.

Although the handwritten *avvisi* structured the content and terminology employed to announce the arrival of Spanish American fleets in Dutch printed newspapers, reports on the arrival of Dutch ships from overseas differed. The Dutch administration depended on their own institutions, and in many cases ships mentioned in the *Courante* were brought in as a prize of war with Spain.

The different origin of vessels informed how they were described. On 9 September 1623, the *Courante* published, within the notices collected at Amsterdam, a list which mentioned the cargo of the ship *De Paltsgraf*. The vessel had arrived in England from the East Indies some days ago. The weight of the ship was mentioned explicitly as 800 barrels (tons). When it came to the merchandise, the list sought to be more precise than information stemming from Spain: instead of using round numbers and summing up the cargo of 40–50 vessels, as in the case of the Spanish treasure fleets, the *Courante* published almost an exact description of the cargo of a single ship. According to the list, the vessel had loaded 221,823 pounds of cloves, 64,513 pounds of nutmeg and 4,043 "pounds of picol catty pepper". Obviously, these were still new expressions for the printer, as he mentioned two Asian and one European weights in one line to address the amount of pepper: picol (approximately 60 kg), catty (approximately 600 g) and pound (almost 500 g). Other goods included, according to the publication, 153 bales of cotton from Masulipatnam, 80 jars, two candied gingers and two pieces of ginger.[45] The jars might have been valuable porcelains and the containers of the ginger. This presentation, albeit in a more refined and accurate form, became common in the *Courante* and was adopted by other printed newspapers. Cargoes were described in detail, ship by ship, indicating the name of each vessel. The adoption and further refinement of the content and language of manuscript newsletters by printed newspapers produced a more precise description of the cargo and enhanced the importance of each voyage.

A similar process happened in the case of prizes of war. Renewed attacks began on Brazil in the summer of 1626, and on 25 July the *Courante* reported that the West India Company had obtained a prize of 600 chests of sugar and other merchandise worth more than 100,000 guilders. The description of the prize obtained by Piet Heyn in September 1626 used similar terminology. On 27 January 1627, the *Courante* informed its readers that the cargo of a Spanish ship brought in by Captain Grau would be sold at Vlissingen. The merchandise included 270 chests of sugar, a good quantity of tobacco, 130 skins, 8 bales of cotton, and 20 barrels of candied fruits.[46] These examples demonstrate how printed newspapers referred to the prizes of war in the same way that they described the arrival of mercantile commodities. As far as possible, they listed the cargo of every ship in the utmost detail, employing the neutral language of handwritten newsletters.

The content and wording of printed newspapers thus depended to a large extent on the example and regulation of their predecessors and competitors: handwritten gazettes. Nonetheless, imprints refined their content further, with detailed descriptions of the whole range of goods aboard an incoming ship and making no distinction between commercial vessels and prizes of war. These refinements stressed, on the one hand, the notion that the booty had been obtained in a just war, eroded the distinction between warfare and commercial enterprise and underlined the importance of Dutch commerce and privateering, all while distancing printed newspapers from handwritten gazettes.

Conclusion

During the sixteenth century, handwritten gazettes provided readers all over Europe with fast and reliable, albeit not completely impartial, information. Reports related to overseas territories and especially to vessels arriving in Europe had already achieved a high level of standardization in the handwritten newsletters of the late fifteenth century. The content and wording of these notices relied heavily on the format employed by the Spanish tax administration. However, the network distributing manuscript newsletters was centred outside of Spanish territory in Venice/Rome and Antwerp/Cologne, and thus mitigated the Spanish influence on the handwritten news about overseas territories.

In 1618, the first weekly newspapers were published in Amsterdam. In order to compete with handwritten newsletters and to avoid any resemblance with occasionally printed broadsheets and pamphlets, the printed *Courante* faithfully adopted the formatting of the already well-established newsletters. Nonetheless, within a very short period of time, small but significant changes appeared, further regulating the external format, content and language of the news.

Dutch printed newspapers altered the established external format in two ways: first, they fixed the position of notices compiled at Amsterdam at the end of each newspaper; and second, they omitted the date and place of editing as a heading and instead printed a single line. Beyond that line and within the news from Amsterdam, almost all reports related to overseas "beyond the line" appeared, especially information about incoming vessels from distant continents. This meant that readers could easily find the latest information concerning overseas events and that Amsterdam occupied a central position within the network of printed news. This guided reading through regulation and subtle enhancement of the deeds of the Dutch Republic avoided the notion of outright propaganda.

Besides the development of the external format, printed newsletters altered the standardization of contents and wording for news related to overseas territories. At first, they adhered to the format of handwritten newsletters and listed the cargo according to the methods of the Spanish tax administration for a whole fleet. But by the beginning of the Thirty Years War, the description of the cargo began to refer to each incoming ship in much more detail, which emphasized the significance of Dutch overseas endeavours. This regulation of the contents set new standards for printing commercial information in the future. In addition, the regulation of the wording used in the announcement of incoming ships made virtually no distinction between commercial enterprises and war booty.

Amsterdam printed newspapers refined and built upon the format of Spanish tax declarations used by handwritten newsletters to announce the cargo of fleets coming from overseas. In contrast to handwritten gazettes, the *Courante* employed additional regulations of the contents, the wording and the format. It presented the prizes of war entering the harbour of Amsterdam in a manner which gave the impression of a fruitful business. This very detailed information could easily be found beyond a line in the newspaper: it guided hurried readers and informed them of the riches to be reaped from further investments overseas against Spain. Without visible propaganda, the Amsterdam *Courante* emphasized through regulation that in times of war, at home there should be "no peace beyond the line".

Notes

1 According to the encompassing lists and study of De Weduwen, *Dutch and Flemish Newspapers*.
2 Rather recent studies are presented by Deen, Onnekink and Reinders, *Pamphlets and Politics*; cf. Niccoli, *Prophecy and People*.
3 For the Netherlands, one of the first studies was Stolp, *De eerste Couranten in Holland*. A recent study on Central Europe: Barbarics-Hermanik, "Handwritten Newsletters".
4 Pieper, *Die Vermittlung einer neuen Welt*.
5 Infelise, *Gazzetta*; North, *Kommunikationsrevolutionen*.
6 Raymond and Moxham, *News Networks*. More specific is the study of Keller and Molino, *Die Fuggerzeitungen*.
7 Cf. Der Weduwen, *Dutch and Flemish Newspapers*, and more specific Arblaster, *From Ghent to Aix*. The importance of the Dutch Republic as a knowledge hub is studied by Huigen, De Jong and Kolfin, *The Dutch Trading Companies*. The Southern Netherlands are addressed by Dupré, De Munck, Thomas and Vanpael, *Embattled Territory*.
8 Crailsheim, *The Spanish Connection*. Many Flemish merchants had strong relations to the Dutch Republic.

9 An overview is presented by Ettinghausen, *How the Press Began*. For the political influence of newspapers, see Van Groesen, *Amsterdam's Atlantic*.
10 Der Weduwen, *Dutch and Flemish Newspapers*; Arblaster, *From Ghent*.
11 Arblaster, *From Ghent*, 122–131.
12 Van Groesen, "(No) News from the Western Front".
13 De Vivo, *Information and Communication in Venice*; Infelise, *Prima dei giornali*.
14 Bauer, *Zeitungen vor der Zeitung*. Cf. Keller and Molino, *Die Fuggerzeitungen*.
15 Zwierlein, "Fuggerzeitungen". Pieper, *Die Vermittlung*.
16 This is also the impression of de Weduwen, *Dutch and Flemish Newspapers*, 16–23.
17 Der Weduwen, *Dutch and Flemish Newspapers*, 89.
18 Infelise, *Prima dei giornali*.
19 "Fuggerzeitungen" from Antwerp 12 April 1598, Cologne 16 April 1598, ÖNB, Cod. 8971, fol. 219r–220r; "Fuggerzeitungen" from Venice 17 April 1598, Rome 12 April 1598, ÖNB, Cod. 8971, fol. 223r–224v.
20 Courante uyt Italien en Duytsch-landt, etc., 23-04-1621, available online at delpher.nl, accessed 15 June 2018.
21 Arblaster, *From Ghent*, 97–105.
22 "Avvisi venuti de Hyspania. Che Clonno, capitaneo del armata hispana, …era arrivato a Cales, e ha portato gran quantitate de oro"—Milano from 23 June to 9 July 1496, in Berchet, *Fonti italiane*, vol. 1, 148.
23 In 1495, the kingdoms of Castile and Aragón were united by the royal marriage of the Catholic Monarchs.
24 Gold certainly referred to the Spanish ducat, by that time an accounting unit which once had been a gold coin. At the end of the sixteenth century, it stood for the value of approximately 34 grams of fine silver. Therefore the cargo consisted, according to the newspaper, of a value approximately equivalent to 240 tons of silver.
25 Approximately 90 tons of cochineal, a red dyestuff from New Spain, today Mexico.
26 "Aus Antorf von 4 de April 1598: Mit gedachten Currier wirdt auch aus Madrill geschrieben wieder die flotta aus Indya inn Seviglia mit 7 Million Gold innkommen auch so inn 8000 arrabas Cutzeniglia angelangt…" "Fuggerzeitungen", from Antwerp 4 April 1598, ÖNB, Cod. 8971, fol 204r–v. anno.onb.ac.at: ANNO, Fugger-Zeitungen, 1598, p. 2, accessed 15 June 2018.
27 For the role of Cádiz, see García-Baquero González, *Cádiz y el Atlántico*. Cf. Brendecke, *The Empirical Empire*.
28 On the control of the network of manuscripts by the Spanish Court, see Pieper, *Vermittlung*.
29 Arblaster, *From Ghent*, 129.
30 Courante uyt Italien en Duytsch-landt, etc., 05-12-1621, "Ut Spanien wert geconfirmeret dat die Vlote upt niew Spanjen vyf ent een half Millionen rijck aencomen was". delpher.nl, accessed 15 June 2018.
31 Thus the cargo of precious metals amounted to the value of around 190 tons of silver.
32 Certainly this is meant to be 24,000 guilders, equivalent to the value of around 240 kg silver.
33 According to the treaty between France and Spain of Cateau-Cambrésis in 1559, there would be no peace beyond the lines. Their peace agreements wouldn't apply south of the Tropic of Cancer and west of the prime meridian passing through Ferro in the Canaries. The phrase "no peace beyond the line" was adopted later to describe warfare between Spain and Portugal on the one hand and France, the Dutch Republic and England on the other hand.
34 This will have been 24 million guilders, approximately 240 tons of silver. Between 1620 and 1624, in Mexico and in Peru total annual silver production reached an average of 270 tons of silver. Garner, "Long-Term Silver Mining Trends", 898–935.
35 Pieper, "News from the New World".
36 Arblaster, *From Ghent*, 129.

37 Espejo Cala and Chartier, *La aparición del periodismo*; Eisenstein, *The Printing Revolution*.
38 Van Groesen, "(No)News".
39 ÖNB, Cod 8969, fol. 177r–v. anno.onb.ac.at: ANNO, Fugger-Zeitungen, 24 October 1596, p. 3, accessed 15 June 2018.
40 As the production of silver amounted to 11.5 million pesos in 1595 and in 1594 to 10.7 million, and in 1594 the fleet didn't leave Spanish America, the 12 million will have been ducats, equivalent to the value of 425 tons of silver. The value of the commodities will have been equivalent to around 70 tons of silver.
41 Around 60 tons of cochineal and 22 tons of indigo. One arroba was equivalent to 11.5 kg and 1 quintal equivalent to 46 kg.
42 Courante uyt Italien en Duytsch-landt, etc., 05-05-1629: "Wt Antwerpen den 18 dito. Eergisteren is tot Brussel eenen Erpxessen uyt Madrid van de Coninck … aengecomen… Den selben Post bringt oock sekere tydinghe dat de Vlote van Terra Firma, rijck seven Millionen in Gout ende Silver ende twee aen Coopmanschappen tot Sivilia … gearrivert ist; hier op is vor den Connick 1 Million ende 200000, ducaten ende de Reste vor de Coopliuyden…" delpher.nl, accessed 15 June 2018.
43 Seven million ducats were equivalent to approximately 250 tons of silver, the value of the commodities was equivalent to 70 tons of silver and the Spanish crown received almost the value of 43 tons of silver.
44 "…die gheschat wordt op ontrent de 200.tonnen Gouts soo aen Gout Silver, 2400 Cassen Indigo ende Consinillie, 37000 Mestcanische Huyden, ende meer andere costelijcke Waren, diemen alle daghen hier te Lande verwachtende is". Courante uyt Italien ende Duytschlandt, etc. 18-11-1628, delpher.nl, accessed 15 June 2018. The amount of precious metals was valued afterwards to almost 12 million guilders (4 million ducats), equivalent to approximately 120 tons of silver.
45 "221823 pound Naghelen, 64513 pound Noten, 4043 pound picol Catty peper, 153 Balen Masilipatanische Calicour, 80 Jarres, 2 Oerhooiden Gember 2 pieces of Gember". *Courante uyt Duytschlandt*, etc. from 9 September 1623, delpher.nl, accessed 15 June 2018.
46 "Op den 26 dieses sal tot Vlissingen int openbaer vercocht werden een Spaensche Berck, up Capiteyn Grau ingebracht, beneffens 270 Kisten sucker, een goede partie Toback, 130 Huyden, acht Balen Catoen, 20 Tonnekens met Confituren …" *Courante uyt Duytschlandt*, etc. from 20 February 1627, delpher.nl, accessed 15 June 2018.

Bibliography

Arblaster, Paul. *From Ghent to Aix: How They Brought the News in the Habsburg Netherlands, 1550–1700*. Leiden and Boston, MA: Brill, 2014.

Barbarics-Hermanik, Zsuzsa. 'Handwritten Newsletters as Interregional Information Sources in Central and Southeastern Europe.' In Dooley, Brendan ed. *The Dissemination of News and the Emergence of Contemporaneity in Early Modern Europe*. London: Ashgate, 2010, pp. 155–178.

Bauer, Oswald. *Zeitungen vor der Zeitung. Die Fuggerzeitungen (1568–1605) und das frühmoderne Nachrichtensystem*. Berlin: Akademie Verlag, 2011.

Berchet, Guglielmo ed. *Fonti italiane per la storia della scoperta del nuovo mondo*. Vol. 1. Roma: Ministerio della Pubblica Istruzione, 1892.

Brendecke, Arndt. *The Empirical Empire: Spanish Colonial Rule and the Politics of Knowledge*. Berlin and Boston, MA: De Gruyter-Oldenbourg, 2016.

Crailsheim, Eberhard. *The Spanish Connection. French and Flemish Merchant Networks in Seville (1570–1650)*. Köln, Weimar, and Wien: Böhlau, 2016.

De Vivo, Filippo. *Information and Communication in Venice: Rethinking Early Modern Politics.* Oxford: Oxford University Press, 2007.

Deen, Femke; Onnekink, David; Reinders, Michel eds. *Pamphlets and Politics in the Dutch Republic.* Leiden and Boston, MA: Brill, 2011.

Dupré, Sven; Munck, Bert de; Thomas, Werner; Vanpaemel, Geert eds. *Embattled Territory. The Circulation of Knowledge in the Spanish Netherlands.* Gent: Academia Press, 2015.

Eisenstein, Elizabeth L. *The Printing Revolution in Early Modern Europe.* Cambridge: Cambridge University Press, 1983.

Espejo Cala, Carmen; Chartier, Rogier eds. *La aparición del periodismo en Europa. Comunicación y propaganda en el Barroco.* Madrid: Marcial Pons, 2012.

Ettinghausen, Henry. 'How the Press Began. The Pre-Periodical Printed News in Early Modern Europe.' *Janus Digital,* Anexo 3 (2015). http://www.janusdigital.es/anexo.htm?id=7, published 14.10.2015, viewed on 26.06.2018.

García-Baquero González, Antonio. *Cádiz y el Atlántico (1717–1778): el comercio colonial español bajo el monopolio gaditano.* Sevilla: Escuela de Estudios Hispano-Americanos CSIC, 1976.

Garner, Richard. 'Long-Term Silver Mining Trends in Spanish America. A Comparative Analysis of Peru and Mexico.' *American Historical Review* 93 (1988): 898–935.

Groesen, Michiel van. '(No) News from the Western Front: The Weekly Press of the Low Countries and the Making of Atlantic News.' *Sixteenth Century Journal* 44, no. 3 (2013): 739–760.

Groesen, Michiel van. *Amsterdam's Atlantic, Print Culture and the Making of the Dutch Brazil.* Philadelphia: University of Pennsylvania Press, 2017.

Huigen, Siegfried; Jong, Jan L. de; Kolfin, Elmer eds. *The Dutch Trading Companies as Knowledge Networks.* Leiden and Boston, MA: Brill, 2010.

Infelise, Mario. *Prima dei giornali. Alle origine della pubblica informazione.* Roma and Bari: Laterza, 2002.

Infelise, Mario. *Gazzetta. Storia di una parola.* Venice: Marsilio, 2017.

Keller, Katrin; Molino, Paola. *Die Fuggerzeitungen im Kontext. Zeitungssammlungen im Alten Reich und in Italien.* Wien-Köln: Böhlau, 2015.

Niccoli, Ottavia. *Prophecy and People in Renaissance Italy.* Princeton, NJ: Princeton University Press, 1990.

North, Michael ed. *Kommunikationsrevolutionen. Die neuen Medien des 16. und 19. Jahrhunderts,* 2nd ed. Wien and Köln: Böhlau, 2001.

Pieper, Renate. *Die Vermittlung einer neuen Welt: Amerika im Nachrichtennetz des Habsburgischen Imperiums 1493–1598.* Mainz: Van Zabern, 2000.

Pieper, Renate. 'News from the New World: Spain's Monopoly in the European Network of Handwritten Newsletters during the Sixteenth Century.' In Raymond, Joad; Moxham, Noah eds. *News Networks in Early Modern Europe.* Leiden and Boston, MA: Brill, 2016, pp. 495–511.

Raymond, Joad; Moxham, Noah eds. *News Networks in Early Modern Europe.* Leiden and Boston, MA: Brill, 2016.

Stolp, Annie. *De eerste Couranten in Holland. Bijtrage tot de Geschiedenis der Geschreven Nieuwstijdingen.* Amsterdam: Academisch Proefschrift, 1938.

Weduwen, Arthur der. *Dutch and Flemish Newspapers of the Seventeenth Century.* 2 vols. Leiden and Boston, MA: Brill, 2017.

Zwierlein, Cornel. 'Fuggerzeitungen als Ergebnis von italienisch-deutschem Kulturtransfer 1552–1570.' *Quellen und Forschungen aus italienischen Archiven und Bibliotheken* 90 (2010): 169–224.

5
LOST IN REGULATION
The Hybrid Stage of Trade Knowledge

Ida Nijenhuis

Mercury's Teachings

In 1766, the Dutch reading public was presented with the first instalment of *De Koopman*, a periodical devoted to commerce which, according to its author, was 'the life and soul of the commonwealth'. The frontispiece of the first bound volume showed a merchant at his desk in his *comptoir*, quill poised, behind him a bookcase filled with folio volumes and Mercury flying towards him from a sea with trading vessels, holding a sheet of paper. Two cherubs are piling up manuals written by Le Long, Ricard, King and De Graaf. A woman representing trade holds a map and leans with her right foot on a globe. She is surrounded by the paraphernalia of trade and navigation: nautical instruments, weights and measures, money and merchandise.[1] This image of a merchant at work epitomizes eighteenth-century views of commerce: it makes entirely clear that the mercantile profession demanded expertise, a comprehensive knowledge of commodities, geography, finance, numeracy, insurance, etc. In part, the merchant could learn this know-how from a specific type of books, the so-called mercantile manuals.

The books of the authors mentioned in the engraving were written with the aim to instruct and inform the (Dutch) merchant and to enlighten those who were interested in trade and everything that was connected with it. Taken together, the books in the frontispiece and *De Koopman* itself represent a crucial stage in the evolution of the trading manual, from a guide for professionals by professionals to a compendium for a broader use and with a mixed content. These publications complied with the practical purposes business manuals usually had, but on a more abstract level, they might also explain the causes of commercial success. Their authors, translators, publishers and editors were mediating figures and formed a motley crowd. In a lot of ways, they resembled Ursula Klein's

DOI: 10.4324/9780429279928-8

eighteenth-century Prussian engineers, learned and technical experts, hybrids of cerebral academics and traditional artisans, who created useful knowledge.[2]

The question this chapter wants to answer is whether and to what extent books on the art of trade came to explain commerce on a theoretical level. Historiography still tends to treat the history of economic thought and that of trade knowledge as totally separate fields. A recent working paper on economic bestsellers, with the promising subtitle 'a fresh look at the history of economic thought', featured a list of eighty publications with at least ten editions, including translations, before 1850.[3] Though the compilers of the list seem to be aware of the hazardous aspects of defining 'economics', they mention the difficulty in delineating economics compared to other sciences in early modern times and the fact that authors tended to cover broader subject areas back then. Still, they are rather myopic in the application of their selection criteria. Following the example of an earlier inventory of economic titles, they exclude practical works and manuals for merchants, farmers and craftsmen, in short the whole genre of *ars mercatoria*, the art of commerce or trade knowledge. As a result, several bestselling publications containing economic knowledge, like Jacques Savary's *Le parfait negociant* (1675) and his sons' sequel, the *Dictionnaire universel de commerce* (1723), do not appear in the list. These manuals contained instrumental information for merchants, but gradually they also featured trade theories, thus adding to their scope as an instructive publication. It is precisely this miscellaneous content that makes eighteenth-century mercantile manuals a primary source for analysing the transfer of knowledge associated with one specific profession to other communities and other languages. Moreover, their history shows how and for how long *ars mercatoria* and political economy were not separate domains of knowledge.

Below we will discuss the conversion of Mercury's teachings into instructions for merchants and how these manuals developed into the hybrid publications of the eighteenth century. By investigating how pin-making was treated in trade manuals and turned into the perfect illustration of Adam Smith's well-known principle of the division of labour, we will demonstrate the amalgam of *ars mercatoria* and political economy. Our focus will be on the Dutch Republic, a country epitomizing commerce during the seventeenth and eighteenth centuries, but always accused by foreigners of having more practice than theory, as Adriaan Kluit (1735–1807), the first Dutch professor in economics, stated in his lecture notes of 1806–1807.[4]

Evolution of the Trade Manual

Training on the job as well as obtaining commercial skills by studying handwritten and printed instructions had been part and parcel of the trading profession for ages. Knowledge of merchandise and markets as well as interpersonal credit was the lifeblood of trading companies, even more so after the discovery of overseas territories. Therefore, apart from being effectively educated in commercial practices, merchants also needed to be up to date. Information on navigation, geography, transnational markets, exotic merchandise, currency, banking, accounting, etc., as well as political news affected their transactions and decisions. Handwritten newsletters, log books of overseas expeditions and recorded conversations with ships' masters and steersmen, all built up to what Jochen Hoock has called the '"Verschriftlichung" kaufmännischen Erfahringswissens' from the late fifteenth century onwards.[5] The invention of the printing press enabled the production of printed merchants' manuals as well as the dissemination of *ars mercatoria*: about 3,200 books and supplements to be used by merchants and read by those interested in commerce were published throughout Europe between 1470 and 1700.[6] In many cases, these manuals, though based on their experience and knowledge, were not or only in part written by merchants. As we will see below, this also applies to the authors mentioned in *De Koopman*'s frontispiece.[7]

We can trace the evolution of the art of commerce into a broad, varied and hybrid body of mercantile knowledge by examining the subject matter index in the impressive bibliography compiled by Jochen Hoock and Pierre Jeannin. After 1600, new categories emerged like banking, stock exchange, history of trade, state-run companies, locations of manufacture and the connections between production and exchange. However, certain late medieval topics get a lot more attention after 1600: accounting, trade terminology, trade geography, coinage, trading community, credit, private companies, measures and weights.[8] Intended to educate as well as to inform, these books and guides on trade matters show a great variety that correspond with the diversity in its writers, publishers and buyers. First of all, they were meant to serve the merchant community in various ways by offering both propositional and prescriptive knowledge. The first type regulated *what* there was to know regarding navigation, geography, transnational markets, exotic merchandise, currency, banking, accounting, etc. Instructions on *how* to go about things in the world of commerce constituted the second category of mercantile knowledge.[9] All kinds of instructions, varying from the correct way to do bookkeeping to which local laws to obey or how best to observe moral guidelines in doing business, make clear they not only reflected specific actions but also prescribed behaviour.[10] Another specific category of users concerns those who wanted to teach business skills and who were in constant need of practical guides and commercial mnemonics.

Writers and publishers were also interested parties, seeing opportunities when exploration of new waters and overseas territories stirred the interest of a non-mercantile readership. In serving this new target group, not per se interested in accounting, numeracy, specie or acceptances, some of them focused on a more general, narrative approach of trade, navigation, geography and commodities. Others opted for combining different types of texts into one volume, like, for instance, Lewes Roberts (1596–1641), a British merchant with the Levant Company, in his *The Merchants Mappe of Commerce* of 1638. The subtitle of the book shows both the author's ambition as well as the expansion of the genre: 'wherein, the universall manner and matter of trade, is compendiously handled'.

Roberts amalgamated cartographical information, knowledge of coinage, accounting and exchange, institutions, commodities, weights and measures and considered this knowledge:

> necessary for all such as shall be imployed in the publique affaires of princes in forreigne parts; for all gentlemen and others that travell abroad for delight or pleasure, and for all merchants or their factors that exercise the art of merchandizing in any part of the habitable world.[11]

Princes, gentlemen and merchants – in that telling order – were to be instructed by Roberts's expertise.

This diversification in subject matter and audience as well as the enormous increase of publications on trade after 1600 reflect the growing appreciation of commerce as a cross-border phenomenon and the concomitant need to regulate the art of commerce. Trade became increasingly viewed as of crucial importance for the wealth and power of a state and mercantile data rapidly developed into an object of desire and debate for merchants and rulers alike. Commerce became a reason of state.[12] More and more, the once handwritten manuals produced by experienced merchants for their own networks developed into comprehensive printed handbooks composed by authors, who occasionally had their roots in commerce but were also linked to government.

The above-mentioned Jacques Savary (1622–1690), author of the seminal *Le parfait negociant* (1675), constitutes an instructive case of this hybrid expertise. He started off as a 'mercier-marchand en gros', a wholesale merchant of haberdashery, and subsequently became a 'fermier des douanes' with the help of Nicolas Fouquet (1615–1680), his patron and superintendent of finances. After Fouquet fell from power, Savary's commercial know-how was still wanted. Chancellor Pierre Séguier (1588–1672) charged him with the adjudication in several trade affairs and Fouquet's successor Jean-Baptiste Colbert (1619–1683) asked him to assist the commission that prepared the new French trade ordinance of 1673. Next, as he explains in the preface to his magnum opus, several members of this committee suggested Savary to publish a work on commerce 'qui pût etre utile aux jeunes gens qui voudroient se metre dans la profession mercantile'. Though he had left the mercantile profession at a time when French trade was unprotected, leading to many bankruptcies, now, in a favourable political climate, his commercial background and experience in arbitrage still made him 'assez capable sur toutes les matieres les plus importantes, et les plus difficiles du commerce'. To stand the test of criticism, Savary had his work checked by two lawyers of the Paris parliament as well as by several traders and bankers throughout the kingdom. The result was a book that incorporated all his accumulated experience and knowledge and went through 32 editions between 1675 and 1800, including translations into Dutch, German, English and Italian.[13]

The Savary-episode demonstrates how the history of the trade manual also becomes the history of 'mercantilism', as the underlying thought of *Le parfait negociant* was to make France more competitive by way of instructing (future) merchants in commercial practices and by making trade acceptable, even honourable, for the French nobility. The book contained instrumental information on trade's technical, juridical and geographical dimensions as well as its multifarious raw materials and products. Its subtitle stated the book's objective: 'instruction generale pour ce qui regarde le commerce de toute sorte de Marchandises, tant de France, que des pays estrangers'. For good reason, Savary dedicated the volume to Colbert, whom he praised for his efforts to establish a flourishing commerce in the monarchy. This connection with state policy ('mercantilism') and the obvious attempt to regulate available trade knowledge define *Le parfait negociant* as a 'Bruchstelle' (Hoock) in the history of *ars mercatoria*.[14]

Printed with the king's privilege, Savary's book allowed wide-ranging information derived from trade's practitioners to get to an audience not strictly mercantile, and its success caused his sons Jacques Savary des Bruslons (1657–1716) and Louis Philémon Savary (1654–1727), both without roots in trade, to expand and reorganize its content. Jacques maintained a trade manual for his work as an 'inspecteur de la douane' and collected printed books on commerce in France and abroad, which Louis Philémon, canon of Saint-Maur, systematized in a card index. Suggestions to produce a 'vocabulaire du commerce français', combined with the permission to explore the royal archives and the request to extend their research to international trade, ultimately resulted in the publication of the brothers' *Dictionnaire universel de commerce* in 1723 (Paris, 2 volumes).[15] Its subtitle did no longer refer to an instructive purpose, but suggested that the lexicon comprised all one had to know about commerce, art and industry all over the globe. Like their father's book, it was printed with the royal privilege and dedicated to an important government official. It opened with a 'Préface historique' that related the evolution of trade since the Phoenicians, a format that was frequently copied by eighteenth-century authors writing on commerce.[16]

Though this act of historicizing commerce and arranging its substance in alphabetical order suggested a definite recording of knowledge, this was not the case. Several new editions as well as translations appeared and demonstrated the lack of finality in this attempt at completeness. Moreover, in these new editions of the *Dictionnaire*, economic theory was added to several entries. According to Perrot, all over Europe one could discern a development in which 'le Manuel des négociants devient timidement Manuel de l'économie politique' between 1730 and 1750.[17] In the 1742 edition of the *Dictionnaire*, the entry on *balance*, for instance, not only described a weighing instrument and the closing of an account, but also discussed the concept of the balance of commerce as analysed by Jean-François Melon (1675–1738) in his *Essai politique sur le commerce*, first published in 1734.[18] The same transformation can be noticed in Malachy Postlethwayt's version of the *Dictionnaire*, which appeared as *The universal dictionary of trade and commerce* in two volumes (London, 1751–1755). Postlethwayt (1707–1767) too integrated knowledge of commercial practice and economic theory and adjusted his publication to the needs of his British clientele. His translation and adaptation of the French original not only wanted to propagate trade knowledge, it also aimed at emulation, 'the desire to imitate and improve on superiors without harming them in the process'.[19] In the prospectus for his publication, he expressly stated that he trusted his version to improve on the French original, implicating this would also enhance British economic power.[20]

Making economic knowledge from abroad available by translation, and thereby allowing the absorption and emulation of the achievements of other nations, became essential in the second half of the eighteenth century, when the already existing transnational debates and exchanges of knowledge and ideas with a view to individual and societal improvement gained momentum. Political economy, the discipline that investigated the optimal relationship between a nation's economy and its politics, became the spearhead in these interchanges and triggered a European movement of economic patriots. They organized themselves in societies, published journals and held competitions to discuss reform plans based on relevant economic texts, but like the Savary's, if possible, they also operated within the corridors of power.[21] The evolution of *ars mercatoria*-publications into hybrids like the aforementioned manuals and dictionaries, containing references to emerging political economists, digressions on the history and the purpose of commerce, descriptions of cities, international treaties, descriptions of goods and where and how they were produced must be appreciated in this context of border crossing public platforms for cultural exchange. In the following section, we will analyse this evolution of the hybrid in the Dutch context.

Manuals for the Dutch Market

As mentioned above, a Dutch translation of *Le parfait negociant* was published in 1683, thus introducing to the Dutch Republic the concept of an all-inclusive trade manual: a single handbook containing up-to-date information concerning all aspects of *ars mercatoria* with the purpose of instruction. *Le parfait negociant* (including its translations) was groundbreaking not just for nations like France that only started to grasp the importance of commerce, but also for a commercial state by birth like the Dutch Republic. Of course, Dutch merchants had been able to use all kinds of manuals, mostly dealing with specific subjects like accounting, insurance and maritime and commercial law. Between 1600 and 1700, without striking ups and downs throughout the century, 299 Dutch authors had produced a manual or treatise on one of these separate fields of mercantile knowledge. For the eighteenth century, we do not have such a precise figure, but here also the production of the single subject guides continued.[22] Two original handbooks in Dutch have titles that suggest a comprehensive approach, but, in fact, are limited in scope. Pieter de Buck's *Den coop-lieden handt-boeck*, published in 1581 in Ghent and reissued in an enlarged edition in 1678, concentrates on weights and measures. The anonymous author of the *Handleiding tot den Hollandsche koophandel, bevattende een beknopt, dog grondig onderwys van dit edel beroep, om door hetzelve tot fortuin te geraken* (Amsterdam, 1754) seems to have found it expedient to suggest a broader scope in order to meet the public's demand. However, apart from an introduction on commerce and its relationship with state government, the book focussed on accounting. Therefore it is justifiable to call the Savary-translation the first complete trade manual in Dutch.[23]

A closer look at both versions may serve to illuminate these qualities. Where the dedication to Colbert in the French original was made by the author himself, in the Dutch version the Amsterdam publishers[24] were the ones to do this. They addressed four 'very distinguished merchants' of that town: Dirck Mels, Theodoro le Roy, Johannes Coymans and Gilbert de Flines.[25] The translator, Gotfried van Broekhuizen (1681–1708 fl.), was not a merchant and by his contemporaries best known for his translations of French publications on history and travel. He followed Savary's original meticulously, except for the preface where he left out the parts in which Savary referred to his own career, his entrance in royal service, his first memoirs on the abuses in French commerce, his proposals regarding their solution by regulation. Also absent in the Dutch 'Voorreden' is Savary's account of the genesis of *Le parfait negociant* in which the author, as explained above, explicitly mentions its function in the training of youngsters who would like to become merchants. This message was, of course, more important to a non-commercial state like France than to a time-honoured trading republic. The fact that he had his work checked (and thus validated) by two lawyers of the Paris parliament as well as by several traders and bankers throughout the kingdom was equally left out by Van Broekhuizen. What stayed was Savary's defence of disclosing *ars mercatoria* to the public. In line with the longstanding practice in merchant communities, Savary justified sharing trade knowledge, knowing that mutual trust and reliable information were of the essence in commercial dealings. Traders that felt their specific expertise should not be divulged were only after their own instead of the common good. They had nothing to fear from future colleagues following the manual's instructions.[26]

In sixty-seven chapters, Savary and his translator next initiated future merchants in the art of trade, including the professional do's-and-don'ts for the merchant-to-be. In chapter three, after having explained the necessity and value of commerce as well as the book's objectives, they made the case for instruction by connecting lack of knowledge, imprudence and ambition to bankruptcies. In the four succeeding chapters, the manual dealt with the talents an aspiring man of commerce should exploit and depicted the course an apprentice had to complete before he could call himself an independent merchant. The other chapters contained factual mercantile knowledge: domestic weights and measures and how to compare them with foreign ones, bills of exchange, all kinds of commodities and manufactured goods and their diverse measurements and qualities, trade and navigation all over Europe, wholesale and retail trade, bookkeeping, how to regulate business in an association what rules apply when selling on credit, which forms and letters to use for various types of affairs and so on. Especially in this factual field, future editions produced corrections and supplements, the prescriptive core remaining as it was. As the introductory 'La Vie de Mr. Savary' in the 1757 edition stated, 'L'autorité du Parfait Négociant augmentant sans cesse, il servit enfin comme de règle pour les affaires du commerce'.[27]

Neither a second Dutch edition of Savary's manual nor an original Dutch equivalent, comprising the latest propositional and prescriptive knowledge of the whole commercial domain, had been published at the time the already mentioned *De Koopman* arrived on the scene in 1768. It is revealing to read why Willem Ockers (1741–1782), in his time better known as a prolific writer of satirical pamphlets, thought it necessary to publish *De Koopman*. He referred to the status quo of what he called 'the science of commerce' in his native country and established that:

> [a]s for the authors on commerce, accounting, navigation etc., our fatherland has few besides the translated works of Mr Le Moine de l'Espine, and Mr Savary. And virtually nothing original, which is surprising in a country like this that, so to speak, has to make a living out of commerce.[28]

De Koopman was supposed to fill this gap and contained exactly the diverse content mercantile manuals following the publication of *Le Parfait Negociant* presented. Of course, *De Koopman* was a periodical and not a trade manual, though its instalments were yearly published as bound books. It was one of the many journals published after 1750 on the above-mentioned wave of a rapidly expanding public involvement in improvement. Be it individual or national. Clearly, Ockers also associated his publication – and in more than one way, as we will see below – with authors like De l'Espine and Savary. For good reason he had the engraver of the frontispiece of *De Koopman* depict the names of acknowledged authors on commerce.

Naturally, we cannot be sure to which titles exactly he wanted to refer to, but contemporaries almost certainly will have recognized the named authors. Isaac le Long (1683–1762), from German Flemish Calvinist descent, born and deceased in Germany, came to Amsterdam in the early eighteenth century to start a career as a publisher. In that capacity, he was responsible for numerous biblical studies and a few commercial handbooks. The most important in the latter category – and perhaps to be viewed as the Dutch Savary – was *Den Koophandel van Amsterdam*, published in 1714. This manual was a revised and enlarged edition of *Le Negoce d'Amsterdam* written by Jacques le Moine de l'Espine's (d.1696), first published in 1694 (also in a Dutch version) and reprinted in 1704. By 1768, already eight editions of *Den Koophandel* had appeared and new, enlarged versions kept being published until 1802.[29]

Ricard may apply to Samuel Ricard (1637–1717) or his son Jean-Pierre Ricard (1674–1728) or to both. Samuel, a Huguenot refugee from France, lived as a *poorter* and merchant in Amsterdam from 1685 onwards and wrote the influential *Traité general du commerce* and *L'Art de bien tenir les livres de comptes en parties doubles à l'Italienne*, which were first published in 1700 and 1709, respectively. Samuel's *Traité* was meant as a complete manual for the merchant and only dealt in part with

Holland's commerce (weights and measures as well as currency). The extended title of the *Traité* reveals how marketable trade knowledge had become. By calling the manual 'plus ample et plus exact que ceux qui ont paru jusques à present, fait sur les mémoires de divers auteurs tant anciens que modernes', the author and publisher appealed to the target group, the professional merchants, claiming that they would be served by his *Traité* with the same ease as a complete library.[30] Samuel's son Jean-Pierre, also a merchant and *poorter* of Amsterdam, was responsible for a revised French version of *Le Negoce d'Amsterdam* in 1722 and he furthermore issued a supplemented edition of his father's work on accounting in 1724.

Charles King, of whom we know next to nothing, compiled miscellaneous documents on commerce in a three-volume set under the title *The British Merchant or, Commerce Preserv'd* (1721).[31] In its physical and intrinsic manifestation, *The British Merchant* may have formed the source of inspiration for Ockers's *De Koopman*. King's volumes contained original articles from the broadsheet *The British Merchant* (1713–1714), pamphlets, letters, numerical data, diplomatic documents and so on. The work discussed the pros and cons of the commercial treaties drafted (but not ratified) in 1713–1715 in the wake of the War of the Spanish Succession between Britain, France and the Dutch Republic. However, it was probably not this debate on international trade that caused the printmaker of *De Koopman* to include *The British Merchant* in his pile of manuals for the merchant, but its Dutch translation of 1728. In this two-volume *Historie van den algemenen en bijzonderen koophandel van Groot Brittannien, door alle gewesten van de waerelt*, the original text was enlarged with listed information on duties, incoming and outgoing trade volumes and the lucrativeness of trade in certain commodities – useful knowledge for merchants combined with political economy.[32]

De Graaf, to conclude, may stand for either Abraham (1635–1713) or his son Isaak (1668–1743). The first was a well-known mathematician and published several, often reprinted works on accounting and navigation, amongst which was a book with the revealing title *Instructie van het Italiaans Boekhouden* (1688). Isaak was a map-maker, and in 1691 received a commission to produce an atlas of Africa and Asia for the VOC, the Dutch East India Company. In 1705, he was appointed official cartographer for the VOC until his death in 1743. Isaak also published financial and mathematical works, amongst others *Jaartafelen van zamengevoegde intrest op winning en verlies* (1714) and *Waardije van lijfrenten naar proportie van losrenten* (1729).

Den Koophandel van Amsterdam

On the whole, the list of authors on the frontispiece of *De Koopman* – of whom only the Ricards are known to have been merchants by profession – showed that a merchant had to be a jack of all trades. He depended on diverse, reliable and actual information on either commercial practices or treaties, a mix of *ars mercatoria* and political economy. With his revisions of and extensions to Le Moine de L'Espine's *Negoce* and by copying parts of Savary's and Ricard's manual into the text, Le Long seems to have met these requirements best. As a second Dutch edition of *Le parfait negociant* did not materialize and Dutch buyers failed to appreciate Ricard's updated French of *Le Negoce d'Amsterdam*, Le Long's Dutch versions swept the market. Between 1714 and 1725, four editions of *Den Koophandel van Amsterdam* were published, and in 1727, Le Long published a second volume with extensions based to a large extent on Ricard. His explicit aim to appeal to a broader reading public than solely merchants and brokers, stating that statesmen wanted to consult his handbook as well, may have boosted the sales of Le Long's manual.[33]

The publishers dedicated Le Long's enlarged and restructured book to the Amsterdam merchants, who were supposed to buy and use it for instructing their apprentices. Unlike *Le parfait negociant, Den Koophandel van Amsterdam* did not contain specific chapters to this end. Remarkablewas the separate chapter Le Long devoted to the *College van Commercie* (Commercial Board), installed by the city government in 1663. This board, consisting of members of the city council and notable merchants, was expected to advise on what measures to take to prevent Amsterdam's trade to relocate due to growing competition. Its short-lived existence (no more meetings were held after 1665) had been called to mind by Johannes Phoonsen (1631–1702) in his well-known *Wissel-stijl tot Amsterdam* (Amsterdam, 1676). In this often reprinted guide for local bill broking, Phoonsen had pleaded for a reinstatement of this type of advisory body in which trade and politics were supposed to produce synergistic effects. Through Le Long, this appeal reappeared in *De Koopman* and other Dutch eighteenth-century texts on trade and politics, especially when discussing the Republic's decline and the means to combat this crisis. On the national level, for example, this propagation of an Amsterdam institution from the past had its parallel in recommending the French *Chambre de Commerce* and the *Conseil de Commerce* as described in the *Dictionnaire*.[34]

Did its wide-ranging contents and its propagation of a commercial board qualify *Den Koophandel van Amsterdam* as a manual in which trade knowledge and political economy met each other? Sporadically, Le Long inserted information taken from other authors than Savary and Ricard and occasionally these extracts suggest acknowledgement of economic principles. One of them, the maxim that commerce depended on hard work, came from William Temple (1628–1699). In his well-known *Observations upon the United Provinces of The Netherlands* (1672), the United Provinces owed this primacy in world trade to its tradition of ingenious diligence or 'industry' being the source of all trade. This 'industry' had been forced upon the Dutch because they lacked means of existence on their populous and narrow territory. Constant repetition had engraved this diligent and frugal attitude so much that it even remained to exist after 'necessity', which had forced the Dutch to be inventive and seek their livelihood outside the state's territory, had gone.[35] In Le Long's manual, this axiom returned in his introductory chapter where he stated that the Dutch were forced to trade and navigation by necessity.[36] However, this example does not mean that Le Long was deliberately looking for a combination of practice and theory. In this respect, it is significant that he published a Dutch translation of Melon's *Essai politique sur le commerce* in 1735, but, unlike the brothers Savary, refrained from integrating the Frenchman's views in the subsequent editions of *Den Koophandel van Amsterdam*.[37] In sum, Le Long's work can be labelled as a hybrid because it bears some evidence of theoretical understanding and links commerce with politics, but this knowledge never materializes in an explicit and systematic way.

Trade Knowledge and Political Economy: Pins and Pin-Making

At the publication of *De Koopman* in 1766/1768, Le Long (but also Ricard, King and De Graaf) were still authorities in mercantile matters, although the first editions of their work dated from around 1700. The contents of their books became more diverse and kept expanding, resulting in, as we have seen, various new, updated editions in multiple volumes throughout the eighteenth century. As we have seen, economic theory gradually entered trade manuals and added to propositional trade knowledge with a varying level of sophistication. This meant that merchants and those interested in commerce increasingly not only read about trade, but also about markets, competition and the various economic segments (trade, agriculture, industry) that created the wealth of nations – all key issues in the European debates on political economy. As a consequence, the importance of industry or manufacturing in trade manuals increased. Until the second half of the eighteenth century, describing manufactured goods as well as their place of production was done in only a few of the trade manuals and on a restricted scale. Merchant-scholar Paul Jacob Marperger (1656–1730) from Nürnberg had been one of the first to outline industrial products and their economic usefulness in his *Neu eröffnetes Manufacturenhaus* (1704).[38] Le Long also paid attention to industry from the 1714 edition of *De Koophandel van Amsterdam* onwards. In two chapters, he discussed commodities produced in Amsterdam (ch. IX) and in several domestic towns, mostly in the province of Holland (ch. XVI), with a view to their marketability. Industry was treated from the perspective of commerce, but the attention assigned to this economic sector in trade manuals grew during the century, a shift that can be deduced from the title of the Ricard editions by Tomás Antonio Marien Y Arrospide from 1781 onwards. To the original heading *Traité general du commerce*, the Spanish editor added 'contenant des observations sur le commerce des principaux états de l'Europe, les productions naturelles, l'industrie de chaque païs'.[39]

However, it would be misleading to think that the process of absorbing or inserting knowledge and information was unilateral. Political economists referred to manuals as well. Melon, for example, had already quoted Savary and the *Dictionnaire* in his essay, as did Antonio Genovesi (1713–1769) in his translation of John Cary's *Essay on the State of England* (1695) and Dirk Hoola van Nooten (1747–1808) in his Dutch translation of Adam Smith's *Wealth of Nations* (1796).[40] These references, however, also show the difference between *ars mercatoria* and political economy: the information from the manuals substantiated the claims of the political economists. Manuals contained 'la règle', the regulated knowledge political economy needed to underpin its theories. Political economists thus did not add to *ars mercatoria*, but used it and went on to create its own regulated knowledge as academic economics. Until they went their separate ways, mercantile manuals and political economy interacted, resulting in an amalgam of what by hindsight we consider to be various knowledge categories, but at the time defying precise classification. Not only qua format divergent works like *The British Merchant* and *De Koopman* are cases in point, the indefiniteness may also be deduced from the various ways publishers and booksellers categorized publications in this field. A limited study of eighteenth-century Dutch sales catalogues demonstrates that auctioneers usually classified trade manuals (hybrids as well as single-issue guides) and works on political economy as belonging to the realm of law and politics. Every now and then, one will find them under philosophy, mathematics and arts.[41] In the 1801 sales catalogue of the books left by two prominent Dutch officeholders, the *Handleiding* and Le Long's *Koophandel van Amsterdam* were categorized under 'Nederlandsche Historien' ('Dutch histories').[42] In the 1802 catalogue of the awe-inspiring library of the well-known Fagel family, a separate category was used for books on trade: *De Re Mercatoria*. This section contained about eighty entries and did not discriminate between political economists like Law, Melon and Forbonnais or the *Tresoor van de Gewichten, Maten en Munten* and the *Dictionnaire* of the Savary brothers.[43]

It is therefore rather complicated to disentangle the threads of trade knowledge that manifest themselves in economic thought. One way to do this is to reconstruct the history of key concepts in economic discourse, like for example the notion of the division of labour. Though Adam Smith (1723–1790) did not invent this concept – Bernard Mandeville (1670–1733) already spoke about 'learning to divide and subdivide labour' in part two of his *Fable of the Bees* of 1729 – he seems to have been the first to apply it to the realm of economic theory, using the case of pin-making to explain the process.[44] Pins had been an item in trade manuals for a long time. As a product that was produced in Limoges or shipped from Normandy to the American isles of America or from Amsterdam to several European areas and as a product liable to export duties, pins are mentioned several times in the manuals by Ricard, Savary, Le Moine de l'Espine and Le Long.

How pins were produced, however, was knowledge that entered the trade manuals with the *Dictionnaire* of the Savary brothers. In the first edition of 1723, the labour factor in producing a single pin was strikingly formulated:

> Il n'y a guères de marchandises qui se vendent mon cher que les Epingles; et cependant il n'y en a point qui passent par plus de mains, avant que de pouvoir être mises en vente. L'on compte jusqu'à plus de vingt-cinq Ouvriers, qui y travaillent successivement, depuis que le fil de leton a été tiré à la filiere, jusqu'à ce que l'Espingle soit attachée au papier.[45]

A few years later, pins and pin-making were also discussed in a non-mercantile setting in the first edition of the *Cyclopaedia* compiled by Ephraim Chambers (c. 1680–1740), one of the first general encyclopaedias in English and 'intended as a course of ancient and modern learning'. Chambers reproduces the description of the *Dictionnaire* when he describes pins as a cheap commodity that employs many hands:

> Notwithstanding that there is scarce any commodity cheaper than pins, there is none that passes thro' more hands e'er they come to be sold. They reckon 25 workmen successively employ'd in each pin, between the drawing of brass-wiar, and the sticking of the pin the paper.[46]

Now one would expect Postlethwayt to do the same, but there is no separate entry for pins and pin-making in his version of the *Dictionnaire* of 1751–1755. However, around the same time, in 1755, an article on this topic by Alexandre Deleyre (1726–1797) was published in the celebrated *Encyclopédie*, another general publication not restricted to commerce. Here, the number of distinct operations to fabricate one pin was 18, the same number Smith mentioned when he illustrated the concept of the division of labour. According to Diderot, Deleyre based his entry on first-hand knowledge, observing the fabrication of pins 'dans les atteliers même des ouvriers'.[47]

This transfer of experience-based and useful knowledge from the (enlarged) realm of trade to a general public and from commercial knowledge to political economy was a European phenomenon. After 1750, political economists started to argue for the integration of trade, agriculture and industry in a more balanced, national economy, thus challenging the commercial paradigm. The description of the way to do or make things, producing and selling them, changed into evidence with which economic principles could be illuminated. This sometimes implied that examples had to be adjusted to the specific audience and its language. In the Dutch context, Smith's example of pin-making did not satisfy his translator, the earlier mentioned Hoola van Nooten. He turned to the example of making clay pipes in the town of Gouda in Holland to explain the effects of the division of labour – and especially machine manufacture – on production. He did this in a footnote to the pin-making passage and described how 32 operations were necessary to produce one perfect clay pipe. When a manufacturer correctly applied the division of labour principle, he could get about 28,000 pipes per week out of circa 40 labourers.[48]

Concluding Remarks

We have seen how regulating trade knowledge meant not only to order and standardize information, but also entailed the adaptation of already available insights. This double meaning of regulation was reflected in the above-discussed process of the slow transformation of the trade manual. Only by analysing *ars mercatoria* and the history of political economy in conjunction, it became possible to discern how both interacted. More of this combined research is needed to grasp the perimeters of knowledge transfer and regulation. For quite a while, 'la règle' in trade knowledge both absorbed and underpinned the work of political economists, but in the end, the hybrid manual like *De Koophandel van Amsterdam* petered out. The production of the ninth edition already demonstrated the difficulty in realizing an updated version. It had been on the agenda of Ockers for quite some time. Scattered throughout *De Koopman*, he had already referred several times to either Le Moine de l'Espine or Le Long and rectified some of their errors. In the 1776 volume, Ockers ventilated the prospect of an updated version of Le Long's manual by means of a fake letter writer.[49] A new edition would be one in octavo, a format easier to handle in the *comptoirs* and just as simple to attach to *De Koopman*. The letter writer said he would gladly be of assistance in correcting the many mistakes *De Koophandel van Amsterdam* still contained.[50] However, in the end it was a Rotterdam bookseller, Reinier Arrenberg (1736–1812), who published both the ninth and the tenth edition in 1780 and 1801–1802, respectively. Ockers seems to have stopped working on the revision halfway through 1778, having completed the first eighteen chapters.[51] After 1802, no more hybrid manuals were published in the Netherlands, though the single issue guides, being more of the propositional type and therefore less vulnerable to changing circumstances, did not suffer that much and are even today available in educational publications. Their expiration, not only in the Netherlands, is connected with the advance of academic economics, a new regulatory development in itself. However, by supplying all-embracing and up-to-date knowledge associated with trade, the hybrids formed a crucial category in regulating and thus instructing those who wanted to understand not only trade skills but also the more abstract aspects of the art of commerce.

Notes

1 Brugmans, 'De Koopman', 64–65. The engraving by Reinier Vinkeles dates from 1767. This representation of the *idealtypischer* merchant was not unique; see for instance the earlier frontispieces in Samuel Ricard's *Traité general du commerce* (1700) and Jacques Savary's Le parfait negociant (1675).
2 Klein, *Nützliches Wissen*, 87–104.
3 Reinert et al., '80 Economic Bestsellers before 1850'.
4 'It is deplorable that foreigners accuse us of having more practice than theory and, in relying upon it, of hardly consulting the set rules that apply to our country too; and it is a pity that (as far as I know) nothing [of this practice] has been brought into a system'. ULL, BPL 2789, 208. See also Nijenhuis, 'Captured by the Commercial Paradigm', 635–656.
5 Hoock, 'Vom Manual zum Handbuch', 163.
6 Kaiser, '*Ars Mercatoria*', 2–3. The volume on the post-1700 publications has not been published (yet).
7 Hoock, 'Vom Manual zum Handbuch', 159. See also Raven, *Publishing Business*, 180–205.

8   For a complete overview, compare *Ars Mercatoria* 1, 402–403, and *Ars Mercatoria* 2, 712–718.
9   Harreld, 'An Education in Commerce', 1; Mokyr, *The Gifts of Athena*, 4–5; Machlup, *Knowledge* 1, 30–31.
10 De ruysscher, 'How Normative were Merchant Guidebooks'?, 144–165.
11 Hoock, 'Vom Manual zum Handbuch', 166, regards *The Merchants Mappe of Commerce* as the first instance of what he calls the 'handelsgeographisches Handbuch'.
12 Hont, *Jealousy of Trade*, 23–24, and for Holland: Hartman and Weststeijn, 'An Empire of Trade', 25.
13 Savary, *Le parfait negociant*, Preface (unpaginated). Perrot, *Une histoire intellectuelle de l'économie politique*, 98. Hoock, 'Vom Manual zum Handbuch', 168–169. The Italian and English translations of *Le parfait negociant* are mentioned by one of Savary's sons in 1721, but until now could not be traced in a library collection. See Pittaluga, *L'Evolution de la langue commerciale*, 114.
14 Lüsebrink, 'Von Savary des Bruslons', *Dictionnaire Universel du Commerce* (1723–1730) zum *Dictionnaire Universel*', 222–223.
15 Perrot, 'Une histoire intellectuelle de l'économie politique', 98–100.
16 This historical introduction was probably taken from Pierre-Daniel Huet's *Histoire du commerce et de la navigation des anciens* (Paris, 17162). See Stapelbroek, 'Between Utrecht and the War of the Austrian Succession', 1032–1033.
17 Perrot, *Une histoire intellectuelle de l'économie politique*, 101, 106.
18 *Dictionnaire universel de commerce* (1742) I, 257–258.
19 Reinert, *Translating Empire*, 2.
20 Postlethwayt, *A Dissertation on the Universal Dictionary of Trade and Commerce*, 23, 30–31, 51–52. Cf. Reinert, *Translating Empire*, 41. Hoock, 'Professional Ethics and Commercial Rationality', 154, considers Postlethwayt's to be the first dictionary to integrate practical information and the principles of political economy, but the earlier 1742 edition of the *Dictionnaire* already contains this merging of two worlds.
21 Reinert, *Translating Empire*, 22, 35, and Nijenhuis, 'For the Sake of the Republic', 1202–1216. On reformist societies, see Stapelbroek and Marjanen, 'Political Economy, Patriotism and the Rise of Societies', 1–25.
22 *Ars Mercatoria* 2, 654. For comparison, English and French authors produced 335 and 336 manuals and treatises during the seventeenth century, showing a strong upward trend around the 1650s and the 1670s respectively.
23 Based on a check of the Short Title Catalogue of the Netherlands, the NEHA catalogue and a limited number of auction catalogues using the Dutch equivalents for manual, guide, instruction, handbook, etc.
    The author of the *Handleiding* is unknown but presents himself as Amsterdam born. A reprint appeared in Bruges in 1784. The book is included in an overview of Dutch books on accounting in the seventeenth and eighteenth centuries: Ten Have, *De leer van het boekhouden*, 293.
24 Hieronymus Sweerts (1664–1692), Jan ten Hoorn (1671–1715), Jan Bouman (1670–1687) and Daniel van Dalen (1673–1700).
25 *De volmaakte koopman*, 'Opdragt'. Coymans also acted as *schepen* of Amsterdam. It is unclear whether the merchants paid for the dedication.
26 Savary, *Le parfait negociant*, 'Preface'. On sharing commercial knowledge, see also Nijenhuis, 'Trading Information', 55.
27 *Le parfait négociant …Nouvelle édition* I, viii.
28 *De Koopman* I, 40:

> Wat de Schryvers over den KOOPHANDEL, het BOEKHOUDEN, de ZEEVAARD enz. aangaan, ons Vaderland bezit 'er weinigen buiten de vertaalde Werkjes van de Heeren LE MOINE DE L'ESPINE, en SAVARY. En genoegzaam niets oorspronkelyks; dat te verwonderen is in een Land als dit, 't welk alleen van de Commerçie zo te zeggen, bestaan moet.

Jongenelen, 'Mordechai', 101–102, produces convincing circumstantial evidence for Ockers to be the author of *De Koopman*.
29 Jansen, *De Koophandel van Amsterdam*, 5, has a table with all the known editions.
30 Jansen, 36. Samuel Ricard's manual went through four editions between 1700 and 1722.
31 The 'King' mentioned in the pile of books cannot be statistician Gregory King (1648–1712), as his work on population and wealth was not published before the end of the eighteenth century.
32 Stapelbroek, 'Between Utrecht and the War of the Austrian Succession', 1028–1030.
33 Jansen, *De Koophandel van Amsterdam*, 23–25, analyses to what extent the chapters on Amsterdam's foreign trade were based on Savary and ibidem, 110–112, on Ricard and the competition Le Long was engaged in with Ricard. See also Stapelbroek, 'Between Utrecht and the War of the Austrian Succession', 1033.
34 Le Long, *Den Koophandel van Amsterdam*, 390–395. Jansen, *De Koophandel van Amsterdam*, 75–76. *De Koopman* II, 334–340, and III, 260, contain references to the *College van Commercie*. Le Long also published an extended version of Phoonsen's *Wissel-stijl* in 1729. Thomas Isaac de Larrey, staying in Paris for negotiations on the commercial treaty with France, suggested in a letter dated 27 May 1750 to *raadpensionaris* Steyn to look up the entries on the French commercial boards in the Savary dictionary with a view to installing one in the ailing Dutch republic; NA, 1.10.29 Collectie Fagel, inv. 1844.
35 Temple, *Observations*, 108 ff. Temple had been an ambassador in The Hague from 1668 to 1670. He returned to the Netherlands after the Peace of Westminster (1674) and helped to negotiate the Peace of Nijmegen (1678–1679). See also Nijenhuis, 'Shining Comet, Falling Meteor', 115–129.
36 Le Long, *Den Koophandel van Amsterdam*, 2–3. Le Long does not mention Temple or another source for this specific statement, but see Jansen, *De Koophandel van Amsterdam*, 60.
37 Melon, *Staatkundige Toetse van den Koophandel*.
38 Marperger had also published the *Neu eröffnetes Kauffmanns-Magazin*, a German and more systematic version of Savary's *Le Parfait Négociant*. *Ars Mercatoria* 2, 244, mentions John Hill's *The exact dealer* (London, 1688) as the first manual to include the description of production locations in England and Wales.
39 On Tomás Antonio Marien Y Arrospide, see Astigarraga, *A Unifying Enlightenment*, 116, 131–134, 228–229.
40 Melon, *Essai politique sur le commerce* (1735) refers to the *Dictionnaire* on p. 25 and to Savary père on pp. 27–29. Genovesi, *Storia del commercio della Gran Brettagna*, I, x. On the same page, Genovesi also referred to Ricard's *Traité*. See Reinert, *Translating Empire*, 263–264. Hoola van Nooten, *Naspeuringen*, 35–37, 116, 122.
41 See, for instance, the sale catalogues of the libraries of the De la Courts (1770) and that of Bout and Levinus (1779).
42 *Catalogus van twee uitmuntende verzamelingen van welgeconditioneerde boeken*, 139, 141.
43 *Bibliotheca Fageliana*, 206–208.
44 Harris, in his *Essay upon Money and Coins*, part 1, § 12, also describes the meaning of division of labour without using the phrase. See Smith, *Wealth of Nations* I, 5 (footnote). Smith had already used the pin example in 1763 in his *Lectures on Jurisprudence* (Glasgow Edition, 341–342).
45 *Dictionnaire universel de Commerce* (1723), column 1882. The whole entry on pins, pin-making and pin-makers covers columns 1880–1886.
46 Chambers, *Cyclopædia*, II, 814.
47 Diderot and d'Alembert, *Encyclopédie*, V, 804–807.
48 Hoola van Nooten, *Naspeuringen*, 17–21 (footnote b).
49 Ockers specifies the use of both authors: *De Koopman* I, 236.
50 *De Koopman* VI, 375–376.
51 Jongenelen, 'Mordechai', 105, 108 n66. See also Jansen, *De Koophandel van Amsterdam*, 235–238, 345.

Bibliography

Anon. *Handleiding tot den Hollandsche koophandel, bevattende een beknopt, dog grondig onderwys van dit edel beroep, om door hetzelve tot fortuin te geraken*. Amsterdam: Steven van Esveldt, 1754.

Astigarraga, Jesús. *A Unifying Enlightenment: Institutions of Political Economy in Eighteenth-Century Spain (1700–1808)*. Leiden and Boston, MA: Brill, 2020.

Bibliotheca Bouttiana, Sive Catalogus Librorum In omni Scientarum genere, summo cum Delectû Collectorum inter quos Eminent Opera Rariora, Eaque Magna atque insignia; Elegantissimè Compacta & Nitidissimè Conservata. The Hague: Johannes Gaillard & Hendrik Bakhuyzen, [1779].

Bibliotheca Selectissima Sive Catalogus Librorum. In Omni Facultate Et Lingua Praestantiorum, Quos Inter Plures Rarissime Occurentes, Constituens Bonam Partem Integrae Bibliothecae. Quam Olim Collegit Vir Doctissimus Petrus De La Court Van Der Voort, Ictus Lugduno Batavus, Poste Aque Auxit Hujus Filius Allardus De La Court, Accedit apparatus insignis Codicum Manuscriptorum, Veterum & Recentium, Numero Quingentorum &c. The Hague: Nicolaas van Daalen, [1770].

Bibliotheca Fageliana. A Catalogue of the Valuable and Extensive Library of the Greffier Fagel, of The Hague … Sold by Auction by Mr. Christie on Monday, March 1, 1802 and the Twenty-Nine following Days. London, 1802.

Brugmans, Hajo. 'De Koopman. Mercurius als spectator.' *Jaarboek Amstelodamum* 10 (1912): 61–135.

Catalogus van twee uitmuntende verzamelingen van welgeconditioneerde boeken [...] mitsgaders een aanzienlyk cabinet van uitmuntende teekeningen en prenten [...] de eerste nagelaten by wylen [...] L.P. van de Spiegel [...] de tweede by wylen [...] Willem van Haarsolte, heer van Yrst [...]: al het welke publicq verkocht zal worden op maandag den 12 october 1801. Utrecht: J. Visch en C. van der Aa, 1801.

Chambers, Ephraim. *Cyclopædia Or, an Universal Dictionary of Arts and Sciences*. 2 vols. London: James and John Knapton, John Darby, Daniel Midwinter, Arthur Bettesworth, John Senex and 13 others, 1728.

De ruysscher, Dave. 'How Normative were Merchant Guidebooks? Of Customs, Practices, and … Good Advice (Antwerp, Sixteenth Century).' In Pihlajamäki, Heikki; Cordes, Albrecht; Dauchy, Serge; Dave De ruysscher eds. *Understanding the Sources of Early Modern and Modern Commercial Law. Courts, Statutes, Contracts, and Legal Scholarship*. Leiden and Boston, MA: Brill/ Nijhoff, 2018, pp. 144–165.

Encyclopédie, ou Dictionnaire raisonné des sciences, des arts et des métiers. Diderot, Denis; Jean Baptiste Le Rond d'Alembert eds. Paris: David Briasson et cetera, 1751–1780.

Genovesi, Antonio. *Storia del commercio della Gran Brettagna scritta da John Cary*. 3 vols. Napels: Benedetto Gessari, 1757–1758.

Harreld, Donald J. 'An Education in Commerce. Transmitting Business Information in Early Modern Europe', paper presented to the XIVth International Economic History Congress, Helsinki, 2006.

Hartman, Jan; Weststeijn, Arthur. 'An Empire of Trade: Commercial Reason of State in Seventeenth-Century Holland.' In Roege, Pernille; Reinert, Sophus eds. *Political Economy of Empire in the Early Modern World* Basingstoke: Palgrave MacMillan, 2013, pp. 11–31.

Have, Onko ten. *De leer van het boekhouden in de Nederlanden tijdens de zeventiende en achttiende eeuw*. Delft: Waltman, 1934.

Harris, Joseph. *An Essay upon Money and Coins*. 2 vols. London: G. Hawkins, 1757–1758.

Hill, John. *The Exact Dealer Being an Useful Companion for All Traders*. London: H. Rhodes, 1688.
Hont, Istvan. *Jealousy of Trade: International Competition and the Nation-State in Historical Perspective*. Cambridge, MA: Harvard University Press, 2005.
Hoock, Jochen. 'Vom Manual zum Handbuch. Zur diskursiven Erweiterung der kaufmännischen Anleitungen im 16. und 17. Jahrhundert.' In Hoock, Jochen; Jeannin, Pierre; Wolfgang Kaiser eds. *Ars Mercatoria. Handbücher und Traktate für den Gebrauch des Kaufmanns. Manuels et traités à l'usage des marchands 1470-1820. Eine analytische Bibliographie. Band 3, Analysen: 1400-1700*. Paderborn: Schöningh, 2001, pp. 157–172.
Hoock, Jochen. 'Professional Ethics and Commercial Rationality at the Beginning of the Modern Era.' In Jacob, Margaret; Secretan, Catherine eds. *The Self-Perception of Early Modern Capitalists*. New York: Palgrave Macmillan, 2008, pp. 147–159.
Hoock, Jochen; Jeannin, Pierre eds. *Ars Mercatoria. Handbücher und Traktate für den Gebrauch des Kaufmanns. Manuels et traités à l'usage des marchands 1470-1820. Eine analytische Bibliographie. Band 1, 1470-1600*. Paderborn: Schöningh, 1991.
Hoock, Jochen; Jeannin, Pierre; Duval, Bernadette eds. *Ars Mercatoria. Handbücher und Traktate für den Gebrauch des Kaufmanns. Manuels et traités à l'usage des marchands 1470-1820. Eine analytische Bibliographie. Band 2, 1600-1700*. Paderborn: Schöningh, 1993.
Hoola van Nooten, Dirk. *Naspeuringen over de natuur en oorzaaken van den rijkdom der volkeren, gevolgd naar het Engelsch van den Heere Adam Smith*. Amsterdam: Wouter Brave, 1796.
Huet, Pierre-Daniel. *Histoire du commerce et de la navigation des anciens*. Paris: Antoine-Urbain Coustelier, 17162.
Jansen, Lucas. *'De Koophandel van Amsterdam': een critische studie over het koopmanshandboek van Jacques Le Moine de l'Espine en Isaac Le Long*. Amsterdam: Nieuwe Uitgevers Maatschappij, 1946.
Jongenelen, Ton. 'Mordechai. Illusie en werkelijkheid in het spectatoriale blad *De Koopman*.' *Mededelingen van de Stichting Jacob Campo Weyerman* 26 (2003): 94–108.
Kaiser, Wolfgang. 'Ars Mercatoria – Möglichkeiten und Grenzen einer analytischen Bibliographie und Datenbank.' In Hoock, Jochen; Jeannin, Pierre; Wolfgang Kaiser eds. *Ars Mercatoria. Handbücher und Traktate für den Gebrauch des Kaufmanns. Manuels et traités à l'usage des marchands 1470-1820. Eine analytische Bibliographie. Band 3, Analysen: 1400-1700*. Paderborn: Schöningh, 2001, pp. 1–26.
Klein, Ursula. *Nützliches Wissen: Die Erfindung der Technikwissenschaften*. Göttingen: Wallstein Verlag, 2016.
Le Long, Isaac. *Den koophandel van Amsterdam, naar alle gewesten des weerelds ... eerst ontworpen door Le Moine de l'Espine*. Amsterdam: Andries van Damme & Johannes Ratelband, 1714.
Lüsebrink, Hans-Jürgen. 'Von Savary des Bruslons' *Dictionnaire Universel du Commerce* (1723-1730) zum *Dictionnaire Universel de la Géographie Commerçante* (1798/99) von Jacques Peuchet. Wissensstrukturen und transkulturelle Dimensionen ökonomischer Enzyklopädien im Frankreich des Aufklärungszeitalters und der Französischen Revolution.' *Das Achtzehnte Jahrhundert* 41/2 (2017): 221–239.
Melon, Jean-François. *Essai politique sur le commerce*. Amsterdam: François Changuion, 1735.
[Melon, Jean-François]. *Staatkundige toetse van den Koophandel of Aanwysinge van proefhoudende Middelen, om den Koophandel op vaste gronden te ondernemen, en met de meeste Voordeelen te verbeteren en uyt te breyden*. Translated by Isaac Le Long. Amsterdam: Jacob ter Beek, 1735.
Machlup, Fritz. *Knowledge: Its Creation, Distribution, and Economic Significance. Vol. 1, Knowledge and Knowledge Production*. Princeton, NJ: Princeton University Press, 1980.

Marperger, Paul Jacob. *Das neu er-öffnetes Manufacturen-Haus.* Hamburg: Benjamin Schiller, 1704.
Mokyr, Joel. *The Gifts of Athena.* Princeton, NJ: Princeton University Press, 2002.
Nijenhuis, Ida. '"Shining Comet, Falling Meteor." Contemporary Reflections on the Dutch Republic as a Commercial Power during the Second Stadholderless Era.' In De Jongste, Jan A.F.; Veenendaal Jr, Augustus J. eds. *Anthonie Heinsius and the Dutch Republic 1688-1720. Politics, War, and Finance.* The Hague: Institute of Netherlands History, 2002, pp. 115–129.
Nijenhuis, Ida. 'For the Sake of the Republic. The Dutch Translation of Forbonais's *Elémens du commerce.*' *History of European Ideas* 40 (2014): 1202–1216.
Nijenhuis, Ida. 'Captured by the Commercial Paradigm: Physiocracy Going Dutch.' In Kaplan, Steven L.; Reinert, Sophus A. eds. *The Economic Turn: Recasting Political Economy in Enlightenment Europe.* London: Anthem Press, 2019.
Nijenhuis, Ida. 'Trading Information: Willem Usselincx (1567-1647) in the Corridors of Power.' In Nijenhuis, Ida; Van Faassen, Marijke; Sluijter, Ronald; Gijsenbergh, Joris; De Jong, Wim eds. *Information and Power in History. Towards a Global Approach.* London & New York: Routledge, 2020, pp. 54–68.
[Ockers, Willem]. *De koopman, of Bydragen ten opbouw van Neêrlands koophandel en zeevaard.* 6 vols. Amsterdam: Gerrit Bom, 1768–1776.
Perrot, Jean-Claude. *Une histoire intellectuelle de l'économie politique, XVIIe-XVIIIe siècle.* Paris : Éditions de l'École des Hautes Études en Sciences Sociales, 1992.
Phoonsen, Johannes. *Wissel-styl tot Amsterdam, : vervattende niet alleen wat men gewoon, maar ook wat een voorsichtigh koopman, tot sijn securiteyt, in de wissel-handel dienstig en noodig is: mitsgaders ordonnantien, willekeuren en reglementen van wisselen.* Amsterdam: Jan van Duisbergh, 1676.
Pittaluga, Maria G. *L'Evolution de la langue commerciale: 'Le parfait negociant' et le 'Dictionnaire universel de commerce.'* Genova: Biblioteca di Letterature, 1983.
Postlethwayt, Malachy. *A Dissertation on the Plan, Use, and Importance, of the Universal Dictionary of Trade and Commerce. Translated from the French of the Late Celebrated Mons. Savary, Inspector-General of the Manufactures of the Custom-House of Paris: With Such Considerable Additions and Improvements, as Will Appear at Large throughout This Dissertation.* London: John and Paul Knapton, 1749.
Raven, James. *Publishing Business in Eighteenth-Century England.* Woodbridge: The Boydell Press, 2014.
Reinert, Erik S., Carpenter, Kenneth; Reinert, Fernanda A.; Reinert, Sophus A. '80 Economic Bestsellers before 1850: A Fresh Look at the History of Economic Thought.' *The Other Canon Foundation and Tallinn University of Technology Working Papers in Technology Governance and Economic Dynamics* 74 (2017).
Reinert, Sophus A. *Translating Empire. Emulation and the Origins of Political Economy.* Cambridge, MA: Harvard University Press, 2011.
Roberts, Lewes. *The Merchants Mappe of Commerce wherein, the Universal Manner and Matter of Trade, Is Compendiously Handled.* London: R. O[ulton, Eliot's Court Press?, Thomas Harper, and Felix Kingston] for Ralph Mabb, 1638.
Savary, Jacques. *Le parfait negociant ou instruction generale pour ce qui regarde le commerce de toute sorte de marchandises, tant de France, que des pays etrangers.* Paris: Louis Billaine, 1675.
Savary, Jacques. *De volmaakte koopman, zynde een naaukeurige onderrechting van alles wat den inlandschen en uitlandschen koophandel betreft.* Translated by Gotfried van Broekhuizen. Amsterdam: Sweerts, Ten Hoorn, Bouman and Van den Dalen, 1683.

Savary, Jacques. *Le parfait négociant, ou Instruction générale pour ce qui regarde le commerce des marchandises de France et des pays étrangers… enrichi d'augmentations par le feu sieur Jacques Savary Des Bruslons, [puis] par M. Philémont-Louis Savary.* Nouvelle édition. Vol. 1. Paris: les frères Estienne, 1757.

Savary des Brûlons, Jacques. *Dictionnaire universel de commerce.* 2 vols. Paris: Jacques Estiennes, 1723.

Savary des Brûlons, Jacques. *Dictionnaire universel de commerce.* Vol. 1. Geneve: Cramer & Philibert, 1742.

Smith, Adam. *An Inquiry into the Nature and Causes of the Wealth of Nations.* Cannan, Edwin ed. London: Methuen & Co., 1904.

Smith, Adam. *Lectures on Jurisprudence.* Meek, R.L.; Raphael, D.D.; Stein, P.G. eds. *The Glasgow Edition of the Works and Correspondence of Adam Smith.* Vol. 5. Oxford: Clarendon Press; Oxford University Press, 1978.

Stapelbroek, Koen; Marjanen, Jani. 'Political Economy, Patriotism and the Rise of Societies.' In Stapelbroek, Koen; Marjanen, Jani eds. *The Rise of Economic Societies in the Eighteenth Century.* Basingstoke: Pallgrave Macmillan, 2012, pp. 1–25.

Stapelbroek, Koen. 'Between Utrecht and the War of the Austrian Succession: The Dutch Translation of the British Merchant of 1728.' *History of European Ideas* 40 (2014): 1026–1043.

Temple, William. *Observations upon the United Provinces of the Netherlands.* Clark, Georg ed. Oxford: Clarendon Press; Oxford University Press, 1972.

PART 3
Instructing

6

INSTRUCTING TRADE AND WAR

Regulating Knowledge and People on Faraway Dutch Voyages ca. 1600

Djoeke van Netten[1]

Introduction

Ships are places like no other; they are places that go from one place to another, and by changing their course they change the course of history. A ship, however, almost never sailed on its own; ships were sent out. This is definitely true for the voyages that appeal most to the imagination: the faraway voyages in what has been called, from a Eurocentric perspective, the 'age of discovery'. From Western Europe, ships were sent out by states and (state-sponsored) companies to faraway lands and unknown faiths. Heads of states and directors of companies attempted to exert control way beyond their spheres of control, trying to discipline people who were impossible to contact after they went offshore. This posed quite a challenge, especially in early modern times, when time and distance were much more closely related than nowadays, when knowledge could not travel faster than the fastest horse could run or a ship could sail.[2]

Regulating knowledge and people on a ship was attempted by giving instructions before departure. Instructing is a regulated form of knowledge regulating. This double regulation makes this genre a perfect case to study the regulating of knowledge in early modern practice.[3] First, as this chapter demonstrates, the written or spoken instructions had titles and forms that made them immediately recognizable as such for contemporaries. The way they were drafted and conveyed was strictly regulated by the directors. Second, and even more important for the central themes of this volume, the instructions that went aboard ships state how to obtain, collect, register, keep, carry, and handle information. Consequently, they enabled practices of knowledge production and knowledge transfer over long distances in time and space. First mentioned type of knowledge transfer, from the authorities on land to the authorities on a ship and via them to the crew, was top-down, one-way, and it involved many practices of secrecy, as

DOI: 10.4324/9780429279928-10

will be shown. The second form of regulation facilitated that knowledge found *en route* was acquired, noted down, labeled,[4] and brought back to where the ships started. Thus, these instructions have shaped global knowledge circulation.

This chapter focuses on the first decades of Dutch navigation to the East Indies at the turn of the seventeenth century. This period can, in hindsight, be seen as the formative years of Dutch overseas trade and expansion. In the 1590s, several routes were planned and sailed; Dutch ships tried to reach the Far East via the north, the south, and the west. In those years, a balance was tipped: away from uncertainty and expectations to knowledge and profit. In 1602, the famous United Dutch East India Company (Vereenigde Oostindische Compagnie [VOC]) was established, which would play a major part in Asian-European trade and politics for almost two centuries.

Examining the faraway Dutch voyages in the late sixteenth and the early seventeenth centuries (1594–1609) through the lens of their instructions reveals the regulating of knowledge in action. Besides, the time frame and the approach help to overcome some of the biases and one-sidedness of the existing historiography. First, most of the literature focuses on trade and expansion in either the East or the West Indies. However, there was no strict east/west divide in practice, definitely not before the monopoly of the VOC and an obligatory route to the Far East were established in the early 1600s. Traditionally, the focus in the historiography has been on the more successful VOC, although in recent years also the Dutch West-India Company (WIC; established 1621) has received some attention.[5]

Second, the historiography on the relation between European expansion and long-distance companies with knowledge almost exclusively concentrates on discoveries and what happened *after* the (first) voyages. Mostly concerning the Spanish Empire, it is shown how from the late fifteenth century onwards new knowledge was encountered in Asia and the New World and how this new-found knowledge from the East and West Indies was brought back to Europe, transformed, disseminated (or kept secret), used to maintain and acquire more power, and in the end how new knowledge transformed European trade, politics, science, and scholarship.[6] Instructions, however, bring our attention to knowledge transfer *before* sailing, trading, and empire-building. Instructions always precede the desired act. Order had to be imposed in advance, instructions had to be drawn up before a voyage; they are pre-scriptions in the literal sense of the word. All these words before the action created the knowledge management thereafter.

Third, most attention has been given to people actually sailing to the Indies or to Europeans receiving, collecting, and publishing (new) knowledge from the Indies. The instructions, however, shift the focus to those who stayed behind, those who initiated, laid out, and determined; we will see their attempts at control, what they *thought* they were doing, and their underlying arguments and justifications.

A fourth problem, closely related to the above-mentioned, is posed by the teleology, which is oftentimes present in studies on so-called discoveries, and especially the VOC. The histories mostly start with the first *successful* voyage to the East Indies in 1595. This expedition is tellingly called the 'first navigation' (*eerste schipvaart*). Consequently, the years 1595–1602 are mostly seen as a prologue, in which 'pre-companies' (*voor-compagnieën*) are only seen as precursors of the great VOC.[7] However, the outcome was yet unknown at the end of the sixteenth century, and we should leave our hindsight bias behind as much as possible to understand the by then available knowledge, expectations, and uncertainties. In this chapter concerning starting points, we do not take into account their unknown unknowns, as, for example, the fact that the Sultan of Bantam was not as co-operative or anti-Portuguese as expected or the impossibility to sail to China via a north-eastern passage.

But even if nowadays, in hindsight, we can tell that certain knowledge was false, they by then did start with certain knowledge. They started with information on known destinations and known products – mostly known from Portuguese, Spanish and English written sources, sometimes complemented with recent personal experience and ancient lore. It is important to add that some of these destinations, like Quinsay in China or the kingdom of Monancabo on Sumatra, were to be found on the map but not to be found on the locations where they were expected or did not exist at all.[8] The same is true for the products they expected to load, like ginger in Brazil or nutmeg in China.[9] We can blame sixteenth-century travellers for the fact that they did not know that those spices did not grow there, but that does not help us to understand their world.

The historiography on the role of the VOC and WIC in the advancement of science and learning provides a nuanced not overtly positive image. It seems, mostly based on mid- and late seventeenth-century case studies, that the companies did not actively hinder the transfer of knowledge from Asia and the Americas to Europe (although in some cases they did) and also not actively promoted scientific enterprises (although in some cases they did). Most importantly, the sheer existence of the companies sending out ships and people and of Dutch commerce and the way merchants dealt with information is seen as having supported and configured the rise of European science, ranging from medicine and botany to economics and ethnology.[10]

The Dutch East India Company itself considered knowledge only useful when it served trade or warfare. To understand the knowledge practices at stake, it is paramount to keep in mind how war and commerce related as the goals of the overseas companies. Profit and politics, however, did not always go well together. As frequently pointed out in the historiography, inherent conflicting characteristics existed in the VOC. The organization was on the one hand a business company, a multinational corporation, and on the other hand an overseas extension of the Dutch government.[11] Trade was the purpose at the outset, warfare was a means to an end, but became also a goal in itself. War could support trade as well as hamper it.

Coming back to the ships with which this introduction started, they are regularly used (in past and present) as a metaphor for the state. The ship of state has been a popular way of commenting on the government of mostly, but not exclusively, republics ever since Plato.[12] In this chapter, the metaphor is flipped; we do not find a ship of state, but the ship as state.[13] It helps to understand the Dutch ships that were sent to the Indies around 1600 as being ruled and regulated as states, literally overseas states. Ships can be considered as an extension of the fatherland. The instructions regulated practices and knowledge management on board. These documents demonstrate how order was imposed.

In this chapter, first a brief international background to the first Dutch overseas voyages will be presented, followed by an explanation on the genre of instructions on board ships. Then, they will be further examined to find out what the directors of the companies mostly worried about, how they tried to discipline captains and crew, and tried to maintain power while also relegating power. In the last part, the focus will be on the instructions on gaining knowledge, recording knowledge, and keeping knowledge. Instructions on secrecy and secret instructions will be singled out, since this can be seen as the most regulated knowledge. Knowledge that explicitly was not allowed to circulate, sheds new light on knowledge practices.

Dutch Companies, Issuing Instructions

Most of Asia was not a total terra incognita for Europeans in the late sixteenth century. The Spanish and the Portuguese had started over a century earlier to 'discover' the world. Backed by Papal authority, the Spanish and the Portuguese had divided the discovered and the yet to be discovered world in two halves by the treaties of Tordesillas (1494) and Zaragoza (1529). However, in the late sixteenth century, other European nations also wanted to take their share in the lucrative trade in spices and other Asian luxuries. As for the Dutch, simultaneous declining supply and increasing demand can be discerned. The former was due to the fact that since 1580, Philip II King of Spain had also become the King of Portugal. The Spanish were at war with the Dutch provinces, so Philip tried to prohibit and prevent Dutch-Portuguese trade. However, despite the revolt against Spain, welfare in especially the coastal provinces Holland and Zeeland grew, as did the desire for exotic delicacies and wonders.

The northern provinces benefitted from the influx of Southern Netherlandish capital and businessmen fleeing war, plunder, and religious persecution. They brought with them some experience in international trade, and an eagerness to damage the Spanish anywhere possible. What they lacked was specific knowledge on places and products. In the early 1590s, this was amended by actively buying and pilfering Portuguese charts and other information.[14] Some Dutchmen returned to Holland after having been in the Indies in Portuguese service; their knowledge based on experience proved extremely useful.[15] At the same time, ancient and medieval sources were also deemed valuable and were used as complementary sources.[16]

One of the main conclusions based on these varied sources was the idea that probably the best route to East Asia would be to sail via the northeast. Thus, from 1594 onwards, several small Dutch fleets attempted to find the passage that had to be there. The historiography on these endeavours mostly emphasizes the heroic wintering on Novaya Zemlya in 1596–1597 and the (hindsight) impossibilities instead of the perceived possibilities back then. When we focus on the outset and the goals, however, these expeditions are very much comparable to the 'first navigation' via the southeast rounding the Cape of Good Hope in the years 1595–1597. This has been seen as a success because it reached a destination in Asia, even though in terms of profit and human lives it can be considered a big failure. This first Dutch fleet rounding the Cape did show the way and pave the way for many more fleets and companies to follow.

At first, in the 1590s, the expeditions of mostly small fleets, exploring different routes, were initiated and financed by individuals, cities, and provinces. Companies were established in Amsterdam, Middelburg, Enkhuizen, Veere, Rotterdam, and Delft. Only in hindsight we know that Amsterdam eventually became much more powerful than the rest.[17] In 1602, after a complex and lengthy process and mostly despite the wishes of the early companies, they were forced together in the United East India Company to overcome falling prices due to their competition.[18]

The company directors, both before and after 1602, mostly did not sail themselves; they had to trust others, they had to entrust others not just with a ship, fully embellished, with money and goods to trade with, but also with power and with knowledge. Since knowledge does not fly freely through the air, it had to be packed and labelled, conveyed to real people, in tangible form.[19] Thus, the directors provided the ships with charts and textual documents, like sailing directions and instructions on how to act at sea and on land.

The still existent instructions are copies in the archives of the companies; the originals that went with the ships were mostly not kept. Their titles, the exact words used, can be enlightening with regard to their intentions. These were not just words, they were calls to action. From the very first written documents in the 1590s, the instructions are mostly called *instructie*. This word is always followed by the proposition *voor* ('for'), to make clear who had to act on the orders: in first instance, the authorities on the ship, that is, the admiral – the highest authority of a fleet – and his council (*scheepsraad*) consisting of skippers, the higher merchants, and some other officers. Sometimes the same kind of documents were called *ordinantie* or *missive* – demonstrating they were authoritative orders or *memorie* – to be remembered. The instructions range from a few to over a dozen pages, divided in short, mostly numbered, paragraphs.

Regarding power and profit, last-mentioned definitely seems to have been the main goal. See for example the *instruxtie ende memorie*, drafted in early 1598 for Cornelis de Houtman, who would be the leader of a small fleet destined from Veere in the Dutch province of Zeeland to the East Indies:

> with all diligence, do everything that is possible and honest to gain cargo [...] we do not specify a destination, place or product, just do everything not to return void, regard the importance of this business.[20]

A little more than a decade after De Houtman, in 1609, a first Dutch Governor General of the East Indies was appointed: Pieter Both. In the instruction for him in this office, the main objective was still commercial, but a few more aims were put forward:

> Do what is possible to continue and enlarge the East-Indian trade, to disseminate the name of Christ, the beatitude of the un-Christians, the honour and reputation of our nation, for the profit of the Company [...] with a view to establish a firm foothold in the Indies, our friendships and trade to God's honour, the welfare of the lands and the profit of the Company.[21]

The 'lands' in the last sentence were of course the Dutch lands. Although even in the *United* East India Company as well as in the West India Company provincial particularism and rivalry between cities did not cease, in the instructions the company always spoke with one voice. And moreover, this voice was presented as serving the fatherland. But still, tellingly, the profit of the company was apparently at least as important as God and the fatherland.

This evocation of a 'national' umbrella becomes even more obvious in another genre of written company documents to be considered as derivatives of instructions: the so-called *artikelbrief*.[22] This document was drawn up by the company directors and in most cases sanctioned by mentioning certain authorities: sometimes the Provincial States of Zeeland or Holland, more often, from the 1590s onwards, by the States General or the Stadholder (Maurice of Nassau) – thus invoking some national authority.[23] Implicitly, this made clear that the laws of a country even were valid far away from the country. Here, we see clearly how the ship was an extension of the country, Dutch overseas territory.

The *artikelbrief* disciplined the crew, as will be elaborated on in the next section. The articles mostly tell the crew what they were not allowed to do and what punishments they awaited when they nevertheless did. *Artikelbrieven* were derived from the instructions and mostly referred to instructions, though the instructions themselves were not meant to be known to the crew.[24] The *artikelbrief* was a more public document, even a public event. It was read out loud on the ship; it seems that this had to happen every month, or six weeks, or even every week.[25] So, written knowledge transfer was followed by regular oral knowledge transfer, even further top-down, regulating the ship as a whole and subsequently demonstrating the hierarchy on the ship. The *artikelbrief* was thus more than a text; it became a performance, a kind of speech act. This was even more emphasized by the oaths that had to be sworn, definitely after the first reading of the *artikelbrief* at the outset of the voyage.[26] The whole crew and the admiral had to swear (separately) an oath of respecting authority and of following the instructions.

The writing and reading out loud of these paper documents thus regulated orderly sailing, gaining profit and gaining new knowledge, and – even more importantly – the instructions aimed to enable to bring profit and knowledge back to the fatherland.

Disciplining at Sea

Every voyage in the first decades of Dutch overseas expansion had its own specific instructions and *artikelbrief*, though not all of them are still kept nowadays. The instructions show some differences and developments, to be discussed later, but mostly they show remarkable resemblances regarding structure, subjects, and even wording. Over the years, the instructions become longer, probably digesting experiences and issues during earlier voyages. Interestingly, they also become more standardized. This is an expected conclusion for the *United* Dutch East India Company, the VOC from 1602 onwards, but more surprisingly, the competing companies in 1590 also demonstrate evermore standardized phrasing and content. This suggests at least some knowledge exchange between these different organizations.

Each particular voyage got its own instructions, more or less resembling the instructions for other voyages. Besides, evermore general instructions for long-distance trade were issued. Not only after the merging of all companies in 1602, but already in 1599, titled 'Instruction by the commissioners of the States of Holland, Zeeland, West-Friesland and Friesland [...] for the merchants [...] destined for the East and West Indies, just as the Guinea-coast and other places'.[27] The VOC issued even more extended instructions for all merchants in 1607 and 1617, and evermore instructions for many other overseas functions and occupations.[28] In short, we can discern how the practice of instructing overseas travel evolved from individual instructions for one voyage, first to more standardization and more encompassing general documents, then to more diversification for specific functions, and plans to attack (see below about 'secret instructions').

When a ship left for the other side of the world, with the instructions also power and knowledge were transferred from the authorities on land to the authorities on the ship, sometimes to the ship as part of a fleet. As we have seen in the *artikelbrieven*, disciplining the crew was something the directors in the Netherlands were very much preoccupied with. The *artikelbrieven* almost always started with lengthy articles on obedience in general. Afterwards, they elaborated on the particularities of how (not) to behave on the ship. The crew was repeatedly warned to obey, respect, do what is said, not to refuse orders, and not to complain.[29] They were told how to conduct oneself on the ship, but not get involved in any plans. Sometimes, they did not even know where they were sailing to. For example, on a voyage led by Simon the Cordes in 1598, where the crew thought they would sail East to trade, while in fact they sailed West to fight.[30] From the instruction for the so-called 'second navigation' (*tweede schipvaart*) departing in 1598, it becomes clear that for the admiral, it was not considered proper to make his plans public.[31] Bottom-up interference with the planning was strictly forbidden. Around the same years, another instruction from Zeeland even stated that mentioning the return trip before the admiral and council confirmed having accomplished their goals would be dealt with as perjury.[32]

To make as much profit as possible, the ships had to be prepared to return as quickly and as fully loaded as possible. We would expect the instructions to deal with many 'in case of' situations so the authorities would know how to react in case of an emergency. It is remarkable, however, how little attention there seems to be given to the most fearful calamities. In contrast with modern-day flights, with the crew being trained and passengers told what to do in case of all kinds of emergencies, in the instructions for specific voyages, nothing is to be found on what we would think of as the worst dangers, like shipwreck, fire, leakage, a broken mast, being stuck in the ice, or infectious diseases. Even on the very first voyages – via the northern as well as the southern route – when the other side of the world was unknown to everyone on board, the possibility of not reaching the destination was completely absent from the instructions.

The only conditional clause to be found concerning accomplishing the set goals is made with respect to the highest authority imaginable: 'if God has provided you with success', 'when this is accomplished with God's help', etc.[33] Probably these references to God indicate part of an explanation: predicting the future was sinful, since what would happen was all in God's hand. Invoking God's providence could be a way of self-protection. Moreover, perhaps horrible what-if scenarios were omitted since they would only scare the crew. Or maybe simpler, it could be that life-threatening calamities were not mentioned since they were simply seen as being beyond control.

The destinations where the ships providentially would arrive were always provided in the first instructions. This was also the case where we (if only in hindsight) can point out the impossibility of the route and the non-existence of some of the destinations, such as the supposed navigable northeast passage and the supposed cities in 'Cathay and China' that lay beyond Novaya Zemlya.[34]

In the aforementioned *tweede schipvaart* via the southern route, the limits of the expedition are a bit more loosely defined, as 'the Philippines or Japan', and the ships should not return before having reached these limits.[35] However, here an escape clause was built in; if the council would unanimously decide to return earlier, this was allowed. A year later, in the so-called 'fourth navigation', the limits were stretched by including China, and even more was left to the decisions of the admiral and council.[36] They are admonished only to visit the Kingdom of China if the commerce in other places did not yield enough profit or if they would have obtained certain knowledge (*seeckere kennis*) on profitable trading possibilities in China. For the rest, they are only advised to prefer nearby commerce over further away commerce.

Apparently, in the course of the second half of the 1590s, there was a tendency to leave more decisions to the authorities on the ship, obviously if only within the greater goal of maximizing profit. This tendency can also be deduced from another calamity of which the instructions do speak: the death of the admiral. This could not be controlled, but what could be controlled, or at least was thought so, was his immediate and smooth succession – so there would be no power vacuum. On the first voyages in 1594 and 1595, there was no appointed one governing admiral per fleet, but every ship had its own master. This had resulted in not so small authority problems, and in losses of lives, ships, and profit.[37]

Afterwards, the power structure was made strictly pyramidal.[38] Naturally, the pyramid always needed a top. Some of the first voyages via the Cape of Good Hope carried, besides instructions and *artikelbrieven*, a closed letter that could only be opened in case of death of one of the leading figures on the ship or fleet. In this letter would have been written the name his successor. On the fleet from Zeeland that departed in 1598, there were four letters marked A, B, C, and D, to be opened when the successor of the successor of the successor of the admiral also died.[39] Whereas in the English East India Company this has remained standard for centuries,[40] the Dutch abandoned this practice already before 1600. In the seventeenth century, the instructions just stated that the council had to vote on who should succeed the admiral with detailed instructions how to vote, but without naming specific individuals.[41] Thus, the company directors left even more in the hands of the council on the ship.

These instructions on voting provide an interesting insight in what the directors of the company thought most indispensable for a successful voyage: unity. Several instructions stated that in case of disagreement in the council, the majority would win and whoever held a minority point of view was not allowed to make that public.[42] As a whole, against the crew, the council must pretend unanimity.[43] Unity was sought for, even if only feigned unity. Consequently, the worst conceivable issue on board was disagreement. 'Discord and strife are the cause of all unhappy voyages' states an instruction from 1598.[44] Not just fighting was forbidden, but also to quarrel or even to disagree was explicitly prohibited.[45] In a document from 1599, the members of the council even had to sign an act of promise of unity, of keeping peace and friendship during the whole voyage.[46] Evidently, this did not guarantee consensus, though it demonstrates how the directors who stayed behind attempted to enforce the unity and concord of the ships they sent out.

Collecting and Keeping Knowledge Overseas

As demonstrated above, instructions on ships regulated life and behaviour on board. So far, we saw top-down transfer of knowledge, from the directors on land to the authorities on the ship and to the crew. The last-mentioned tier was only told what to do on a daily basis, and not known in the goals and destinations of their ship. This section zooms in on specific sections of the instructions for the masters of the ship, namely the orders that explicitly dealt with the regulation of gaining and presenting new knowledge along the way. These orders are most prominent in the first northbound voyages. The ships had written sailing instructions also for the route beyond Novaya Zemlya, but they had nothing comparable with the detailed Portuguese charts on board the first southbound navigation. The known unknowns on these expeditions were far greater than on the southern route, and the instructions mirrored this. Consequently, in the instructions from 1594 and 1595, there were many orders on inspecting and exploring islands and coasts in the northern seas to find out if people lived there and if the places could be used to harbour, trade, or even settle.[47] There are also many orders on sketching, keeping written notes, and keeping tracks and logs.[48] The commanders even had to swear an oath that they would keep daily notes concerning navigation and trade.[49]

Even though, for voyages to Asia via Africa and via South America, more charts and information on places were already known and on board, they also carried instructions managing the production of new knowledge. The authorities on the ship were encouraged to carry out research, to find new profitable destinations, and to ask for information. The aim of these information-finding-explorations was clear: commerce, as is for example demonstrated in the instructions regarding a voyage to South America that departed in 1598:

> With all diligence explore and sail unto all rivers, harbours and places from Rio de la Plata along the coast of America till Terra Nova and do not return from there unless these places are researched to the contentment of the authorized [the admiral and his officers], if some profitable trade can take place.[50]

Another instruction, also dated 1598, stated what to do when having arrived at the island of Principe, on the African west coast:

> Find out if there is someone with experience on the coast of Zephala [Mozambique] or the East Indies, and if there is someone, obtain good information … and try to bring this person with you, so to have better knowledge of your commerce.[51]

Apparently, the Dutch were also looking for embodied knowledge.

After collecting knowledge *en route*, we encounter an interesting paradox, since this knowledge had to be transferred and kept secret at the same time. On the one hand, the acquired knowledge could be used in service of more profit, so it had to be circulated again to subsequent captains, merchants, and other company employees. On the other hand, this knowledge had to be kept secret, especially with regard to competitors – the Portuguese, the English, and in the 1590s, also explicitly other Dutch companies.[52] Just as obedience and discipline, secrecy was something that the directors in the Netherlands tried to control as much as possible. For the *eerste schipvaart*, no secret-keeping articles or oaths can be found, but just before the departure of the *tweede schipvaart* in 1598, the merchants, skippers, and mates had to swear and sign an oath of secrecy that they would hand over:

> all the logs, charts, notes, drawings of lands, cities, streams, harbours, capes, astronomical observations, courses […] made, annotated, written or obtained on the voyage, […] to the admiral or directors, if or if not requested, without holding back or making public any copy or sketch.[53]

In almost all later instructions the parts on secrecy are less elaborate; however, it is always present. Mostly, it is stated that 'the officers are bound to keep secret, everything the admiral orders them not to make public. Especially and importantly the contents of this instruction'.[54] Although the crew had less sensitive knowledge at their disposal, they were also warned, for example, in an *artikelbrief*, stating that sharing knowledge considered advantageous to the voyage with Portuguese, Spanish, and other foreigners would be punished.[55]

Regarding the relations with foreigners, in the instructions of the mid-1590s, we encounter instructions that explicitly advise against attacking other ships, even enemy ships. Concerning the *eerste schipvaart*, we read that 'other nations' should not be injured. Only in case of attack, one was permitted to defend oneself, but it would be better to try to talk first.[56] Also in 1595, for the second northbound voyage, it was added that not even public enemies (*openbare vyanden*) must be injured.[57] It should be emphasized here that the Dutch were at war with Spain (and thus Portugal) during these years. However, for example, in the aforementioned instruction for Houtman in 1598, it is stated that Spanish, Portuguese, and all indigenous peoples were not to be trusted but should not be harmed and violence should not be used.[58] From these individual instructions, we should conclude a non-aggressive policy in the first years of the early companies, which has not much been singled out in the historiography.

The general 'Instruction by the commissioners of the States' of 1599, mentioned before, marked a policy change. Issued even before the successful, abundantly loaded *tweede schipvaart* had returned, this was an instruction for *all* merchants going East and West, to Africa, and to other places. The world, especially the seas, were presented in its entirety, a place where no nation should be attacked. But thereafter, one big exception was proclaimed: it was permitted to attack and overpower Spanish ships and everyone trading or allied with the Spanish. To this new rule, an exception was made: 'Indians' should never be attacked, not even when trading with Spain.[59]

All fleets from this time onwards set off with this awareness. The 1599 instruction is not much researched, probably since it is not directly linked with the famous VOC. However, it has had many consequences for the decade thereafter. The best known one is probably the capture of the Portuguese carrack *Santa Catarina* by the Dutch in 1603, for which this general instruction can be seen as at least partly a justification.[60] Mostly this capture is seen as the start of many developments thereafter, most importantly the VOC asking Hugo Grotius to write a justification, resulting in his 'De Indis' (only much later published under the better known title *De Jure Praedae*), of which a part became his influential *Mare Liberum* (1609), arguing the freedom of the seas.[61]

Considering instructions thus helps us to understand later practices and publications. The other way round, looking back from Grotius helps us to understand the language of the instructions. To explain this, we must make a diversion to the history of political thinking. Grotius may have been the first to directly apply reason-of-state theory to Dutch overseas sailing in scholarly writing.[62]

Reason-of-state discourse, however, can already be found in the instructions that were drafted for the Dutch long-distance voyages in the 1590s. They do not contain explicit references to Botero, Lipsius, let alone Machiavelli, but the language of these political writers is omnipresent. From the very first Dutch long-distance voyages, we find their discourse, indicating how to rule with reason to secure welfare.[63] Also other characteristics of what has been brought forward as 'raison d'état' can be discerned, like how moral and religious issues were secondary (or just absent) to the government, just as we can consider the company as a power machine and envisage the mechanisms used to preserve power and produce discipline and obedience.[64] One of these mechanisms was the emphasis on necessity as a valid argument to deviate from normal practice, as for example can be seen in the justification of attacking Spanish and Portuguese ships from 1599 onwards.[65] Another one was the explicit admonition in some instructions to the admiral and his officers to pretend and even outright lie to the crew and to passing foreigners about their destination, their aims, and their successes.[66] The regulation of knowledge covers the regulation of fake knowledge as well.

The consequences of the 1599 general instruction by the States of Holland and its line of thinking can also be recognized in a new subgenre of instructions, which were issued in the years 1603 till 1609, namely secret instructions. The very first official fleet under the VOC banner, with Steven van der Hagen as its admiral, sailed in 1603 with a 'secret' instruction much less innocent than the ones before 1599. It was preceded by some sort of 'war manifesto' justifying attacking enemy ships.[67] The King of Spain and Portugal was presented as 'the enemy of our general prosperity' and, as daily experience had demonstrated, his 'indecent, violent means, evil and false practices' the Dutch were forced (*genootsaeckt*) to 'do offence to Spaniards, Portuguese and their adherents'.[68] This emphasis on necessity is easily associated with reason-of-state thinking.[69]

Another example can be found in 1607, when admiral Pieter Willemsz Verhoeff got an instructive *Memorie* about trade and destination, and a secret instruction that was explicitly not to be known by everyone on the ship. It ordered to be as detrimental to the enemy (*den vijandt affbreuck doen*) as possible, be it in Mozambique, Goa, the Malabar coast, or the Philippines.[70] The instruction ordered to research accurately which places could possibly be conquered.[71] Whereas a decade earlier exploring places was explicitly put in service of commerce, here it is commanded with war as its final aim.

In the same years, secret instructions were issued for the admirals Paulus van Caerden and Cornelis Matelief with comparable recommendations to attack and damage Portuguese, Spaniards, or their goods.[72] Matelief and his council were ordered to regulate themselves after the instruction and the secret instruction, and if they were incompatible, the secret instruction would prevail.[73] We see how, at this point, war definitely prevailed over commerce as the most important goal of VOC ships in the East.

After 1609, no more secret instructions were issued, which has to do with the Twelve Years' Truce between Spain and the Dutch Republic concluded in that year.[74] 1609 was also the year of the above-mentioned instruction for the first Governor General Pieter Both. This document is full of orders to inform (*informeren*), examine (*examineren*), and research (*ondersoecken*). Both is advised to find, keep, and if possible, enlarge good intelligence to judge and to know the state of affairs, trade, persons, and nations in several parts of the Indies.[75] Thus, an interesting step from information to intelligence (*intelligentie*) is made. Not in the sense of the current use of the Dutch word *intelligentie* (brainpower), but here the word definitely is used compared to its English counterpart (to be translated with *inlichtingen* nowadays), mostly in state service. Whereas early modern secret intelligence has been extensively researched for the English and, for example, the Venetian case, it would be rewarding to analyse the VOC knowledge practices in Asia through this lens.[76]

Conclusions and Reflections on Regulating Knowledge by Instructions

To conclude, the instructions for faraway travels regulated knowledge transfer. To begin with, from the authorities in the Dutch Republic to the authorities on the ship and (via *artikelbrieven*) to the crew, the instructions attempted to impose order on board. The instructions also ordered how new knowledge had to be acquired, presented, and brought back, thus enabling the global knowledge circulation in which especially Amsterdam came to play a central role in the seventeenth century. As to the VOC and its demeanour with regard to knowledge, research into the instructions at first sight confirms the general picture of the existing literature.[77] The companies did not actively promote science or scholarship, but by sending out ships and people, they did facilitate new knowledge flows from Asia to Europe – and the other way round.

Examining the knowledge processes that were actively regulated by the companies, it has proved insightful to ask in what interest collecting, transferring, and keeping knowledge was advised and performed. The instructions demonstrate that from an institutional, company viewpoint, only knowledge with immediate advantages concerning profit, warfare, and politics should be collected, and if obtained, only strictly regulated or not at all be disseminated outside the ship and the company headquarters.

While first all activities of the early companies were in the service of commerce and maximizing profit, from 1599 onwards warfare became an additional aim and then top priority. This seems to have changed again with the Truce of 1609. But even when commerce was the ultimate aim of a ship, it can be concluded that overseas trade was from early on perceived as a reason of state, and the instructions were infused by raison d'état discourse. To approach these instructions regulating knowledge from the angle of contemporary political thought has made their language and the surrounding practices more comprehensible.

Moreover, these instructions are and should be understood as one genre, not just individual documents related to one voyage or one person, as they have been analysed hitherto. The focus on the years before plus the years after 1602 helps to overcome the historiographical divide between East and West and to overcome the teleological tendencies which resulted in presenting the early travels and companies only as a prologue to the VOC or to Dutch colonial history.

Obviously, instructions are only one genre of many written documents produced by the early companies and by the VOC.[78] After setting sail, practice could be resilient, unity difficult to enforce, bottom-up agency never totally absent, supposedly known destinations proved out of reach, and unknown unknowns became known in the end, changing the playing field and the game. Eventually, to achieve a much more complete picture, other sources like logs, journals, published travel texts, correspondence, and much more of the company's archives should be taken into account.

There are more research desiderata. The best route to the Indies did not change much after 1600, probably that is why the emphasis shifted from collecting knowledge *en route* to intelligence on land. This probably had to do as well with the VOC evermore presenting itself as a stately power in the Indies. Procuring secret intelligence in service of the VOC screams for more attention from researchers. It would be interesting as well to know more about how the instructions after 1609 developed, in the VOC as well as the WIC. Another much needed approach must be to bring other countries into the picture, whereby this chapter can hopefully act as a starting point. International comparisons are yet too few and too little elaborated on. The Portuguese, Spanish, and English situations provide many more starting points to place the Dutch in a bigger context and oversee the world as a whole.[79]

As long as most ships sailed, definitely till the age of steam and telegraphs, they had to be instructed by written documents, which disciplined the people on the ship and at the same time bestowed them with a certain power, sometimes even state power. To understand their course, we should not just focus on what they brought back, but also on how they started out. These sources do not show results or what actually happened, though they do provide insights in the prevailing rules and regulations. We read what they, in early modern times, planned to achieve, to control, and to regulate.

Notes

1 Many thanks to the team (see all the other contributors to this volume): research group IV of the collaborative project Creating a Knowledge Society in a Globalizing World and the Netherlands Institute for Advanced Studies (NIAS). This research was also made possible by a Veni grant from the Dutch Research Council (NWO). Besides the team, thanks to Lisa Kattenberg, Isabel Casteels, and Erling Sandmo for thinking along.
2 McCusker, 'The Demise of Distance'.
3 In general, see the Introduction to this volume. As to the terms knowledge and information, see also Van Netten, 'Sailing and Secrecy'.
4 Howlett and Morgan, eds., *How Well Do Facts Travel?*
5 For example, in Friedrich, Brendecke, and Ehrenpreis, eds., *Transformations of Knowledge*. See also Schmidt, *Inventing Exoticism*; Van Groesen, *Amsterdam's Atlantic*.

6 Among others: Elliott, *The Old World and the New*; Grafton, *New Worlds, Ancient Texts*; Bayly, *Empire and Information*; Harris, 'Long-Distance Corporations'; Drayton, 'Knowledge and Empire'; MacLeod, ed., *Nature and Empire*; Barrera-Osorio, *Experiencing Nature*; Delbourgo and Dew, eds., *Science and Empire in the Atlantic World*; Portuondo, *Secret Science*; Brendecke, *The Empirical Empire*.
7 Gaastra, *The Dutch East India Company*, and, in fact, all historiography on the VOC. Literature on the early companies on their own is very scarce.
8 L'Honoré-Naber, ed., *Reizen van Willem Barentsz* II, 220; De Jonge, *De Opkomst van het Nederlandsch Gezag* I-1, 502.
9 Ijzerman, ed., *Journael van de Reis naar Zuid*-Amerika, 83; 'Waeren die men met groote winste uijt desen landen soude connen voeren in den Coninckrycken van China'. Manuscript Voorbereiding Eerste Schipvaart, 201.
10 Davids, *Zeewezen en Wetenschap*; Van Goor, 'Handel enWetenschap'; Davids, 'Navigeren in Azië'; Van Berkel, 'Een Onwillige Mecenas?'; Blussé and Ooms, eds., *Kennis en Compagnie*; Cook, *Matters of Exchange*; Huigen, De Jong, and Kolfin, eds., *The Dutch Trading Companies as Knowledge Networks*. Friedrich, Brendecke, and Ehrenpreis, 'Introduction', 4, sketches the same picture of the role of the VOC and state this in need of revision. However, basically they confirm more than revise.
11 Gaastra, *The Dutch East India Company*, 20–25; Gelderblom, De Jong, and Jonker, 'The Formative Years'.
12 See Slechte, 'Het Spotschip'.
13 Cf. (for the English case) Ogborn, 'Writing Travels', 164.
14 Zandvliet, *Mapping for Money*, 30–32, 37–49; Van Netten, 'Sailing and Secrecy'.
15 Van Gelder, Parmentier, and Roeper, eds., *Souffrir pour Parvenir*; Bossaers e.a., *Dirck Gerritsz Pomp*.
16 Van Netten, 'The Richest Country in the World'.
17 Casteels, 'De Wereld in Enkhuizen', argues the importance of Enkhuizen over Amsterdam in the 1590s.
18 See Witteveen, *Een Onderneming van Landsbelang*; Gaastra, *The Dutch East India Company*, 20–23.
19 Howlett and Morgan, eds., *How Well Do Facts Travel?*
20 '... doet alle naersticheyt, die mogelijck ende eerlijck is, om uwe ladinge te becommen [...] wy en limiteeren u geen oordt, plaets noch specie van laedinge, doet in alles soo dat ghy niet leedich te huys en coompt, regardt nemende op de importansie van de saecke'. Unger, ed., *De Oudste Reizen van de Zeeuwen*, 31. See also De Jonge, *De Opkomst van het Nederlandsch Gezag* I-1, 222–226.
21 '... omme den Oostindische handel tot verbreidinge van de name Christi, salicheyt der onchristenen, eere ende reputatie van onse natie, ter proffite van de Compagnie ... te continueren [en] ... te vergroten'. 'Ten einde onsen voet in India vast, onse vruntschappen en traficque tot Godes eere, der landen welvaert ende der Compagnies proffijt gevordert ende gedreven'. Rietbergen, *De Eerste Landvoogd Pieter Both*, 214–215 (no. 10), 218–219 (no. 21).
22 Literally an 'article letter', that is, a letter consisting of several articles.
23 Instructions on authority States General or States of Zeeland: L'Honoré-Naber, ed., *Reizen van Jan Huyghen van Linschoten naar het Noorden*, 140–141; Unger, ed., *De Oudste Reizen van de Zeeuwen*, 8; De Jonge, *De Opkomst van het Nederlandsch Gezag* III, 147. *Artikelbrieven* signed by Maurits: L'Honoré-Naber, ed., *Reizen van Willem Barentsz* II, 211–217; De Jonge, *De Opkomst van het Nederlandsch Gezag* I-1, 204; Unger, ed., *De Oudste Reizen van de Zeeuwen*, 24–30, 116–121; Keuning, ed., *De Tweede Schipvaart* I, 152; Ijzerman, ed., *Journael van de Reis naar Zuid-Amerika*, 87–98; Van Opstall, ed., *De Reis van de Vloot* I, 17.
24 For this research, I gratefully rely on later published instructions and *artikelbrieven* found in the indispensable works of Pieter van Dam (edited by F.W. Stapel), P. Mijer, J.K.J. de Jonge, and numerous volumes in the series of the Linschoten Vereeniging (https://www.linschoten-vereeniging.nl/nl/werken). Only later in the seventeenth

century, some instructions were printed, but in that case, only the parts on the crew and not the specific instructions for the admiral and the council. Generally on these documents, Van Foreest and De Booy, ed., *De Vierde Schipvaart*, 15–26.
25 Keuning, ed., *De Tweede Schipvaart* I, 160–162; Van Dam, *Beschryvinge* I-1, 590 (no. 1).
26 L'Honoré-Naber, ed., *Reizen van Jan Huyghen van Linschoten*, 261–262; Unger, ed., *De Oudste Reizen van de Zeeuwen*, 121–122; Keuning, ed., *De Tweede Schipvaart* I, 161–162; Ijzerman, ed., *Journael van de Reis*, 97–98; Moree, ed., *Dodo's en Galjoenen*, 138–140.
27 De Jonge, *De Opkomst van het Nederlandsch Gezag* I-1, 249–253.
28 Van Dam, *Beschryvinge* I-1, 370–404, 568–601; Mijer, *Verzameling van Instructiën*.
29 For example Keuning, ed., *De Tweede Schipvaart* I, 157, 159; Moree, ed., *Dodo's en Galjoenen*, 138–140.
30 Wieder, *De Reis van Mahu*, 19–28. See also L'Honoré-Naber, ed., *Reizen van Willem Barentsz* II, 186.
31 Keuning, ed., *De Tweede Schipvaart* I, 157.
32 Unger, ed., *De Oudste Reizen van de Zeeuwen*, 27.
33 For example, L'Honoré-Naber, ed., *Reizen van Willem Barentsz* II, 185, 197–198, 219, 222–223; L'Honoré-Naber, ed., *Reizen van Jan Huyghen van Linschoten*, 261; Unger, ed., *De Oudste Reizen van de Zeeuwen*, 30.
34 L'Honoré Naber, ed., *Reizen van Linschoten*, 231, 257. On China and/or Cathay, see also Van Netten, 'The Richest Country in the World'.
35 Keuning, ed., *De Tweede Schipvaart* I, 150.
36 De Jonge, *De Opkomst van het Nederlandsch Gezag in Oost-Indië* II, 501. On the difference in limits, see Van Foreest and De Booy, ed., *De Vierde Schipvaart*, II, 22.
37 Particularly regarding the *eerste schipvaart* and the northbound voyages.
38 And in case of possible misbehaviour of the admiral, justice could only be done after, not during, the voyage. This was also informed by the experience of the *eerste schipvaart*. Keuning, ed., *De Tweede Schipvaart* I, 160.
39 De Jonge, *De Opkomst van het Nederlandsch Gezag* I-1, 201–212, 212–215, 226–227; also in Unger, ed., *De Oudste Reizen van de Zeeuwen*, 34–35.
40 Ogborn, 'Writing Travels', 164.
41 See, for example, Keuning, ed., *De Tweede Schipvaart* I, 147–152.
42 Keuning, ed., *De Tweede Schipvaart* I, 151.
43 Ijzerman, ed., *Journael van de Reis naar Zuid-Amerika*, 83–86.
44 '… alle twyst ende twedracht [sijn] oorsaecke […] van quaede ende ongeluckige reysen'. Unger, ed., *De Oudste Reizen van de Zeeuwen*, 30.
45 De Jonge, *De Opkomst van het Nederlandsch Gezag* I-1, 206, 231; Keuning, ed., *De Tweede Schipvaart*, 155.
46 Van Foreest and De Booy, ed., *De Vierde Schipvaart*, 193.
47 L'Honoré-Naber, ed., *Reizen van Willem Barentsz* II, 185.
48 L'Honoré-Naber, ed., *Reizen van Willem Barentsz* II, 197–198 (first voyage), 218–224 (second voyage); L'Honoré-Naber, ed., *Reizen van Linschoten*, 140–141 (second voyage).
49 L'Honoré-Naber, ed., *Reizen van Linschoten*, 261.
50 'Met alle naersticheydt ende vlijt verzouckende ende aenzeijlende alle Rijvieren, Reeden ende plaetsen van Rio de la Plata aff de geheele Custe van America langs tot Terra Nova toe ende niet weder van enige derzelver te zeijlen ten zij de zelfde plaetsen tot contement van de geauctoriseerde wel ondersocht zijn, ofte oock enige profijtelicke handel aldaer zoude connen geschieden …' Ijzerman, ed., *Journael van de Reis naar Zuid-Amerika*, 83.
51 '… soo sult … vernemen offer niemand en is, die op de coste van Zephala oft Oost-Indes bekent is, indien daer imanden is, ghy sult goede informatie nemen … ende oock middel soucken om deselve met u t nemen, opdat ghy te beter kennisse van uwe negocie mocht hebben'. De Jonge, *De Opkomst van het Nederlandsch Gezag* I-1, 238.
52 This paradox is dealt with for the Spanish case by Sandman, 'Controlling Knowledge'.

53 'dat wy alle Journalen, Caerten, Schriften, affteijckeningen van Landen, Steden, Stromen, Reden, Hauenen, Capen ofte Hoecken, Hemelsteyckenen, Coursen ... op dese voyage gemaect, geannoteert, geschreuen ofte vercregen ... in handen vanden Admirael offte Bewinthebberen hetsy dat wy daertoe versocht werden offte niet sonder daer off enige copie ofte cladden te mogen achterhouden ofte andere mede te delen'. Keuning, ed., *De Tweede Schipvaart* I, lxviii.
54 Keuning, ed., *De Tweede Schipvaart* I, 151; Van Foreest and De Booy, ed., *De Vierde Schipvaart*, 153.
55 Unger, ed., *De Oudste Reizen van de Zeeuwen*, 27–28. More on companies and secrecy in Van Netten, see 'Sailing and Secrecy'.
56 De Jonge, *De Opkomst van het Nederlandsch Gezag* I-1, 213–215.
57 L'Honoré-Naber, ed., *Reizen van Willem Barentsz* II, 221.
58 Unger, ed., *De Oudste Reizen van de Zeeuwen*, 31.
59 De Jonge, *De Opkomst van het Nederlandsch Gezag* I-1, 248. The term 'Indians' must be understood as a very broad category encompassing all indigenous peoples in the Americas, Africa, and Asia.
60 As pointed out by Van Ittersum, 'Hugo Grotius in Context', 520–526 and Van Ittersum, 'The Long Goodbye'.
61 See note 60. See also Van Ittersum, *Profit and Principle*; Wilson, *Savage Republic*; Borschberg, *Hugo Grotius*.
62 Keller, 'Mining Tacitus'.
63 It is tempting to allude to a commercial reason of state, but that concept has been reserved for republican thinking later in the 17th century and involves much more freedom and less authoritarian rule. Weststeijn, *Commercial Republicanism*; Hartman and Weststeijn, 'An Empire of Trade'.
64 In general, Viroli, *From Politics to Reason of State*; Burke, 'Tacitism, Scepticism, and Reason of State'; Tuck, *Philosophy and Government*.
65 Kattenberg, *The Power of Necessity*.
66 For example, L'Honoré-Naber, ed., *Reizen van Willem Barentsz* II, 186.
67 De Jonge, *De Opkomst van het Nederlandsch Gezag* III, 146, calls it an 'oorlogs-manifest'.
68 Ibidem, 146–147.
69 Kattenberg, *The Power of Necessity*.
70 Van Opstall, ed., *De Reis van Verhoeff*, 20–23, 183.
71 Ibidem, 187.
72 De Booy, ed., *De Derde Reis van de VOC*, 121–125.
73 Akveld, ed., *Machtsstrijd om Malakka*, 286.
74 Van Opstall, ed., *De Reis van Verhoeff*, 7–8.
75 Rietbergen, *Pieter Both* I, 214–215, 218.
76 See the chapter of Ioanna Iordanou in this volume. Iordanou, *Venice's Secret Service*, and, for example, Hutchinson, *Elizabeth's Spymaster*.
77 See footnote 10.
78 Van Meersbergen and Birkenholz, 'Writing That Travels'.
79 Comparison between the companies of different countries is scarce. For the eighteenth century, see Nierstrasz, *Rivalry for Trade*. A little comparing the Dutch (cartography) case with Portugal, see Zandvliet, *Mapping for Money*, 39, 49.

Bibliography

Akveld, Leo ed. *Machtsstrijd om Malakka: De reis van VOC-admiraal Cornelis Cornelisz. Matelief naar Oost-Azië, 1605–1608*. Zutphen: Walburg Pers, 2013.

Barrera-Osorio, Antonio. *Experiencing Nature: The Spanish American Empire and the Early Scientific Revolution*. Austin: University of Texas Press, 2006.

Bayly, C.A. *Empire and Information: Intelligence Gathering and Social Communication in India, 1780–1870*. Cambridge: Cambridge University Press, 1996.

Berkel, K. van. 'Een Onwillige Mecenas? De Rol van de VOC bij het Natuurwetenschappelijk Onderzoek in de Zeventiende Eeuw.' In Bethlehem, J.; Meijer, A.C. eds. *VOC en Cultuur: Wetenschappelijk en Culturele Relaties tussen Europa en Azië ten Tijde van de Verenigde Oost-Indische Compagnie*. Amsterdam: Schiphouwer en Brinkman, 1993, pp. 39–58.

Booy, A. de ed. *De Derde Reis van de VOC naar Oost-Indie onder het Beleid van Admiraal Paulus van Caerden, Uitgezeild in 1606*. The Hague: Nijhoff, 1972.

Borschberg, Peter. *Hugo Grotius, the Portuguese and Free Trade in the East Indies*. Singapore: NUS Press, 2008.

Bossaers, K.W.J.M.; Boon, P. A. *Dirck Gerritsz Pomp alias Dirck China*. Enkhuizen: Vereniging Oud Enkhuizen, 2002.

Blussé, L.; Ooms, I. eds. *Kennis en Compagnie: De Verenigde Oost-Indische Compagnie en de Moderne Wetenschap*. Amsterdam: Balans, 2002.

Brendecke, Arndt. *The Empirical Empire: Spanish Colonial Rule and the Politics of Knowledge*. Berlin and Boston, MA: De Gruyter, 2016.

Burke, Peter. 'Tacitism, Scepticism, and Reason of State.' In *The Cambridge History of Political Thought 1450–1700*. Cambridge: Cambridge University Press, 1991, pp. 477–498.

Casteels, Isabel. 'De Wereld in Enkhuizen. Kennis van Overzeese Gebieden tussen 1580 en 1600.' *Holland* 51 (2019): 149–158.

Cook, Harold. *Matters of Exchange: Commerce, Medicine, and Science in the Dutch Golden Age*. New Haven, CT: Yale University Press, 2007.

Dam, P van. *Beschryvinge van de Oostindische Compagnie*. Vol. I-1. Ed. Stapel, F.W. The Hague: Nijhoff, 1927.

Davids, C.A. *Zeewezen en Wetenschap: De Ontwikkeling van de Navigatietechniek in Nederland tussen 1585 en 1815*. Amsterdam: De Bataafsche Leeuw, 1986.

Davids, Karel. 'Navigeren in Azië: De Uitwisseling van Kennis tussen Aziaten en Navigatiepersoneel bij de Voorcompagnieën en de VOC, 1595–1795.' *Tijdschrift voor Zeegeschiedenis* 9 (1990): 5–18.

Delbourgo, James; Dew, Nicolas eds. *Science and Empire in the Atlantic World*. New York: Routledge, 2008.

Drayton, Richard. 'Knowledge and Empire.' In Marshall, P.J. ed. *The Oxford History of the British Empire*. Vol. 2. Oxford: Oxford University Press, 1998, pp. 231–252.

Elliott, J.H. *The Old World and the New, 1492–1650*. Cambridge: Cambridge University Press, 1970.

Foreest, H.A. van; Booy, A. de ed. *De Vierde Schipvaart der Nederlanders naar Oost-Indië onder Jacob Wilkens en Jacob van Neck, 1599–1604*. Vol. II. The Hague: Nijhoff, 1981.

Friedrich, Susanne; Brendecke, Arndt; Ehrenpreis, Stefan eds. *Transformations of Knowledge in Dutch Expansion*. Berlin: De Gruyter, 2015.

Gaastra, F. *Geschiedenis van de VOC: Opkomst, Bloei en Ondergang*. Zutphen: Walburg Pers, 2012.

Gelder, Roelof van; Parmentier, Jan; Roeper, Vibeke eds. *Souffrir pour Parvenir: De Wereld van Jan Huygen van Linschoten*. Haarlem: Arcadia, 1998.

Gelderblom, Oscar; Jong, Abe de; Jonker, Joost. 'The Formative Years of the Modern Corporation: The Dutch East India Company, 1602–1623.' *The Journal of Economic History* 73 (2013): 1050–1076.

Goor, J. van. 'Handel en Wetenschap.' In Bethlehem, J.; Meijer, A.C. eds. *VOC en Cultuur: Wetenschappelijk en Culturele Relaties tussen Europa en Azië ten Tijde van de Verenigde Oost-Indische Compagnie*. Amsterdam: Schiphouwer en Brinkman, 1993, pp. 1–16.

Grafton, Anthony. *New Worlds, Ancient Texts: The Power of Tradition and the Shock of Discovery.* Cambridge, MA: The Belknap Press of Harvard University, 1992.

Groesen, Michiel van. *Amsterdam's Atlantic: Print Culture and the Making of Dutch Brazil.* Philadelphia: University of Pennsylvania Press, 2017.

Harris, Steven J. 'Long-Distance Corporations Big Sciences and the Geography of Knowledge.' *Configurations* 6 (1998): 269–304.

Hartman, Jan; Weststeijn, Arthur. 'An Empire of Trade: Commercial Reason of State in Seventeenth-Century Holland.' In Reinert, Sophus; Røge, Pernille eds. *The Political Economy of Empire in the Early Modern World.* Basingstoke: Palgrave Macmillan, 2013, pp. 11–31.

Howlett, Peter; Morgan, Mary S. eds. *How Well Do Facts Travel? The Dissemination of Reliable Knowledge.* Cambridge: Cambridge University Press, 2011.

Huigen, Siegfried; Jong, Jan L. de; Kolfin, Elmer eds. *The Dutch Trading Companies as Knowledge Networks.* Leiden: Brill, 2010.

Hutchinson, Robert. *Elizabeth's Spymaster: Francis Walsingham and the Secret War That Saved England.* London: Phoenix, 2007.

IJzerman, J.W. ed. *Journael van de Reis naar Zuid-Amerika door Hendrik Ottsen, 1598–1601.* The Hague: Nijhoff, 1918.

Iordanou, Ioanna. *Venice's Secret Service: Organising Intelligence in the Renaissance.* Oxford: Oxford University Press, 2019.

Ittersum, M.J. van. 'Hugo Grotius in Context. Van Heemskerck's Capture of the *Santa Catarina* and Its Justification in *De Jure Praedae* (1604–1606).' *Asian Journal of Social Science* 31 (2003): 511–548.

Ittersum, M.J. van. *Profit and Principle: Hugo Grotius, Natural Rights Theories and the Rise of Dutch Power in the East-Indies, 1595–1615.* Leiden: Brill, 2006.

Ittersum, M.J. van. 'The Long Goodbye. Hugo Grotius' Justification of Dutch Expansion Overseas, 1615–1645.' *History of European Ideas* 37 (2010): 386–411.

Jonge, J.K.J. de. *De Opkomst van het Nederlandsch Gezag in Oost-Indië: Verzameling van Onuitgegeven Stukken uit het Oud-Koloniaal Archief.* Vol. I-1. The Hague: Nijhoff, 1869.

Kattenberg, Lisa. 'The Power of Necessity: Reason of State in the Spanish Monarchy, ca. 1590–1650.' Unpublished PhD-thesis, University of Amsterdam, 2018.

Keller, Vera. 'Mining Tacitus: Secrets of Empire, Nature and Art in the Reason of State.' *British Journal for the History of Science* 45 (2012): 189–212.

Koolen, G.M.J.M. *Een Seer Bequaem Middel: Onderwijs en Kerk onder de Zeventiende-Eeuwse VOC.* Kampen: Kok, 1993.

Keuning, J. ed. *De Tweede Schipvaart der Nederlanders naar Oost- Indië onder Jacob Cornelisz. van Neck en Wybrant Warwijck, 1598–1600.* Vol. I. The Hague: Nijhoff, 1938.

L'Honoré-Naber, S.P. ed. *Reizen van Willem Barentsz, Jacob van Heemskerck, Jan Cornelisz Rijp en Anderen naar het Noorden, 1594–1597.* Vol. I. The Hague: Nijhoff, 1914.

L'Honoré-Naber, S.P. ed. *Reizen van Willem Barentsz, Jacob van Heemskerck, Jan Cornelisz Rijp en Anderen naar het Noorden, 1594–1597.* Vol. II. The Hague: Nijhoff, 1917.

MacLeod, Roy ed. *Nature and Empire: Science and the Colonial Enterprise.* Ithaca, NY: University of Chicago Press, 2000.

McCusker, John J. 'The Demise of Distance: The Business Press and the Origins of the Information Revolution in the Early Modern World.' *The American Historical Review* 110, no. 2 (2005): 295–321.

Meersbergen, Guido van; Birkenholz, Frank. 'Writing That Travels: The Dutch East India Company's Paper-Based Information Management.' In Brock, Aske Laursen; Meersbergen, Guido van; Smith, Edmond eds. *Trading Companies and Travel Knowledge in the Early Modern World.* New York: Routledge, 2021, pp. 43–70.

Mijer, Pieter. *Verzameling van Instructiën, Ordonnanciën en Reglementen voor de Regering van Nederlandsch-Indië*. Batavia: Lands-drukkerij, 1848.

Moree, P.J. *Dodo's en Galjoenen: De Reis van het Schip 'Gelderland' naar Oost-Indië, 1601–1603.* Zutphen: Walburg Pers, 2001.

Netten, Djoeke van. 'Sailing and Secrecy: Information Control and Power in Dutch Overseas Companies in the Late Sixteenth and Early Seventeenth Century.' In Nijenhuis, Ida; van Faassen, Marijke; Sluijter, Ronald; Gijsenbergh, Joris; de Jong, Wim eds. *Information and Power in History: Towards a Global Approach*. New York: Routledge, 2020, pp. 157–171.

Netten, Djoeke van. 'The Richest Country in the World. Dutch Knowledge of China and Cathay and How to Get There in the 1590s.' In Weststeijn, Thijs ed. *Foreign Devils and Philosophers: Cultural encounters between the Chinese, the Dutch and other Europeans, 1590–1800*. Leiden: Brill, 2020, pp. 24–56.

Nierstrasz, Chris. *Rivalry for Trade in Tea and Textiles: The English and Dutch East India Companies (1700–1800)*. Basingstoke: Palgrave Macmillan, 2013.

Ogborn, Miles. 'Writing Travels: Power, Knowledge and Ritual on the English East India Company's Early Voyages.' *Transactions of the Institute of British Geographers* 27 (2002): 155 171.

Opstall, M.E. van ed. *De Reis van de Vloot van Pieter Willemsz Verhoeff naar Azië, 1607–1612.* Vol. I. The Hague: Nijhoff, 1972.

Portuondo, Maria. *Secret Science: Spanish Cosmography and the New World*. Chicago, IL: University of Chicago Press, 2009.

Rietbergen, P.J.A.N. ed. *De Eerste Landvoogd Pieter Both (1568–1615): Gouverneur-Generaal van Oost-Indië (1609–1614)*. Vol. I. Zutphen: Walburg Pers, 1987.

Sandman, Alison. 'Controlling Knowledge: Navigation, Cartography, and Secrecy in the Early Modern Spanish Atlantic.' In Delbourgo, James; Dew, Nicolas eds. *Science and Empire in the Atlantic World*. New York: Routledge, 2008, pp. 31–51.

Schmidt, Benjamin. *Inventing Exoticism: Geography, Globalism, and Europe's Early Modern World*. Philadelphia: University of Pennsylvania Press, 2015.

Slechte, Henk. 'Het Spotschip: Maritieme Metaforen op Politieke Prenten, en hun Bronnen.' *De Boekenwereld* 15 (1998): 238–261.

Tuck, Richard. *Philosophy and Government, 1572–1651.* Cambridge: Cambridge University Press, 1993.

Unger, W.S. ed. *De Oudste Reizen van de Zeeuwen naar Oost-Indië, 1598–1604*. The Hague: Nijhoff, 1948.

Viroli, Maurizio. *From Politics to Reason of State: The Acquisition and Transformation of the Language of Politics, 1520–1600*. Cambridge: Cambridge University Press, 1992.

Weststeijn, Arthur. *Commercial Republicanism in the Dutch Golden Age. The Political Thought of Johan & Pieter de la Court*. Leiden: Brill, 2011.

Wieder, F.C. *De reis van Mahu en Cordes door de straat van Magelhaes naar Zuid-Amerika en Japan, 1598–1600*. Vol. 1. The Hague: Nijhoff, 1923.

Wilson, Eric. *The Savage Republic: "De Indis" of Hugo Grotius, Republicanism, and Dutch Hegemony within the Early Modern World System (c.1600–1619)*. Leiden: Nijhoff, 2008.

Witteveen, Menno. *Een Onderneming van Landsbelang: De Oprichting van de Verenigde Oost-Indische Compagnie in 1602*. Amsterdam: Amsterdam University Press Salomé, 2002.

Zandvliet, Kees. *Mapping for Money: Maps, Plans and Topographic Paintings and Their Role in Dutch Overseas Expansion during the 16th and 17th Centuries*. Amsterdam: De Bataafsche Leeuw, 1998.

'Waeren die men met groote winste uijt desen landen soude connen voeren in den Coninckrycken van China.' Manuscript Voorbereiding Eerste Schipvaart; Maritime Museum, Amsterdam; inv.nr. A.4592.

7
REGULATING THE TRANSFER OF SECRET KNOWLEDGE IN RENAISSANCE VENICE

A Form of Early Modern Management

Ioanna Iordanou

In the late 1560s, the Venetian ambassador in Constantinople, who was casually termed *bailo* by the Venetians,[1] was ordered to desist from the 'very dangerous' practice of using 'lemon juice' (an euphemism for invisible ink) when relating 'the secret matters that take place daily' in the Ottoman capital in his letters to the Venetian government. Instead, he was admonished to revert to the widely accepted use of ciphers because the Sultan's envoy in Venice, Ibrahim Bey, had grown increasingly suspicious of the *bailo*'s clandestine method of correspondence.[2] This appeal followed a formal request by the Sultan via Ibrahim Bey for the *bailo* to actually stop using ciphers altogether in his communication with the Venetian authorities or to submit the cipher keys to the Sultan, a request that the Venetians rejected, arguing that letter interception and the widely accepted use of ciphers as a common diplomatic practice precluded such a concession.[3] In response, the Sultan, who was irrevocably resolute, demanded a clause to the capitulation of the peace treaty with Venice, forbidding the use of methods of encryption. The Venetians retorted, however, that without ciphers, they would not be able to render favours to his majesty, transporting secret messages to his grandees across the Mediterranean.[4] This response related to a favour the Venetians had rendered to the Sultan two years earlier, transporting, in secret, letters sent by their Grand Vizier (the Sultan's prime minister) Sokollu Mehmet Pasha to a grandstanding military commander who was sailing across the Mediterranean with his fleet, after he had played an instrumental role in the Siege of Malta (1565) by the Ottomans.[5]

In a separate incident, a few years later, the Venetian authorities instructed their governor in Trogir – at that time a Venetian colony – to employ a Turkish spy, tasked with travelling to the Ottoman Empire, in order to deliver a letter to the *bailo* who, at the time, was under house arrest. The commission came with detailed instructions: the spy was to hide the letter in a waterproof piece of cloth, which had been duly provided by the Venetian Council of Ten – the executive committee responsible for the security of the Venetian state.[6] Then, he was to stich up the concealed letter in a way that it created a secret compartment inside his clothes. Upon arrival in *Pera*, the suburb of Constantinople where the Venetian embassy was situated, he would hand over the letter to the *bailo* through a window and wait until the *bailo* had composed and handed him a reply for the Venetian authorities, which he would consequently transport back.[7]

This chapter will focus primarily on 'secret' knowledge, that is, privileged knowledge or confidential information on political, military, economic, social, and even cultural matters that were of geostrategic significance for the Venetian state and thus ought to be protected and concealed. Within the context of state security, where this chapter is situated, this type of privileged knowledge or confidential information fell under the term 'intelligence', which indicated knowledge or information of political, economic, social, or even cultural value that was worthy of secrecy, evaluation, and potential covert (at times even overt) action by the Venetian government in the name of state security. The two aforementioned episodes are representative of two significant features in the dissemination of secret knowledge in the early modern world – and this chapter. First, official state secrecy, the accomplishment of which enabled the transfer of privileged knowledge that had to be concealed in order to cross both geographical as well as societal borders, moving in the courier's bag, through diverse local sites of interaction – such as the home, the workshop, the marketplace, and the government – to a variety of recipients.[8] Second, formal processes of regulating – or, as it will become more evident as the chapter unfolds, managing – the transfer of secret knowledge through official decrees on the use, provision, classification, and disposal of widely accepted methods of encryption. These were primarily ciphers, an encryption technique through which a message was concealed by means of changing the characters in which it was composed.[9]

The chronological and geographical focus of this chapter is sixteenth-century Venice, a sprawling maritime empire, encompassing vast parts of northern Italy, the Balkan Peninsula, and several mainland and island territories in the Levant, covering part of what is contemporary Greece. This territorial expansion was crucial for Venice, because it enabled her to control the most strategic Mediterranean and European trade routes, dominating the commerce of luxury items like silk and spices from India and Egypt and overseeing their distribution to the rest of Europe.[10] For this reason and following the exponential growth of diplomacy in the early modern period,[11] the Venetians had delegated the administration of their territorial state to formally appointed governors, while official ambassadors across Europe played the role of the intermediary between the Venetian government and foreign rulers.[12]

As a result of its imperial make up and the significance of defending its territories in order to protect its economic prominence, early modern Venice marshalled into existence one of the world's earliest centrally organised state intelligence organisations.[13] At the helm of this process was the Council of Ten, the governmental committee responsible for all matters of the security of the Venetian Republic.[14] The Council was actually made up of seventeen men, including ten ordinary members who served annual terms, the Doge's six ducal councillors – who did not have voting rights – and the Doge as the ceremonial figurehead.[15] Every month, three ordinary members took turns at heading the Ten's operations. They were called *Capi del Consiglio dei Dieci*, the Heads of the Council of Ten.[16]

In an era when written correspondence was the most prevalent method of long-distance communication,[17] letters and dispatches became the cornerstone of political and diplomatic exchanges.[18] Accordingly, for the Council of Ten, correspondence provided the main communication link between the government and their formally appointed representatives within and beyond the Venetian empire. Innumerable such epistles pertaining to matters of state security were sent on a daily basis from and to the Doge's Palace – Venice's political nucleus situated in Saint Mark's Square overlooking the Venetian lagoon – most of them written in cipher for secrecy purposes. A great number of them have survived in Venice's State Archives, primarily because the Council of Ten kept a 'secret' archive called *Cancelleria Secreta*, the storehouse for official state knowledge that had to be kept secret.[19]

In fact, secrecy, that is, official state secrecy, had a pervasive aura engulfing the Venetian government's state security pursuits. For this reason, the Council of Ten institutionalised it, issuing several formal decrees on the necessity and accomplishment of secrecy for the benefit of effective knowledge transfer.[20] These decrees were complemented by regulations – that is, legally binding directives – on the provision, use, classification, and disposal of ciphers to enable the transfer of secret knowledge. For the Venetian authorities, such regulations had a specific function: they determined and dictated uniform and interdependent ways of working across all different operations of Venice's state bureaucracy and intelligence apparatus. They are thus indicative of a primordial form of managing human action through commonly accepted working patterns, an enlightening insight, which renders the process of regulating the transfer of secret knowledge more significant than the content and revelatory nature of secret knowledge itself.

This chapter will start by exploring the Venetian regulations on secrecy, first those pertaining to official state secrecy and consequently those relating to the provision, use, classification, and disposal of methods of encryption. Drawing from early theorisations of bureaucratic organisation, the chapter will then proceed to analyse the process of regulating the transfer of secret knowledge and exclusive information as a primordial form of management, that is, managing coordinated ways of working, more often than not, at a distance. Finally, through the use of social theorisations of secrecy, the process of intentional concealment will emerge as an enabler of knowledge transfer, facilitating interactions that helped transcend geographical and even societal barriers for the purpose of communicating privileged knowledge. As an outcome of this analysis, it will become apparent that official state secrecy made concessions that open knowledge could not proffer.

The Ten's Regulations on Official State Secrecy

Sixteenth-century Venice was renowned for its obsession with secrecy. As a territorial state with commercial – and by extension, political – interests across Europe and Anatolia, this fixation pertained primarily to official state secrecy, that is, secrecy of state affairs that were dealt with by the government. They were thus debated and deliberated upon by the numerous deliberative bodies that made up the Venetian government. Therein lay the difficulty in the accomplishment of official state secrecy: the large number of patricians participating in the Venetian governmental committees. More specifically, the Venetian Senate – the government's debating committee and primary legislative organ up until the mid-sixteenth century – was made up of 300 men, while the Great Council (*Maggior Consiglio*), the assembly of the entire body of Venetian male patricians, was composed of 2,000 men.[21] Aside from their extended family networks, most of these councillors had an entourage of servants and gondoliers accompanying them to the Doge's Palace on a daily basis, the majority of whom were, more often than not, keen to overhear and prattle about what was discussed within the Palace's halls.[22] For this reason, from the beginning of the sixteenth century, the Council of Ten had decreed that all patricians who partook in Venice's governing bodies were legally required to keep the content of discussions and debates taking place during formal assemblies strictly confidential.[23]

This was only one of a series of decrees on the necessity and accomplishment of official state secrecy for the preservation of privileged knowledge that had to be protected at any cost. 'Everyone in this Council [...] knows how necessary secrecy is [...], since without it our State cannot be governed effectively', the Ten declared, when they introduced a slew of regulations institutionalising secrecy as a vital instrument of statecraft.[24] In fact, for the Venetian government, and especially for the Council of Ten, secrecy embodied confidentiality, harmony, and civic concord. It was primarily for both these 'functional' and 'symbolic' purposes that secrecy was 'inherent in Venice's Republican ideology', and therefore was glorified as one of the government's most potent virtues.[25] Hence, the string of regulations, from the fifteenth century, intended to protect secrecy and ultimately to institutionalise it. These regulations involved a variety of affairs, including the dealings of governmental bodies with secret matters of the state, the encounters of patricians with foreign princes and their emissaries, and the safeguarding of the formal correspondence and other relevant documentation of Venetian envoys serving within and beyond the *Dominante*, as Venice was known across the Venetian dominion.[26]

As we have already seen, from the beginning of the sixteenth century, Venetian patricians were strictly forbidden to communicate any matter discussed in the Senate or other deliberative bodies, either orally or in writing, to any outsider of these committees, for a fine of 1,000 ducats and in extreme cases, even the death penalty.[27] The impending punishments were extremely harsh, considering that the annual salary of a patrician serving as an ambassador overseas ranged from

2,400 to 7,200 ducats.[28] Sanctions were even more stringent for members of the Council of Ten for whom any attempt to disobey this law entailed forfeiting their rights to statecraft for a decade.[29] Additionally, patricians who partook in governmental councils were prohibited from revealing any debates or instances of conflict and discord during assemblies. The Ten were particularly preoccupied with disclosures of debates and disagreements that arose during governmental committees, as these would tarnish the image of Venice as *La Serenissima*, the most Serene Republic. For this reason, they decreed against such ventures under the extraordinary pain of death and the subsequent confiscation of all personal possessions.[30]

The Ten's unyielding preoccupation with minimising disclosures ensuing from governmental assemblies went hand in hand with their stout-hearted resolve to limit Venetian patricians' encounters with foreign grandees and dignitaries. For this reason, from the 1480s, members of the Venetian ruling class were strictly forbidden to discuss state matters when consorting with foreign emissaries for a fine of 1,000 ducats and a two-year exile.[31] Moreover, when a Venetian nobleman wished to visit a foreign dignitary in the city, he was required by law to obtain a special permission.[32] In 1569, for instance, when an imminent visit of the Archduke of Austria to Venice was rumoured, Girolamo Lippomano, who had served as the Venetian ambassador to the Archduke's court two years earlier, hurried to obtain a licence from the Heads of the Ten to call on the imperial visitor.[33]

These decrees on official state secrecy served a fundamental purpose: they constituted commonly accepted patterns – that is, standardised and thus mutually accepted practices – of conduct that demarcated the passages, boundaries, and obstacles of the direct communication of official secret knowledge. Accordingly, they determined who was included or excluded from access to privileged knowledge or exclusive information. This was fairly evident in the protection of state secrets that had to be communicated via written correspondence between Venetian diplomats serving overseas and the Venetian authorities stationed in the Doge's Palace. For this reason, from the fifteenth century, a series of regulations had been issued to safeguard the secrecy of these communications. According to them, formal Venetian representatives serving within and beyond the *Dominante* were not allowed to divulge information on their mission or on relevant matters of the state in their correspondence with relatives, friends, and other acquaintances.[34] Similarly, when Venice's diplomatic legations were run by distinguished state secretaries, such as in the case of Milan and Florence, *Residenti*, as they were called, were strictly ordered to write their missives personally under the pain of loss of their diplomatic prerogatives and other public benefits.[35] Importantly, when communicating with the government and its representatives on state affairs – particularly on issues of state security – using methods of encryption, especially cryptography, was compulsory by law.[36] So instrumental was the use of ciphers in the official communication between the Venetian government (especially the Senate and the Council of Ten) and their formal representatives that another string of regulations issued by the Ten pertained to their use, classification, and disposal.

The Ten's Regulations on Writing in Cipher

Cryptography, that is, the art of writing in cipher,[37] provided the basis for written communication between the Council of Ten and their formal representatives within and beyond the territories of the Venetian dominion. Its significance, therefore, was immense for Renaissance Venice's diplomatic and, by extension, intelligence operations. For this reason, early modern Venice created one of the world's earliest professional departments of cryptology. This was housed in the *Palazzo Ducale* and occupied some of the most gifted cipher secretaries of the period.[38] Aside from breaking enemy ciphers, the main responsibility of the Venetian state cryptographers was to produce ciphers for the official clandestine communication between the Venetian government and their formal representatives – including Venetian ambassadors, governors, and military commanders – stationed beyond the watery confines of the lagoon city. For this reason, the Ten issued a slew of regulations on the provision, use, classification, and disposal of Venetian ciphers.

The first string of the Ten's regulations involved the provision of enciphering and deciphering facilities for the representatives of the *Serenissima*. On a basic level, this meant that all secretaries accompanying Venetian ambassadors in overseas missions ought to have been trained in methods of encryption and decryption in order to handle the correspondence responsibilities on behalf of the envoys they served. In practice, this meant developing the ability to wield the designated cipher in order to encipher and decipher official letters. In consequence, the systematic study and development of a working knowledge of ciphers was an essential aspect of their job.[39] Moreover, as Venetian governors and military chiefs were required to communicate in cipher regularly, they had to either be conversant with cryptography or to be provided with secretaries adept at methods of encryption and decryption. This was particularly important for high-ranking naval commanders such as the *Capitano Generale da Mar* – the commander-in-chief of the Venetian fleet, who frequently communicated information to the Ten that would nowadays be deemed classified. For this reason, in 1577, the Ten unanimously decreed that navy chiefs should be provided with a secretary who would be responsible for enciphering and deciphering the *Capitano*'s letters to the Council of Ten and their state representatives.[40]

The second string of regulations involved the actual use of formal ciphers. Already from the 1540s, the government had decreed that all major diplomats had to be granted a distinct cipher for their direct communication with the Council of Ten. For security purposes, this cipher would differ from other ciphers provided for the communication amongst Venetian diplomats. The same decree was reiterated in 1589, clearly stating that Venetian envoys had to be furnished with two distinct ciphers, one for their written interactions with the Ten and another one for their communication with the Ten's legates and other state servants.[41] By the seventeenth century, the Venetian system of encrypted communication distinguished between two types of cipher: the *zifra grande*, which was reserved for the communication between the Ten, their ambassadors, their governors, and their *Provveditori Generali*, and the *zifra piccola* that was allocated to lesser representatives, such as Venetian consuls in areas where Venice did not have diplomatic representation but strong commercial presence and naval commanders of a lesser rank such as *capitani*.[42] At times of diplomatic tribulations or impending dangers, however, temporary decrees were issued to increase the security of methods of encryption. In the summer of 1590, for example, the Ten ordered the Venetian ambassador in Savoy to combine two major ciphers in constructing different parts of his epistles in order to boost their inaccessibility.[43]

Regulations surrounding the use of methods of encryption were not to be taken light-heartedly by Venetian state representatives. Instead, those who ignored them were severely scolded and chastised. The Venetian envoy in Milan was once reprimanded for neglecting the Ten's order to write in cipher, especially when names of important dignitaries were mentioned in his epistles.[44] Secretaries who misused the cipher were threatened with a raft of punishments, including the loss of one year's salary or even their job. In November 1577, a secretary in the employ of the Duke of Candia – the Venetian ruler of the island of Crete – lost both, as a result of mishandling the designated cipher and compromising thus the security of the Venetian state.[45]

For the appropriate cipher to be used by Venetian state officials, it had to be distributed to them in a secure manner, ensuring that outdated ciphers were returned safely to the Venetian intelligence headquarters in the Doge's Palace. Accordingly, every time a fresh cipher was introduced, it was sent to the relevant dignitaries, who were expected to start using it imminently while carefully restoring the old one to the Council of Ten. In January 1591, for example, the Venetian governor in Dalmatia was sent the key to a new cipher with the instruction to consign the old one to any Venetian representative on his way to Venice through the Dalmatian coast, ensuring that a formal receipt of consignment was produced.[46] At the close of the sixteenth century, Iseppo Gregolin, the secretary of the *Provveditore Generale da Mar*, wrote to the state cryptographer Ferigo Marin informing him that he had received the newly allocated cipher. In his epistle, he proposed to return the outdated one in person in order to escape the risks involved in a postal consignment.[47] In a territorial state like Venice, however, the coordination of the distribution of the designated cipher did not always go according to plan, causing mismatches and halting the flow of correspondence. In 1605, for instance, the governor of Zante informed the *Capi* that his cipher was different to the one used by his counterpart in Cerigo (the contemporary Greek island of Kythira in south-eastern Peloponnese), causing a communication breakdown between the two islands.[48] The main cause of these discrepancies was the regular update of ciphers that occurred when the Ten had confirmation or even suspicion that a cipher had been broken. In such cases, they ordered the immediate halt of a cipher's use and its instant substitution with a fresh one.[49]

Detailed instructions on such updates were sent to formal cipher users and reminders were communicated when deemed necessary. In the summer of 1583, for example, the *Capi* reminded the *bailo* in Constantinople that he should desist from using a cipher already deemed outdated by the Ten. The Ten became aware of the *bailo*'s gaffe when the Venetian governor of the city of Crete, stationed in the city of Candia, contacted them to inform them that he was unable to read enciphered letters sent to him by the Venetian diplomat in Constantinople, as he was no longer in possession of the out-of-date key the *bailo* was using. To rectify the issue, the Ten supplied the *bailo* with the new cipher and updated the *Provveditore* in Crete on this final development, in order to restore the secret communication between the two officials.[50]

The great speed with which ciphers were updated bore the need for a third string of regulations. These pertained to their classification and, importantly, to the disposal of outdated ciphers. Already by 1578, ducal secretaries had been ordered to produce lists of all those who received the cipher keys, making a note of the proposed manner in which the keys would be returned after their use.[51] As the number of ciphers gradually proliferated by the beginning of the seventeenth century, especially since Venice deployed several permanent embassies and ruled over a large number of geographically dispersed strongholds, fresh decrees were issued for their cataloguing. More specifically, in 1605 official state cryptographers were asked to register all ciphers and their keys in two formal books, one for the Venetian colonies in the Mediterranean and one for the Venetian-dominated territories in the Italian mainland. Furthermore, they were requested to take a note of the date and the person to which keys were consigned, in addition to the proposed return date. They were also ordered to create two copies of these books that were to be stored in secret locations. Importantly, due to the miscommunication problems caused by the misplacement of outdated keys, the Ten also decreed that older keys no longer in use were to be burned from time to time so that they would not be misperceived for keys currently in use.[52]

Regulating the Transfer of Secret Knowledge: A Form of Management?

The formal regulations discussed above – both on official state secrecy and on the provision, use, classification, and disposal of state ciphers – were issued by the Venetian Council of Ten for the purpose of protecting the transfer of privileged knowledge pertaining to the security of the sprawling Venetian empire. In essence, they constituted commonly accepted norms, stemming from formal governmental decrees, on official state secrecy and methods of encryption for the written communication of knowledge – usually of diplomatic, political, and military value – that, in order to be transferred, had to be protected and concealed. In this respect, these regulations had two distinct functions. First, they served as commonly accepted patterns of conduct that delineated the channels and boundaries of knowledge transfer, determining who was included or excluded from access to privileged knowledge. Second, transcending the purpose of mere instructions to their formal representatives and state officials, they assumed a managerial overtone, even an outright managerial function. This observation becomes more clear if we consider the fundamental nature of management as a set of rules that create a certain degree of homogeneity in the way people work. To do so, we must resort to contemporary terminology and basic theoretical conceptualisations of management.

Since we are dealing with the development of an emergent, early modern state bureaucracy, it is prudent to draw on the work of one of the foundational thinkers of the bureaucratic management theory, the German sociologist Max Weber (1864–1920).[53] According to Weber, in its purest form, management is built on regulations, knowledge of which constitutes 'special technical expertise' that leads to a certain degree of consistency and homogeneity in the way human action is organised.[54] Accordingly, the Ten's directives and regulations on official state secrecy and encrypted correspondence constituted what Weber described as 'an administrative order' that communicated 'general rules and regulations which are more or less stable, more or less exhaustive, and which can be learned'.[55] These rules and regulations dictated the actions of not only administrative staff but anyone involved directly with the organisation of work within Venice's state bureaucracy and intelligence apparatus.[56] In this respect, in both their functions, regulations regarding encrypted communication became enablers in the dissemination of knowledge that had to be concealed and therefore protected. Their enabling capacity lay in their governing 'organized action' by dictating some consistency and homogeneity in the way methods of encryption were wielded by their users.[57] In a way, then, regulations acted as techniques 'to handle controversies by breaking them down into mundane technical details'.[58] It is for this reason that regulating the concealment and transfer of secret knowledge and exclusive information assumed an outright managerial function.

The instrumentality of regulations in the coordination of enciphered communication between the Council of Ten and their formal representatives across Europe, the Near East, and even Northern Africa necessitates further elaboration. The series of formal decrees and regulations that the Ten deliberated upon and issued determined the systematic, interdependent ways of working across all different operations of Venice's state bureaucracy and intelligence pursuits. Such regulations conferred a legal authority, indicating that 'powers of command' were 'legitimated by that system of rational norms', not the ruler's influence or institutional right.[59] In practice, this meant that those serving in Venice's secret service were expected to bestow obedience less on the Ten's power of command and more on the decrees and directives issued by them, a trait widely different to other early modern states that employed more conventional forms of power and control imposed primarily by tradition or charisma.[60] Accordingly, it was the implementation of such norms and regulations stemming from the Ten's formal decrees that rendered the protection and transfer of secret knowledge possible, indicating, once again, their function as a primordial form of management, that is, managing human action through interwoven ways of working.

Undeniably, in the era of wind and sail, the communication of these regulations was achieved through enciphered epistles. Accordingly, while the regulations surrounding the encrypted transfer of knowledge became a form of management, official correspondence became the tool through which management was accomplished. Under this light, (encrypted) correspondence became less a means of knowledge or information transfer and more a vital tool of management, which involved complex processes of issuing, sending, receiving, executing, and reporting on written instructions and regulations. The focus of both superiors and subordinates on the instructions conveyed by an epistle rather than the subject matter disclosed or undisclosed in it further supports this claim. The string of directives and regulations surrounding state secrecy and official methods of encryption further reinforces the managerial function of written communication as a process requiring and dictating uniformity of action. It is for this reason that the Ten's decrees served as commonly accepted patterns of conduct that demarcated the boundaries, passages, or obstacles of knowledge transmission.

By and large, in both their functions, regulations on the accomplishment of official state secrecy and the provision, use, classification, and disposal of encrypted communication acted as enablers in the communication of knowledge that had to be concealed and hence protected. In this respect, secrecy itself became a vehicle rather than the obstacle of the communication of secret knowledge between, in the Venetian case, the government and the governed. This social aspect of secrecy that enables the transfer of secret knowledge or exclusive information by protecting it from the prying eyes of outsiders has been overwhelmingly neglected by historians of the early modern period and merits further analysis.[61]

Secrecy as an Enabler of Knowledge Transfer

Trying to delineate the concept of secrecy in the early modern period is, as historian Daniel Jütte has astutely remarked, 'an elusive task'.[62] To do so, once again, one must turn to contemporary theorisations of secrecy. Sociologist and philosopher Sissela Bok defined secrecy as the process of 'intentional concealment', echoing sociologist Georg Simmel's interpretation of the concept as 'consciously willed concealment'.[63] In their definitions and interpretations of the term, both literati put the emphasis on the social process of concealing rather than on the knowledge that must be concealed. Nevertheless, defining secrecy in terms of concealment or even in terms of who remains excluded from privileged knowledge or confidential information offers the historian limited ground for scholarly analysis. This is because, while secrets (and their keepers) can be arresting for researchers (and their audiences), they offer little more than momentary thrill. On the contrary, exploring secrecy as a 'communicative event' premised upon ongoing social interactions necessary for the transfer of knowledge that must be concealed in order to be communicated[64] offers more fertile ground for deep historical analysis.

Let us explore this contention further. The Council of Ten's formal regulations on secrecy, including those on methods of encryption as a means to conceal privileged knowledge that ought to be protected, demarcated the behaviours and actions of their formal representatives and other functionaries. In consequence, these decrees enabled and nurtured social interactions amongst those involved in the protection and transfer of secret knowledge. Borrowing from social theorisations of secrecy might help elaborate on this contention further. Secrecy, as a process, enables the creation of social boundaries between two separate entities, a privileged inner circle of those *in the know* and everyone else not *in the know*. The exclusivity of being *in the know* can boost the sense of distinctive inclusiveness in the inner circle and, by extension, cement one's identification with it.[65] In the case of the Ten's formal deliberations and ensuing decrees on state secrecy and encryption methods, this is evident not only in the inclusion of a variety of individuals in the 'circle of secrecy' – including the Council of Ten, their state representatives within and beyond the Venetian Republic's confines, and the state secretaries responsible for Venice's cryptologic pursuits as well as the ordinary messengers and spies who were entrusted with transporting secret knowledge – but in the 'strongly accentuated exclusion' of everyone else who should not be privy to the privileged knowledge shared between those in the 'circle of secrecy'.[66] Viewed from this prism, secrecy became a legitimate method of handling privileged knowledge and organising its secret diffusion.[67]

While instances of breach of secrecy were inevitable, the conscious awareness of being the designated custodians of state secrets and the sense of specialness in being entrusted with official, privileged knowledge of state affairs may have reinforced those officials' inclination towards ongoing intentional concealment. Sustaining this intentional concealment served a dual purpose. First, from a practical (and moral) perspective, it helped maintain the Venetian patricians' social standing, as they were threatened with enforced withdrawal from their duties if they deliberately attempted to breach secrecy. In such cases, they would risk being ousted from statecraft, a grave punishment indeed for someone belonging to the Venetian ruling class. Second, from a social perspective, it rendered them members of a privileged inner circle, potentially enhancing their sense of distinctive inclusiveness in it and, by extension, cementing their identification with it.[68] Especially in the context of contemporary official state secrecy, intelligence historian Michael Herman went as far as to argue that the 'mystique' of secret knowledge can have 'therapeutic functions due to the group bonding it provides' and can even generate a 'wry professional pride in secrecy'.[69] While extending the applicability of this claim to the early modern period is inappropriate, primarily due to overwhelming lack of self-narratives of the custodians of secret knowledge, based on contemporary social theorisations of secrecy, we can infer that state secrecy created a dynamic and enduring relationship between the Venetian government and its formal representatives.

On the whole, official secrecy served several purposes in Renaissance Venice. First, it enabled the concealment of both the keeper of secrets and the privileged knowledge of the secret, especially in situations of conflict or competition. Second, underpinned by the notion of *arcana imperii*, emerging from the scriptures of Roman historian and senator Tacitus (c. 56 AD–c. 120 AD) and sanctioned by Renaissance diplomat and political thinker Nicolò Machiavelli, secrecy helped preserve governmental power. Importantly, secrecy enabled the Council of Ten to shape and stage-manage working relationships within the Venetian intelligence apparatus. This relationship building aspect of secrecy has been analysed effectively by Nobel laureate Elias Canetti, who showed how rulers mobilise secrecy to mould their relationship with subordinates as well as relations between subordinates. They do so by creating a system of secrets, and quietly observing and controlling information flows and the institutional loyalty that may ensue from this endeavour. Through the use of secrecy, Canetti argued, rulers, as the sole possessors of panoramic views of knowledge, create an aura of mystery around them.[70] While writing within the context of dictatorships, Canetti's ruminations are relevant to Venice's official secrecy pursuits. This is because, in early modern Venice, secrecy became 'an ongoing accomplishment of social interactions',[71] creating a space, ostensibly concealed from the public's eyes, to debate, to strategise, and to take decisions for the benefit of the Venetian state.

On the whole, it is this social aspect of secret communication that renders Renaissance Venice's official state secrecy pursuits such a fascinating object of historical study and analysis. As evidenced in the above-mentioned instances, this is due to the paradox of secret communication that lay, on the one hand, in erecting cognitive barriers between those *in the know* and those not *in the dark*, and on the other hand, in demolishing barriers that would be needed if no means existed to conceal and protect the transfer of privileged knowledge or confidential information. During this demolition process, societal barriers were also temporarily taken down, as privileged information was shared between individuals of diverse social standing, including the individual in power, his formal representatives overseas, and the lowly messenger who materialised the communication between them through transporting their enciphered epistles – and, more often than not, could become privy to some of the 'classified' information – in addition to the cipher secretary who, billeted in the Venetian black chamber, enciphered and deciphered privileged knowledge. Through this lens, secrets became 'specific modes of knowledge exchange and social action' that mobilised idiosyncratic ways of communication and interaction, primarily because of the possibility for intentional concealment.[72] In consequence, despite the enduring challenge in its upholding, secrecy was a performative and social praxis that transcended the static nature of a secret's content to enable social interactions amongst individuals who, without the shield of concealment, would not have been able to interact.

Conclusion

In the early modern era there were different channels of knowledge exchange and transfer; secrecy was only one of them. Indeed, the early modern world had an unyielding fascination with secrecy, which spawned several cultural, intellectual, and political outlets. The literary genre of the *secreta* that dealt with secrets and their disclosure was one of them.[73] This flourished in parallel with a distinct profession, that of the *professori dei secreti* – the professors of secrets, who pursued the study of nature's secrets.[74] And, of course, in the era of state formation and the gradually ensuing governmental bureaucracies, the imperative role of secrecy for *arcana imperii* – the secrets of the state – sprung from published copies of Machiavelli's political doctrines to become the cornerstone of early modern politics.[75] Additionally, secrecy was tightly intertwined with the protection, even regulation, of intellectual and commercial rights which materialised with the advent of the patent system.[76] Accordingly, secrecy was an instrumental tool of knowledge protection and knowledge transfer. It was for this reason that the early modern period saw the institutionalisation of official state secrecy. Renaissance Venice, the state that boasts one of the earliest centrally organised state intelligence organisations, pioneered this process with the Council of Ten, the governmental committee responsible for the domestic and foreign security of the sprawling Venetian empire, at the helm.

In the fifteenth and sixteenth centuries, the Venetian government issued a slew of regulations for the accomplishment of official state secrecy as well as the provision, use, classification, and disposal of official state ciphers. Both types of regulations served two important functions. First, they acted as commonly accepted patterns of conduct that enabled the communication of privileged knowledge or information that had to be protected in order to be transferred by clearly delineating the passages and boundaries of its transmission. This type of knowledge and information crossed both geographical and societal borders. Second, and following from the first function, regulations became a primordial form of what nowadays is termed 'management', which, in its purest form, is made up of norms that create a certain degree of uniformity in the way human action is organised.[77]

To be sure, it would be challenging to interpret early modern regulations as primordial forms of management that enable and organise homogenous action without drawing on contemporary theorisations of both management and secrecy. Drawing on such sources enables us to cast the spotlight on the process of regulating the transfer of secret knowledge across geographical as well as societal borders rather than the actual content of knowledge itself. Seen this way, the enciphered transfer of knowledge matters less as a means of information exchange and more as a vital form of management, involving complex processes of issuing, sending, receiving, executing, and reporting on written instructions, which ultimately enabled the *regulators* (in our case, the almighty Council of Ten) to control their underlings' behaviour and choreograph their actions across vast distances. And while those regulators' power of command was sanctioned through their regulations rather than through their institutional right to power, one wonders who regulated those who issued those regulations. In other words, invoking Roman poet Juvenal's timeless aphorism 'Quis custodiet ipsos custodes'? (*Satire* VI, 347–348), it is worth asking: who regulated the regulators of knowledge and its transfer in the early modern era? In the era of fake news and post-truth, the answer to this question remains as much of a challenge now as it was in the early modern era.

Notes

1. On the Venetian *bailo* in Constantinople, see Lazari, 'Cenni intorno alle legazioni venete'; Bertelè, *Il palazzo degli ambasciatori*; Preto, 'Le relazioni dei baili a Constantinopoli'; Dursteler, 'The Bailo in Constantinople'; Hanß, 'Baili and Ambassadors'; Gürkan, 'Laying Hands on *Arcana Imperii*'.
2. Archivio di Stato di Venezia (hereafter ASV), Consiglio di Dieci (hereafter CX), *Deliberazioni Secrete*, Registro (hereafter Reg.) 8, carta (hereafter c.) 82 verso (hereafter v.) (3 April 1567). Unless otherwise stated, all dates have been converted to the Gregorian calendar.
3. Ibid., cc. 76 v.–77 recto (hereafter r.) (27 January 1567).
4. Ibid., c. 78 v.–80 r. (18 February 1567).
5. Ibid., cc. 38 v.–40 r. (14 August 1565).
6. On the Venetian Council of Ten, see Macchi, *Storia del Consiglio dei Dieci*; Finlay, *Politics in Renaissance Venice*.
7. ASV, CX, *Deliberazioni Secrete*, Reg. 10, cc. 73 v.–74 r. (14 November 1572).
8. The word 'transfer' is used purposely here, to indicate the direct and controlled communication of privileged knowledge or confidential information as opposed to any type of free flow or wider circulation of knowledge.
9. Kahn, *The Codebreakers*, xv.
10. On the economy of sixteenth-century Venice, see Luzzatto, *Storia economica di Venezia*; Lane, *Venice*; Lanaro ed., *At the Centre of the Old World*.
11. On the development of diplomacy in the early modern period, see the classic work of Mattingly, *Renaissance Diplomacy*. For revisionist view, see Lazzarini, *Communication and Conflict*; Lazzarini, 'Renaissance Diplomacy'.
12. Iordanou, *Venice's Secret Service*.
13. Ibid. See also Iordanou, 'What News on the Rialto'?
14. On the Council of Ten as Venice's spy chiefs, see Iordanou, 'The Spy Chiefs of Renaissance Venice'.
15. Cozzi, 'Authority and the Law', 308.
16. Macchi, *Istoria del Consiglio dei Dieci*; Finlay, *Politics*.
17. On correspondence and epistolary exchange in the early modern period, see Schneider, *The Culture of Epistolarity*; and the essays in Bethencourt and Egmond, eds., *Correspondence and Cultural Exchange*.
18. On epistolarity as a political tool in early modern Italy, see Boutier, Landi, and Rouchon, *La politique par correspondance*. Generally on the role of diplomatic correspondence and reportage in early modern Italy, see Hyde, 'The Role of Diplomatic Correspondence and Reporting'.
19. On the *Cancelleria Secreta*, see De Vivo, 'Ordering the Archive'; De Vivo, 'Cœur de l'Etat, Lieu de Tensión'; Antonini, 'Historical Uses of the Secret Chancery'.
20. See Iordanou, *Venice's Secret Service*, esp. ch. 2.
21. On a synthesis of the inner workings of the Venetian political system, especially in the sixteenth century, see Viggiano, 'Politics and Constitution'. On the *Maggior Consiglio*, especially the requirements for admission and its prerogatives, see Maranini, *La costituzione di Venezia*, esp. 41–46, 78–102.
22. Walker, De Vivo, and Shaw, 'A Dialogue on Spying in 17th Century Venice', 325.
23. ASV, CX, *Deliberazioni Secrete*, Reg. 3, c. 2 r./v. (31 March 1529); Ibid., Reg. 14, cc. 129 v.–130 r. (28 November 1605).
24. Deliberation of the Council of Ten dated 19 April 1583 in Romanin, *Storia documentata di Venezia*, Vol. VI, 130.
25. De Vivo, *Information and Communication in Venice*, 41.
26. Lonardi, 'L'anima dei governi', 209.
27. Romanin, *Storia documentata*, 121–122 (the deliberation is dated 12 February 1532 *more veneto* – meaning the calendar year started on 1 March, as was customary in early modern Venice).

28 Zannini, 'Economic and Social Aspects', 127.
29 Romanin, *Storia documentata*, 523–534 (*Capitolare* of the Ten dated 22 December 1578).
30 Ibid., Reg. 14, cc. 129 v.–130 r. (28 November 1605). See also Romanin, *Storia documentata*, 138; De Vivo, *Information and Communication*, 43.
31 Romanin, *Storia documentata*, 116–117. This regulation already existed in a more basic form from 1403. See Lonardi, 'L'anima dei governi', 209, fn. 577.
32 ASV, CX, *Deliberazioni Secrete*, Reg. 9, c. 213 r. (8 February 1572).
33 ASV, CCX, *Licenze per visitare ambasciatori e personali esteri* (4 and 16 May 1569).
34 ASV, CX, *Deliberazioni Miste*, Reg. 16, c. 120v. (23 May 1464).
35 See, for example, ASV, CX, *Deliberazioni Secrete*, Reg. 19, cc. 85 r.–86 r. (11 July 1641). On the Venetian *Residenti*, see Zannini, 'Economic and Social Aspects', 112, 133.
36 See, for example, ASV, CX, *Deliberazioni Secrete*, Reg. 4, c. 34 r. (25 September 1539).
37 Cryptography has been defined as the transformation of a text in a way that it becomes unintelligible to outsiders without a key. See Kahn, *The Codebreakers*, xv.
38 Ioanna Iordanou, 'The Professionalization of Cryptology'.
39 ASV, CX, *Deliberazioni Miste*, Reg. 35, c. 114 c./v. (14 July 1512); ASV, CX, *Deliberazioni Comuni*, Reg. 30, c. 130r./v. (4 August 1572).
40 ASV, CX, *Deliberazioni Secrete*, Reg. 11, c. 135 r. (3 July 1577).
41 Ibid., Reg. 13, cc. 57 r.–58 r. (18 April 1589).
42 Ibid., Reg. 14, cc. 126 r.–127 r. (31 August 1605).
43 Ibid., Reg. 13, c. 73 v. (19 June 1590).
44 ASV, CCX, *Lettere Secrete*, filza 3 (1 August 1543).
45 ASV, CCX, *Lettere dei Rettori e di altre Cariche*, b. 286 (20 November 1577).
46 ASV, CCX, *Lettere Secrete*, filza 11 (21 January 1591).
47 ASV, *Inquisitori di Stato*, b. 399 (14 December 1599).
48 ASV, CCX, *Lettere dei Rettori e di altre Cariche*, b. 296, fol. 130 (28 May 1605).
49 See, for example, ASV, CX, *Deliberazioni Secrete*, Reg. 13, cc. 52 v.–53 v. (13 July 1584); Ibid., c. 85 r. (3 April 1591); ASV, CCX, *Lettere Secrete*, filza 11 (29, 30 March 1591).
50 ASV, CCX, *Lettere Secrete*, filza 10 (25 June 1583).
51 ASV, CX, *Deliberazioni Secrete*, Reg. 11, cc. 166 r.–167 r. (18 August 1578).
52 Ibid., Reg. 14, cc. 126 r.–127 r. (31 August 1605).
53 On a well-rounded review of the significance of Max Weber's work on organisation and management studies, see Cummings and Bridgman, 'The Relevant Past'; Cummings, Bridgman, Hassard, and Rowlinson, *A New History of Management*, 118–147.
54 Weber, *Economy and Society*, Vol. 2, 958.
55 Ibid.
56 Weber, *Economy and Society*, Vol. 1, 52.
57 Max Weber called this attribute 'Verwaltungsordnung'. See Weber, *Economy and Society*, Vol. 1, 51.
58 Ruef and Harness, 'Agrarian Origins of Management Ideology', 604.
59 Weber, *Economy and Society*, Vol. 2, 954.
60 Ibid., Vol. 1, p. 48.
61 An exception here is the phenomenon of secret groups and societies, especially in the eighteenth and twentieth centuries. See, for example, Van Dülmen, *Der Geheimbund der Illuminaten*, on the Enlightenment-minded secret order of Illumitati; Kosseleck, *Critique and Crisis*, on eighteenth-century freemasonry; Johnson, 'Secretism and the Apotheosis of Duvalier'; and also, Johnson, *Secrets, Gossip, and Gods*, for insightful discussions on the notion of 'secretism' in twentieth-century South America.
62 Jütte, *The Age of Secrecy*, 98.
63 Bok, Secrets, 5; Simmel, 'The Sociology of Secrecy and Secret Societies', 449.
64 Bellman, 'The Paradox of Secrecy', 2.

65 On social theorisations of secrecy, see Simmel, 'The Sociology of Secrecy'.
66 Ibid., 464.
67 Bellman, 'The Paradox of Secrecy', 8.
68 On the social link between secrecy and group identity, see Ibid.
69 Herman, *Intelligence Power in Peace and War*, 329–330.
70 Canetti, *Crowds and Power*, 290–297. See also Costas and Grey, *Secrecy at* Work, 21–22.
71 Ibid., 7.
72 Jütte, *The Age of Secrecy*, 10.
73 For a useful overview of this type of literature, see Ferguson, *Bibliographical Notes*.
74 Eamon, *Science and the Secrets of Nature*; Jütte, *The Age of Secrecy*.
75 Pesic, 'Secrets, Symbols, and Systems', 19–20, 56–57.
76 On the emergence of the patent system in Renaissance Venice, see Hulme, 'History of the Patent System'. On a revisionist view, see Sichelman and O'Connor, 'Patents as Promoters of Competition'.
77 Weber, *Economy and Society*, Vol. 2, 958.

Bibliography

Antonini, Fabio. 'Historical Uses of the Secret Chancery in Early Modern Venice: Archiving, Researching and Presenting the Records of State.' Unpublished Ph.D thesis, Birkbeck College, University of London, 2016.
Bellman, Beryl L. 'The Paradox of Secrecy', *Human Studies* 4 (1981): 1–24.
Bertelè, Tommaso. *Il palazzo degli ambasciatori di Costantinopoli a Venezia*. Bologna: Apollo, 1932.
Bethencourt, Francisco; Egmond, Florike eds. *Correspondence and Cultural Exchange in Europe, 1400–1700*. Vol. 3 of Muchembled, Robert; Monter, William eds. *Cultural Exchange in Early Modern Europe*. Cambridge: Cambridge University Press, 2007.
Bok, Sissela. *Secrets: On the Ethics of Concealment and Revelation*. New York: Vintage, 1989.
Boutier, Jean; Landi, Sandro; Rouchon, Oliovier. *La politique par correspondence: Les usages politiques de la lettre en Italie (XIVe-XVIIIe siècle)*. Rennes: Presses Universitaires de Rennes, 2009.
Canetti, Elias. *Crowds and Power*. Trans. Stuart, Carol. New York: Continuum, 1981.
Coco, Carla; Manzonetto, Flora. *Baili veneziani alla Sublime Porta: Storia e caratteristiche dell' ambasciata veneta a Constantinopoli*. Venice: Stamperia di Venezia, 1985.
Costas, Jana; Grey, Christopher. *Secrecy at Work: The Hidden Architecture of Organizational Life*. Stanford, CA: Stanford University Press, 2016.
Cozzi, Gaetano. 'Authority and the Law.' In Hale, John R. ed. *Renaissance Venice*. London: Faber & Faber, 1973, pp. 293–345.
Cummings, Stephen; Bridgman, Todd; Hassard, John; Rowlinson, Michael. *A New History of Management*. Cambridge: Cambridge University Press, 2017.
Cummings, Stephen; Bridgman, Todd. 'The Relevant Past: Why the History of Management Should Be Critical for our Future.' *Academy of Management, Learning and Education* 10, no. 1 (2011): 77–93.
De Vivo, Filippo. 'Cœur de l'Etat, Lieu de Tensión: le Tournant Archivistique vu de Venise (XVe-XVIIe Siècle).' *Annales. Histoire, Sciences Sociales* 68, no. 3 (2013): 699–728.
De Vivo, Filippo. 'Ordering the Archive in Early Modern Venice (1400–1650).' *Archival Science* 10, no. 3 (2010): 231–248.
De Vivo, Filippo. *Information and Communication in Venice: Rethinking Early Modern Politics*. Oxford: Oxford University Press, 2009.

Dursteler, Eric R. 'The Bailo in Constantinople: Crisis and Career in Venice's Early Modern Diplomatic Corps.' *Mediterranean Historical Review* 16, no. 2 (2001): 1–30.
Eamon, William. *Science and the Secrets of Nature: Books of Secrets in Medieval and Early Modern Culture.* Princeton, NJ: Princeton University Press, 1994.
Finlay, Roberts. *Politics in Renaissance Venice.* London: Ernst Benn, 1980.
Ferguson, John. *Bibliographical Notes on Histories of Inventions and Books of Secrets.* Glasgow: Glasgow University Press, 1883.
Gürkan, Emrah Safa. 'Laying Hands on *Arcana Imperii*: Venetian Baili as Spymasters in Sixteenth-Century Istanbul.' In Maddrell, Paul; Moran, Christopher; Iordanou, Ioanna; Stout, Mark eds. *Spy Chiefs Volume II: Intelligence Leaders in the Europe, the Middle East, and Asia.* Washington, DC: Georgetown University Press, 2018, pp. 67–96.
Hanß, Stefan. 'Baili and Ambassadors.' In Pedani, Maria Pia ed. *Il Palazzo di Venezia a Istanbul e i suoi antichi abitanti / İstanbul'daki Venedik Sarayı ve Eski Yaşayanları.* Venice: Edizioni Ca' Foscari, 2013, pp. 35–52.
Herman, Michael. *Intelligence Power in Peace and War.* Cambridge: Cambridge University Press, 1996.
Hulme, Edward Wydham. 'History of the Patent System under the Prerogative of the Common Law.' *Law Quarterly Review* 12 (1896): 141–154.
Hyde, John Kenneth. 'The Role of Diplomatic Correspondence and Reporting.' In Waley, Daniel Philip ed. *Literacy and its Uses: Studies on Late Medieval Italy.* Manchester: Manchester University Press, 1993, pp. 217–259.
Iordanou, Ioanna. *Venice's Secret Service: Organizing Intelligence in the Renaissance.* Oxford: Oxford University Press, 2019.
Iordanou, Ioanna. 'The Professionalization of Cryptology in Sixteenth Century Venice.' *Enterprise and Society* 19, no. 4 (2018): 979–1013.
Iordanou, Ioanna. 'The Spy Chiefs of Renaissance Venice: Intelligence Leadership in the Early Modern World.' In Maddrell, Paul; Moran, Christopher; Iordanou, Ioanna; Stout, Mark eds. *Spy Chiefs Volume II: Intelligence Leaders in the Europe, the Middle East, and Asia.* Washington, DC: Georgetown University Press, 2018, pp. 43–66.
Iordanou, Ioanna. 'What News on the Rialto? The Trade of Information and the Early Modern Venice's Centralised Intelligence Organisation.' *Intelligence and National Security* 31, no. 3 (2016): 305–326.
Johnson, Paul C. 'Secretism and the Apotheosis of Duvalier.' *Journal of the American Academy of Religion* 74, no. 2 (2006): 420–445.
Johnson, Paul C. *Secrets, Gossip, and Gods: The Transformation of Brazilian Candomblé.* New York: Oxford University Press, 2002.
Jütte, Daniel. *The Age of Secrecy: Jews, Christians, and the Economy of Secrets, 1400–1800.* Trans. Riemer, Jeremiah. New Haven, CT: Yale University Press, 2015.
Kahn, David. *The Codebreakers: The Story of Secret Writing.* London: Weidenfeld and Nicolson, 1966.
Kosseleck, Reinhardt. *Critique and Crisis: Enlightenment and the Pathogenesis of Modern Society.* Cambridge: MIT Press, 1988.
Lanaro, Paola ed. *At the Centre of the Old World: Trade and Manufacturing in Venice and on the Venetian Mainland (1400–1800).* Toronto: Centre for Reformation and Renaissance Studies, 2006.
Lane, Frederic. *Venice: A Maritime Republic.* Baltimore, MD: Johns Hopkins University Press, 1973.
Lazari, Vincenzo. 'Cenni intorno alle legazioni venete alla porta ottomana nel secolo XVI.' In Albèri, Eugenio ed. *Relazioni degli Ambasciatori Veneti al Senato*, Series III. Vol. III. Florence: Società Editrice Fiorentina, 1855, pp. xiii–xx.

Lazzarini, Isabella. *Communication and Conflict: Italian Diplomacy in the Early Renaissance, 1350–1520*. Oxford: Oxford University Press, 2015.

Lazzarini, Isabella. 'Renaissance Diplomacy.' In Gamberini, Andrea; Lazzarini, Isabella eds. *The Italian Renaissance State*. Cambridge: Cambridge University Press, 2012, pp. 425–443.

Lonardi, Simone. 'L'anima dei governi. Politica, spionaggio e segreto di stato a Venezia nel secondo Seicento (1645–1699).' Unpublished Ph.D thesis, University of Padua, 2015.

Luzzatto, Gino. *Storia economica di Venezia dall'XI al XVI secolo*. Venice: Centro Internazionale delle Arti e del Costume, 1961.

Macchi, Mauro. *Storia del Consiglio dei Dieci*. Milan: G. Daelli, 1864.

Maranini, Giuseppe. *La costituzione di Venezia dopo la serrata del Maggior Consiglio*. Venice: La Nuova Italia Editrice, 1931.

Mattingly, Garrett. *Renaissance Diplomacy*. London: Jonathan Cape, 1955.

Pesic, Peter. 'Secrets, Symbols, and Systems: Parallels between Cryptanalysis and Algebra, 1580–1700.' *Isis* 88, no. 4 (1997): 674–692.

Preto, Paolo. 'Le relazioni dei baili a Constantinopoli.' *Il Veltro* 23 (1979): 125–130.

Romanin, Samuele. *Storia documentata di Venezia*. Vol. VI. Venice: Pietro Naratovich, 1857.

Ruef, Martin; Harness, Alona. 'Agrarian Origins of Management Ideology: The Roman and Antebellum Cases.' *Organization Studies* 30, no. 6 (2009): 589–607.

Schneider, Gary. *The Culture of Epistolarity: Vernacular Letters and Letter Writing in Early Modern England, 1500–1700*. Newark: University of Delaware Press, 2005.

Sichelman, Ted; O'Connor, Sean. 'Patents as Promoters of Competition: The Guild Origin of Patent Law in the Venetian Republic.' *San Diego Law Review* 49, no. 129 (2012): 1267–1282.

Simmel, Georg. 'The Sociology of Secrecy and Secret Societies.' *American Journal of Sociology* 11, no. 4 (1906): 441–498. Trans. Small, Albion.

Van Dülmen, Richard. *Der Geheimbund der Illuminaten: Darstellung, Analyse, Dokumentation*. Stuttgart-Bad Cannstatt: Fromann, 1975.

Viggiano, Alfredo. 'Politics and Constitution.' In Dursteler, Eric R. ed. *A Companion to Venetian History, 1400–1797*. Leiden and Boston, MA: Brill, 2013, pp. 47–84.

Walker, Jonathan; De Vivo, Filippo; Shaw, James. 'A Dialogue on Spying in 17th Century Venice.' *Rethinking History: The Journal of Theory and Practice* 10, no. 3 (2006): 323–344.

Weber, Max. *Economy and Society: Outline of Interpretive Sociology*. Vol. 1. Ed. Roth, Guenther; Wittich, Claus. Berkeley: University of California Press, 1978.

Weber, Max. *Economy and Society: Outline of Interpretive Sociology*. Vol. 2. Ed. Roth, Guenther; Wittich, Claus. Berkeley: University of California Press, 1978.

Zannini, Andrea. 'Economic and Social Aspects of the Crisis of Venetian Diplomacy in the Seventeenth and Eighteenth Centuries.' In Frigo, Daniela ed. *Politics and Diplomacy in Early Modern Italy: The Structure of Diplomatic Practice, 1450–1800*. Cambridge: Cambridge University Press, 2000, pp. 109–146.

PART 4
Disciplining

8
RISKING PRIVATE VENTURES

The Instructive Failure of a Well-Traveled Artist, Cornelis de Bruyn

Harold J. Cook

In the first decade of the eighteenth century, an artist and traveler, Cornelius de Bruyn,[1] arranged to undertake a private knowledge-gathering expedition through Russia and Persia and on to the Dutch East Indies. By acquiring accurate information of exotic places associated with contemporary Dutch geopolitical interests, preferably of the tangible and picturable varieties that could be conveyed on paper, De Bruyn expected to further his fame and fortune. His success, however, depended on his reputation for precise description. The patricians who governed the decentralized Dutch Republic, some of whom also participated in the international Republic of Letters, sought accurate information for profit and power as well as for edification and pleasure. The ideals of their community aimed to let nature speak for itself as reported by unembellished words and images. But representations of the world can differ, and shortly after De Bruyn returned and printed an illustrated book, its pictorial faithfulness was compared with other recent images and doubted. In the circumstances, he could not appeal to a formal body to prove the truth of his version of Persepolis; he could only appeal to individual persons. So he resorted to publishing a detailed comparison of his work vis-à-vis those of his rivals to show his superior accuracy. It may have been impolitic to argue for correctness in every detail, but what else could he do to save his reputation? The effort did not save him. Despite years of hard traveling and careful work, De Bruyn's fortune declined: he went bankrupt and died in obscurity. We do not even know with certainty the date of his death.

De Bruyn's failure is instructive. He made strenuous efforts to disentangle the physically real from speculation and imagination, which points to the high value the leading members of the Dutch Republic placed on acquiring accurate information. In defending their polities and profits, the *regenten* faced enormous pressures from adversaries – at the time, especially from France – requiring them to be efficient in identifying the impersonal facts at issue as a groundwork for the collective negotiations necessary to determine what courses of action to take.[2] Those daily disciplines also encouraged curiosity and accuracy in leisure activities, with many of the *regenten* identifying themselves as *liefhebbers*: lovers of things and knowledge about things, the kind of people elsewhere called *virtuosi*.[3] In describing worldly objects, they gave pride of place to careful description. Put another way, in the objective mode, images were meant to depict physical things rather than meaningful abstractions.[4] Not only did the Royal Society of London chose for its motto *nullius in verba* ('take the word of no one') but artists like De Bruyn were enjoined to draw 'from life' (*ad vivem* or *naar het leven*), a phrase he placed on the title page of his finished work: 'All depicted *from life* by the author himself with great accuracy, and never before brought to light.'[5] The last phrase reminds that he also presented himself as cultivating curiosity (*nieusgierigheid*), being a person with a nose for uncovering new things.[6] For instance, when staying at the country house of a Dutch merchant in Russia, he spotted several sorts of unusual turnips and set about painting them in watercolor; when he showed the painting shortly afterward, however, his audience 'would not believe that they were done after Nature, till I produced the very Turnips; a Sign that they are not curious there about such things.'[7] In implied contrast, of course, his own curiosity had been fine-tuned. Careful illustration of an object by someone trained like himself counted as a proof of real existence.

When his reputation was later threatened, De Bruyn therefore stood his ground by insisting on his studied ability to depict things accurately and without embellishment. The facts as De Bruyn knew them were meant to be both tangible and picturable, true no matter the time or place in which they were first encountered or later contemplated. They were mobile because they were impersonal. But disentangling real nature from the embellishments of others without a formal refereeing process proved to yield uncertain results. His example illuminates the strengths and weaknesses of the relatively free and decentralized political economy of the Republics to which he belonged: the Dutch Republic and the Republic of Letters.

Visual Reportage

De Bruyn has been carefully studied in recent years.[8] His two most important publications were commercial ventures, the first of which was a success, the second a loss for the author in more ways than one. The first, the richly illustrated *Reizen door Klein Asia* (*Travels through the Near East*), printed in Dutch in 1698 and in French in 1700 – containing eye-opening engravings of the pyramids and Sphinx near Cairo and the holy sites of Jerusalem – had been composed as a kind of afterthought from his nearly two decades of travel. The project was a kind of accident resulting from his ambition to become an accomplished painter of histories (the most highly regarded genre of the time). De Bruyn had first apprenticed with Theodoor van der Schuer, a court painter from his native city of Den Haag, but after the disastrous French invasion of his homeland in 1672 he traveled to Rome, where he joined the community of artists from the Low Countries known as the Bentvogels. There he could study classical architecture and sculpture. Since most of the biblical, mythical, and ancient scenes admired by buyers were set in the Mediterranean, he found an opportunity to travel along trading routes into the Ottoman Near East (1678–1684), where he carefully recorded cityscapes, ancient monuments, and the enormous variety of costumes found in the city and court. De Bruyn's audience found his images of modes of dress to be of great help in visualizing the multiple world cultures of the time.[9] Between 1684 and 1692, he put his knowledge to work in the Venetian studio of Johann Carl Loth, who was much admired for his life-like paintings of past events.[10]

After nearly twenty years abroad, De Bruyn returned to the Dutch Republic, bringing along antiques and visual studies of the Eastern Mediterranean, which he sold to collectors. It was not, however, an auspicious time to set up as a history painter, especially without established contacts among potential patrons. The Prince of Orange had recently also become King of England, and he and Mary II were refurbishing Hampton Court palace rather than extending Het Loo or other Dutch residences. At the same time, the Nine Years' War against France was going badly for William III in the southern Low Countries and the resulting high taxes were squeezing everyone. De Bruyn nevertheless found a way to capitalize on his experiences by assembling what he knew into an impressive book containing over 200 copper plate engravings. The project attracted 624 subscribers who promised to buy 1,330 copies (of an initial print run of 3,000 or 4,000).[11] Many of its written descriptions of the places he had visited in the Near East were supplemented with passages lifted from other well-regarded travel accounts, but the images were from his own hand, depicting details not previously represented.[12] De Bruyn also demonstrated his innovative energies and expertise: at least one copy of the Dutch edition and one of the subsequent French edition appeared using a new method for color printing invented by Johannes Teyler. Because of the labor and expense of publishing the plates in color, they were presumably produced to signal the work's importance and possibly to advertise it to eminent persons.[13] It brought De Bruyn a fine reputation.

The book presented De Bruyn as an especially observant visual artist. Even his depiction of a place he was unable to visit himself boasted of exacting scrutiny: Palmyra. Because of a successful English expedition to the site in 1691, many previously unknown details had come to light, and in the mid-1690s the Royal Society of London published accounts of the findings along with a view of the ruins. Given the excitement about new information on a place thought to have been founded by King Solomon, De Bruyn could hardly publish on the Near East without an account of 'Tamor' (or in English, 'Tadmor'). As he later explained, however, when he was in Aleppo (during 1682 and 1683) he could not reach the city because an earlier group attempt had failed miserably.[14] But while working on his book, he had become acquainted with one of the most eminent antiquarians of the period, Gisbert Cuper, who through his own informant in

Aleppo, Dutch consul Coenraad Calckberner, had been sent not only copies of the English accounts of the recent venture but a painting of the ruins. The latter was depicted on a four meters wide wood panel by a little-known Dutch artist who had been in the Ottoman lands for some time, Hofsted van Essen. On the basis of that painting or a common original, an engraving of the remains of the ruins appeared with the reports of the expedition's findings in the *Philosophical Transactions of the Royal Society* in 1695 (Figure 8.1).[15] Based on Cuper's work, De Bruyn was able to publish both a Dutch translation of the English report and a corrected version of the engraving:

> the same has been improved by me, through a small addition, to wit, from a piece of a round porphery column, lying on the ground, beside the six standing columns, which are shown in the middle of the print, depicted in the foreground, indicated by the letter G.[16]

The additional detail in De Bruyn's engraving was an advertisement for his sharp eye. He explained that 'despite my never having set foot here,' he had been able to make the correction because he has seen the painting made 'from life' by his compatriot. He further noted that the original painting had recently been

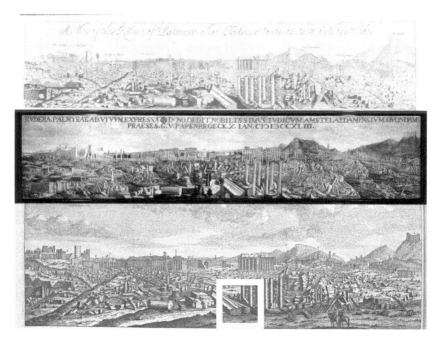

FIGURE 8.1   Three views of Palmyra. Top, from *Philosophical Transactions*, 19 (1695), p. 129; middle, Hofsted van Essen's oil on wood panel, Allard Pierson Museum, Amsterdam; bottom, Cornelis de Bruyn, *Reizen I*, p. 335, with base of fallen column (item G) highlighted.

brought to Amsterdam by a young man named 'Heer' Henrico Lub; perhaps they had become friends when both were in Aleppo, since many years later, De Bruyn resided with Lub near Haarlem.[17] Despite not having been there himself, then, it was De Bruyn's engraving of Palmyra that was chosen for Bernard de Montfaucon's five-volume encyclopaedia, where De Bruyn was declared 'one of the most accurate Travelers of that time.'[18]

The success of De Bruyn's *Reizen door Klein Asia* therefore depended on contemporary enthusiasm among the *liefhebbers* for objectivity as well as novelty: objects carefully studied, handled, described, and depicted. He decided to capitalize on his abilities. As De Bruyn later explained: 'the care I had taken, upon my return, to consult with men of learning and curiosity, persuaded me I might possibly make discoveries of greater importance than I had been able to make in my former travels.'[19] He therefore decided to embark on an even more ambitious project along the same lines, this time with deliberate preparation.

As De Bruyn looked around him for other places where he could profit from observations made with a fresh eye, he understandably settled on Russia and Persia. In the period when he was getting his first book ready for the publisher, Tsar Peter the Great himself was spending most of the year of 1696 in Amsterdam, stirring up great excitement; and at the time Dutch interests in Russia also connected with Persia, both of which were adversaries of the Ottomans, who were, in turn, mainly aligned with France. De Bruyn would therefore choose to record the people, places, and things on the borderlands between Europe and Asia.

Perhaps, however, we should consider De Bruyn to have been a kind of personal representative of one of the most powerful figures in the Dutch Republic, Nicolaes Witsen. Witsen had earlier developed an acquaintance with the Tsar and acted as one of his hosts in Amsterdam. He was also a director of the Dutch East India Company (VOC) and many times burgomaster of Amsterdam, sat as a member of the national States General, and acted as a diplomat, while also being an author and collector: he had purchased at least twenty-four of De Bruyn's paintings of costumes of the Ottoman court, subscribed for seven copies of the book, and kept up a friendship with Cuper, who was at that moment helping De Bruyn with information about Palmyra.[20] Some decades earlier, Witsen's father had arranged for drawings to be made during a diplomatic mission to China, which that resulted in a richly illustrated book that helped to inspire the chinoiserie of period, and the younger Witsen continued to be eager for visual evidence of people, places, and objects.[21] He would arrange for passports and letters of introduction in Russia for De Bruyn.[22] Since De Bruyn was also welcomed to Isfahan by an officer of the company of which Witsen was a director, the VOC, the second half of his journey might also be said to have been under his aegis.

Witsen's interests in the world beyond Europe were deep, and his curiosity about what was then called Tartary – all the lands east of Moscow and north of the Himalayas and China – led to active efforts to acquire information.[23] Witsen's family had been involved in commerce with Russia, so in the mid-1660s, shortly after taking his law degree, he took part in a diplomatic mission to Moscow that was seeking new trading privileges.[24] Although the outcome was unsuccessful, he took a keen interest in the Muscovites and not only made several well-placed friends – most importantly, Peter's tutor and advisor, Andrej Winius – but retained a strong and well-informed personal interest in Russia from then on.[25] As Peter came of age, Witsen sent him a copy of his book on shipbuilding (of 1671) while also acting as the Tsar's intermediary in overseeing the commissioning of a personal warship – a galleon – at Amsterdam in 1693.[26] When the Tsar arrived in Amsterdam, it was Witsen who arranged for him to work in the VOC dockyards 'incognito.' He also introduced Peter to many of the local *liefhebbers* and their collections of objects.

For Dutch officials like Witsen, good relations with Russia were important for both commercial and geopolitical reasons. Witsen sought out and kept track of information about Russian territories east of Moscow by placing them on a map he developed (apparently drawing on copies of manuscript maps of Siberia originally made by Semyon Ulianovich Remezov).[27] An early version was sent to the Royal Society of London, eliciting praise from its president for being 'Columbus like, the Discovery of a New World; ... For it looks in one Part no less difficult, than a Geographical Description of the Bottom of the Sea.'[28] In 1690, as Witsen readied the map for publication, he wrote to both the young Tsars about it; its six large sheets appeared a year later (with a second edition in 1705).[29] A fuller description in word and image of what he had found was published in Witsen's book, *Noord en Oost Tartarye* (*North and East Tartary*), first appearing in 1692 but mainly circulating in the edition of 1705.[30]

Equally important, recent events in Russia also promised to open up trade routes to Persia and China. The Dutch commanded most of the trade from Russia to Europe via its one seaport at Archangel. The Russia trade included not only furs, caviar, and other local products, but also merchandise from Persia, including silk. Partly because of the links to Persia, the Russian connection grew into one of the most lucrative 'rich trades' in the hands of Dutch merchants, and booksellers found avid readers for accurate reports of the region.[31] Moreover, with the expansion of Russia through Siberia to the Pacific, hopes also grew that Dutch commerce with China could also be established via Archangel. Witsen was corresponding with Tsar Peter about such a trade route by 1693, no doubt as a part of his work with a German merchant, Evert Ysbrants Ides, who from 1692 to 1695 led a trade embassy from Moscow to Peking.[32] Originally from Glückstadt, Ides had become one of the chief foreign merchants in Moscow and also hoped for direct trade with China. The embassy included a large party of merchants and armed guards as well as an artist, and it proved to be a great financial success for Ides.[33] While news of the outcome was circulating almost immediately, the narrative Ides produced (with only a few illustrations, the artist having died on the journey) first appeared only in 1704 in a large folio edition in Dutch, to which was added a description of China written about 1674 by one 'Dionysius Kao.' One suspects that one of Witsen's Russian associates brought Ides's account along with the Tsar on his visit to Amsterdam at the end of the

1690s and that Witsen arranged for its translation and publication. In any case, Ides thanked Witsen publicly for an early version of Witsen's map, which 'I made use of as a Guide throughout my Journey.'[34] He revised it as he went, resulting in a new map printed with Ides's book.

Moreover, a recent and intriguing voyage of another German, Engelbert Kaempfer, was also well known to Witsen and probably provided the example for the route taken by De Bruyn. Kaempfer had first settled in Sweden and then was recruited for service on a royal embassy that was seeking to establish trade with Persia.[35] Beginning in 1683, the Swedish embassy traveled via Moscow and the Volga to the Caspian Sea and on to Isfahan. There, Kaempfer met Herbert de Jager, who had become a client of Witsen's within the VOC because of his talent for Oriental languages.[36] Kaempfer and De Jager together made a short side-trip to the ancient ruin of Persepolis. When diplomatic negotiations bogged down, Kaempfer took a position as a surgeon with the VOC, and no doubt at De Jager's urging wrote to Witsen about what he had seen, hoping for patronage; he then traveled to Japan and other Asian destinations. When he finally resigned from the VOC, in Amsterdam, he enrolled at the university in Leiden and presented a medical thesis about the medical practices and curiosities he had observed, for which he obtained a medical doctorate in April 1694, promptly presenting a copy of his work to Witsen.[37] That, in turn, probably induced Witsen to pass on to an English acquaintance a drawing of Persepolis made by De Jager, which was published by the Royal Society.[38] De Bruyn would take almost the identical route to Kaempfer's (although not going on to East Asia). It must have been on the basis of what he learned from Kaempfer and De Jager that Witsen gave written instructions to De Bruyn for his own journey, drawing special attention to making accurate drawings of the little-known Persepolis (Figure 8.2).[39]

But Witsen was not only interested in commerce, costume, and antiquities, he was also interested in natural history. De Bruyn therefore trained himself for the gathering of specimens. The subject was at the time a kind of obsession

FIGURE 8.2 Herbert de Jager's portrayal of Persepolis in *Philosophical Transactions*, 18 (1694), p. 117. Gate of All Nations depicted on right.

among the *liefhebbers*, many of whom had impressive gardens and collections. Witsen introduced the Tsar to many of them, and on his second visit to The Netherlands in 1716–1717, Peter made a point of seeking to purchase the most important for his own museum in St. Petersburg, including the cabinets of Levinius Vincent, Albert Seba, and Frederick Ruysch.[40] De Bruyn was therefore following in the footsteps of people like yet another traveler, artist, and sometime client of Witsen's, Maria Sibylla Merian. An accomplished artist with considerable knowledge of insects and botany, she had visited Witsen's personal collections as well as other fabulous cabinets and took particular notice of the remarkably beautiful butterflies that came from the Dutch settlements in Surinam. Undoubtedly with Witsen's help, she managed to obtain an unusual grant from the city of Amsterdam to help support the travel of herself and her daughter from 1699 to 1701 to the Dutch colony in South America in order to study its natural history, giving special attention to the insects.[41] Just about the time that De Bruyn left for Russia, Merian returned to Amsterdam with specimens and paintings of previously unknown plants and insects, creating quite a stir among collectors. She sold many of the objects, while she and her daughters later worked on turning the illustrations into *Metamorphosis insectorum Suranamensium*, published in Latin and Dutch in 1705. They acted as publishers, working with a printer and selling the copies privately to keep the profits in their own hands. So would De Bruyn.[42]

'Elated' by his first success among *liefhebbers* like Witsen, therefore, De Bruyn added new kinds of expertise to the repertoire of his investigative methods. As he would later write, he 'carefully visited and examined several collections of rarities, and learned how to keep all sorts of birds, beasts and fishes in spirits, and to prepare them so as to bring them home without decaying.' He also resolved 'to paint after the life many productions of the sea, as well as flowers, plants, fruits and the like.' But while these were important additional arrows in his quiver, he remained focused on the antiquarian studies of distant places that had dominated his first book.[43]

The Risks of a Private Scientific Expedition

De Bruyn aimed to capitalize on the visual interests of the *liefhebbers*, but to do so he had decided on something quite unusual: a private scientific expedition. It might bring additional fame and fortune but it carried risks, and not only ones related to the difficulties of the journey. To imagine that a private scientific venture could be financially successful was possible only because of the exceptional information economy of the Dutch *regenten* and *liefhebbers*, where collectors were rapidly expanding their holdings and almost every year a large, illustrated folio volume on natural history was published. But even in the Republic, a purposely designed private and self-supporting venture for the acquisition of new images and objects was unknown, the pioneering effort of Merian having not yet been brought to a conclusion.[44] Other expeditions in the period were supported by governments or princes, like Ides's diplomatic mission to Peking or by employment in a trading company, as with Kaempfer's travels in South and East Asia, or by private commerce, as with Jean-Baptiste Tavernier, a French gem merchant who traveled for both adventure and wealth. Publication afterward was a kind of side-line. Some decades later, Carl Linnaeus would encourage his students to undertake private travel for the sake of science, although his own trip to Lapland in 1732 was underwritten by the Royal Swedish Academy of Literature and Science in Uppsala. De Bruyn had recommendations and instructions from Witsen, and possibly from others, but there is no evidence of people like them underwriting the venture.[45] His plan therefore suggests that around 1700, it was for the first time possible to imagine succeeding in a private venture deliberately undertaken to searching out objects and accurate representations of the world.

De Bruyn left The Hague on 28 July 1701, and on 2 August was in the North Sea headed for Archangel, where he arrived at the end of the month. From then on, he mentions spending time with merchants, officials, and princely figures, and traveling along well-established trade routes. Once the weather changed, he journeyed by sled to Moscow (arriving on 4 January 1702) and conversed with Tsar Peter in Dutch; after moving about with the court for over a year, in mid-April 1703, with the permission of Peter he traveled to the Volga and down to Astrakhan in the company of Armenian merchants (at least one of whom had spent time in Amsterdam and spoke Dutch) and then (from 12 July) over the Caspian Sea to the Persian cities of Qom and Isfahan (arriving in mid-December). There he resided for a prolonged period in the Armenian caravanserai of New Julfa, although he also sometimes attended the Shah's court to paint members of it.[46] From 26 October 1704 to 27 January 1705, he made a side-trip to record the ruins of Persepolis, as Witsen had requested, living on site for several weeks in order to take measurements, to draw everything accurately, and to collect a stone relief and other fragments (Figure 8.3). Finally, in July 1705, he headed from Isfahan to Gamron on the Persian Gulf and took ship with the VOC for Ceylon and the capital of the Dutch East Indies, Batavia (now Jakarta), which he reached in March 1706. Given a war for the throne of Mataram that was then in progress, he could not travel around Java widely, and De Bruyn was now suffering from several problems with his health as well. He decided not go on to the Coromandel coast of India or other parts of VOC East Asia. After a half year spent as the guest of the Governor General Joan van Hoorn (whose portrait he painted), he decided to head back to Amsterdam. Given French action against Dutch shipping due to the War of Spanish Succession, he sent back his baggage by a VOC ship but himself set out for home on 25 August 1706 by the same route he had come. Although he was caught up in the Great Northern War and almost lost his life in 1708 when a Swedish army blocked his planned route through the Baltic, he arrived in Amsterdam via Archangel in October 1708, a little more than seven years after his departure.

FIGURE 8.3 Cornelis de Bruyn, first view of Persepolis from *Reizen II*.

Once back in the Dutch Republic, De Bruyn set up his cabinet in Amsterdam, having collected shells, bottles containing preserved animal specimens, and ancient relics as well as drawings and paintings, all of which were for sale to visitors. When in March 1711 Zacharias Conrad von Uffenbach visited De Bruyn – whom he described as more 'courtly' in appearance than 'curious' – he was disappointed that most of the collections had already been sold.[47] De Bruyn also began the effort of writing and engraving a book about his findings, an ambitious folio-sized work with hundreds of images. He was no doubt in close contact with Witsen about its contents, since in the book he inserted a section lifted from the book by Ides on Siberia along with further comments by Witsen on why the Arctic sea could not be navigated further east, as had been hoped, due to the ice.[48] We know that De Bruyn was also communicating with Cuper on antiquities, particularly asking about whether the cuneiform inscriptions at Persepolis (which he had carefully recorded) could be translated. For that part of the project he also worked with a certain H. Praetorius of Haarlem, who wrote the chapters in the book that discussed Persepolis from the available evidence of ancient literature.[49] De Bruyn contracted with Willem and David Goeree for printing 1,000 copies of the work, which he intended to sell privately. As advertised on the title page, his book contained over 300 engravings, many of them large foldouts, making it one of the most richly illustrated works of the era. (Merian's famous book, by contrast, contained a mere sixty plates.) It was published in 1711, dedicated to the owner of a famous cabinet, Anton Ulrich, Duke of Brunswick-Wolfenbüttel.

De Bruyn organized his book as a kind of travelogue, but one clearly aiming at an unvarnished record of things and events. Ides, too, had explained that 'solely aiming at Truth, we have represented her naked, without any Hyperbolical or Ornamental Illustrations to render her the more agreeable and surprising.'[50] De Bruyn echoed the sentiment by declaring, 'I have made it an indispensible Law to myself, not to deviate in any respect from the Truth, merely to give an ornamental Air to this Work.' Instead, he promised 'that nothing will be found here, but what I have seen with my own Eyes, and have examined with the utmost Attention and Care' and that 'there are no Facts but what are related with the strictest Veracity.' Moreover, 'I have drawn with my own hand, and immediately from the Life, all the Plates now presented to the Public.'[51] Unembellished eyewitness accounts, in simple words and clear lines, were the marks of truth.

But the project did not bring him riches. Instead, he soon found himself in financial difficulty. Since his return, he had been moving from house to house, staying with acquaintances. Now, despite a good notice or two – the *Republyk der Geleerden* noted that he needed no introduction to its readers – the book sold only 240 copies in three years. Part of the reason must be that it was expensive and that De Bruyn had published it as a private venture without the connections necessary to generate the kind of publicity that would make the booksellers eager. In May 1714, he was forced to auction off the remaining unsold copies and their copper plates along with the unsold copies of the French edition of his first book. Hendrik Wetstein handled the auction and his sons Gerard and Rudolph Wetstein bought up the property and then, in combination with two other booksellers, slipped in new title pages and sold the copies for a profit.[52] In 1718, they also produced a French edition of the second book, and in 1720 a three-volume edition of both of De Bruyn's voyages appeared in London, and an English edition in two volumes (bound together in the copies I have seen) was brought out in 1737.[53] In other words, once the publishers became the chief vehicles for printing and distribution, with their understanding of the market and their international contacts, the book did well despite its cost. Nevertheless, the book remained expensive, for that reason causing one author to lift a large extract from De Bruyn's travels and add it to a work about Russia for the benefit of ordinary readers who would otherwise not know it.[54] Jacob Campo Weyerman, not always a faithful reporter, later wrote that De Bruyn himself had been driven to live in a tiny house in Vianen, a 'free city' whose separate jurisdiction made it a refuge for criminals and bankrupts. He later lived from the hospitality of an old friend, David van Mollem, a wealthy silk manufacturer who owned an estate with a magnificent garden on de Vecht outside of Utrecht.[55]

Perhaps another reason why his books did not sell was the fading bloom of Dutch-Russian relations. Witsen remained supportive of Peter, purchasing technology for him such as dredging machines, fire hoses, and printing presses. He also arranged secret supplies of weapons and munitions via Archangel during the Great Northern War, for which he received a personal letter of thanks and a specially made gilded sloop from the Tsar. But the same year (1702) had seen the death of William III, exacerbating frictions in the Anglo-Dutch alliance, and while the English slowly moved towards the side of Sweden, Witsen continued to lobby for Russia in the Dutch States General.[56] More importantly, perhaps with Russia now establishing itself on the shores of the Baltic there was less chance for European merchants to control the internal traffic from China or Persia. In 1715, Peter would even try to stop exports from Archangel in order to drive the trade to the new St. Petersburg.[57] In the circumstances, visual details about Russia and Persia represented in De Bruyn's expensive volume might now be taken to be more curious than important.

For *liefhebbers*, therefore, the book's most signal contribution to knowledge was the depictions of the famous palace at Persepolis; but on that point De Bruyn had even greater misfortune: his reputation for accuracy was questioned. On the heels of his *Reizen over Moskovie*, two other works were published that presented images of Persepolis that were at variance with De Bruyn's. Also in 1711, and from a commercial Amsterdam house, Jean-Baptise Chardin brought out a new and illustrated edition of his *Voyages en Perse et autres lieux de l' Oriént*. 'Sir John' Chardin was a French jeweler who had spent time in Istanbul and Isfahan in the later 1660s through the mid-1670s, later settling in England and gaining a knighthood. A year later, Engelbert Kaempfer's *Amoenitates exoticarum* (Lemgo, 1712) appeared. Although he had only three days on site in the 1680s, Kaempfer had made detailed sketches and taken measurements of the site.[58] Both their illustrations presented the monuments of Persepolis differently than De Bruyn. Where De Bruyn had, for instance, depicted the sphinxes at the Gate of All Lands with missing or partly destroyed faces, Chardin represented them as having lion-like heads (Figures 8.4–8.6).

Questions therefore arose among De Bruyn's patrons about the authenticity of his renderings, weakening their support for his project. Cuper, for instance, had at first been enthusiastic about De Bruyn's reports and illustrations of Persepolis. He had circulated copies of De Bruyn's renderings of cuneiform inscriptions to his learned colleagues around Europe (none of whom could decipher their meaning). But he shared his concerns about the differences between De Bruyn's renderings of Persepolis and Chardin's in a letter of 19 October 1712 to Mathurin Veyssiere de la Croze, librarian to the Elector of Brandenburg and one of the foremost Orientalists. Cuper was soon able to consult Kaempfer's book, too, and he wrote to his friend, Witsen.[59]

Witsen remained firmly supportive of De Bruyn, but without wishing to attack the other two authors nor to upset his long-standing friendship with Cuper. He assured Cuper, for instance, that he knew Kaempfer well and considered him to be a learned and reliable person. He therefore promised to pass the word to De Bruyn that he needed to explain why his own images differed. At the new year, Witsen wrote to Cuper that he had spoken to De Bruyn about his doubts, also enclosing a personal letter from De Bruyn to Cuper.[60] Witsen assured Cuper that De Bruyn had explained the inaccuracies of Chardin's depictions as not being done according to art (*na de konst*) because Chardin had been on site only briefly and had not made the drawings himself. The result was that Chardin made errors (*mismaektheyt*), so that his drawings did not conform to the truth. Witsen himself held De Bruyn to be an expert depicter (*tekenaer*) of

Risking Private Ventures **181**

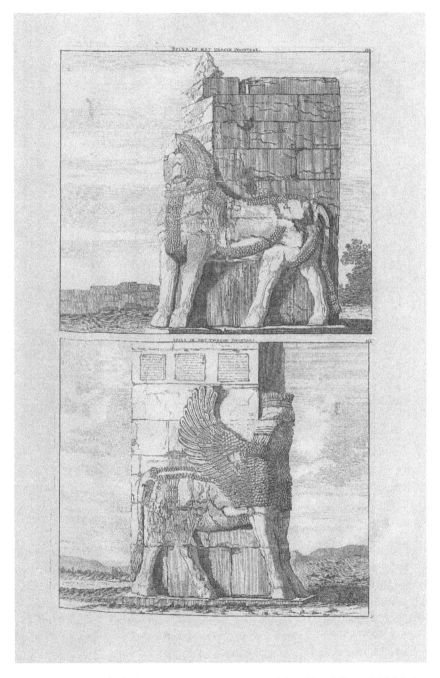

FIGURE 8.4 Cornelis de Bruyn, two monuments on either side of Gate of All Nations, *Reizen II*, plates 122 and 123.

FIGURE 8.5 Jean Chardin, two monuments on either side of Gate of All Nations, *Voyages*, vol. 3, plate LVI.

good character, having known him for many years to be an honest person whose art was his forte. Witsen conceded that people understandably also thought well of Chardin, whom Witsen had also met in person, and he considered Chardin's understanding of Persian culture to be far better than De Bruyn's. But when it came to the drawings, De Bruyn was clearly to be preferred.[61] Cuper initially accepted Witsen's explanations and accepted that the errors (*misgrepen*) were on the part of Chardin and Kaempfer.[62]

By then, Witsen had advised De Bruyn that a direct and robust reply to the doubts being raised was necessary. They met in person, allowing De Bruyn to share his findings. De Bruyn must have felt that he held a winning hand, since by the middle of February he had decided to publish a detailed rebuttal.[63] He

Risking Private Ventures **183**

FIGURE 8.6 Kaempfer, two monuments on either side of Gate of All Nations, *Amoenitatum Exoticarum,* Fasciculus II, p. 337.

also enrolled his friend Praetorius in writing a comparison between what he (Praetorius) had published in De Bruyn's book on the ancient literature about Persepolis and what Chardin and Kaempfer had to say about it. These two detailed replies were then published, and translations of them were later published as an appendix to the English edition of De Bruyn's *Travels*.[64]

Since he had to be careful not to insult well-regarded rivals, De Bruyn's public defense focused on his ability to depict the world without embellishment. He conducted his examination of the other two versions of Persepolis with the 'utmost exactness,' doing so in order to find out 'what has been advanced, either with inconsideration or solidity' by the two authors 'without reflecting in the least on the reputations of those illustrious travellers whose plates and sentiments differ from mine; or pretending to derogate from their merit and learning in any other particular.' He even made excuses for them: Chardin, he stated, had found it necessary to employ 'some mercenary draughtsmen' for the purpose since he 'could not draw himself, as he acknowledges in his writings, and has likewise assured me in conversation,' while his engravers 'have committed egregious errors.' He then went on at length to criticize Chardin's plates in contrast to his own, one after another.[65] He did the same for Kaempfer's book, noting that in its preface, the author apologized for the quality of the engravers 'who succeeded very ill in copying in little, those original designs, which he drew on the spot with all possible exactness.' But since Kaempfer held no knighthood, De Bruyn felt it possible to add that 'It seems very improbable ... that all these faults should be chargeable on the meer negligence, or unskillfulness of the engravers.' In the end, De Bruyn based his case on his own refusal to attempt any reconstruction of what the sculptures might have looked like when they were new. For instance, one image in Kaempfer clearly intended to offer 'a more perfect work' by turning a ruin into an image of a lovely and bejeweled woman, whereas his own rendering of same item included all its defects. The additional document by Praetorius went a step further still, arguing for historical and cultural relativism:

> For my part, I am persuaded, there is no more similitude between the habits of the pagan *Indians* of these days, and those of the ancient *Persians*, than there is between our manner of dress and that of our ancestors.

Others might resort to embellishment and hypothesis but he did not. The final argument from De Bruyn resorted to material evidence: if the reader had further doubts he could seek out the 'entire figure from the rocks of *Persepolis*' that he brought back – the bas-relief had already gone into Witsen's collection – 'together with several other curious pieces' (Figure 8.7).[66]

FIGURE 8.7 De Bruyn, bas-relief, *Reizen II*, plate 142.

The question is still debated.[67] Defenders of De Bruyn write that:

> Photographs of the ruins of Persepolis will show the modern reader at once that De Bruijn was as good as his word. His engravings of Persepolis were certainly by far the most accurate representations that had been made until then.[68]

Or 'Even if he made some minor mistakes ... we now know that his artistic skills and his painter's eye contributed to the best report on Persepolis available to an eighteenth century audience.'[69] But a defender of Kaempfer quotes a visitor to Persepolis from a few decades later, the founder of Assyriology, Carsten Niebuhr, who condemned the 'severity' of De Bruyn's criticism of his competitors. Niebuhr thought that 'It would therefore have been better had he not published his remarks about Chardin and Kaempfer; for in these he often accuses those travellers of errors in order to defend his own faulty drawings.'[70]

Cuper may have taken a similar line, agreeing that De Bruyn was correct but that his vigorous defense was impolite. Chardin had died at the beginning of 1713 and *De mortuis nihil nisi bonum*. Cuper continued to be very eager to make his mark on antiquarian studies in Europe, dominated by the French-language Republic of Letters, and he managed to maintain his own reputation despite his engagement on behalf of the allies during the War of Spanish Succession. In 1715, only months after the war's conclusion, he would be voted a member of prestigious Parisian *Acadèmie des Inscriptions et des Belles Lettres*. Neither he nor Witsen is known to have gone public in support of De Bruyn, nor to have helped him in his financial difficulty. 'Sir John' Chardin held the field.

Conclusions

In Niebuhr's estimation then and probably in Cuper's, De Bruyn was not being politic. In mounting an energetic defense of his own accuracy, De Bruyn could not help but compare his work to that of the others, finding them wanting. But going on the attack in print and insisting on one's own rightness did not comport with polite behavior. Witsen backed De Bruyn privately and Cuper might concede privately that De Bruyn was correct, but that did not turn either into an advocate within the Republic of Letters. Nor did De Bruyn have institutional backing, nor the support of a prince, nor did he have minions to fight battles on his behalf.[71] Although Praetorius acted as his second, his learned friend was almost unknown to the international community of antiquarians. The Dutch Republic had governmental procedures to decide matters of fact when necessary, but the Republic of Letters had no courts of justice. It was up to him alone to defend his reputation, and he was heading for destruction. What Niebuhr's sense of academic generosity overlooked, therefore, was why De Bruyn felt compelled to defend himself: he had been charged with making inaccurate drawings of an ancient monument, and accuracy was the coin of his realm.

De Bruyn had worked hard to disentangle the real from embellishments of human imagination. But no institution existed that could rule on his success in rendering them *naar het leven*. In his final printed words, he pointed to the few tangible proofs available, but they implied his condition: 'I have likewise taken the pains to paint several extraordinary pieces of drapery, both of men and women, which the curious may see at my house, together with a variety of *Indian* fish, fruits, and birds.'[72] It was now 1714 and auctioning off his books and engravings, the capstone of all his labor, loomed on the horizon. De Bruyn still had pictures to sell, but the reward for his exacting efforts would be slight.

Notes

1 I use the spelling 'De Bruyn' rather than the alternative 'De Bruijn,' to be consistent with the usage of the Koninklijke Bibliotheek.
2 't Hart, *Making of a Bourgeois State*; idem, *Dutch Wars of Independence*; Tracy, *Founding of the Dutch Republic*.
3 Jong, Meijers, Westermann, and Woodall, eds., *Virtus*; Cook, *Matters of Exchange*; Hochstrasser, *Still Life and Trade*; Jorink, *Reading the Book of Nature*; Margócsy, *Commercial Visions*.
4 For elaborations of this view of 'objectivity', see Cook, 'Early Modern Science and Monetized Economies.'
5 'Alles door den Auteur zelf met groote naeukeurigheit na 't leven afgetekent, en noit voor dezen in 't ligt gebragt,' which appears at the end of the full title of De Bruyn, *Reizen over Moskovie* (hereafter *Reizen II*); for the phrase 'naar het leven,' Marr, 'Picturing Collections.'
6 Daston, 'Moral Economy'; Ball, *Curiosity*.
7 While I have worked from the original Dutch, for English quotations I have used the contemporary English translation; De Bruyn, *Travels into Muscovy* (hereafter *Travels*), 8.
8 For instance, Drijvers, 'Cornelis De Bruijn'; De Hond, 'Cornelis de Bruijn'; Jurriaans-Helle, Scheepers, Drijvers, Hannema, Sancisi-Weerdenburg, and Gnirrep, *Cornelis de Bruijn*; Jona Lendering, 'Cornelis de Bruijn,' http://www.livius.org/bn-bz/bruijn/cornelis_de_bruijn.html#Holland; Hayden, 'Cornelis De Bruyn.'
9 Most of the surviving drawings ascribed to De Bruyn are studies of people and costumes. They can be found, for example, by searching for his name on the public webpages for the Rjiksmuseum, Teyler's Museum, and similar public institutions. For the importance of costumes, see Hunt, Jacob, and Mijnhardt, *Book That Changed Europe*. The figure of their study, Bernard Picart, was also one of the engravers for De Bruyn's (earlier) *Reizen II*.
10 A dependable summary of his life is De Hond, 'Den Vermaarden Cornelis de Bruyn.'
11 De Bruyn, *Reizen door Klein Asia* (hereafter *Reizen I*), list at the end of the preface to the reader; Drijvers, 'Deez Tekende en Schreef.'
12 Versteeg, 'Zich te bedienen van den arbeid van anderen.'
13 Smolenaars, 'Cornelis de Bruijn and Colour Printing'; Jurriaans-Helle et al., *Cornelis de Bruijn*, 60–64; Hannema, 'Groot Gelt Gespilt.'
14 The attempt of 1678 is reported on 130–138 of Lanoy and Goodyear, 'Extract of the Journals'; translated in De Bruyn, *Reizen I*, 331–334.
15 For the details, see De Hond, 'Treffelyke Ruïnen en Overblyfzelen,' 111–128. Van Essen went on from Aleppo to Persia, perhaps to help in teaching perspective drawing to Shah Abbas II, like the Shah's drawing master, Philips Angel II; both Van Essen and Angel made drawings of Persepolis; Sancisi-Weerdenburg, 'Introduction,' 13.
16 De Bruyn, *Reizen I*, 335. The Dutch account was based on Halifax, 'A Relation of a Voyage.' The translation had been prepared by Cuper and his friend Johann

Georg Graevius, but because they could not find anyone who understood English well enough to make a Latin translation, too, they had to abandon their plans to have it printed in Utrecht by François Halma; Chen, 'Wat van Ver Komt,' 27.
17 De Bruyn, *Reizen I*, 335. De Hond, 'Den Vermaarden Cornelis De Bruyn,' 19.
18 De Hond, 'Treffelyke Ruïnen En Overblyfzelen,' 123.
19 De Bruyn, *Travels*, 2.
20 Drijvers, 'Deez Tekende en Schreef,' 63; Brienen, 'Nicolaes Witsen's Collection,' 229; De Bruyn, *Reizen I*, list at the end of the preface to the reader. While Drijvers accepts De Bruyn's own comment that he was sometimes mistakenly identified as Kornelis de Bruyn who plotted to kill Johan de Witt in 1672, Judy Haden suggests that he was really that person; Hayden, 'Cornelis De Bruyn,' 153–161. If Haden is correct, then that would open an even earlier and much more political relationship between De Bruyn and the Orangist, Witsen. Moreover, the illustrations of persons collected by De Bruyn that passed through Witsen's hands – one survives in the Bibliothèque Nationale de France, Smith-Lesouëf, 233 – were later very influential for European representations of the Persian and Mogul empires; Subrahmanyam, *Courtly Encounters*, 200–207.
21 Nieuhof, *Gezantschap der Neêrlandtsche Oost-Indische Compagnie*; for an authoritative account of Witsen's intellectual interests more generally, see Peters, *Wijze Koopman*.
22 De Hond, 'Beroep Reiziger,' 68.
23 See especially Naarden, 'Witsen's Studies of Inner Asia.'
24 The Witsens do not seem to have been involved directly; there are very few references to the Witsen family in Veluwenkamp, *Archangel: Nederlandse Ondernemmers*, or Wijnroks, *Handel*. But Witsen's early biographer thinks that they may have conducted the business through the house of Vogelaer, whose members were certainly numerous and energetic in the trade; Gebhard, *Het Leven van Witsen*, 1:45.
25 Gebhard, 33–43; Wladimiroff, 'Kaart van een Verzwegen Vriendschap,' 261–262.
26 Wladimiroff, 'Kaart van een Verzwegen Vriendschap,' 261.
27 Goldenberg, 'Russian Cartography,' 1901. My thanks to Susan Danforth for pointing out this connection.
28 Sir Robert Southwell, *Philosophical Transactions*, 17, no. 193 (1 January 1686): 492–494.
29 Gebhard, 1:421–425.
30 It has recently been made available in Dutch and Russian: http://resources.huygens.knaw.nl/retroboeken/witsen/#page=0&accessor=toc&view=homePane (accessed 7 July 2018).
31 An earlier example is Olearius and Von Mandelslo, *Persiaensche Reyse*.
32 Wladimiroff, 'Kaart van een Verzwegen Vriendschap,' 280; more generally, Monahan, *Merchants of Siberia*.
33 Deutsche Biographie (https://www.deutsche-biographie.de/sfz36259.html), accessed 12 June 2018.
34 Ides, *Three Years Travels*, chapter 19, 90; first published as Ides, *Driejaarige Reize naar China*. For an example of an image of a place (Tobol'sk) circulated through the hands of Witsen, see Monahan, 'Moving Pictures.'
35 A letter of Witsen to Cuper in November 1712 explains that Kaempfer took the post of Latin secretary to Ambassador Lodewijk (or Ludwig) Fabritius, who was originally a Hollander and an old friend of Witsen's; Gebhard, 2:347.
36 Sancisi-Weerdenburg, 'Introduction,' 13. For what is known of De Jager, whose papers disappeared with his death, see Peters, *Wijze Koopman*, 229–237.
37 Drijvers, 'Skilled Artist,' 90–91; Haberland, *Engelbert Kaempfer*, 89.
38 Image and letter of Witsen to Martin Lister, *Philosophical Transactions*, 18, no. 210 (1694): 117–118; Letter of Witsen to Cuper, 1 January 1713, in Gebhard, 2:353.
39 Witsen to Cuper, Gebhard, 2:353: 'en ik heb aen hem voorschrijvingen gegeven gehandt toen hij de reyse aenvong, en instructie gegeven en bijsonder aen hem gerecommendeert sig vlijtig te leggen om dit persepolis aft te beelden ….' The

printing of De Jager's depiction 'was de reden dat ik Sr de Bruyn belaste of versogt hadde agt op dit werk te slaen.' On what was known of Persepolis at the time, see Sancisi-Weerdenburg, 'Introduction,' 1–35.
40 For good introductions to the rich literature on natural history and collecting in the period, see Jorink, *Reading the Book of Nature*; Margócsy, *Commercial Visions*; Van Gelder, ed., *Bloeiende Kennis*; Bergvelt and Kistemaker, eds., *Wereld Binnen Handbereik*.
41 On Merian and Witsen, see Peters, *Wijze Koopman*, 420–421; on Merian more generally, see Schiebinger, *The Mind Has No Sex?*, 68–79; Davis, *Women on the Margins*, 140–202; Kinukawa, 'Art Competes with Nature'; Hochstrasser, 'Butterfly Effect,' 59–101.
42 Merian's *Metamorphosis*, sold by subscription, contained sixty plates, being advertised for 15 guilders in black and white or three times that for an edition hand-colored by herself or one of her daughters; Veenhoff and Smolenaars, 'Maria Sibylla Merian's Flowers and Insects,' 26.
43 De Bruyn, *Reizen II*, 2.
44 A market for specimens already flourished, but there were as yet very few people who made their living from traveling for the purpose of collecting; Bergvelt and Kistemaker, eds. *Wereld Binnen Handbereik*; Margócsy, *Commercial Visions*.
45 De Hond, 'Beroep Reiziger,' 67–69.
46 In the mid-seventeenth century, Shah Abbas II had been taught drawing by two Dutch painters in residence at his court, Hendrick Boudewijn van Lockhorst and Philips Angel; Subrahmanyam, *Courtly Encounters*, 172–173.
47 De Hond, 'Cornelis De Bruijn,' 63; De Hond, 'Beroep Reiziger,' 18; Brienen, 'Nicolas Witsen and His Circle,' 442.
48 De Bruyn, *Travels*, 96–138.
49 Drijvers, 'Deez Tekende en Schreef,' 69–73, 65. Uffenbach also met Praetorius, but the latter is otherwise little known. Witsen described him as a High German from Courland who was married to a well-to-do woman of Haarlem; Gebhard, II:359.
50 Ides, *Three Years Travels*, 134–135.
51 De Bruyn, *Travels*, quotations from sigs. A and 4.
52 Hannema, 'Groot Gelt Gespilt,' 41–42.
53 Smolenaars, 'Cornelis De Bruijn and Colour Printing,' 36.
54 Comment of the last page of the Preface to the English translation of Weber et al., *Present State of Russia*.
55 Hannema, 'Groot Gelt Gespilt,' 39; De Hond, 'De Vermaarden Cornelis de Bruyn,' 19–20. De Bruyn made out his will in 1701 in Van Mollem's Amsterdam house; De Hond, 'Beroep Reizeger,' 68.
56 Wladimiroff, 'De Kaart,' 262–263; Gebhard, I:448–475.
57 Veluwenkamp, *Archangel*, 153.
58 On Kaempfer at Persepolis, see Haberland, *Kaempfer*, 41–46; some of his manuscript sketches are reproduced in those pages as well.
59 Drijvers, 'Skilled Artist,' especially 95–104.
60 The Witsen letters to Cuper are held at the National Library in The Hague, KW 72 C 32, but for ease of reference I cite the published version in Gebhard, 2:351 (Witsen to Cuper, 1 January 1713).
61 Gebhard, 2:351–353.
62 UvA: Be 68 a: 'Cuper (Gÿsb) aan Witsen (Nic.),' February 1713.
63 Drijvers, 'Deez Tekende en Schreef,' 74–76; Gebhard, 2:359.
64 De Bruyn, *Aenmerkingen*, translated as 'Remarks of Cornelis le Bruyn, On the Plates of the Antient Palace of Persepolis. Published by Sir John Chardin and Mr. Kempfer' and 'A Letter Written to the Author on the Subject of His Remarks, By a Lover of Antiquity'; *Travels*, 2:198–223. I have been unable to see the original publication at the library of the University of Amsterdam because it is currently (summer of 2018) being digitized.

65 He offered criticisms of plates no. 52, 53, 55, 57, 58, 59, 60, 61, 62, 63, 64, 65, 66, 67, and 69.
66 De Bruyn, *Travels*, 2:198, 199, 208, 211, 214, 222–223, 214; Peters, *Wijze Koopman*, 392, reports that the item was listed in the 1728 auction catalogue of Witsen's possessions.
67 For a careful comparison, see De Jong, 'Tot Meerder Naeukeurigheit.'
68 De Hond, 'Cornelis De Bruijn,' 63.
69 Jurriaans-Helle et al., *Cornelis de Bruijn*, 47.
70 Haberland, *Kaempfer*, 46, quoting from Carsten Niebuhr, 2:149. Niebuhr was a member of an expedition organized by Frederick V of Denmark to study the Near East, publishing on the cuneiform inscriptions of Persepolis in 2 volumes, 1774–1778.
71 On the importance of politeness in academic and scientific debate, see, for example, Shapin, *Social History of Truth*, and Biagioli, 'Etiquette, Interdependence, and Sociability,' 193–238; but also see the more complicated picture of Goldgar, *Impolite Learning*.
72 De Bruyn, 2:214.

Bibliography

Ball, Philip. *Curiosity: How Science Became Interested in Everything*. Chicago, IL: University of Chicago Press, 2013.

Bergvelt, Ellinoor; Kistemaker, Renée eds. *De Wereld Binnen Handbereik: Nederlandse Kunst- en Rariteitenverzamelingen, 1585–1735: Catalogus*. Zwolle: Waanders Uitgevers/ Amsterdams Historisch Museum, 1992.

Biagioli, Mario. 'Etiquette, Interdependence, and Sociability in Seventeenth-Century Science.' *Critical Inquiry* 22 (1996): 193–238.

Brienen, Rebecca P. 'Nicolaes Witsen's Collection, His Influence, and the Primacy of Image.' In Cashion, Debra Taylor; Luttikhuizen, Henry; West Ashley D eds. *The Primacy of the Image in Northern European Art, 1400–1700*. Leiden: Brill, 2017, pp. 222–238.

Bruyn, Cornelis de. *Reizen Door Klein Asia*. Delft: Henrik van Kroonveld, 1698 (*Reizen I*).

Bruyn, Cornelis de. *Reizen over Moskovie, door Persie en Indie*. Amsterdam: Dedrukt voor den Auteur, door Willem en David Goeree, 1711 (*Reizen II*).

Bruyn, Cornelis de. *Aenmerkingen over de Printverbeeldiingen van de Overblijfzelen van het Oude Persepolis, Onlangs Uitgegeven door de Heeren Chardin en Kempfer, Waer in Derzelver Mistekeningen en Gebreken Klaer Worden Aengewezen; Mitsgaders het Oordeel over Dezelve, Vervat in een Brief van een Liefhebber der Oudheid*. Amsterdam: R. en G. Wetstein, J. Oosterwyk, and H. van de Gaate voor den autheur, 1714.

Bruyn, Cornelis de. *Travels into Muscovy, Persia, and Part of the East-Indies*. A. Bettesworth, C. Hitch, S. Birt, C. Davis, J. Clarke, S. Harding, D. Browne, A. Millar, J. Shuckburgh, and T. Osborne, 1737 (*Travels*).

Chen, Bianca. 'Wat van Ver Komt … Gijsbert Cuper en de Zeventiende-Eeuwse Interesse voor de Tastbare Oudheid van Verre Streken.' Afstudeerscriptie, Universiteit van Amsterdam, 2005.

Cook, Harold J. *Matters of Exchange: Commerce, Medicine and Science in the Dutch Golden Age*. New Haven, CT: Yale University Press, 2007.

Cook, Harold J. 'Early Modern Science and Monetized Economies: The Co-Production of Commensurable Materials.' In Füssel, Marian; Knäble, Philip; Elsemann, Nina eds. *Wirtschaft Und Wissen: Expertenkulturen und Märkte vom 13. bis 18. Jahrhundert*. Göttingen: Vandenhoeck & Ruprecht, 2017, pp. 97–114.

'Cuper (Gÿsb) aan Witsen (Nic.).' February 1713, MS, UvA: Be 68 a.

Daston, Lorraine. 'The Moral Economy of Science.' *Osiris* 10 (1995): 3–24.
Davis, Natalie Zemon. *Women on the Margins: Three Seventeenth-Century Lives.* Cambridge, MA: Harvard University Press, 1995.
Drijvers, Jan Willem. '"Deez Tekende en Schreef Niet Anders dan Hij Zag" (Cornelis De Bruijn, Nicolaes Witsen en Gysbert Cuper).' *Phoenix* 35 (1989): 63–80.
Drijvers, Jan Willem. 'Cornelis De Bruijn and Gijsbert Cuper: A Skilled Artist and a Learned Discussion.' In Sancisi-Weerdenburg, Heleen; Drijvers, Jan Willem eds. *Through Travellers' Eyes: European Travellers on the Iranian Monuments.* Leiden: Nederlands Instituut voor het Nabije Oosten, 1991, pp. 89–107.
Drijvers, Jan Willem; Hond, Jan de; Sancisi-Weerdenburg, Heleen eds. *'Ik Hadde de Nieusgierigheid': De Reizen door het Nabije Oosten van Cornelis de Bruijn (ca. 1652–1727). Vol. 31, Mededelingen en Verhandelingen van het Vooraziatisch-Egyptisch Genootschap 'Ex Oriente Lux'.* Leiden and Leuven: Ex Oriente Lux, Peeters, 1997.
Gebhard, Johan Fredrik. *Het Leven van Mr. Nicolaas Cornelisz. Witsen (1641–1717).* 2 vols. Utrecht: J.W Leeflang, 1881.
Gelder, Esther van ed. *Bloeiende Kennis: Groene Ontdekkingen in de Gouden Eeuw.* Hilversum: Verloren, 2012.
Goldenberg, L.A. 'Russian Cartography to ca. 1700.' In Woodward, David ed. *The History of Cartography, Vol III, Cartography in the European Renaissance, Part 2.* Chicago, IL: University of Chicago Press, 2007, pp. 1852–1903.
Goldgar, Anne. *Impolite Learning: Conduct and Community in the Republic of Letters, 1680–1750.* New Haven, CT: Yale University Press, 1995.
Haberland, Detlef. *Engelbert Kaempfer, 1651–1716: A Biography.* London: The British Library, 1996.
Halifax, W. 'A Relation of a Voyage from Aleppo to Palmyra in Syria; Sent By the Reverend Mr. William Halifax to Dr. Edw. Bernard (Late) Savilian Professor of Astronomy in Oxford ....' *Philosophical Transactions* 19 (1695): 83–110.
Hannema, Kiki. '"Groot Gelt Gespilt": De Boekuitgaven van De Bruijn.' In Drijvers, Jan Willem; Hond, Jan de; Sancisi-Weerdenburg, Heleen eds. *'Ik Hadde De Nieusgierigheid': De Reizen Door het Nabije Oosten van Cornelis de Bruijn (ca. 1652–1727).* Leiden and Leuven: Ex Oriente Lux, Peeters, 1997, pp. 21–42.
Hayden, Judy A. 'Cornelis De Bruyn: Painter, Traveler, Curiosity Collector--spy?' In Hayden, Judy A.; Matar, N.I. eds. *Through the Eyes of the Beholder: The Holy Land, 1517–1713.* Leiden and Boston, MA: Brill, 2013, pp. 141–164.
Hochstrasser, Julie B. *Still Life and Trade in the Dutch Golden Age.* New Haven, CT: Yale University Press, 2007.
Hochstrasser, Julie B. 'The Butterfly Effect: Embodied Cognition and Perceptual Knowledge in Maria Sibylla Merian's *Metamorphosis Insectorum Surinamensium*.' In Huigen, Siegfried; Jong, Jan L. de; Kolfin, Elmer eds. *The Dutch Trading Companies as Knowledge Networks.* Leiden and Boston, MA: Brill, 2010, pp. 59–101.
Hond, Jan de. 'Cornelis De Bruijn (1652–1726/7): A Dutch Painter in the East.' In Gelder, Geert Jan van; Moor, Ed de eds. *Eastward Bound: Dutch Ventures and Adventures in the Middle East.* Amsterdam: Rodopi, 1994, pp. 51–80.
Hond, Jan de. '"Den Vermaarden Cornelis de Bruyn": Een Korte Biographie.' In Drijvers, Jan Willem; Hond, Jan de; Sancisi-Weerdenburg, Heleen eds. *'Ik Hadde de Nieusgierigheid': De Reizen Door het Nabije Oosten van Cornelis de Bruijn (ca. 1652–1727).* Leiden and Leuven: Ex Oriente Lux, Peeters, 1997, pp. 9–20.
Hond, Jan de. '"Treffelyke Ruïnen En Overblyfzelen": Beschrijving Van Palmyra.' In Drijvers, Jan Willem; Hond, Jan de; Sancisi-Weerdenburg, Heleen eds. *'Ik Hadde de*

Nieusgierigheid': De Reizen Door het Nabije Oosten van Cornelis de Bruijn (ca. 1652–1727). Leiden and Leuven: Ex Oriente Lux, Peeters, 1997, pp. 111–128.

Hunt, Lynn; Jacob, Margaret C.; Mijnhardt, Wijnand. *The Book That Changed Europe: Picart and Bernard's 'Religious Ceremonies of the World'*. Cambridge, MA: Bellknap/Harvard, 2010.

Kinukawa, Tomomi. 'Art Competes with Nature: Maria Sibylla Merian (1647–1717) and the Culture of Natural History.' Ph.D. dissertation, University of Wisconsin-Madison, 2001.

Ides, Evert Ysbrants. *Driejaarige Reize naar China, te Lande Gedaan door den Moskovischen Afgezant, E. Ysbrants Ides, van Moskou af, over Groot Ustiga, Siriania, Permia, Sibirien, Daour, Groot Tartaryen tot in China*. Amsterdam: François Halma, 1704.

Ides, E. Ijsbrants. *Three Years Travels from Moscow Over-Land to China: Thro' Great Ustige, Siriania, Permia, Sibiria, Daour, Great Tartary, etc. to Peking*. London: for W. Freeman, et al., 1706.

Jong, Jan de; Meijers, Dulcia; Westermann, Mariët; Woodall, Joanna eds. *Virtus: Virtuositeit en Kunstliefhebbers in de Nederlanden. Vol. 54, Nederlands Kunsthistorisch Jaarboek 2003*. Zwolle: Waanders Uitgevers, 2004.

Jorink, Eric. *Reading the Book of Nature in the Dutch Golden Age, 1575–1715*. Trans. Mason, Peter. Leiden: Brill, 2010.

Jurriaans-Helle, Geralda; Scheepers, Esthers; Drijvers, Jan Willem; Kiki Hannema, Sancisi-Weerdenburg; Gnirrep, Kees. *Cornelis de Bruijn: Reizen van Rome naar Jeruzalem en van Moskou naar Batavia*. Amsterdam: Allard Pierson Museum, 1998.

Lanoy, Timothy; Goodyear, Aaron. 'An Extract of the Journals of Two Several Voyages of the English Merchants of the Factory of Aleppo, to Tadmor, Anciently Call'd Palmyra.' *Philosophical Transactions* 19 (1695): 129–160.

Margócsy, Dániel. *Commercial Visions: Science, Trade, and Visual Culture in the Dutch Golden Age*. Chicago, IL: University of Chicago Press, 2014.

Marr, Alexander. 'Picturing Collections in Early Modern Europe.' *Intellectual History Review* 20, no. 1 (2010): 1–4.

Monahan, Erika. *The Merchants of Siberia: Trade in Early Modern Eurasia*. Ithaca, NY: Cornell University Press, 2016.

Monahan, Erika. 'Moving Pictures.' *Canadian-American Slavic Studies* 52, no. 2–3 (2018): 261–289.

Naarden, Bruno. 'Witsen's Studies of Inner Asia.' In Huigen, Siegfried; Jong, Jan L. de; Kolfin, Elmer eds. *The Dutch Trading Companies as Knowledge Networks*. Leiden and Boston, MA: Brill, 2010, pp. 211–239.

Nieuhof, Johan. *Het gezantschap der Neêrlandtsche Oost-Indische Compagnie, aan den grooten Tartarischen Cham, den tegenwoordigen keizer van China*. Amsterdam: Jacob van Meurs, 1665.

Nieuhof, Jan. *An Embassy from the East India Company of the United Provinces to the Grand Tartar Cham Emperor of China*. Trans. Ogilby, John, 1669. Facs., Menston and Harrogate: Scholar Press and Palmyra Press, 1972.

Olearius, Adam; Mandelslo, Johann Albrecht von. *Persiaensche Reyse, Uyt Holsteyn, door Lijflandt, Moscovien, Tartarien in Persien, door Philippus Crusius, en Otto Brughman, Gesanten des Doorl : Hoogh : Heere, Heer Frederick. Hertog van Sleswijck en Holsteyn, &c. aen den Koninck van Persien: En van daer te Landt naer Oost-Indien*. t'Amsterdam: Voor Jan Jansz, 1651.

Peters, Marion. *De Wijze Koopman: Het Wereldwijde Onderzoek van Nicolaes Witsen (1641–1717), Burgemeester en VOC-Bewindhebber van Amsterdam*. Amsterdam: Bert Bakker, 2010.

Sancisi-Weerdenburg, Heleen. 'Introduction: Through Travellers' Eyes: The Persian Monuments as Seen by European Visitors.' In Sancisi-Weerdenburg, Heleen; Drijvers, Jan Willem eds. *Through Travellers' Eyes: European Travellers on the Iranian Monuments.* Leiden: Nederlands Instituut voor het Nabije Oosten, 1991, pp. 1–35.

Schiebinger, Londa. *The Mind Has No Sex? Women in the Origins of Modern Science.* Cambridge, MA: Harvard University Press, 1989.

Shapin, Steven. *A Social History of Truth: Civility and Science in Seventeenth-Century England.* Chicago, IL: University of Chicago Press, 1994.

Smolenaars, Marja. 'Cornelis De Bruijn and Colour Printing.' *Antiquarian Book Monthly* 25, no. 11, no. 291 (1998): 34–36.

Subrahmanyam, Sanjay. *Courtly Encounters: Translating Courtliness and Violence in Early Modern Eurasia.* Cambridge, MA: Harvard University Press, 2012.

't Hart, Marjolein C. *The Making of a Bourgeois State: War, Politics and Finance during the Dutch Revolt.* Manchester: Manchester University Press, 1993.

't Hart, Marjolein C. *The Dutch Wars of Independence: Warfare and Commerce in the Netherlands 1570–1680.* London: Routledge, 2014.

Tracy, James D. *The Founding of the Dutch Republic: War, Finance and Politics in Holland, 1572–1588.* Oxford: Oxford University Press, 2008.

Veenhoff, Ann, and Smolenaars, Marja. 'Maria Sibylla Merian's Flowers and Insects.' *Antiquarian Book Monthly* 25, no. 285 (1998): 26–27.

Veluwenkamp, Jan Willem. *Archangel: Nederlandse Ondernemers in Rusland, 1550–1785.* Amsterdam: Balans, 2000.

Versteeg, Annemarie. '"Zich te Bedienen van den Arbeid van Anderen": Bronnen voor de Beschrijving van Turkije.' In Drijvers, Jan Willem; Hond, Jan de; Sancisi-Weerdenburg, Heleen eds. *'Ik Hadde de Nieusgierigheid': De Reizen Door het Nabije Oosten van Cornelis de Bruijn (ca. 1652–1727).* Leiden and Leuven: Ex Oriente Lux, Peeters, 1997, pp. 71–82.

Weber, Friedrich Christian; Lange, Lorenz; Müller, Johann Bernhard; Bruyn, Cornelis de; Taylor, William; Innys, William; Innys, John; Osborn, John. *The Present State of Russia: Being an Account of the Government of That Country, Both Civil and Ecclesiastical.* Vol. 1. London: Printed for W. Taylor, J. Innys, and J. Osborn, 1722.

Wladimiroff, Igor. 'De Kaart van een Verzwegen Vriendschap: Nicolaes Witsen en Andrej Winius en de Nederlandse Cartographie van Rusland.' Ph.D. dissertation, University of Groningen, 2008.

Wijnroks, Eric H. *Handel Tussen Rusland en de Nederlanden, 1560–1640: Een Netwerkanalyse van de Antwerpse en Amsterdamse Kooplieden, Handelend Op Rusland.* Hilversum: Verloren, 2003.

9
ON CENSORS AND BOOKSELLERS
Curial Elites and the Regulation of Roman Book Trade in the Seventeenth Century

Andreea Badea[1]

Over the past 400 years, the circulation of knowledge and participation in its consumption and production have come to occupy a central position in scholarly discourse in a process that has been closely connected to an emerging Republic of Letters.[2] However, they also do relate to actual reflections on and to modes of sharing knowledge with wider audiences beyond the scholarly world, an ideal that was exemplified by the eighteenth-century program of "Volksaufklärung" or "Enlightenment for the people". Although similar discourses on free participation in knowledge gained ground at least since the Enlightenment, it is imperative to keep in mind that these sprang, to a great extent, from contemporary measures to *control* the consumption and production of knowledge through the regulation of the printing and publishing business and through various forms of censorship. Different mechanisms were employed in various ways within early modern communities and contributed significantly to the formation of a *Dispositif*, while allowing for strata-specific variations.[3] In addition to their familiarity with formal regulations, subjects of early modern states generally could muster a reasonable understanding of the informal limits on the production and consumption of knowledge.

While censorship constituted the norm in early modern European governance, the feasibility and the rigor of censorship varied, depending on the variable regulative regimes that were installed by different styles of governance. In England, for instance, censorship was part of a moral and economic regime that aimed at a certain coordination, but it wasn't in the position to follow its idea of a strict monitoring of information flows. In the United Provinces, however, there have been repeated attempts to institutionalize a thoroughly organized system of censorship, but there was no uniform authority to control such obstacles.[4] In other regions, by contrast, censorship could be installed as a constitutive element of an articulated set of control tools wielded by ecclesiastical and secular institutions. In this area, the Italian Peninsula is a case in point, hosting papacy which was at once a dual monarchy in temporal and spiritual affairs, temporal ruler of the States of the Church in Central Italy and as the head of the Roman Catholic Church respectively. Historians of censorship have convincingly argued that harsh punitive measures tended to nurture a climate of uncertainty and fear that conversely could be managed by a sophisticated repertoire of dissimulation practices.[5]

Alongside the repressive features of censorship stressed by much of modern scholarship, however, it is interesting to note that pastoral concerns lay at the heart of Roman Catholic efforts to control the circulation of knowledge: on the bumpy path to salvation, the faithful, and notably the "weak, rustic, simple" folks among them, needed to be protected by their shepherds from pernicious knowledge. The elitist flavor of similar concerns raises additional questions, however: if censorship formally affected all the faithful in order to protect the "weak", how did the watchmen of safe knowledge know how to define a canon of legitimate knowledge and permissible books? Through which channels did they gather intelligence concerning the book market and how could they secure their own purchases? This contribution seeks to address these questions via an in-depth investigation of the Roman Curia as an example of a censoring and regulating institution. After a brief discussion of Roman censorship as a social disciplining, I turn to an analysis of readers who were allowed to participate in the sharing of both safe and prohibited knowledge based on their social or professional position. Moving upwards in the Roman network of educated readers and censors, I then discuss official channels of information flow to and from Northwestern Europe, notably the Apostolic Book Commissioner at the Frankfurt Book Fair.[6] I conclude with an investigation of the practical, unofficial means of surveying the book market and purchasing pivotal works and the efforts to protect discreet distribution channels, which allowed Roman Inquisitors and censors to stay connected to the production of knowledge outside Italy.

Censorship and Early Modern Roman Curia

The Roman Inquisition or the Holy Office was a congregation of cardinals founded in 1542 by Pope Paul III to assist the Pontiff in matters pertaining to Catholic doctrine and charged with the monitoring and coordinating extant local Inquisitions. Although universal in scope, chronology suggests its main task originally consisted in the protection from and elimination of Lutheran thought in Italy, which was to be achieved through the criminal prosecution of suspected individuals as well as through the prohibition or expurgation of dangerous intellectual content. Censorship, of course, has been practiced since Antiquity[7] and found its most iconic expression in the notorious indexes of forbidden books. Similar indexes had been published in the middle of the sixteenth century by several universities – Paris, Salamanca, and Louvain – that claimed a doctrinal authority on par with local bishops and the papacy.[8] The papacy sought to draw on this pivotal tool to discipline the book market with the controversial Roman, "Pauline" Index of 1559, which was moderated by the Tridentine Index of 1564 and updated in various editions in the following centuries.

However, the multiple agendas within the Roman Holy Office led to further institutional differentiation of curial governance. The Fathers of the Council of Trent and the papacy experimented with new agencies, the jurisdictions of which overlapped with those wielded by the Supreme Congregation of the Holy Office with dynamics that culminated in the epochal reorganization of the Roman curia in fifteen congregations of cardinals in 1588 by Pope Sixtus V.[9]

The Sacred Congregation of the Index, established in 1571 by Pope Pius V, had originally been envisaged as a temporary college charged with the revision of the Index of prohibited books. It evolved into a permanent congregation, however, after the publication of a new Index in 1596, which by then was already considered outdated and incomplete.[10] The consequences were twofold: first, the move implied that the sharing and division of competences with the Holy Office became a feature of curial governance. Initially, competition and conflict between the two congregations had been rife; however, in the course of the seventeenth century, they had outgrown their competing nature. Second, the consolidation of the Congregation of the Index contributed to the fine-tuning of censorial practices and procedures that had to counter the haphazard and arbitrary nature of sixteenth-century bureaucracy.

The control of the circulation and sharing of knowledge was by consequence the new congregation's main brief. This implied that the congregation's cardinals and the consultors engaged by the pope to assist them, examined and in most cases prohibited the books that had been reported to the Congregation by Inquisitors, church officials, and diplomatic channels. However, the formal prohibition of a book didn't necessarily drive its Catholic readership into non-existence. Another important task of the Congregation of the Index consisted in "the regulation of the exception of the rule". On request, a permission or "reading license" (*licentia legendi*) could be granted if the supplicant was deemed resilient to error, as determined by a consideration of his (or occasionally her) education, reputation, and scholarly record.[11] Yet, the Congregation was not the only authority to regulate and grant such exceptions. It was assisted (and frequently sidelined) by other congregations (notably the Inquisition), by diverse religious orders and by bishops and different local entities.[12]

Resulting dynamics of competition and cooperation between Roman congregations in the battle against common enemies, in tandem with the volatility of papal decisions that routinely allocated the authority to grant reading licenses to various curial actors, suggest that the jurisdictions of different institutions were not the expression of a given normative order; rather, they were claimed and occupied in a performative manner – an assessment that also applies to other fields as well. Because of its standing as the *Suprema*, the Congregation of the Holy Office shared almost every aspect of its set of duties with at least one of the other congregations. Presided over by the Pope himself, the Holy Office was often approached by petitioners as a supreme court of appeal. Its jurisdiction in matters pertaining to censorship were more extensive, including, as they did, surveillance of the redaction and printing process prior to publication, measures to prevent dissemination, and the granting of the Imprimatur (printing licenses) or the *publicetur* (license of circulation in a specific jurisdiction). Alongside this set of tools pertaining to "preventive" censorship, the Holy Office also assumed similar functions to those of the Index Congregation in the proscription of books. The censors and the cardinals of the *Suprema* tended to focus on works of Divinity rather than history or law though, which were more likely to end on the desk of the Secretary of the Index Congregation.[13]

It is important to note that the Congregation of the Inquisition was the only Roman dicastery that could tap into the activities of a dense web of local inquisitions in Northern and Central Italy. Local inquisitors wielded highly diversified tools of control and punishment that enabled them to mold the orthodox and orthopraxical society they sought to establish in their capacity as local branches of the Holy Office in Rome.[14] At the crossroads of secular and sacral spheres, these tribunals represented a pivotal mediator of Roman centralization while fostering the notion that sin was a criminal offence.[15] This mixture of theological and disciplinary instruments was designed to have an enormous impact on the knowledge flow and on the erudite lives on the Peninsula.

However, many of the Roman and Italian instruments of censorship were only superficially implemented in other Catholic territories. Even though the papacy claimed to be the one universal authority for Catholic faithful, the Index of forbidden books remained highly controversial in many quarters and was even rejected by some Catholic sovereigns as an intrinsic part of a normative order. By consequence, the European impact of Roman censorship had to be negotiated continuously, depending on the diplomatic relations with the different territories and on the actors within these networks.[16]

Who Was Allowed to Read What?

The Inquisition's regulations above all affected the less educated, the so-called "animae simplices", who constituted the main target of most of the Roman disciplining measures. In official discourse, keeping this category of people protected from unsafe and dangerous knowledge was one of the main concerns of the entire Roman censorial apparatus.[17] It is not surprising then that scholarship of the last four decades has revealed the depth of the harm inflicted on the "ignorant and illiterate, on those social categories that were unfamiliar with Latin and did not habitually frequent the courts or academies".[18] Yet, from the offenders' point of view, displaying ignorance could also be a successful strategy in order to avoid harsher penalties. By this logic, better educated defendants were expected to understand more of the suspected texts they were accused of reading and were consequently let off the hook less easily. However, this system required a further scaling within the literates in favor of those scholars who were thought to be immune to contamination by perilous contents.[19] Ecclesiastical authorities had been developing a wide set of evasion tools since the Middle Ages. Members of religious orders had always enjoyed the privilege of reading books classified as dangerous or even as prohibited, but diverse scholars, theologians, physicians, lawyers, and noblemen also claimed the right to participate in the circulation of more exclusive – academic – knowledge. It is in this context that rather than condoning the existence of a black market under the cloak of rigorous prohibitions, curial administrations developed ways to control not only the rule but also the exception via the above-mentioned reading licenses. These reading licenses were highly coveted and, by consequence, evolved into a central tool in early modern Catholic scholarship, even though the practical implementation gave rise to endemic conflicts of competences between the *Magister Sacri Palatii* (the Pope's first theologian since the High Middle Ages), the congregations of cardinals involved in book censorship, religious orders, and diocesan and other local actors.[20] However, in line with Roman *mores*, no clear-cut regulation of the system of distribution was found up to the Napoleonic era. Instead, the diverse entities established a pragmatic coexistence that was likely to weaken their respective authority but that nonetheless fueled a certain awareness of control within large strata of the faithful.

Among the four groups who were considered to be trustworthy enough to be allowed to request and possess reading licenses, noblemen hoped to advance their social, political, and diplomatic careers by reading prohibited books, generally on matters dealing with history or politics, while theologians needed prohibited texts to boost their position as controversialists within the Catholic cosmos. However, the largest group of petitioners was comprised of lawyers and physicians, who depended on books published north of the Alps, as many Catholic authors had become rather cautious in the wake of the Council of Trent. To an extent, censorship and the very selective approach to the diverse fields of Canonical law deteriorated the situation of Catholic law, which made it absolutely necessary to rely on books written by Protestants. By consequence, Law courses at Catholic universities in the Holy Roman Empire as well as in Spain were based primarily on Lutheran jurisprudence. As a matter of fact, in the late seventeenth century, even the cardinals of the Congregation of the Index did not balk at consulting prominent Lutheran authors like Hermann Conring or Benedikt Carpzov.[21] Every single book written by these authors was presented twice during the Congregation's meetings and was intensely discussed before being prohibited, while the books of lesser figures frequently were not even regarded worthy of purchase prior to proscription. Matrimonial law was a case in point, as Catholic authorities preferred to maintain a Janus-faced reluctance to produce general rulings and preferred to decide on individual cases rather than risking disobedience (and disavowal) on behalf of the faithful.[22] Scholars seeking more systematic teachings in this field therefore had to turn to Protestant scholarship. The situation of Catholic physicians was very similar to that of the lawyers. They too needed to solicit reading licenses in order to keep up with the state of knowledge epitomized in the works of authors like Leonhart Fuchs or Johann Jacob Wecker,[23] to name a few. In addition, they were also required to request permission from Roman dicasteries to delve into the rather exotic branches of their craft propagated by the whims of scholarly fashion. Enter the case of the physician Paolo Bettucci, who in 1688 submitted a letter of supplication to the Sacred Congregation of the Index for a reading license that was to cover works on Astrological Medicine. His request amply referred to his success as an esteemed physician, celebrated by the local college of physicians, who had never lost a single patient, as well as to his urgent need to keep it that way by practicing (and studying) Astrological Medicine. It obviously struck the right note, as the cardinals benignly granted Bettucci's request.[24] That astrological medicine had been highly fashionable at the European courts since the sixteenth century may reduce the surprise somewhat in the eyes of the historian assessing his case.[25] That other physicians were less fortunate, however, illustrates the arbitrariness of the process. Hannah Marcus's research into 5,137 reading licenses issued by the Congregation of the Index in the last decades of the sixteenth and the first decades of the seventeenth centuries highlights the haphazardness of Roman decision-making, as the cardinals apparently did not flinch from rejecting requests for authors or books they had licensed in the same session to other petitioners.[26] Certainly, this could be considered a question of trust, but the ambiguity of the selection criteria and the randomness of the decisions also contributed to maintaining a certain mystification of the decision.

However, the same assessment applies to professors in Divinity for that matter, who felt even compelled to forge reading licenses. Similar practices came to the limelight in the 1680s, when the diligent Secretary of the Index Congregation, Giulio Maria Bianchi, introduced registers of reading licenses to counter the widespread practice among petitioners to submit a request for the "renewal" of licenses that had, in fact, been granted to friends, peers, or colleagues with similar names.[27]

Information from Frankfurt

It has been widely acknowledged that carefully staged public abjurations, periodic raids on individual homes, or even public executions and pyres had a highly theatrical dimension, aiming as they did at the visualization and selective accentuation of authority. Similar methods were also deployed toward reading as a knowledge practice. Yet, most of these means targeted booksellers and book printers: beyond their own clandestine printings, they were often connected with foreign centers of knowledge production and therefore more likely to attract inquisitorial suspicion because of their contacts, dating back from the sixteenth century, with the book trade of the Empire, lines of contact that frequently passed through the Frankfurt Book Fair or the Swiss cantons. Unsurprisingly, similar contacts with the German (and Protestant) book market also provided the infrastructure of a flourishing "black market" of smuggled books that conversely proved highly vulnerable to the relentless persecution on behalf of Italian authorities.[28] It is probably in this context that in 1604, the apostolic Nuncio to the Emperor in Prague eventually honored the efforts of the imperial Book Commissioner to the Frankfurt Fair, Valentin Leucht, putting him (and his successors for the next two centuries) on the Curia's payroll as a joint imperial and apostolic book commissioner.[29] Leucht (and his predecessor) had already been engaged by subsequent nuncios for smaller assignments well before 1604. As a Catholic in imperial service, his work mainly consisted in reorienting the German book market along Catholic lines through the redaction of Catholic book lists for commercial purposes rather than through direct restrictions on or control over Protestant publishing. Despite its expectation of free labor from unpaid censors, the Curia footed the bill for its outer guard in the Empire in order to stay informed about the Frankfurt and German book markets.[30] The Holy Office was the only congregation endowed with a patrimony of its own and paid salaries to its consultors. The Index, by contrast, had to rely on the goodwill of the religious orders to finance the permanence in Rome of co-religionaries they had assigned to the congregation.[31] Meanwhile, at Frankfurt, a multiconfessional and imperial city, the commissioner was bound to act on his imperial brief when discretely pursuing the tasks linked to his (equally secret) apostolic assignment.[32] In fact, he had never been accredited by the diverse authorities of the Empire as a *papal* official. While the curia could thus enjoy a free ride on the back of imperial institutions,[33] the duality of the office remained a subject of rumors and speculation for two centuries. Turning to the activities of the apostolic book commissioner to the Frankfurt Fair, it is difficult to overstate the importance of the lists of Catholic books redacted by him. Additionally, he dispatched Fair catalogues to Rome at regular intervals in order to protect the borders of Italian states from potentially dangerous books.[34] However, the nature of the commissioner's services also exposes a fundamental flaw in Roman censorial endeavors: the commissioner was unable to dispatch the books themselves to Rome. A fair amount of his energy went into ensuring compliance on reluctant booksellers and printers with his requests to hand over one copy of newly printed books to his office, implying that, in the absence of a dedicated budget, dispatching yet another copy to Rome was not a possibility.[35] The financial requirements for knowledge regulation not only affected the book commissioner's activities, however. In the absence of financial means to purchase the books themselves, the Congregation of the Index did not balk at prohibiting many books after a summary scrutiny of titles and authors rather than after reading the actual works.

Readers and Sinners

The Frankfurt catalogues were an important source of information on new publications and trends of the book trade. However, in order to attain copies of the books, Roman cardinals and officials had to turn to other networks. Some of these churchmen actively participated in the lively scholarly exchanges across confessional borders as members of the Republic of Letters.[36] In this quality, they could draw on their learned correspondence in order to stay informed about new publications or to participate directly in the exchange of manuscripts and prints.[37]

Roman censors could take a walk to the book shop next door, but their own hold on local booksellers had led to a rather restricted supply of transregional books.[38] Even if a book was not explicitly prohibited in the Index of Forbidden Books, its readership was still bound by the ten Index Rules that, starting with the Tridentine Index of 1564, had furnished the opening chapter of subsequent Roman (and Spanish and Portuguese) Indices, although indices as such had already been known at that time.[39] In the case of Protestant theological books, the danger was easy to grasp; in many other cases, by contrast, the faithful were more likely to stumble into sin by reading suspect content that they had not recognized as proscribed, leaving it up to readers whether they were willing to exploit such uncertainties to satisfy their curiosity or not. In other cases, some contents remained in a shady zone that even within the Roman congregations proved difficult to demarcate clearly, with some best-selling authors – such as, for instance, Isaac Vossius – haunting Cardinals and Censors for many years.[40] Needless to say, a bookseller had to select his stock of new publications with caution. As much as erudite books and manuals printed not only in Protestant territories were widely sought after, so too were other forms of unconventional and disreputable reading. These texts were in great demand among a broad and learned readership, and the popularity of authors and books was likely to also attract the attention of censors. By consequence, Roman dicasteries seeking to channel the knowledge flow in a way that provided them with access to potentially dangerous books leaned toward protecting at least some of the local dealers.

One of the most prominent among these local booksellers was the Frenchman Jean Crozier, who set up his business in Rome during the late 1670s. He appears twice in the sources of the Holy Office, in situations that were, to put it mildly, somewhat particular.

In 1681 the Roman Inquisition registered the self-denunciation of the young merchant Luca Bellonti for owning and reading Machiavelli's "Istorie fiorentine".[41] The man had been sent to the Inquisition by his confessor, since heresy, including the reading of heretical books, was a reserved case that could only be absolved by the Pope (or his delegates). This entanglement between (obligatory) sacramental confession and confession in front of the Inquisitor, evidenced by the countless protocols listing "spontaneous" self-denunciations, can be considered one of the most effective tools of social and religious disciplining on the Peninsula.[42] In Bellonti's case, "his" protocol recorded how he had bought the book from a young man in Crozier's shop at Monte Giordano, but at the very beginning of his interrogation, the penitent specified that Crozier himself had not been present in the shop and that the French bookseller had at no time handled or owned the book himself. Bellonti reportedly had planned to buy some "gallant" books and had tried to find them in the French book shop, but instead of selling him the requested titles, Crozier's alleged servant had offered him "the Machiavelli". Unfortunately, he was incapable of remembering the servant's name. He only remembered the average stature of the young servant, his red hair, his scraggy face, and his moss-tinted long tunic.[43] The bleak presentation of a complete stranger, whom nobody ever saw again, appears as irritating as Bellonti's description of the book. Already a quick glance makes clear how improbable it was that a book of similar quality could simply be possessed or traded by a servant. According to the records, it was a leather-bound octavo with a golden cut, an expensive adorned piece of work that hardly fitted the story of the poor servant in search of quick money.

However, the young Bellonti was well prepared to answer the inquisitor's questions, emphasizing that he hadn't known exactly how explicitly the book had been prohibited. Even though he admitted awareness of the prohibition, he still stressed the fact that he thought it might trespass "contro bonos mores", but did not belong among the heretical works in the first class.[44] Of course, these explanations were part of a well-known strategy of defense, but Bellonti's testimony also reveals an important detail about his knowledge or ignorance regarding Roman censorship: Pope Alexander VII had abolished the three classes of prohibition with the revision of the Index in 1664.[45] Obviously, the idea of hierarchy within banned authors and books had been deeply ingrained in the minds of readers to the extent that even in Rome readers did not understand the new, simplified system even two decades after its reform. That the inquisitor didn't comment on this confusion suggests that this kind of uncertainty and rudimentary knowledge regarding the mechanism of control were widespread and that authorities were well aware of this state of affairs. This same uncertainty could also keep more scrupulous readers away from books whose risks were difficult to assess. Bellonti, conversely, conveniently exploited this confusion with reference to his naïve curiosity. He additionally explained that he had not read the book carefully, but in a state of distraction and without much interest. Ultimately, his case was with a quick abjuration "de levi" in front of the Inquisitor and behind closed doors and with only the usual salutary penitence.[46]

Strikingly, Bellonti managed to return home without having been forced to reveal further information. Other self-denunciations resulted in dramatic house searches and yet more denunciations, as in the case of the young doctor Marco Ruccoli from Anagni who had turned himself in at the Roman seat of the Inquisition in 1647 for having read "the" Machiavelli. Ruccoli himself was released, but the dealer he named in his deposition as well as a certain Ceceroni to whom he reportedly had lent the book after having read it himself were severely prosecuted for the possession and reading of heretical books.[47] Self-denunciations normally held severe consequences for the entourage of the confessed sinner. Decades later, by contrast, Bellonti, was not interrogated on possible accessories to his offence and Crozier's bookshop was left alone, even though reading Machiavelli, whose books and ideas were among the most severely persecuted, was still considered a serious crime and routinely failed to obtain the permission of the Roman congregations in petitions for reading licenses.[48] All this suggests that Crozier enjoyed discreet yet considerable protection by powerful friends, because it was not only Bellonti who took care not to involve the bookseller in his story of sin and atonement, but also the inquisitor himself, who carefully disculpated Crozier from any complicity in the affair.

Crozier's Loophole

The second record of the Holy Office concerning Jean Crozier sheds further light on why everyone seemed so keen to protect his name during Bellonti's interrogation.

In 1696, the vicar of the local inquisitor of Rimini stumbled upon a partially opened chest with books addressed to Crozier at the port of Pesaro. After having examined the contents, he had deemed it necessary to report his findings to his superior. The Inquisitor dispatched his vicar's report through the proper official channels to the Holy Office on May 31, and afterwards furnished the additional specification that his vicar had discovered two issues of the *Acta Eruditorum* from 1695, which he expected to be banned.[49]

The vicar had been alarmed by the contents of the diverse book reviews in the *Acta Eruditorum* and had tried to understand above all the mathematical texts under discussion in the journal. After a first revision, he was convinced that the two issues contained multiple cases of heresy, requiring, as he saw it, a due process.

In the meantime, however, Crozier himself had also called on the Inquisition to act. Afraid to forfeit his merchandise, he complained about the incident, demanded that the inquisitor be rebuked, and that the chest be handed over to him, claiming that the authority of the Master of the Sacred Apostolic Palace and the Congregation of the Holy Office had been infringed upon by the investigations in Pesaro. Consequently, in Crozier's view, an order from the Holy Office to dispatch the chest to Rome came down to a due reassertion of its authority.[50]

Taken at face value, this arrogance may seem astonishing; after all, Crozier was dictating to the highest-ranking Roman congregation how he should proceed in order to preserve the interests of a mere bookseller. Yet, the Holy Office complied with his request and defended its authority following Crozier's script and borrowing the wording of its orders to the Pesaro office directly from Crozier's petition.[51]

It should be noted that Crozier's case was exceptional. Other booksellers were less fortunate in their encounters with the Inquisition. In 1679, the Roman Inquisition dealt with the Milanese bookseller Giorgio Mederni, who was denounced by his brother because of his business with a merchant from Basel. The denunciation protocol focused above all on Lutheran books, even though Mederni owned a well-stocked shop, judging by the reports of the house search following the accusations. The *familares* of the Holy Office discovered a couple of books written by Ariosto alongside Pallavicino's "Retorica delle puttane", but they also found Hospinian's "De festis judeorum" and a fair share of best-selling works on sorcery.[52] The books on his shelves suggest that Mederni sought to offer a selection to a heterogeneous public rather than supporting Lutheran missionary campaigns, but the Holy Office in Rome considered him a heretic who had had contact to a heretic merchant and assigned the local inquisitor to torture him "leviter" in order to learn the names of possible accomplices. The unfortunate bookseller was to remain in custody prior to the defamatory public abjuration "de vehementi" to which he had been sentenced and was threatened with harsh corporal punishment should he ever relapse into owning or trading forbidden books.[53] The Mederni case illustrates how Crozier, for his part, had managed to carve out for himself a special position within the Roman book market and within European learned networks, and was treated accordingly by the Inquisition. But there is more to this footnote in the history of the Inquisition and the Roman book market. The issues of the *Acta Eruditorum* that had alarmed Inquisition officials at Pesaro and Rimini happened to be destined for two princes of the Church in Rome: the Cardinal-Inquisitor Girolamo Casanate was one of them. The other one could not be identified. Casanate was a former Assessor of the Holy Office and chief librarian of the Vatican Library who was to become, in 1698, Prefect of the Index Congregation.[54]

Crozier didn't sell books only to Casanate himself, but was also one of the chief suppliers of the Bibliotheca Vaticana, a position of eminent importance within the Roman circles of power,[55] a position that was due, in large part, to his connections with printers and booksellers in Leipzig, Lyon, and Switzerland. Every cardinal knew Crozier's name and bought his books, and important European scholars wanted to be introduced to him. Antonio Magliabecchi corresponded intensively with him and Jaque Benigne Bossuet sent him expensive gifts.[56] Even though everybody seemed keen to buy Crozier's books, however, potential buyers may well have had to take their precautions before paying an actual visit to his bookshop. The Dutch printer Jacob Krijs recorded in his 1701 Roman diary that it was wise to remain incognito in Crozier's shop, as rumors went that his customers were carefully screened by the Inquisition – a regime of surveillance the diary's author specified he had not been subjected to himself, however.[57] While the Roman Inquisition let Crozier off lightly, the entry in Krijs's diary suggests that his customers did expect the same treatment at the hands of the Holy Office.

Enter one of the two Roman subscribers to the *Acta Eruditorum*, Cardinal Girolamo Casanate. Casanate had become famous for his extensive library in which he had collected a vast number of books, including Protestant works and other prohibited books that came both under the general Index rules and under specific proscriptions by the Roman congregations. The composition of such a library undoubtedly met academic needs and mirrored the individual scholarly interests of the day. However, it simultaneously functioned as a censorship "thesaurus" of sorts that facilitated the daily work of the Holy Office's experts and cardinal-Inquisitors.[58]

Casanate's personal library was larger than others but is also representative for other libraries of cardinals, who, thanks to reading licenses or membership of the Holy Office and the Index, collected many prohibited books and who were likely to engage in an intense intellectual correspondence. The libraries of noble families in Rome provided scholars with a suitable platform to balance (and connect) the responsibilities of curial office with scholarly activities in the Republic of Letters. Such scholars often performed as librarians for cardinals, acted as brokers in their Roman patronage channels to advance the careers of other scholars, and even published in the *Acta Eruditorum*.[59] This constituted Crozier's loophole: he needed to access a book market that encompassed both books that were eligible for soft or hard censorship and works that allowed scholars to secure their very own participation in the Republic of Letters. While their learned activities theoretically could lead to accusations and harsh criminal procedures before their own tribunal, the censors' ability to keep up with current scholarly debates simultaneously guaranteed the efficiency of knowledge control. However, in the case of the *Acta Eruditorum*, there were only two copies of every volume which reached Rome at regular intervals. By the end of the seventeenth century, the cardinals apparently felt that the journal's benefits in terms of information and documentation outweighed possible damage to highly educated scholars and censors who were not likely to step into the same pitfalls as the "rustici" and the "infirmiores". Although this perspective would change in the following years, the journal was still considered a pivotal instrument for the practice of censorship. It would continue to be purchased by the Biblioteca Casanatense, which was closely linked to the Dominicans (and therefore to the Index and the Holy Office) at Casanate's death. Even after the first prohibition of the *Acta Eruditorum* in 1702, the books under review in the journal continued to be listed as separate volumes on par with the books that were physically present in the other collections in order to facilitate the retrieval of bibliographic data.[60] It is quite telling that proceedings against the journal were only initiated after Casanate's death in 1700.[61]

Conclusion

In light of the available evidence, we should conclude that unhindered access to the *Acta Eruditorum* was indeed considered an obligatory passage point for censorial practice. This attitude toward the journal, but above all toward intermediate actors like Crozier, sheds light on the paradoxical position of the censor caught between personal interests and duty. On the one hand, it was the scholar's curiosity that kept him in touch with current channels of knowledge diffusion. On the other hand, it was the very same curiosity that, in the censor's mind and practice, constituted the first step to heresy and blasphemy, a view that, from Paul's persuasion of the magicians in Ephesus through the middle ages, fed the general notion in censorial circles and institutions on hunger for knowledge as a huge danger to the spiritual safety of the faithful.[62] By the end of the seventeenth century, it had become clear that control of the entire book market and of learned debates was no longer possible. This awareness fueled a curious duplicity how Roman experts and cardinals valued censorship procedures, which continued to serve traditional purposes of banning or expunging books on the one hand, but which, on the other hand, also kept eager censors up to date about recent intellectual developments. These interests were complementary. The knowledge obtained in censorship proceedings guaranteed a means of staying connected in the plural and stratified world of scholarship, which, in turn, facilitated improved control measures. Curial actors relied on the evasion of their own tools of repression in order to not disrupt the flow of information they depended on both as scholars and censors.

It should be remembered that this kind of knowledge could be shared by the top tiers of Roman Early Modern Catholicism, those officials and experts who carved out, with the Index of Forbidden Books as well as through the daily activities of the Congregations, a kind of yardstick for the dissemination of knowledge in a multilevel society that had to embody a singular, if often poorly defined, idea of Catholicism. They did this by providing new prohibitions of books that formally applied to all faithful. However, in the same stroke the guardians of this Catholicism stratified their censoring activities through the demonstration of a normative order that was never fully enforced on all faithful and that created, by consequence, a space of both evasion, threat, and a semblance of surveillance.

Notes

1 I would like to thank my colleague Bruno Boute for his diligent and critical proofreading of the manuscript, Hannah Marcus for linguistic help and constructive criticism and Werner Thomas for the critical revision of the final draft.
2 For a detailed analysis of the flow of information within the republic of letters see the contribution of Dirk van Miert in this volume.
3 "Dispositif" has to be understood in this context in terms of Michel Foucault. It means the totality of certain conceptually comprehensible preliminary decisions within which discourses and social interactions can unfold. They find expression in linguistically, pragmatically relevant aspects of recording, describing and shaping the lifeworld of a society.
4 Groenveld, "The Mecca of Authors"; see also Shuger, "Civility and Censorship", especially 91–92, and van Eijnatten, "Van godsdienstvrijheid naar mensenrecht". On alternative, literary forms of dealing with dangerous knowledge, see Renate Dürr's Kapilte in the same volume.
5 Fragnito, *Proibito capire*, 232–259, and Paolin, "Bibelleserinnen zwischen Schweigen und Wort", especially 243–244. For the special political and social situation within the peninsula, see Prodi, *Il sovrano Pontefice*, 167–207. For a basic reading, see Prosperi, *Tribunali della coscienza*, especially 103–116.
6 My focus is on the flow of information concerning the acquisition of knowledge. Regarding a transfer of secret state knowledge, see Ioanna Iordanou's chapter in this book.
7 For a deepher reading regarding cesorship and censura as quality control, see the contributions of Irene van Renswoude and Werner Thomas in this volume.
8 Bujanda,"Thesaurus de la littérature interdite au XVIe siècle", 18–20.
9 Del Re, *La Curia Romana*, 20.

10 For a detailed overview of the first years of the congregation, see Frajese, *Nascita dell'Indice*, 282–345. See also Wolf, *Index*, 35–41.
11 On reading licenses, see Frajese, "Le licenze di lettura tra vescovi ed inquisitori", 769–770, 793, and Frajese, *Nascita dell'Indice*, 208–220. See also Marcus, "Bibliography and Book Bureaucracy", 433–434, 436–443.
12 See also Hasecker, *Quellen zur päpstlichen Pressekontrolle in der Neuzeit*, 121–131.
13 Hasecker, *Quellen zur päpstlichen Pressekontrolle in der Neuzeit*, 75–120.
14 Still fundamental today is Prosperi, *Tribunali della coscienza*, 57–134, 135–153, and Romeo, *L'Inquisizione nell'Italia moderna*, 101–105. See also Black, "Relations between Inquisitors in Modena and the Roman Congregation in the Seventeenth Century", 97–103. On the difficult system of balancing authority between the diverse entities, see Fosi, *Papal Justice*, 105–118.
15 Lavenia, *L'infamia e il perdono*, 392.
16 Hasecker, *Quellen zur päpstlichen Pressekontrolle in der Neuzeit*, 109–114.
17 See Infelise, *I libri proibiti*, 42–49, for the sharp controls among the less literates. See also Fragnito, "La censura ecclesiastica in Italia".
18 Caravale, "Illiterates and Church Censorship in Late Renaissance Italy", 93.
19 On censoring texts within a learned readership and in consequence without being afraid of possible damages, see Renswoude, *The Censor's Rod*.
20 Regarding the competing and correlated practices of the institutions of censorship, see Fragnito, "La censura libraria tra Congregazione dell'Indice, Congregazione dell'Inquisizione e Maestro del Sacro Palazzo (1571–1596)", 163–175.
21 Regarding the Spanish lectures, see Beck Varella, "Verdammt zum Vergessen", 26–39. For the universities of Würzburg and Bamberg, see Beiergrößlein e.a., "Das Naturrecht", 181–182, 187–188.
22 See Windler, "Uneindeutige Zugehörigkeiten", 334–339.
23 Marcus, "Bibliography and Book Bureaucracy", 448. For a deeper, more detailed reading conf. Marcus, *Forbidden Knowledge*.
24 ACDF, Index Diari 9 (1688–1692), 6r/v and ACDF Index Prot. 46 (1688–1689), fol. 155r; 156v.
25 Kalf, "Eine zu elitäre Wissenschaft", 139–141.
26 Marcus, "Bibliography and Book Bureaucracy", 435, 447–448.
27 Badea, "Nach bestem Wissen ein schlechtes Gewissen?", 142–145.
28 Braida, *Stampa e cultura in Europa*, 107–108. See also Infelise, *I libri proibiti*, 105–108.
29 Einsenhard, "Die kaiserliche Aufsicht", 82–84; see also Becker, "Die Berichte des Kaiserlichen und Apostolischen Bücherkommisars", 427. The Congregation of the Index conferred Leucht the status, but it didn't pay the money. The salary was paid by the Segretaria di Stato, conf. ACF Index Diari 1 (1571–1606), fol. 185r; see also Pelgen, "Das Apostolische Bücherkommissariat", 246–247.
30 Cavarzere, "An Interrupted Dialogue", 33.
31 Marino, "L'attività economica: la tenuta di Conca", 48.
32 Einsenhard, "Die kaiserliche Aufsicht", 82–89.
33 Pelgen, "Das Apostolische Bücherkommissariat", 246.
34 The Congregation of the Index collected them in its archives, see, for instance, ACDF Tit. Libr. 1694–1697, 63.
35 Becker, "Der kaiserliche Bücherkommissar", 428.
36 For further reading, see the work of Daniel Stolzenberg on the relations between a Dutch publisher who contacted the Holy Office to protect his merchandise, Stolzenberg, "The Holy Office in the Republic of Letters", especially 16–18.
37 Ever since Antiquity letters were a common place for the presentation of knowledge and for *disputations*; they can even be considered as the starting point for the development of the early modern learned journals. See Gierl, "Korrespondenzen, Disputationen, Zeitschriften", 420, 432–433. For a general overview regarding the evolution of learned letters, see van Mierth, "Letters and Epistology".

38 On the relation of the Roman dicasteries to diverse booksellers, see also Stolzenberg, "The Holy Office in the Republic of Letters".
39 Bujanda, "Thesaurus de la littérature interdite au XVIe siècle", 22–23.
40 Badea, "Über Bücher richten?", 358–364.
41 ACDF, St. St. O-2-m (4), fol. 35v.
42 Prosperi, "Die Beichte und das Gericht des Gewissens", 183, 189, 193. However, Prosperi's monography is still basically on this topic; see Prosperi, *Tribunali della coscienza*, 219–257.
43 ACDF, St. St. O-2-m (4), fol. 55v.
44 ACDF, St. St. O-2-m (4), fol. 55r.
45 Rebellato, *La fabbrica dei divieti*, 139–142. See also Hasecker, *Quellen zur päpstlichen Pressekontrolle in der Neuzeit*, 107.
46 ACDF, St. St. O-2-m (4), fol. 55v. 56r.
47 ACDF, St. St. O 2m (5), fol. 112r/v.
48 Urban VIII had forbidden the reading of Machiavelli by decree on 30 October 1631, Hasecker, *Quellen zur päpstlichen Pressekontrolle in der Neuzeit*, 606–607. For a very differentiated view on Machiavelli's European reception see Zwierlein, "Machiavellismus / Antimachiavellismus", especially 904–905, 927.
49 ACDF, Tituli librorum (1694–1697), Nr. 64, (1) and (3). Schmidt, *Virtuelle Büchersäle*, 241–244.
50 Ibid., (2).
51 Ibid., (4).
52 ACDF, St. St. O 2m (12), fol. 190r.
53 Ibid.
54 Schmidt, *Virtuelle Büchersäle*, 239.
55 Grafinger, "I cardinali di Santa Romana chiesa", 216.
56 Regarding Crozier's networks, see Lebrun, "Autour du quietisme", 405–406. For his book trade, see also Schmidt, *Virtuelle Büchersäle*, 187–88.
57 Schoon, "Making Church History in Rome", (10).
58 For the importance of the library for Casanates censorial work as well as his ambiguous learned and official persona, see Palumbo, "La 'bibliotheca haeretica'", 22, 27; see also Palumbo, "Casanate", 289. The composition of the libraries of Roman cardinals is discussed in Schmid, *Virtuelle Büchersäle*, 153–166.
59 Laeven, *The "Acta Eruditorum" under the editorship of Otto Mencke*, 183.
60 Schmidt, *Virtuelle Büchersäle*, 156. As an example for such lists, see the catalogue "Theologia", Biblioteca Casanatense, Ms. Cas. 463/8.
61 ACDF Index Diari 12 (1700–1704), fol. 84r–90r and Ibid., Prot. 62 (1702), Bl. 310r.
62 Ibid., Prot. 46 (1688–1689), fol. 223r/v.

Bibliography

Badea, Andreea. 'Über Bücher richten? Die Indexkongregation und ihre Praktiken der Wissenskontrolle und Wissenssicherung am Rande gelehrter Diskurse.' In Brendecke, Arndt ed. *Praktiken der Frühen Neuzeit. Akteure – Verfahren – Artefakte*. Cologne e.a.: Böhlau, 2015, pp. 354–367.

Badea, Andreea. 'Nach bestem Wissen ein schlechtes Gewissen? Selbstanzeigen bei der Römischen Inquisition und die Vergabe von Leselizenzen im 17. und 18. Jahrhundert.' In Cristellon, Cecilia; Schorn-Schütte, Luise eds. *Grundrechte und Religion in Europa der Frühen Neuzeit*. Göttingen: V&R unipress, 2019, pp. 133–147.

Beck Varella, Laura. 'Verdammt zum Vergessen – oder zum Erinnern? Kirchliche Zensur und juristische Literatur im Spanien des 18. Jahrhunderts.' In Oliver, Brupbacher;

Röder, Tilmann; Osterkamp; Grotkamp, Nadine eds. *Erinnern und Vergessen – Remembering and Forgetting*. München: Martin Meidenbauer, 2007, pp. 26–39.

Becker, Rotraud. 'Die Berichte des Kaiserlichen und Apostolischen Bücherkommisars Johann Ludwig von Hagen an die römische Kurie (1623–1649).' *Quellen und Forschungen aus italienischen Archiven und Bibliotheken* 51 (1971): 422–465.

Beiergrößlein, Katharina; von Dorn, Iris; Klippel, Diethelm. 'Das Naturrecht an den Universitäten Würzburg und Bamberg im 18. Jahrhundert.' *Zeitschrift für Neuere Rechtsgeschichte* 35 (2013): 172–192.

Black, Christopher. 'Relations between Inquisitors in Modena and the Roman Congregation in the Seventeenth Century.' In Aron-Beller, Katherine; Black, Christopher eds. *The Roman Inquisition. Centre versus Peripheries*. Leiden and Boston, MA: Brill, 2018, pp. 91–117.

Braida, Lodovica. *Stampa e cultura in Europa*. Bari: Laterza, 82010.

De Bujanda, Jesús Martínez; Davignon, René; Stanek, Ela; Richter, Marcella eds. *Thesaurus de la littérature interdite au XVIe siècle: auteurs, ouvrages, éditions avec addenda et corrigenda*. Scherbrook: Librairie Droz, 1996.

Del Re, Niccolò. *La Curia Romana. Lineamenti storico-giuridici*. Vatican City: Libreria editrice Vaticana, 41998.

Caravale, Giorgio. 'Illiterates and Church Censorship in Late Renaissance Italy.' In Vega, María José; Nakládalová, Iveta eds. *Lectura y culpa en el siglo XVI. Reading and Guilt in the 16th Century*. Barcelona: Universitat Autònoma di Barcelona, 2012, pp. 93–106.

Cavarzere, Marco. 'An Interrupted Dialogue? Italy and the Protestant Book Market in the Early Seventeenth Century.' In Zwierlein, Cornel; Lavenia, Vincenzo eds. *Fruits of Migration: Heterodox Italian Migrants and Central European Culture 1550–1620*. Leiden and Boston, MA: Brill, 2018, pp. 27–44.

Eisenhardt, Ulrich. *Die kaiserliche Aufsicht über Buchdruck, Buchhandel und Presse im Heiligen Römischen Reich Deutscher Nation (1496–1806). Ein Beitrag zur Geschichte der Bücher- und Pressezensur*. Karlsruhe: C. F. Müller, 1970.

Fosi, Irene. *Papal Justice. Subjects and Courts in the Papal State, 1500–1750*. Washington, DC: The Catholic University of America Press, 2011.

Fragnito, Gigliola. 'La censura libraria tra Congregazione dell'Indice. Congregazione dell'Inquisizione e Maestro del Sacro Palazzo (1571–1596).' In Rozzo, Ugo ed. *La censura libraria nell'Europa del secolo XVI*. Udine: Forum, 1997, pp. 163–175.

Fragnito, Gigliola. 'La censura ecclesiastica in Italia: volgarizzamenti biblici e letteratura all'Indice. Bilancio degli studi e prospettiva di ricerca.' In Vega, Marìa Josè; Weiss, Julian; Cesc, Esteve eds. *Reading and Censorship in Early Modern Europe*. Barcelona: Universitat Autònoma di Barcelona, 2010, pp. 39–56.

Fragnito, Gigliola. *Proibito capire. Chiesa e volgare nella prima età moderna*. Bologna: Il Mulino, 2015.

Frajese, Vittorio. 'Le licenze di lettura tra vescovi ed inquisitori. Aspetti della politica dell'Indice dopo il 1596.' *Società e Storia* 86 (1999): 767–818.

Frajese, Vittorio. *Nascita dell'Indice. La censura ecclesiastica dal Rinascimento alla Controriforma*. Brescia: Morcelliana, 2008.

Gierl, Martin. 'Korrespondenzen, Disputationen, Zeitschriften. Wissensorganisation und die Entwicklung der gelehrten Medienrepublik zwischen 1670 und 1730.' In van Dülmen, Richard; Rauschenbach, Sina eds. *Macht des Wissens. Die Entstehung der modernen Wissenschaft*. Cologne e.a.: Böhlau, 2004, pp. 417–438.

Groenveld, Simon. 'The Mecca of Authors? States Assemblies and Censorship in the Seventeenth-Century Dutch Republic.' In Duke, Alastair C.; Tamse, C.A. eds.,

Too Mighty to Be Free. Censorship and the Press in Britain and the Netherlands. Zutphen: Walburg Press, 1987, pp. 63–86.

Hasecker, Jyri. *Quellen zur päpstlichen Pressekontrolle in der Neuzeit (1487–1966).* Paderborn e.a.: Schöningh, 2017, p. 107.

Infelise, Mario. *I libri proibiti.* Rome and Bari: Laterza, 82008.

Kalf, Sabine. 'Eine zu elitäre Wissenschaft. Astrologische Verfahren als Ausweis medizinischer Gelehrsamkeit von Thomas Bodier bis Giovanni Antonio Magini.' In Mulsow, Martin; Rexroth, Frank eds. *Was als wissenschaftlich gelten darf: Praktiken der Grenzziehung in Gelehrtenmilieus der Vormoderne.* Frankfurt/Main and New York: Campus Verlag, 2014, pp. 139–160.

Laeven, Hubert. *The "Acta Eruditorum" under the Editorship of Otto Mencke. The History of an International Learned Journal between 1682 and 1707.* Amsterdam: APA-Holland University Press, 1990.

Lavenia, Vincenzo. *L'infamia e il perdono. Tribunali, pene e confessione nella teologia morale della prima età moderna.* Bologna: Il Mulino, 2004.

Lebrun, Jaques. 'Autour du qiétisme. Correspondance inédite de l'abbé Bossuet (1696–1699).' *Revue d'Histoire Ecclésiastique* 68 (1973): 405–428.

Marcus, Hannah. 'Bibliography and Book Bureaucracy: Reading Licenses and the Circulation of Prohibited Boons in Counter-Reformation Italy.' *The Papers of the Bibliographical Society of America* 110 (2016), pp. 433–457.

Marcus, Hannah. *Forbidden Knowledge Medicine, Science, and Censorship in Early Modern Italy.* Chicago, IL: University of Chicago Press, 2020.

Marino, Mario. 'L'attività economica: la tenuta di Conca – Economics: the Conca Estate.' In Cifres, Alejandro; Pizzo, Marco eds. *Rari e preziosi. Documenti dell'età moderna e contemporanea dall'archivio del Sant'Uffizio.* Rome: Gangemi, 2010, pp. 48–63.

Mejia, Jorge; Grafinger Christine M.; Barbara Jatta. *I cardinali bibliotecari di santa romana Chiesa: la quadreria nella Biblioteca Apostolica Vaticana.* Vatican City: Biblioteca Apostolica Vaticana, 2006.

Miert, Dirk van. 'Letters and Epistolography.' In Grafton, Anthony; Most, Glen; Settis, Salvatore eds. *The Classical Tradition.* Cambridge, MA: Harvard University Press, 2010, pp. 520–523.

Palumbo, Margherita. 'La "bibliotheca haeretica" del cardinal Girolamo Casanate.' In Bonani, Vittoria Bonani ed. *Dal torchio alle fiamme. Inquisizione e censura. Nuovi contributi dalla più antica Bibliotheca Provinciale d'Italia.* Salerno: Biblioteca Provinciale di Salerno, 2005, pp. 21–32.

Palumbo, Margherita. 'Casanate, Girolamo.' In Adriano Prosperi; Vincenzo Lavenia; John Tedeschi eds. *Dizionario storico dell'Inquisizione.* Vol. 1. Pisa: Edizioni della Normale, 2010, p. 289.

Pelgen, Franz Stephan. 'Das Apostolische Bücherkommissariat unter Franz Xaver Anton von Scheden (1766–1779).' In Wolf, Hubert ed. *Inquisition und Buchzensur im Zeitalter der Aufklärung.* Paderborn e.a.: Schöningh, 2011, pp. 245–262.

Paolin, Giovanna. 'Bibelleserinnen zwischen Schweigen und Wort. Frauen und die Heilige Schrift in den norditalienischen Inquisitionsdokumenten.' In Giordano, Maria Laura; Valerio, Adriana eds. *Das katholische Europa im 16.-18. Jahrhundert.* Stuttgart: Kohlhammer, 2019, pp. 241–259.

Prodi, Paolo. *Il Sovrano Pontefice. Un corpo e due anime. La monarchia papale nella prima età moderna.* Bologna: Il Mulino, 1982.

Prosperi, Adriano. 'Die Beichte und das Gericht des Gewissens.' In Prodi, Paolo; Reinhard, Wolfgang eds. *Das Konzil von Trient und die Moderne.* Berlin: Duncker & Humblot, 2001.

Prosperi, Adriano. *Tribunali della coscienza. Inquisitori, confessori, missionari.* Turin: Einaudi, 22009.
Rebellato, Elisa. *La fabbrica dei divieti. Gli Indici dei libri proibiti da Clemente VIII a Benedetto XIV.* Mailand and Cremona: Edizioni Sylvestre Bonard, 2005.
Romeo, Giovanni. *L'Inquisizione nell'Italia moderna.* Bari: Laterza, 52010.
Schmidt, Bernward. *Virtuelle Büchersäle. Lektüre und Zensur gelehrter Zeitschriften an der römischen Kurie 1665–1765.* Paderborn e.a.: Schöningh, 2009.
Schoon, Dirk. 'Making Church History in Rome: Fr. Jacob Krijs, Apostolic Vicar Petrus Codde and Their Anti-Jesuit Networking Mission.' Lecture at the symposium 'Only a small village? Dutch church history in a global perspective (17th and 18th century).' https://www.uu.nl/en/file/31285/download?token=T0ZolBtT (31.10.2018).
Shuger, Debora. 'Civility and Censorship in Early Modern England.' In Post, Robert C.; Roth, Michael eds. *Censorship and Silencing: Practices of Cultural Regulation.* Los Angeles, CA: The Getty Research Institute, 1998, pp. 89–110.
Stolzenberg, Daniel. 'The Holy Office in the Republic of Letters: Roman Censorship, Dutch Atlases, and the European Information Order, circa 1660.' *Isis* 110 (2019): 1–23.
van Eijnatten, Joris. 'Van godsdienstvrijheid naar mensenrecht. Meningsvorming over censuur en persvrijheid in de Republiek, 1579–1795.' *Bijdragen en mededelingen betreffende de geschiedenis der Nederlanden* 118 (2003): 1–21.
Van Renswoude, Irene. 'The Censor's Rod. Textual Criticism, Judgment, and Canon Formation in Late Antiquity and the Early Middle Ages.' In Teeuwen, Mariken; Renswoude, Irene van eds. *The Annotated Book in the Early Middle Ages. Practices of Reading and Writing.* Turnhout: Brepols 2018, pp. 555–595.
Wolf, Hubert. *Index. Der Vatikan und die verbotenen Bücher.* Beck: Munich, 2007.
Windler, Christian. 'Uneindeutige Zugehörigkeiten. Katholische Missionare und die Kurie im Umgang mit "Communicatio in sacris."' In Pietsch, Andreas; Stollberg-Rillinger, Barbara eds. *Konfessionelle Ambiguität. Uneindeutigkeit und Verstellung als religiöse Praxis in der Frühen Neuzeit.* Gütersloh: Gütersloher Verlagshaus 2013, pp. 314–345.
Zwierlein, Cornel. 'Machiavellismus / Antimachiavellismus.' In Jaumann, Herbert ed. *Diskurse der Gelehrtenkultur in der Frühen Neuzeit. Ein Handbuch.* Berlin and New York: De Gruyter, 2011, pp. 903–951.

10
REGULATING THE EXCHANGE OF KNOWLEDGE

Invoking the 'Republic of Letters' as a Speech Act

Dirk van Miert

Introduction

The early modern history of knowledge is characterized by dramatic changes in European people's conceptualization of the world they were living in. The advance of print capitalism, the encounter with and subjugation of the Americas, the Reformation, the wars of religion, the developments in historical and textual criticism, the rise of natural sciences all concurred to new and sometimes radical ideas associated with the Enlightenment. These changes shook the world of learning to the core, both physically and metaphysically. Huge differences in interpretations of God and man, of the kosmos and the world, of nature and culture, of man and history divided the world of learning, and these divisions were played out in unpublished and published texts. Yet, it is a well-established fact that learned men and women kept on communicating across all sorts of political, religious, linguistic, and social boundaries. How was this possible without written rules about how to communicate knowledge? Books and manuscripts were easily lost in transmission and dispatching letters was a costly business. Up until the end of the seventeenth century, there were no explicit reflections about the rules of engagement in the exchange of knowledge. There was an increasing awareness of something like intellectual ownership and true authorship, but these were not translated into copyrights that were respected outside of sovereign jurisdictions. Pirating ideas and texts was daily business, and libraries were notoriously difficult to get access to.

The question therefore rises how people in the early modern period could build enough trust amongst each other to expect fair treatment and reciprocity. This article seeks to answer this question by adopting a socio-linguistic approach. I will analyze the way in which early modern learned letter writers employed the phrase 'Republic of Letters' as a speech act in the Austinian sense:

an illocutionary act.[1] The repetition of these acts created patterns of behavior that, overtime, started to act as regulative 'rules' about what and how to communicate. The 'Republic of Letters' is hence regarded in this article as a speech community with shared norms that became more and more explicit and finally even codified.

Although this explicit codification near the end of the seventeenth century is acknowledged by historians, scholars routinely describe the Republic of Letters as an early modern phenomenon tout court without taking head of its discursive development.[2] The aim of this article is not to describe this development in terms of its ideals, but to analyze seventeenth-century usages of the term from a functional perspective, answering the question what scholars were doing when they employed the term. In the last part of the article, I do review some normative codifications that explicitly regulated the exchange of knowledge in a century which preceded such codifications, but I ignore most of the content. This article then is not so much an exercise in the history of ideas, but a historical socio-linguistic experiment.

Already in 1996, Marc Fumaroli called for a conceptual history of the Republic of Letters, mapping the semantic field of its usage, and for an account of the shifting institutional and intellectual contexts in which the term Republic of Letters operates.[3] Fumaroli discussed a number of occurrences of the term, but the image remains patchy. We still know very little of the career of this concept in terms of its popularity and its functionality. The current article takes a first step in quantifying its use, drawing on a body of 20,000 scholarly letters. Subsequently, it tries to bridge the gap between conceptual and sociological history by adopting a socio-linguistic approach.

Defining the Republic of Letters

As is well known, early modern scholars and scientists often referred to the learned world they inhabited by using the expression *respublica literaria* (or *res publica literarum*): the Learned Republic, Commonwealth of Learning, or Republic of Letters. The phrase makes a first solitary appearance in the historical archive in 1417, then drops from the radar until it resurfaces in the 1480s, after which Aldus Manutius and Erasmus make the concept popular.[4] It then remains in use throughout the sixteenth, seventeenth and eighteenth centuries, after which it becomes a more nostalgic idea or even a mere historiographical category.

In the second half of the twentieth century, the Republic of Letters became a beloved category of historians to describe the early modern world of learning, and its currency has increased ever since. Much of the popularity of the term is due to the fact that it is not a label that has retroactively been stuck on a community. It therefore appears to be less normative than labels like the 'Renaissance' or 'humanism'. Even the 'Enlightenment', a concept that is closely associated with the Republic of Letters, is a category that was not in use during much of the period to which it is today applied. In other words, the Republic of Letters is an actor's category: a phrase that learned men and occasionally women in the early modern period used to denominate some kind of learned commonality.

Exactly what they meant with this label is open to interpretations that vary from one scholar to the other, and much of that variety is caused by the different periods on which modern interpreters focus or by the changing contexts in which early modern people themselves employed the phrase. Despite the abundance of rhetoric praising good behavior, in particular liberality in sharing knowledge, early modern scholars were seldom naively fooled by high-spirited protestations of mutually shared purposes. But the fact that they usually employ the phrase 'Republic of Letters' when they praise the services that their interlocutors contributed to the learned common good (*res litteraria, bonae litterae*, i.e. the learned cause, the arts and sciences) was performative as well as discursive, for it meant not only a description of merits, but also a prescription to heed codes of conduct that were not laid down but that were socially constructed and transmitted. The Republic of Letters was, in other words, not merely a utopian intellectual ideal, but discursive practice.[5] One of the things I want to show in this contribution is how this worked: how did mentioning the 'Republic of Letters' become a speech act or how did a discursive ideal transform into discursive practice? The political overtones of the very word 'Republic' invite such a discursive analysis; the idea that the Republic of Letters is associated with republican ideals readily offers itself – not least because so many of the humanists we assume to have been its members used Cicero as their stylistic model.[6] To be sure, there were alternative terms in use that referred to the same concept of learned commonality.

Early modern alternative indications such as the *orbis literarius/-atus/-arum*, the *sodalitas doctorum*, the *mundus eruditorum, omnis literatorum cohors, omnes literarores, ordo litteratus, chorus literatorum, res litteraria*, the Commonwealth of Learning, and *Gelehrtenrepublik* (*Republik derer Gelehrten, gelehrte Republik*) seem to capture both the idea that this was a social world of learned people as well as a wider 'world' that included not only people but also institutions and infrastructure. Indeed, some early modern scholars thought of the Republic of Letters as the assembly of learned institutions such as universities and societies.[7] In conducting a discourse analysis, we therefore have to make sure that we do not miss out on alternative labels that point to the same referent (the world of learning).

Method and Theory

Rather than attempting to come to a universally applicable and generally acceptable definition of what the Republic of Letters entailed, it is wise to acknowledge that early modern scholars themselves failed to agree as much as modern historians do. In other words, we need to accept the multiplicity of meanings of the Republic of Letters and its varying reaches across time and space.

This article will limit itself to a distinct epistolary corpus (that of the *ePistolarium*) that resulted from the correspondences of people who were active in the seventeenth-century Dutch Republic. This corpus is geographically anchored in the Low Countries, but covered a wider compass, with links to France, England, and Germany, and to lesser extents with Spain, Portugal, Italy and Nordic, Central European, and Eastern European countries. In terms of chronology, it covers a full century with letters written from 1594 to 1707, although the bulk of the corpus dates from the 1640s and 1650s. In this article I will not draw any conclusions regarding development over time of the use of the 'Republic of Letters' and will simply regard the seventeenth-century uses of the term at large. The method of analysis is that of discourse analysis: I will analyze particular passages in scholarly letters where the phrase 'Republic of Letters' occurs, with the purpose of teasing out what letter writers tried to convey or accomplish in using this phrase. Theoretically, I draw on the idea of performativity: calling on the Republic of Letters is in fact a speech-act. Letter writers were *doing* something with it: they praise, encourage, beg, ask, mourn, complain, or warn against something, and more often than not try to move the recipient into a certain action. In other words, the Republic of Letters is not a dismissable rhetorical flourish or inconsequential embellishment, but an indirect illocutionary act with the aim to smoothen the exchange of knowledge, keep the stream of information going, seek patronage, etc.

My assumption is that some kind of border needed to be crossed: maybe a difference in confession, or perhaps a linguistic boundary, or a generation gap. As such, the Republic of Letters functioned as a 'regime' governing a speech community, a discursive practice meant to regulate the exchange of knowledge within and between social groups.

Occurrences and Languages

A keyword search of the phrase 'Republic of Letters' in the *ePistolarium* yields 44 hits, but the search is not without problems. First of all, the corpus is multilingual, which forced us to reiterate searches across different languages. In addition, there are variants in spellings in each language, and Latin requires searching for the keyword in at least four cases.[8] A survey yielded the following results (hits refer to letters, not to instances in letters, but since there is only one case in which the phrase occurs twice in the same letter, this distinction can be almost collapsed) (Table 10.1).

For this article, I have looked at all instances listed in the tables above. The occurrences have been grouped in two major categories: usage in which the 'Republic of Letters' is employed to cement relations between letter writers and usage which goes one step further, i.e. when the 'Republic of Letters' is mentioned to make something happen.

There was no German occurrence of the term. As far as the English corpus is concerned, it appears as the *Commonwealth of Learning* and *Republick of Learning*

TABLE 10.1 Search terms and hits

Search Term	Hits
Commonwealth of Learning	1
Republick of Learning	1
Republique des Lettres	7
Republica Litteraria (it.)	2
Repubblica Letteraria (it.)	1
Literatorum Republica	1
Reipublicae Litterariae	5
Rempublicam Litterariam	2
Remp. Literariam	1
Republica Litteraria	4
Respublica Literaria	1
Reipublicae Literariae	9
Reip. Literariae	1
Rempublicam Literariam	4
Republica Literaria	2
Reipublicae Literarum	1
Literariae Reipublicae	1
Subtotal	**44**

Search Term	Hits
Orbis Literarii	1
Orbe Literario	1
Literarum Orbe	1
Litterati Orbis	1
Orbis Litterati	1
Orbis Literati	2
Literati Orbis	2
Orbi Literato	1
Orbem Literatum	1
Literato Orbe	1
Subtotal	**12**

Search Term	Hits
Ordo Litteratus	1
Omnis Literatorum Chorus	1
Geleerde Werelt	7
Omnes Literati	10
Subtotal	**19**
Total	**75**

(each only once).[9] This should be no surprise since less than 3% of the corpus is in German or English. This is too small a corpus to conclude that our current English historiographical label Republic of Letters is not a seventeenth-century actor's category in English. Yet, less than 1% of the corpus is Italian, and there are three occurrences of the term in that language (all from Leopold de Medici). More surprisingly, the expression *Republiek/-que der Letteren* does not occur in Dutch, although over one-third of the corpus is in Dutch (37.1%). Slightly more than a quarter of the letters are in French (26.5%), rendering seven hits in that language. The vast majority of the hits are in Latin, which makes up 32.8% of the corpus.[10]

The term 'Republic of Letters' thus seems to be most peculiar to the use of Latin and less characteristic of French, to say nothing of its virtual absence in English, German, and Dutch. In absolute terms, the chance is 4.4 times larger than a hit is in Latin than in French. In relative terms, in the *ePistolarium* only 0.13% of the French letters mention the *République des Lettres* against 0.46% of the Latin ones. The chance of coming across the Republic of Letters in a random Latin letter is therefore 3.6 times higher than in a random French letter. Thus, the currency of the term is clearly predominantly Latin.

I have included the phrase 'the learned world' in the search (again, in different languages and spelling variants), but have drawn the line with 'the world of the learned [men]'. *Literatorum coetus, eruditorum orbis, omnes literatores*, and the like have not been taken into account, despite the fact that praising Claude Saumaise (1588–1653) as the 'literatorum princeps' is semantically hardly distinguishable from the 'reipublicae literariae princeps'.[11] The criterion is that there was a collective singular noun involved, like 'state' or 'world' or 'society', and not a mere plural referring to people, such as *gens de lettres* or *homines literati/literatores*, not even if accompanied by the adjective 'all'.[12]

'Republic' or 'Republic of Letters'?

The letters in the *ePistolarium* betray an ambiguity of the term 'republic': Nicolaas Heinsius (1620–1681) used 'republic' in emphatic opposition to the world of learning.[13] But in other letters, the 'res publica' denotes not a state or state affairs, but the common interest of learning, as in a letter from Georg Michael Lingelsheim (1556–1636) to Hugo Grotius (1583–1645) of 1617 or one from Constantijn Huygens (1596–1687) to Claude Saumaise of 1644.[14]

Sometimes, the word 'republic' is used to denote a particularly Christian public interest with or without a connection to learned services to Christianity. Thus, the Lutheran Swedish diplomat Johann Adler Salvius (1590–1652) in a letter to the (remonstrant) Dutch ambassador of Sweden Hugo Grotius in 1639 deplores the early death of the Duke Bernhard von Sachsen-Weimar (1604–1639) as 'injurous for the evangelical republic', that is, for the 'prostestant public cause' (his death strengthened the position of both France and of the Holy Roman Empire).[15] When Willem de Groot (1597–1662) in 1640 admonished his brother Grotius to continue to serve the common good in a variation of a much used formula, he wanted him to 'continue to help the Christian republic'. This phrase must be understood in the context of Grotius's idealistic ecumenical arguments for a reunification of the Protestant and Catholic Churches.[16]

Analysis of Occurrences: Cementing and Using the 'Republic of Letters'

Cementing Relations

The cementing of relations aims to build trust among the correspondents. Praising the interlocutor (or a third person) is meant to invest in a new relation, to maintain an existing relation, or to make it better. The praise can be straightforward, but can also be expressed through the use of honorary titles, for example, by addressing the recipient as the consul or prince of the Republic.[17] Surprisingly, the recipient of many such praises, Hugo Grotius, himself never employed the phrase 'Republic of Letters'; in all his extent letters, the term occurs not a single time. There is just one anonymous letter to the States General in which the Republic of Letters is mentioned, but according to the modern editors of his correspondence, this letter is 'probably not written by Grotius: style and content make ascription to Grotius unlikely'.[18] The letter praises Grotius contributions to the commonwealth of learning, stating that he merely wanted to be important in the Republic of Letters and not to stir up any civil unrest.[19] All instances of the use of the phrase are found in letters *to* Grotius. This one letter is almost the only instance in the entire *ePistolarium* in which an author would have praised his own services to the common good; the context of Grotius defending himself against his former prosecutors could explain this boastfulness, but more likely this letter was drafted by someone else to exonerate Grotius. The fact that the Republic of Letters is usually employed in a context of praise suggests that Grotius never praised his correspondents the way they praised him. In other words, Grotius occupied a high place in the intellectual hierarchy of the Republic of Letters, at least high enough to get away with being not as deferential as his correspondents. It might also mark a certain skepticism on Grotius's part about the vitality of a Republic of Letters. After all, Grotius was very aware of his own talents and felt wronged ever since he was imprisoned at Loevestein. When he was appointed ambassador to the queen of Sweden, his brother ensured him he had heard that his friends Gerard Vossius (1577–1649) and Caspar Barlaeus (1684–1648) had thanked the Swedish chancellor Axel Oxenstiern (1583–1654) on account of 'all the learned men'.[20] Correspondents were aware of Grotius's sensitivity: in 1643, one of them ensured a third correspondent that he had always spoken highly of Grotius 'with the reverence that all learned men owed to his huge merits'.[21] It is well known that Grotius showed himself angry that some correspondents failed to address him with the honorary titles that he was entitled to as a royal ambassador.[22] Grotius also never used the phrase 'orbis literarius', although he speaks four times of 'all the learned men'. The only other occasion where he referred to a collective noun ('the whole chorus of learned men') is in a letter that he wrote with obvious deference as a seventeen-year-old to the much older professor of Greek Bonaventura Vulcanius (1538–1614), whose accomplishments together with those of Joseph Scaliger (1540–1609) he takes as encouragement not to rest in his zeal for studying.[23] In short, invoking the Republic of Letters to praise an interlocutor is to place oneself below the addressee in terms of intellectual standing. Of course, star scholars also praised their students, but they did not mention the Republic of Letters – a great servant of the Republic of Letters was an honorary title reserved for the ones who had proved themselves. Not all great citizens of the Republic of Letters were assumed to sit on a high horse, though. Henry More (1614–1687) praised and thanked Descartes in a letter, not because Descartes or the Republic of Letters needed that, but simply because he learned so much from Descartes's writings.[24] A similar move is made by Matthias Bernegger (1582–1640), who praised Grotius in a cover letter to a book he presented: a freshly published edition of Tacitus in which he applied part of Grotius's studies to public use. He did not do this for Grotius himself, who stood above childish glory, but for the Republic of Letters, which he believed would benefit much from Grotius's work.[25]

Yet, as said, the letter to the States General purportedly written by Grotius is *almost* the only example in the *ePistolarium* of someone praising himself. All other instances are found in an entirely different context: in Dutch letters from Anthoni Leeuwenhoek (1632–1723) in which he defends himself as a vernacular underdog in the world of learning. Moreover, he uses the phrase 'learned world' rather than 'Republic of Letters'. 'I have understood with great satisfaction that the learned world takes pleasure from the labour I have invested', he wrote in 1683, boasting that his observations were published by a French journal.[26] In other letters, Leeuwenhoek claims that the whole Learned World would support him[27] or takes on an otherwise defensive tone: he would serve the Learned World if he could.[28] In letter to the Elector Palatine, he offers some of his observations and claims to make them clear for the entire Learned World to silence obstructionists; the context is again that of a defense or an attack.[29] Drawing a contrast with an overly confident adversary, he claims to have adopted a much more careful tone in presenting discoveries that were new to the learned world.[30] Indeed, he assumes the Learned World is wise enough not to belief certain phantasies.[31] These examples suggest that Leeuwenhoek, writing in Dutch, felt the urge to defend his own accomplishments; it is the same context as the one in which Grotius supposedly claimed services to the Republic of Letters. It indicates that Leeuwenhoek obtained a low position in the authorial hierarchy of the Learned World: the tone of his letters points to a feeling of being wronged. But as any author of grant proposals in the twenty-first century knows, authority cannot be desperately claimed but ought to be sovereignly implied. Leeuwenhoek's use of the phrase 'Learned World' thus confirms what his biographers have observed: 'this self-taught man was businesslike, sensitive to status'. Such a habitus did not match the ideal of the learned scholar and ideal citizen of the Republic of Letters, in particular not because Leeuwenhoek struggled with Latin and was not trained in the learned and literary canon. His claim to merit for the common learned good is exceptional in the corpus, and it confirms his exceptional position as an autodidactic vernacular scholar.[32] In other words, the study of the phrase 'Republic of Letters' seems to confirm the already existing biographical interpretations.

Less obviously titular are expressions such as 'utter delight', 'ornament', or 'propitious support' of the learned community.[33] Even unspecified members of the Republic of Letters are affectionally described as the '*corculi* (intelligent little hearts) to whom it is given to dwell in the world of learning' – and for whom the great Vossius, as one correspondent of Grotius reports, had no time to do anything, since his work was all day long, constantly interrupted by people who wanted something from him.[34] Grotius's brother shows himself relieved that Grotius does have time to splendidly help the Republic of Letters.[35] This brings us to praise that is not expressed in terms of titles of honor, but in terms of the services paid to the learned community: through his merits, Grotius illuminates and enriches the Republic of Letters.[36] With these, he obliges the other scholars (e.g. by sharing books)[37] and earns glory[38] and fame.[39]

Letter writers not only praise the merits and services of their correspondents, but frequently encourage them or pray to God to carry on the good work. Here, the Latin signal words are 'perge' and 'insiste': carry on, go on, continue to oblige, adorn, promote, serve, or enrich the (good of the) Republic of Letters and gain glory for yourself in the process. Such wishes are most frequently expressed in the valedictions.[40]

Very close to this category is the wish or prayer that the correspondent be kept safe and sound. These phrases are usually variants on the Latin phrase 'Deus te Reipublicae literariae incolumem (con)servet'.[41] The wish that a correspondent remain healthy for the good of the Republic of Letters also betrays anxiety: to share fear about the well-being of the addressee in connection with the well-being of the Republic of Letters at large creates a communal identity, in which both interlocutors are assumed to identify with the common good or common interest of learning (*res publica literaria*). Often such utterances of anxiety take the form of prayers. A long letter from Vossius about the precariousness of his own health is followed by the news that Saumaise is recovering from illness, to the huge benefit of the Republic of Letters.[42] When a scholar died, he was praised by noting that his death was a loss for the Republic of Letters at large. For example, when the Amsterdam printer Cornelis Blaeu (ca. 1610–1642) died, Vossius showed himself relieved that he had left his money to his brother Joan, saving the large Blaeu firm from bankruptcy – which would have been 'an even larger blow to the Republic of Letters'.[43] When Caspar Barlaeus mourned the death of the Italian scholar Domenico Molino (1572–1635), he thought it was 'a loss for the Republic of Letters', in particular for the Paduan scholarly community, who in him lost a Mecenas, an Apollo, a Pallas, and a curator.[44]

Despite such mourning, there are surprisingly few complaints about the dismal state of affairs in the Republic of Letters. Of course, there are people who fail to live up to the codes of conduct in the Republic of Letters. Christiaan Huygens (1629–1695) in 1661 complained about the monks who guarded the Spanish Royal Library at El Escorial. They were sitting on an enormous treasure of manuscripts and books, but had no clue of what was happening in the wider world of learning, and they failed to care for scholarship and science.[45] Complaints of malicious monks who shielded of libraries were commonplace in the protestant provinces of the Republic of Letters.[46] In fact, the very word 'monk' was for scholars like Joseph Scaliger a pejorative term.[47] But Christiaan Huygens himself was also not very obliging, even if numerous correspondents praised his contributions to the Republic of Letters. John Collins (1625–1683) condemned the way in which the mathematician and astronomer James Gregory (1638–1675) rebutted Christiaan Huygens – 'it were to be wisht, that Mister Gregory had been more mild with yt generous person, who hath deserv'd well of ye republick of Learning' – even if Huygens himself was partly to blame because he had held Gregory in slight esteem.[48] In other words, a reputable citizen of the Republic of Letters could have enough credit to treat others disrespectfully while maintaining an honorable position. But that credit could be lost. Vossius, for example, accused his colleague Daniel Heinsius (1580–1655) of 'constant betrayal of everyone who has an excellent reputation in the Republic of Letters'. He hoped that Saumaise would teach him a lesson in modesty, and that he would stop believing 'the flatterers who instead of actually honouring him, heap honorary titles of Fenix, Dictator and Atlas of Studying on him'.[49]

These three complaints are indirect: they concern third parties and the interlocutor was not meant to bring that third party to better conduct. But, very often, the Republic of Letters was invoked to regulate the flow of knowledge, that is, to make knowledge exchange happen. We will now move on to this more explicitly performative use of the Republic of Letters.

Using the Republic of Letters

The Republic of Letters referenced a collectively held value: 'res literaria' (the learned good or cause, or the interest or sake of learning) that could be used whenever a member of the group actually wanted something for his own benefit. In such cases, the private interest was presented as an instance of the public interest. In 1614, the librarian Janus Gruterus (1560–1627) in Heidelberg was working on an edition of Cicero, inspired by the working notes of Janus Gulielmus (1555–1584) who had died three decades before at a young age. Gruter realized there was a lot of good material amongst the handwritten and unpublished commentaries by Gulielmus and he resolved to publish the commentaries of Gulielmus and add them to his own edition. But he wanted more: he asked Grotius to share with him any commentaries or annotations that Grotius might have written down about Cicero, promising Grotius to publish these. Evidently, Gruter wanted to use the fame of the deceased Gulielmus and of the living Grotius on the title page of his own edition to boost the sales and increase Gruter's own fame. How could he sponge off the fame of better scholars to put himself in the spotlight? By telling that Grotius was not indebted to him, but to the Republic of Letters:

> Right now I am working on Gulielmus' papers on Cicero. If you can support that with any insight or endeavour of your own, as I think you can, please share this and add it your other services to the Republic of Letters and communicate it swiftly with me. It will be published in good faith under your own name, not without honour and all due praises.[50]

This letter turns the tables on Grotius by not asking for a favor, but by allowing Grotius to fulfill his public duties to the common learned good.

Membership of the Republic of Letters comes with obligations. Robert Boyle (1627–1691) obliged himself to obey Robert Moray (1608–1673) and Christiaan Huygens who are 'persons, that have deserved so well of the commonwealth of learning, that J should think myself unworthy to be looked upon as a member of it, if J declined to obey them, or to serve them'.[51] Inability to share material leads to feelings of sadness; Constantijn Huygens was 'sad for the Republic of Letters and for myself in particular' that he had no manuscript of Aulus Gellius to send to the philologist Johannes Fredericus Gronovius (1611–1671) to thank this friend.[52] This time, Huygens takes personal responsibility: the Republic of Letters is sad, but Huygens is even sadder.

In 1636, Leiden professor Marcus Zuerius Boxhorn (1612–1653) wrote to Constantijn Huygens about Jean-Louis Guez de Balzac's (1597–1654) critical discussion of Heinsius's play *Herodes infanticida* (1632), a play that 'the whole *ordo litteratus* read, flabbergasted with admiration'. Balzac seemed the only critical reader. Heinsius, the 'prince of ingenious men' responded to Balzac with a letter. Boxhorn edited this letter, not with the aim of annoying Balzac, but to serve those who have the courage to admit that they can still learn something. 'I thought it was in the interest of the learned world to prevent these things from getting lost because of the modesty of the author'.[53] This passage smacks of a carefully arranged scenario, of course. It seems far more likely that Heinsius asked Boxhorn to act as an intermediary so that he himself could pose as indifferent to having the last word in print. As we have gathered from Vossius's letter to Grotius, the reputation of Heinsius was rather ambiguous.[54] The Republic of Letters is invoked here as a reason to publish the letter: publishing is a service to the common learned good.

Correspondents often referred to the collective interest to encourage each other to publish material. Grotius was eager for Isaac Casaubon (1559–1614) to publish his convictions regarding predestination, right in the middle of the Arminian controversies over the subject – at a time that Casaubon himself was considered the mouthpiece of the English King James I (1566–1625). Casaubon, however, was reluctant, given the precariousness of the Arminian controversy in relation to the Anglican Church. Grotius therefore tries to convince Casaubon by reminding him to live up to the love for learning and learned men that he has always claimed he had. 'If in anything you want to bear witness to the love with which you follow not only all learned men but also all lovers of learning, I beg and implore you not to refuse me this favour'.[55] Here, Grotius comes close to referencing the Republic of Letters, but limits himself to 'all the learned men' in an attempt to persuade Casaubon to publish something that could raise confessional antagonism.

Similarly, Willem de Groot asked his brother to expand a set of critical notes on a work of André Rivet (1572–1651) into 'a book that all learned men and lovers of fine literature will always greatly appreciate', deploring that his work is not yet available.[56] In another letter, the same Willem de Groot deplores that fact that Johannes Arnoldi Corvinus (1580–1650) has authored a juridical treatise that remains unpublished, as many other writings by Corvinus 'much to the detriment of the Republic of Letters'.[57] There is one rare case in which the letter writer thought that publishing was *not* necessary and that the manuscript that was printed had been too easily communicated: Ismael Boulliau (1605–1694), writing to Nicolaas Heinsius, made sure to first praise the ones who had supplied the manuscript (the brothers Pierre [1582–1651] and Jacques Dupuy [1591–1656]), only to note subsequently that the edition was 'of little interest to the kingdom [of France] and to the Republic of Letters' – not that the edition would really stir things up, but it was not the best work to refute an opponent.[58]

Another act to which letter writers took refuge to bring their correspondents to perform and deliver was to take care of a student. This occurred in the familiar genre of the recommendation letter. The student is worthy of attention on account of his fine disposition to the Republic of Letters and his love of letters (students usually had no actual track record of services already paid). Good behavior gives the student credit, even if he has not yet published anything. 'The young man is morally very upright, devoted to letters, and a lover of *all learned men*, a devotee and admirer above all of your name', Vossius wrote to Grotius in Paris, recommending the bearer of the letter.[59] Grotius used the same language himself. Writing to Meric Casaubon (1599–1671) in 1639, he vouched for the excellence of Justus Rijckwart (b. 1607) by reminding Casaubon of his eagerness to oblige learned men (just as he had asked Casaubon's father Isaac 25 years earlier to live up to his love for learned men):

> I know you are such a good man that you not only seize every opportunity offered to oblige all men of letters, but also to seek opportunities actively and therefore I thought I would do what I must to do, both: acquainting him with you, together with your virtues, and recommending him to you.[60]

Apart from publishing books and helping students, the Republic of Letters was invoked to add force to petitions for collaboration. Thus, mathematician René-François de Sluse (1622–1686) (writing in Liège) petitioned Christiaan Huygens in The Hague to make available and communicate 'to the learned world' observations of the comet of 1664–1665. Bad weather conditions had obscured his own view. Sluse reported that colleagues in Leuven had observed that the comet's tail subtended an arc of 80 degrees when it appeared between the constellations of Crater and Corvus. He hoped people in Rome, with their accurate telescopes, could observe the same matter.[61] Clearly, the *orbis literatus* here serves to connect the shared interests of astronomers in Rome, Liège, Leuven, and The Hague.

Codification of the Republic of Letters

From the seven occurrences of the phrase 'République des Lettres' in French, three are actually references to Pierre Bayle's (1647–1606) journal *Nouvelles de la République des Lettres*. By using this phrase in the title of the first ever review journal, Bayle institutionalized the idea of the Republic of Letters. It is interesting to note that these three letters in the *ePistolarium* read more like reports or articles, headed by a bibliographical reference to the journal than like actual letters: this suggests that institutionalization also stimulated a matter-of-fact style.[62] One such letter suggests that the combination of 'nouvelles' with 'république des lettres' stuck in scholars' minds. 'There is no real news at all in the Republic of Letters', Henri Justel (1619–1693) wrote in 1690 from London, somewhat apologetically, to Christiaan Huygens in The Hague, 'although they write to me more from Paris, I knew they weren't doing anything there. You can only see malicious booklets there, not worth reading'. Note that 'news' relates here to 'newly published books'.[63] Leeuwenhoek referred to the journal by mentioning a 'booklet, entitled *Nouvelles de la Republique*', leaving out the crucial 'des lettres' from its title. In quoting from it, he translated an original Latin reference to unspecified *eruditi* as 'the learned world' (*de geleerde werelt*), for whom observations were 'made common' (*vulgari*), that is, published.[64]

Bayle gave the journal a specific program. In the preface to the first issue of 1684, he put it thus:

> on doit donc mettre bas tous les termes qui divisent les hommes en différentes factions, & considerer seulement le point dans leque ils se réünissent, qui est la qualité d'homme illustre dans la République des Lettres. En ce sens-là, tous les Savans se doivent regarder comme freres, ou commes d'aussi bonne maison les uns que le autres. Ils doivent dire,
> Nous sommes tous égaux
> } comme enfans d'Apollon.[65]
> Nous sommes tous parents

This idea of the Republic of Letters of all scholars constituting an egalitarian community is closely connected to the idea of tolerance, primarily religious tolerance. In drafting his program, Bayle drew on tropes that characterized earlier occasional reflections about the Republic of Letters. Take for example the letter of Jacques Dupuy to Nicolaas Heinsius of 1649:

> the Free traffic of letters (i.e. *commercium literarium*) with Heinsius is one of the best results of the peace of Rueil [which ended the first Fronde]. War and social disorder had a negative impact on free traffic and communication within the Republic of Letters.[66]

Such explicit terminology about the norms of the Republic of Letters is relatively scarce in the seventeenth century. They anticipate the words, uttered a hundred years later in 1751, by Voltaire (1694–1778):

> Jamais la correspondance entre les philosophes, ne fut plus universelle; Leibnitz servait à l'animer. On a vu une république littéraire établie insensiblement dans l'Europe malgré les guerres, et malgré les religions différentes. Toutes les sciences, tous les arts ont reçu ainsi des secours mutuels; les académies ont formé cette république. L'Italie et la Russie ont été unies par les lettres. L'Anglais, l'Allemand, le Français allaient étudier à Leyde. Le célèbre médecin Boerhaave était consulté à la fois par le pape et par le czar. Ses plus grand élèves ont attiré ainsi les étrangers, et sont devenus en quelque sort les médecins des nations; les véritables savants dans chaque genre ont resserré les liens de cette grande société des esprits, répandue partout et partout indépendante. Cette correspondance dure encore; elle est une des consolations des maux que l'ambition et la politique répandent sur la terre.[67]

It is this high-minded discourse of a 'spiritual society' uniting Europe that continues to dominate the historiography of the Republic of Letters. Before Bayle, Voltaire and other French and primarily German scholars writing in the eighteenth century theorized the Republic of Letters, only few treatises had dealt with the phenomenon: *De politia litteraria*, authored around 1450 by Angelo Decembrio (1415–after 1467) but published only in 1540, describes an idealized learned community at the court of Ferrara; Trajano Boccalini (1556–1613) describes the Parnassus, an allegory of the Republic of Letters, in his *Ragguagli di Parnaso* (1612) as a politically autonomous community.[68] Diego de Saavedra Fajardo (1584–1648) satirized the overload of bad books in his *La republica literaria* (written perhaps around 1612, but published posthumously in 1655/1670), in the tradition of Erasmus's *Praise of Folly*. But even if these works evocate a community of learning, the ways in which members of this community should interact with each other is not necessarily explicit. For more generalized ideas about the codes of conduct, loose instances scattered in letters are probably more representative of normative ideas and practices.

The letters in the *ePistolarium* suggest that there was an increasing generalized idea of the codes of conduct. Thus, the private teacher of the Constantijn Huygens's children, the ill-fated Henrick Bruno (1617–1664), reported to

Huygens in 1639 that he had stopped with the lessons in poetry composition because they had reached a level that 'will be comparable, through usage and constant exercise, to the whole Republic of Letters'. Apparently, they had learnt to write poems like any other member of the Republic of Letters and thus ticked the box of one skill that any learned citizen had to master.[69]

But what were these skills? As noted, Boccalini and Saavedra Fajardo gave no detailed instruction on how to become a good citizen of the Republic of Letter. There were, of course, handbooks on proper behavior, such as Baldassare Castiglione's (1478–1529) *Il Cortegiano* (1528), Erasmus's (1466–1536) *De civilitate* (1530), Henry Peacham's (b. 1578) *The Compleat Gentleman* (1622), and others, but such books do not specifically deal with the conduct of a scholar. Erasmus's writings give ample and detailed instruction on how to write well and compose effective letters. Petrarch (1304–1374) and Macchiavelli (1469–1527) offered models of behavior, but there was no treatise that treated the Republic of Letters anthropologically as a social or historical phenomenon in its own right. Surely, the phrase was used to denote the world of learning, but more normative descriptions occurred only in the second half of the seventeenth century.

In 1659, we learn from a letter of Boulliau that the recently deceased Paolo del Buono (1625–1659), member of the Accademia del Cimento, had thought of establishing a *Republica litteraria ac philosophica*:

> It was the plan of a high mind and a man born to do great things; but it must not look for a place amongst the Europeans in our times, because in all kingdoms and states of our world, no society can be formed that is not suspect for the ruling powers.[70]

Boulliau, in other words, was pessimistic about the chances of constituting a truly independent scholarly community.

In 1667, astronomer Stanislaas Lubienietzki (1623–1675) published a thick *Theatrum cometicum* that reflected on the comet of 1664–1665. The sections in the book take the form of letters written to famous men. Lubienietzki time and again refers to the *Respublica litteraria* and to related concepts such as *res literaria*. In a letter to Christiaan Huygens, entitled *Commentatio Hugeniana* and printed in this 'Theatre', he declares that if anyone, it is Huygens who 'knows best what laws should be lived by in the Republic of Letters'. And he continues to expand the metaphor in style: 'I call upon the Philosophical Senate, now that I am made consul, not through my own merit, but through the sole Queen of good minds, the Liberty that is devoted to the Republic of Letters.'[71] Interestingly, the 'theatre' metaphor suggests a centralized concentration from a circle of onlookers: on 'orbis' of learned men acknowledging the value of the lessons taught by an individual who works from an elevated space.[72] This idea of a circle returns in the bleaker expression *orbis literatus*, which might read not merely as the 'learned world', but also as 'learned circle'. Lubienietzki is one of the few people who reflected on the idea of a *respublica literaria*: he sees the liberty to think, the *libertas philosophandi*, as constitutive of this republic. In Lubienietzki's letter to Huygens, we see how he internalized knowledge of how to behave as a scholar: he refers not merely to implicit patterns of conduct in the moral economy, but to explicit 'laws'. Such articulations were anticipated by Decembrio's *De politia litteraria* (written around 1450) and Erasmus's *Anti-Barbari* (written around 1494).[73] We do come across incidental references to the Republic of Letters in book titles, such as in the inaugural address of the professor of Greek Cosme Damian Çavall (fl. 1520–1530) at Valencia (1531)[74] or a hundred years later in the title of a funeral address (1633) praising the deceased as 'de Republica literaria meritissimus'[75] or other funeral speeches (for Jacobus Thomasius [b. 1622] in 1684 and for Valentin Alberti [b. 1635] in 1697), using the same phrase[76] – precisely the expression that occurs often in the vicinity of the expression in the letters studied above. Likewise in 1670, there appeared an anthology of study programs authored by Heinrich Bullinger (1504–1575), Erasmus, Juan Luis Vives (1493–1540), Johann Jacob Breitinger (1575–1645), and François du Jon (1545–1602), *de Ecclesia christiana et Republica literaria meritissimi*.[77] When physician Johann Hannemann (1640–1724) in 1694 published four letters to famous scholars, he praised them in the title as *in Republica literaria primates*.[78] Elsewhere in that same year, he observes:

> we already live in an age in which the Republic of Letters is experiencing its largest growth. For whole peoples [*gentes*] are coming together in an already laudable initiative to enhance the cause of learning [*rem literariam*] and are founding Colleges and Societies that study Nature and Man with the utmost zeal.[79]

In short, the Republic of Letters is gaining official currency in the second half of the seventeenth century.

The rising popularity of the term should be seen as part of a growing self-awareness of the Republic of Letters, symptomized by the emergence of *Historia literaria*. This 'learned history' was envisioned by Francis Bacon (1561–1626) in *The Advancement of Learning* (1605), but spearheaded only at the end of the seventeenth century by Daniel Morhof (1639–1691) in his *Polyhistor*. It is in this tradition that the Republic of Letters started to assume a modern history of its own. In the wake of *historia literaria*, countless disputations, dissertations, and treatises about the Republic of Letters started to appear. They included reflections on the conduct proper (or not) of scholars.[80] A German student in 1698 publicly defended 'an academic dissertation about the Republic of Letters'.[81] The great Ludovico Muratori (1672–1750) in 1704 pseudonymously published his *Primi disegni della Repubblica letteraria d'Italia esposti al pubblico*, which outlines the plan for a society dedicated to literature in the Italian vernacular.[82] Christoph August Heumann (1681–1764), a central figure in the early history of *historia literaria*, gave further boost to the Republic of Letters as an institution in his *Overview of the Republic of Letters or a Map to the History of Letters, Opened Up for the Studious Youth* of 1718 (republished eight times, the last time posthumously in 1791).[83] For Heumann, the Republic of Letters and the history of learning were interchangeable. Note that 'history' of learning means not primarily the 'past' but has retained the Greek and Latin meaning of a 'description'.[84] When Johann Friedemann Schneidemann (1669–1733), professor in Halle, gave a valedictory address in 1727, he translated the Latin title of his *Oratio solemnis de forma reipublicae litterariae* as 'von der besten Art zu regieren in der Republic der Gelehrten'.[85] In short, although ideals about the Republic of Letters were occasionally explicated before the second half of the seventeenth century, substantial theorizing of what it required to become a member of this society increased dramatically from this period onwards.

Conclusion

In the first decades of the eighteenth century, then, we can observe that codes of conduct were codified into ethical rules on how to behave. The performative regulative discourse of a Republic of Letters became institutionalized into explicit prescriptive regulations, which involved religious toleration, awareness of hierarchy, and gentlemanly conduct. As such, the discourse of the Republic of Letters became only stronger in the course of eighteenth century as a way to regulate the exchange of knowledge across religious and political borders.

That type of discourse only took off because it drew on existing practices that are revealed in the daily communications of scholars. These letters show that invoking the Republic of Letters was not an inconsequential rhetorical embellishment, but an appeal to a supranational regime: a moral economy with certain patterns of conduct that one was supposed to heed to become fully integrated into the speech community. The conscious accounts of what the Republic of Letters was and what it entailed to be part of it do not necessarily reflect the actual practices of how scholars benefitted from such a shared regime. These practices demonstrate that the Republic of Letters helped to regulate the communication of knowledge through mutually understood and socially constructed patterns of conduct that were recognized time and again, calling for more systematic treatments. The regime thus constructed proved immensely popular in the eighteenth century. What happened to the regime of the Republic of Letters after the end of the *Ancien Régime* itself is altogether the subject of another analysis, but the institutionalization of formal regulation and communication in domestically oriented universities is bound to have been a competitor in catering to the demand of regulating the exchange of knowledge.

Notes

1 Austin, 'How to Do Things with Words'.
2 The most recent general account, Bots, *De Republiek der Letteren*, 14, 16, 17, observes that the notion of the *Respubica litteraria* as a *community* of scholars is developed near the end of the seventeenth century, but Bots's subsequent description of the main characteristics of the Republic of Letters across the whole early modern period draws heavily on these normative descriptions without providing a chronological development.

3 Fumaroli, *La République des Lettres*, 37.
4 See Van Miert, Hotson, and Wallnig, 'What Was the Republic of Letters'?, 33–34, for a list of occurrences of the phrase near the end of the fifteenth century.
5 For an example on how the necessity to communicate via letters created similar discursive practices (rather than explicit intellectual reflexion) in a community that partly overlapped with the Republic of Letters, see Trivellato, 'A Republic of Merchants?', 145, 149.
6 Carel Peeters in his review of Bots's *De Republiek der Letteren* (Peeters, 'De Republiek der Letteren is van iedereen') makes this connection with 'republicanism' much more forcefully than scholars tend to do, which betrays a lack of historical sensitivity. In modern usage, the word 'Republic' takes on an anti-royalist meaning, whereas the first early modern connotation was with that of a political body or 'state'. Yet, the fact that famous scholars were styled as 'consuls', 'triumviri', and 'principes' and not as 'rex' betrays humanists' sensitivity toward the political overtones of the concept of 'res publica'.
7 Hans Bots has recently styled the Republic of Letters as the 'intellectual world of Europe' and described it not only anthropologically as a community of people bent on the exchange of knowledge, but also as a 'world' that included practices such as epistolary traditions, institutions such as universities and societies, commercial stakeholders such as the book printers and traders, and a reflective discourse embodied in the medium of the journal; Bots, *De Republiek der Letteren*.
8 In Latin, the word *literaria* can have a double *tt*; the adjective *literaria* is often replaced by the genitive plural *lit(t)erarum*; the word *respublica* is sometimes separated as *res publica* (although never as *publica res*) and the word order is sometimes switched to *literaria respublica*. Each form can occur at least in the single nominative, genitive, accusative, or ablative (the dative being isoform in some cases to the genitive). The total number of permutations in the Latin expression is 192 (see skillnet.nl/blogs). Unfortunately, the Lucene query syntax of the *ePistolarium* seems unable to cope with combining wildcards and double quotes. The formula 'Re*publica* lit*erar*' OR 'lit*erar* re*publica*' proved too complex and even 'Re*publica* lit*erar*' gave no hits.
9 The terms 'Gelehrtenrepublik', 'gelehrte Republik' and 'Republic of Letters', 'Republick of Letters', 'Literary Republic', 'Literary republick', and 'Republic of Learning' yielded no hits.
10 For the percentages, see the breakdown in *ePistolarium*, 'Corpus Metadata'.
11 Grotius (Paris) to Etienne de Courcelles (Amsterdam), 23 June 1640 (Grotius, *Briefwisseling* 11, no. 4705; *ePistolarium* groo001/4705): 'Bene admodum fecisti, quod et literatorum principi Salmasio et aliis piis atque eruditis libellos illos legendi fecisti copiam'.
12 The word 'literatores' occurs 26 times, but only as genitive: *lit(t)eratorum*, never in the other cases.
13 Nicholas Heinsius to Christiaan Huygens, 4 February 1662 (CHC, no. 966): 'Nuper epistolas nonnullas ad alios amicos exaratas tibi curandas commisi, quod literas ad rem publicam non pertinentes negligentius a Bisdommero haberi sim expertus'.
14 Georg Michael Lingelsheim to Grotius, 9 August 1617 (Grotius, *Briefwisseling* 1, no. 524; *ePistolarium* groo001/0524):

> Mihi longe gratissimum fuit cognoscere ex scripto tuo multa acerrimo iudicio excogitata; liber est refertus exacta doctrina, ac multa noviter explicata magno iudicio. Sic perge bene mereri de re publica. Iam librum tuum habet sub manibus Scultetus noster, a quo obtinebo quoque censuram suam, quam etiam ad te mittam.

Constantijn Huygens to Claude Samaise, 23 September 1644 (Huygens, *Briefwisseling* 4, no. 3773): 'Perge tu vero, summe vir, implere saeculum sublimioris momenti eruditissimis commentarijs, quae aut affecta nunc, aut parata habes, et a quibus qui te his talibus nimis avocarent, equidem de re publica parum bene mereri statuerem'.

15 Johann A. Salvius to Grotius, 2 August 1639 (Grotius, *Briefwisseling* 10, no. 4235; *ePistolarium* groo001/4235): 'Angit nos hodie appulsus de immatura ducis Vinariensis morte nuncius, rei publicae evangelicae hoc tempore magnopere nocivus. Sed solabimur nos Dei dispositione cuncta, etiam quae nobis mala videntur, in bonum vertentis'.

16 Willem de Groot to Grotius, 24 September 1640 (Grotius, *Briefwisseling* 11, no. 4849; *ePistolarium* groo001/4849): 'Vale, frater optime, et tuis consiliis et studiis rem publicam christianam juvare perge'. Whether the juxtaposition of the Church (or the *Respublica Christiana*) and the Republic of Letters was a typically protestant idea is a question I reserve for another article.

17 Matthias Bernegger (1582–1640) (Strasbourg) to Grotius (Paris), 10 July 1630 (Grotius, *Briefwisseling* 4, no. 1523; *ePistolarium*; groo001/1523):

> Instituti mei rationem tibi Robertinus credo meus explicavit; et ego nunc amplius, cum tibi, tum itaque veluti civis in literatorum hac republica sub Ex[cellen]tiae v[es]trae patrocinio protectum ultra omnia cupio. Salmasio, hoc est incomparabili illi consulum in republica litteraria pari explicarem.

Grotius and Saumaise together constitute 'that incomparable pair of consuls of the Republic of Letters', to whom Bernegger enfolds his plans in detail. Stanislas Lubienietzki (1623–1675) (Hamburg) to Christiaan Huygens (The Hague), 30 October 1665 (Huygens, *OC* 5, no. 1490; *ePistolarium* huyg003/1490): 'Senatum voco Philosophicum, nullo meo merito, a sola Regina bonarum mentium Libertate Reipublicae literariae Studiosissima, Consul creatus'. Here, the metaphor of the Republic of Letters is extended to not only have a consul but also a senate under the reign of Liberty. Gustaf Rosenhane (1619–1684) (Stockholm) to Grotius (Paris) 8 June 1641 (Grotius, *Briefwisseling* 12, no. 5223; *ePistolarium* groo001/5223): 'Sufficiat una mihi laus constanter amavisse litteras et litteratos et horum si licet fateri principem, quem titulum etiam mea natio Excellentiae vestrae attribuit. Itaque veluti civis in literatorum hac republica sub Excellentiae vestrae patrocinio protectum ultra omnia cupio'. Rosenhane not only claims that Sweden has bestowed on Grotius the title of prince of the learned men, but inscribes himself as a 'citizen' of this republic of the learned under Grotius's patronage.

18 Grotius, *Briefwisseling* 17, 276, note 1.

19 Anonymous to States General (Den Haag), August 1625 (Grotius, *Briefwisseling* 17, no. 995A; *ePistolarium* groo001/0995A):

> Quantum etiam reipublicae literariae profuerim testantur libri mei tam in iure quam literis editi. Ea in republica gubernanda mea ratio fuit, non ut seditiones moverem aut Belgium contra semet ipsum armarem, ut multi fecere, sed ad id vos incitarem unde respublica utilitatem, vos gloriam ac magnanimitatis nomen referre possetis.

20 Willem de Groot (Den Haag) to Grotius (Paris), 29 July 1635 (Grotius, *Briefwisseling* 6, no. 2202; *ePistolarium* groo001/2202):

> Narravit et mihi ille [Christoffel Sticke, lord of Breskens] Vossium et Barlaeum cancellario Oxensterniensi gratias omnium litteratorum egisse, pro dignitate in te collata: consules item Amstelodamenses ostendisse id gratum sibi esse: ipsumque cancellarium dixisse non cogitasse se tam multis gratam futuram fuisse tui promotionem.

21 Martinus Ruarus (1588/1589–1657) (Straszyn) to Paulus Pels (1587–1659) (Gdansk), 1 October 1643 (Grotius, *Briefwisseling* 14, no. 6464, appendix; *ePistolarium* groo001/6464-01]:

> Non bene memini omnium quae antehac scripsi ad dominum Mercierum de facto domini legati Sueciae, attamen conscientia mihi mea testatur me nunquam

neque locutum esse neque scripsisse de viro hoc magno, nisi cum reverentia quam omnes literati maximis eius debent meritis.

22 Nellen, *Hugo Grotius*, 667–668.
23 Grotius (The Hague) to Bonaventura Vulcanius (1538–1614) (Leiden), 1600 (Grotius, *Briefwisseling* 1, no. 14; *ePistolarium* groo001/0014): 'Quo modo enim nos, quibus fervet aetas maximum animo adminiculum, quiescere poterimus, ubi Musageten Scaligerum, ubi te quoque ipsum cogitatione perpendimus, qui fugientis aevi supremo gratissimos omni literatorum Choro foetus quotidie parturitis obstetricante Camoenarum Collegio'.
24 Henry More (Cambridge) to Descartes (Egmond-Binnen), 11 December 1648 (More, 'Epistolae quatuor', 234; *ePistolarium* desc004/8648): 'Quorsum autem haec? Non quod putarem, vir Clarissime, aut tua interesse aut Reipublicae Literariae, ut haec conscriberem; sed quod mirabilis illius voluptatis ac fructus, quem ex scriptis tuis percepi, conscientia extorqueret hoc, qualecunque est, animi in te grati testimonium'.
25 Matthias Bernegger (Strasbourg) to Grotius (Paris), 26 February 1638 (Grotius, *Briefwisseling* 9, no. 3469; *ePistolarium* groo001/3469):

> Quo fine Tacitum hunc opera mea generique Freinshemii recens editum muneri mitto; gratiosum vel ideo uti spero futurum, quod in eo tuorum quoque studiorum partem usibus publicis applicatam conspicies, quod quidem factum adeo non excuso, ut imputem etiam si non tibi, qui virilibus curis intentus iuvenilium laborum gloriolam non captas, at certe reipublicae litterariae, quam crediderim ex ista parallelorum locorum collectione tua non multo minus quam ex iusto commentario profecturam.

26 Leeuwenhoek (Delft) to Antoni Heinsius (1641–1720) (Paris), 14 October 1683 (Leeuwenhoek, *Alle de Brieven* 4, no. 78; *ePistolarium* leeu027/0078):

> dat mijne Stellingen, aldaar veel geestimeert waren, als mede dat eenige van mijne observatien, in Frankrijk in soo danige agtinge waren, dat deselvige in het journaal de Medicine, dat nu met den jare 83 was begonnen, waren ingelijft, en andere stonden omme daar mede ingesteld te werden, welke saaken ik met groot aen genaamheijt heb verstaan, om dat hier uijt blijkt dat mijn arbeijt, die ik daar aan besteet heb, de geleerde Werelt, daar in een goet behagen schept.

27 Leeuwenhoek (Delft) to the Royal Society (London), 30 March 1685 (Leeuwenhoek, *Alle de Brieven* 5, no. 84; *ePistolarium* leeu027/0084):

> Ik en twijffel niet, bij aldien in voorgaande tijden de geleerde Werelt soo kundig hadde geweest, ende met mij hadden gesien, dat in alle mannelijke Zaaden levende dierkens waren, ende daarop mijne stellingen van voorttelingen hadde gehoort, off, daarmen nu 70 autheuren weet op te halen, die tegen mijn gevoelen hebben geschreven men geen een vandeselve soude gevonden hebben, die vande Eijeren ende Eijernesten souden gedroomt hebben.

28 Leeuwenhoek (Delft) to the Royal Society (London), 6 August 1687 (Leeuwenhoek, *Alle de Brieven* 7, no. 102; *ePistolarium* leeu027/0102):

> Soo ik wist dat ik de Geleerde Werelt dienst konde doen, met de angel van de Luys die hy in 't hooft draagt, den angel die hy achter in 't lijf draagt, en het mannelijk lit van deselve aan te wijsen, ik soude deselve laten afteikenen.

29 Leeuwenhoek (Delft) to Johann Wilhelm von Pfalz-Neuburg (1658–1716) (Düsseldorf [de]) 18 September 1695 (Leeuwenhoek, *Alle de Brieven* 11, no. 157; *ePistolarium* leeu27/0157):

> Hier heeft zijn Doorlugtigste Keurfurst mijne aantekeninge die ik gehouden heb in de na speuringe van de voortteelinge der twee byzondere Schulp-vissen, …

was het niet alle, wy zouden ten minsten voor het meerendeel, hare voortteelinge ontdekken, ende dezelve de geleerde werelt voor de oogen leggen, en alzoo, die geene die nog willen beweeren dat de Schulp-vissen van zelfs, ofte uit slik voortkomen, zoodanige dwars-dryvers nog meer de mont stoppen.

30 Leeuwenhoek (Delft) to Hamen van Zoelen (1625–1702) (Rotterdam), 17 December 1698 (Leeuwenhoek, *Alle de Brieven* 12, no. 196; *ePistolarium* leeu027/0196):

Dat de Heer Hartsoeker de woorden voert, dat hy, na zyne kennisse, de eerste van allen is, die het zaad der Dieren met de vergroot-glasen heeft beginnen te ondersoeken, komt my vreemt voor. Ik hebbe in myne ontdekkingen, die al veel zyn, waar van de Geleerde Werelt geen kennisse hadde, soodanige taal niet willen voeren, maar liever het oordeel daar van laten vellen aan anderen.

31 Leeuwenhoek (Delft) to NN, 16 June 1700 (Leeuwenhoek, *Alle de Brieven* 13, no. 213; *ePistolarium* leeu027/0213):

Dog ik hebbe soo nu als dan daar maar een weynig in gesien. Ik beeld my in, dat de Geleerde Werelt nu wijser is, als sulke en diergelijke verdigtsels aan te nemen, en het geene ik van desen kome te seggen, dat sullen na alle aparentie andere van my seggen.

32 Jorink, *Reading the Book of Nature*, 241.
33 Rutgerus zum Bergen (1603–1661) (Strassbourg) to Grotius (Paris), 6 March 1630 (Grotius, *Briefwisseling* 4, no. 1483; *ePistolarium* groo001/1483):

S.P. Literas tuas, clarissime vir, summa literatorum omnium voluptas, recte accepi, quas quanta cum voluptate legerim, tam exiguo papyri spatio vix deformari, nedum accuratius depingi queat. Quem enim vel morosissimum non penissime officiant tam abundantes eruditione, humanitate, officio, et, quod palmarium puto, ab Hugone Grotio hominum fidem quali et quanto viro scriptae! Cuius nomen ob amplas ingenii dotes iam dudum aequissimo, nec inconsulte propitio literati orbis suffragio divinitati transscriptum est.

Note the use of both 'omnes literati' and 'literatus orbis'. Vossius (Amsterdam) to Grotius (Paris), 2 September 1641 (Grotius, *Briefwisseling* 12, no. 5358; *ePistolarium* groo001/5348): 'Cum gaudio intellexi ex literis filii Isaaci, ut salvus Parisios venerit, Excellentiam t[uam] compellarit et, quod fore sciebam, acceptissimus fuerit; clarissimum Salmasium, alterum orbis literati decus, cum dolore suo non repererit, eo quod in Burgundiam abiisset'. Vossius praises Saumaise as the 'other/second ornament of the literate world', implying that Grotius is the first. Note that Bernegger paired Saumaise and Grotius as the consuls of the Republic of Letters (see above, note 17). Leeuwenhoek (Delft) to Antonio Magliabechi (1633–1714) (Firenze), 20 February 1698 (Leeuwenhoek, *Alle de Brieven* 12, no. 191; *ePistolarium* leeu027/0191): 'Vale multum diuque, Vir Illustrissime, Orbis Literati Decus et Ornamentum, et mihi meisque, ut coepisti, favere perge'. Leeuwenhoek (Delft) to Magliabechi (Firenze), 17 April 1698 (Leeuwenhoek, *Alle de Brieven* 12, no. 192; *ePistolarium* leeu027/0192): 'Vale tandem Vir Illustrissime, Orbis Litterati Decus et Ornamentum, Vale aeternum, et mihi, ut coepisti, favere perge'.

34 Harald Andersson Appelboom (1612–1674) (Amsterdam) to Grotius (Paris), 2 July 1640 (Grotius, *Briefwisseling* 11, no. 4716; *ePistolarium* groo001/4716):

Quod saepe facio, hesterno die compellavi clarissimum Vossium, qui impense petiit, ut suo nomine vestram Excellentiam salutarem plurimum. Me viri miseret, quem sic a mane ad vesperam civium studiosorum et peregrinantium compellationibus video distringi. Conqueritur hanc potissimum esse caussam, cur tam pauca praestare possit, probanda iis, quibus in literato orbe corculis esse datum est.

35 Willem de Groot (1597–1662) (The Hague) to Grotius (Paris), 14 November 1639 (Grotius, *Briefwisseling* 10, no. 4386; *ePistolarium* groo001/4386): 'gaudeo tantum tibi a publicis curis superesse otii, ut tam luculenter rempublicam litterariam juvare possis'.
36 Martinus Fogelius (1634–1675) (Hamburg) to Christiaan Huygens (Paris), 6 October 1666 (Huygens, *OC* 6, no. 1561; *ePistolarium* huyg003/1561): 'Ceterum diu est, quod tua merita in rempublicam literariam aestimem, & propterea valde desideravi tuam amicitiam'. Willem de Groot (The Hague) to Grotius (Paris) 14 September 1637 (Grotius, *Briefwisseling* 8, no. 3252; *ePistolarium* groo001/3252): 'Ex iis magna cum voluptate didici, quam multa et varia ad illustrandam rempublicam litterariam tibi in promtu sint'.
37 Jean-Paul de la Roque (d. 1691) (Paris) to Christiaan Huygens (The Hague), 12 July 1684 (Huygens, *OC* 8, no. 2349; *ePistolarium* huyg003/2349):

> Je verray pour cet effet Mons. Cassini, aujourdhuy, et je luy demanderay l'exemplaire que vous luy en auez enuoyé, et qu'il ne fera sans doute pas difficulté de me prester. Les Sçauans vous ont de grandes obligations d'enrichir ainsy la Republique des lettres, de vos excellentes productions.

38 H. Coets (fl. 1687) (Leiden) to Christiaan Huygens (The Hague), 25 October 1687 (Huygens, *OC* 9, no. 2499; *ePistolarium* huyg003/2499):

> illis … qui praeclara inventa ex ignorantiae abysso in lucem trahendo, sibi gloriam et orbi literato commodum pepererunt haud contemnendum. In quorum numero te nulli secundum esse, cum omnes uno ore exclament, quotquot sunt studii mathematici cultores facile veniam dabis, si non statim fidem datam liberaverim.

39 Grotius Paris (Paris) to Nicolas-Claude Fabry de Peiresc (1580–1637) (Belgentier), 6 September 1630 (Grotius, *Briefwisseling* 4, no. 1539; *ePistolarium* groo001/1539):

> Haec cum mihi persuadeant Nicolai Damasceni esse, quibus hoc nomen in *Eclogis* tuis inscribitur, valde mihi gratum hoc accidit, quod eadem opera haud sane gravi licuit et tibi, nostro saeculo viro apud omnes literatos celeberrimo, morem gerere et illius viri suo saeculo celeberrimi memoriam suscitare.

40 Willem de Groot (1597–1662) (The Hague) to Grotius (Paris), 21 December 1637 (Grotius, *Briefwisseling* 8, no. 3393; *ePistolarium* groo001/3393): 'Perge de republica litteraria et magis etiam de ecclesia bene mereri; nos qui nihil aliud possumus, votis certe favebimus et te tuosque ardentibus precibus Deo commendabimus'. René François de Sluse (Liège) to Christiaan Huygens (The Hague), 20 July 1663 (Huygens, *OC* 4, no. 1137; *ePistolarium* huyg003/1137): 'Tu, vir Praestantissime, perge orbem literatum tuis εὑρήμασιν ornare, meque quo soles affectu semper prosequere'. Frans van Schooten (1615–1660) (Leiden) to Christiaan Huygens (The Hague), 19 September 1658 (Huygens, *OC* 2, no. 517; *ePistolarium* huyg003/0517):

> Id solum opto, ut, quo coepisti pede non desistas, sed in ijs, quae Rempublicam Literariam promovere valent, aut utilitati publicae inservire possunt, meditandis continuo alacriter pergas; ut tua fama, quae jam per totum terrarum orbem illucere coepit, indies magis magisque inclarescat.

Frans van Schooten (1615–1660) (Leiden) to Christiaan Huygens (The Hague) 13 February 1659 (Huygens, *OC* 2, no. 587; *ePistolarium* huyg003/0587): 'Tu modo, vir Amicissime, ut coepisti, perge tuis praeclarissimis inventis Rempublicam Literariam continuo ornare. Vale'. Leopoldo de Medici (1617–1675) (Firenze) to Christiaan Huygens (Paris), 5 November 1660 (Huygens, *OC* 3, no. 802; *ePistolarium* huyg003/0802): 'Resta che Vostra Signoria si compiaccia al suo ritorno di Francia di arricchire il Tesoro della Republica Litteraria con nuoui parti del suo sapere, come ella mi accenna'. The phrasing is original; the common good of the Republic of

Letters is metaphorically referred to as a 'treasure'. Leopoldo de Medici (Firenze) to Christiaan Huygens (Paris), 16 August 1666 (Huygens, OC 6, no. 1558; *ePistolarium* huyg003/1558):

> Sequiti pure Vestra Signoria le sue degne fatiche sotto la direzione di un Rè così grande, et vniuersale protettore della Virtù, e de Virtuosi, onde per la Republica litteraria, e per il mondo tutto, mercè della di lui regia munificenza si può aspettare utili, e gloria grande nei nostri Tempi.

Leopoldo de Medici (Firenze) to Christiaan Huygens (Paris), 1673 (Huygens, OC 7, no. 1941; *ePistolarium* huyg003/1941): 'io le rendo grazie del libro ... godendo intanto sommamente di udire, che ella si sia liberata dalle sue indispozioni a segno che abbia potuto applicare ad arricchire la repubblica letteraria di nuove gemme erudite, parti del suo intelletto'. Johannes Hevelius (1611–1687) (Gdansk) to Christiaan Hugyens (The Hague), 19 February 1663 (Huygens, OC 4, no. 1099; *ePistolarium* huyg003/1099): 'Bene Vale, et non istum duntaxat, quem Dei gratia exorsi sumus; sed et plures insecuturos annos, quos Tibi Divina destinavit Providentia faustos felicesque experire; tum magno Reipublicae Literariae bono, magnis conatibus insiste' (earlier on in this letter, the term 'commercium literarium' is used: 'alacriter commercium literarium vicissim aggredior'). René François de Sluse (1622–1685) (Liège) to Christiaan Huygens (The Hague), 19 October 1658 (Huygens, OC 2, no. 538; *ePistolarium* huyg003/0538): 'Multa in libro reperi de quibus alias tecum, quando feriatum intellexero. Timeo enim, vt ait ille, ne in publica commoda peccem, si longo sermone morer tua tempora, quae studijs reipublicae litterariae vtilioribus impendis'.

41 Gerardus Vossius (Amsterdam) to Grotius (Paris), 1 July 1635 (Grotius, *Briefwisseling* 6, no. 2166; *ePistolarium* groo001/2166): 'Deus Optimus Maximus te, illustrissime domine, cum familia tota, diu, Christiani orbis bono et reipublicae literariae conservet'. Willem de Groot (The Hague) to Grotius (Paris), 14 October 1641 (Grotius, *Briefwisseling* 12, no. 5417; *ePistolarium* groo001/5417): 'Interea Deus Opt. Max. te nobis totique ecclesiae et reipublicae litterariae diu servet incolumem'. Daniel Lipstorp (1631–1684) (Leiden) to Christiaan Hugyens (The Hague), 20 April 1653 (Huygens, OC 1, no. 156; *ePistolarium* huyg003/0156):

> Equidem non diffiteor extollendos esse istos Tuae Nobilitatis liberales conatus, quibus continuo Rempublicam literariam sibi devincire studes, cuius oculos in te defixos esse non ignoras, esse autem cum discrimine salutis famae pericula tentanda non approbo, sed potius valetudinis habendam esse rationem suadeo, ut diutius de Orbe literario benemereri queas.

René François de Sluse (1622–1685) (Liège) to Christiaan Huygens (The Hague), 19 October 1657 (Huygens, OC 2, no. 416; *ePistolarium* huyg003/0416): 'Interest nedum Reipublicae vestrae sed litterati orbis vniuersi eum [parentem tuum] cito restitui'. Anna Maria van Schurman (1607–1678) (Utrecht) to Constantijn Huygens (The Hague), 22 June 1666 (Huygens, *Briefwisseling* 6, no. 6566 *ePistolarium* huyg001/6566): 'Deumque Opt[imum] Max[imum] veneror, ut te diu ecclesiae, patriae, reipublicae literarum et tuorum omnium ingenti bono servet incolumem'. Matteo Campani (1620–1678) (Rome) to Christiaan Huygens (The Hague), 2 December 1664 (Huygens, OC 5, no. 1304; *ePistolarium* huyg003/1304): 'Vale literariae Reipublicae bono: et me ama, ut ipse te diligo atque ueneror'. Bernhardus Fullenius, (1640–1707) (Franeker) to Christiaan Huygens (The Hague), 10 August 1683 (Huygens, OC 8, no. 2317; *ePistolarium* huyg003/2317): 'Vale diu feliciterque Reipublicae litterariae et publico bono, et amica me responsione dignare'. Note the juxtaposition of the Republic of Letters and the public good. Grotius (Hamburg) to Gerardus Vossius (Amsterdam), 22 October 1632 (Grotius, *Briefwisseling* 6, no. 1794; *ePistolarium* groo001/1794): 'Deus te cum conjuge ac liberis sospitem diu Batavis literatisque omnibus praestet'.

42 Gerardus Vossius (Amsterdam) to Grotius (Paris), 4 June 1639 (Grotius, *Briefwisseling* 10, no. 414; *ePistolarium* groo001/414): 'Simul illud addo magnum Salmasium, - quem diu salvum ac sospitem esse non paullo majoris interest Reipublicae literariae – post morbum gravissimum nunc convalescere magis et magis'.

43 Gerardus Vossius (Amsterdam) to Grotius (Paris), 17 June 1642 (Grotius, *Briefwisseling* 13, no. 5752; *ePistolarium* groo001/5752):

> exquiram ex Blauwio: sic enim, non Blauwiis, nunc scribendum mihi, fratrum eo qui iunior erat paucos ante menses defuncto. Magis ea res obesset reipublicae literariae, nisi fratrem propemodum ex asse haeredem fecisset. Absque eo foret qui superest impar esset sumptibus faciendis tantis, quippe, ut mittam caetera, typographiae ergo alit quotidie supra homines XL.

44 Caspar Barlaeus (Amsterdam) to Cornelis van der Myle (1579–1642) 16 December 1635 (Barlaeus, *Epistolarum liber*, no. 312; *ePistolarium* barl001/0312): 'Nec minus Respublica literaria, Patavina praesertim, in eodem viro Mecoenatem amisit, quo gaudebat; Apollinem, cujus se hortatu monitisque erigebat: Palladem, cujus se aegide tuebatur; purpuram, qua spendescebat; curatorem, a quo fovebatur tenerius'.

45 Christiaan Huygens (The Hague) to Nicolaas Heinsius, 13 October 1661 (Huygens, *OC* 3, no. 907; *ePistolarium* huyg003/0907):

> Pater meus ante paucos dies in Galliam profectus est, Arausionensis arcis restitutionem Principis nomine a Rege petiturus. Comitem habet fratrem Ludoicum qui non multo ante ex Hispania redierat. Rogas quid ibi rerum gesserit; atque ego pro illo tibi respondeo, in ea quidem re quam illi commendaveras aliquid egisse, sed minus quam optaverat. Varias lectiones aliquot ex optimo Ovidij manuscripto ac pervetusto descripsit, in quo frequenter easdem quoque emendationes quae a te proditae sunt se reperisse dicebat. In ijs quas collegit nullae sunt admodum magni momenti; sed nec multas colligere licuit, quod res non ferebat ut diutius in Bibliotheca regia moraretur. Caeterum incredibilem inscitiam socordiamque tum monachorum illorum qui in celeberrimo Escurialiensi Coenobio degunt, tantaque librorum optimorum copia potiuntur, tum omnium in universum Hispanorum, satis praedicare non poterat; quippe qui non tantum literas scientiasve non curent, sed nec quid in reliquo literarum orbe rerum geratur aut norint aut nosse laborent.

46 Scholten and Pelgrom, 'Scholarly Identity and Memory'.

47 See, e.g., Joseph Scaliger (Leiden) to Richard Thomson (1569–1613) (Cambridge), 26 December 1600: '…quando cloacae illae et colluvies monachorum sese in Europam effuderint, ut Loiolitae odie et Capuccini', in Scaliger, *Correspondence* 3, 551, ll. 12–13.

48 John Collins (1625–1683) (London) to Robert Moray (1608–1673) (London), February 1669 (Huygens, *OC* 6, no. 1709; *ePistolarium* huyg003/1709):

> Vpon ye whole, Monsieur Hugens seems blameable for beginning these comparisons, quasi ex animo vilipendendi, as appears from his reason rendred, why Gregory's quadrature of ye Hyperbola should not seem new to ye Royal Society; on the other side it were to be wisht, that Mister Gregory had been more mild with yt generous person, who hath deserv'd well of ye republick of Learning.

49 Gerardus Vossius (Amsterdam) to Grotius (Paris), 25 September 1639 (Grotius, *Briefwisseling* 10, no. 4310; *ePistolarium* groo001/4310):

> Facile credo hanc contentionem non parum detracturam nomini Heinsiano, sed partim eo me solor, quod nemo ignoret ipsum sibi hoc malum intrivisse, dum perpetuus est in traducendis omnibus, quorum praeclarum est in republica literaria nomen, partim ac imprimis isto, quod contentionis hujus bonum sperare liceat eventum. Sine dubio enim multa etiam doctissimos quosque docebit Salmasius et fortasse etiam Heinsius hinc discet modestius de se sentire caeterisque suis

laudibus hanc addet, ut ne tam credulus sit palpatoribus, qui eum phoenicis, dictatoris, Atlantis studiorum elogiis onerant verius quam honorant.

50 Janus Gruterus to Grotius, 13 April 1614 (Grotius, *Briefwisseling* 1, no. 325; *ePistolarium* groo001/o325): 'Ego quieti devotus, adhucdum versor in Cicerone Gulielmiano: cui si quid ingenio industriave adstruere potes, ut potes, da quaeso id quoque ceteris tuis in remp[ublicam] literariam meritis, ac nobiscum ocyus communica. Bona fide sub nomine tuo publicabitur, non sine honorifico, hoc est, debito tibi praeconio'.
51 Robert Boyle (1627–1691) (Oxford) to Robert Moray (London), December 1663 (Huygens, *OC* 4, no. 1193 *ePistolarium* huyg003/1193).
52 Constantijn Huygens (The Hague) to J.F. Gronovius (Leiden), 16 September 1670 (Huygens, *Briefwisseling* 6, no. 6769; *ePistolarium* huyg001/6769): 'A. Gellium, si inter membranas meas repertus fuisset, illico misissem; non fuisse, et reipublicae literariae et mea praecipue caussa doleo, quod hanc occasionem tibi, tanto amico, gratificandi occupare non contigerit'.
53 Marcus Zuerius Boxhorn, Marcus (Leiden) to Constantijn Huygens (The Hague), 12 July 1636 (Huygens, *Briefwisseling* 2, no. 1405; *ePistolarium* huyg001/1405):

> [Balsaci] *Herodem*, scilicet, *Infanticidam*, tragoediam, ut breviter hoc dicam, excitatam et coelestem, quam universus ordo litteratus cum stupore admirationis legit, praedicatque. ... Multa quippe ex ultima antiquitate, qua sacra, qua profana, singulari cum genio hic eruuntur, quae ne modestia authoris perirent, orbis literarii interesse existimabam.

54 For Heinsius's dubious character, see the most devastating character murder by a modern scholar ever committed of his early modern intellectual subject, viz. Ter Horst's 1934 dissertation *Daniel Heinsius*.
55 Grotius (Rotterdam) to Isaac Casaubon (London), 20 April 1614 (Grotius, *Briefwisseling* 1, no. 329; *ePistolarium* groo001/0329):

> Siquid, vir citra comparationem doctissime, meae in te reverentiae, quae summa est, tribuendum putas, siqua in re testari cupis amorem, quo omnes non literatos modo sed et literarum amatores prosequeris, unum hoc beneficium ne mihi deneges oro te atque obtestor.

On the contexts, see Hardy, *Criticism and Confession*, 94–100.
56 Willem de Groot (The Hague) to Grotius (Paris), 19 January 1643 (Grotius, *Briefwisseling* 14, no. 6045; *ePistolarium* groo001/6045):

> De iis quae ad Rivetum notasti cogitabo, sed id si solum prodiret, vereor ne et tu deridiculo futurus sis ob nimiam brevitatem. Florum sparsionem tuam magna ex parte legi, et volupe mihi fuit videre aliorum scriptorum cum iurisconsultis consonantiam in arte aequi et boni. Correctionibus vero tuis, paucis quidem illis sed insignibus, ut accedam, non suades, sed cogis. Liber iste apud omnes eruditos et politioris litteraturae amantes semper fiet maximi, quare dolet exempla tua nondum comparere.

57 Willem de Groot (1597–1662) (The Hague) to Grotius (Paris), 8 July 1639 (Grotius, *Briefwisseling* 10, no. 4194; *ePistolarium* groo001/4194):

> [J.A. Corvinus] vir optimus, jam laborat in pertexendis juris Erotematis, quorum ego jam partem aliquam in formam manualis vidi impressam. Scio id opus a te expectari nimisque jam diu suppressum ut et alia ejus viri scripta magno cum reipublicae litterariae incommodo.

58 Ismael Boulliau (Paris) to Nicolaas Heinsius (The Hague), 30 July 1660 (Huygens, *OC* 3, 508, no. 762A; *ePistolarium* huyg003/0762a):

> Illustrissimos Viros Petrum et Jacobum Puteanos sine Laudum titulis mihi nunquam nominandos in concedenda Historiae Concilii Florentini e Regio codice

transcriptione minus faciles ac indulgentes optassem; illam enim vulgari, et publici juris fieri nec Regni, nec Reipublicae Literariae multum intererat. tantas tamen turbas inde excitandas non praevideo; neque ad Leonis Allatii revincendam erroneam assertionem illa historia opus erat, aut unquam erit.

59 Geradus Vossius (Amsterdam) to Grotius (Hamburg), 5 April 1634 (Grotius, *Briefwisseling* 5, no. 1923; *ePistolarium* groo001/1923): 'Juvenis est eximiae probitatis literarumque cultor literatorumque omnium amantissimus, tui imprimis nominis et cultor et admirator'.

60 Grotius (Paris) to Meric Casaubon (Canterbury), 19 March 1639 (Grotius, *Briefwisseling* 10, no. 4025; *ePistolarium* groo001/4025):

Ego qui te norim ea esse bonitate, ut omnes literatos demerendi occasiones non arripias tantum oblatas, sed et quaeras ultro, facturum me putavi, quod utrique debeo, si te ipsi [Justo Richewartio] notum cum virtutibus tuis facerem, ipsum autem tibi commendarem.

61 René François de Sluse (Liège) to Christiaan Huygens (The Hague), 26 December 1664 (Huygens, *OC* 5, no. 1292 *ePistolarium* huyg003/1292):

Cometae aspectum qualem optarem, tum aedes vicinae, tum vel maxime pluuium illud et turbidum coelum hactenus mihi inuident. Ex Lovaniensium relatione intellexi, cum nuper inter Craterem et Coruum obseruatus est, totos octodecim gradus cauda subtendisse. Certiora tu orbi literato propones si coelo clementiore vsus es, aut nostri saltem Romani obseruatores, qui accuratis illis telescopijs ipsam etiam fortassis cometae materiam scrutari poterunt.

62 Christiaan Huygens (The Hague), 8 October 1687 to (Gottfried Wilhelm Leibniz [1646–1716]) (Huygens, *OC* 9, no. 2489 *ePistolarium* huyg003/2489): 'Solution du Probleme proposè par M. Leibnitz dans les nouvelles de la Republique des Lettres du Mois de Septembre 1687'. Leibniz (Hannover) to Christiaan Huygens (The Hague), January 1688 (Huygens, *OC* 9, no. 2512 *ePistolarium* huyg003/2512): 'vostre figure dans les Nouvelles de la republique des lettres mois d'octobre 1687'. Christiaan Huygens (The Hague) to (Leibniz), September 1690 (Huygens, *OC* 9, no. 2490 ePistolarium huyg003/2490): 'Problema propositum a D[omino] Leibnitz in diario Eruditorum (*Nouvelles de la République des Lettres*) mensis Sept. 1687'.

63 Henri Justel (London) to Christiaan Huygens (The Hague), 19 May 1690: (Huygens, *OC* 9, no. 2593 *ePistolarium* huyg003/2593): 'il ny a aucune nouuelle considerable dans la Republique des lettres, quoy qu'on ne m'ecriue plus de Paris, i'ay sceu qu'on ny faisoit rien. on ny uoit que de mechans petits liures qui ne meritent pas d'estre leus'.

64 Leeuwenhoek (Delft) to the Royal Society (London), 9 June 1699 (Leeuwenhoek, *Alle de Brieven* 12, no. 200; *ePistolarium* leeu027/0200):

Tis sulks, dat seker Doctor Medicine mij ter hand stelt een Boekje genaamt *Nouvelles de la Republique*, en toonende mij daar in op het 552. bladzijde, een extract int Latijn uijt een Brief geschreven vande Heer Dalepatius, aan de schrijver vande *Nouvelle de la Republique*.

This Dalepatius (astonomer François de Plantade [1670–1741]) is quoted (accurately) as 'having wanted, in the meantime, to make this public for the Learned World to say what they feel about it' ('Ondertusschen hebben wij dit willen gemeen maken, op dat de geleerde werelt uijten zoude, wat zij hier van gevoelen'). For the source, see Dalenpatius, 'Article V, Extrait d'une Lettre', 554: 'Interim haec vulgari voluimus, ut Eruditis, quid hac in re sentiant edere velint'.

65 Bayle, 'Preface' [March 1784], printed in: Bots and De Vet, *Stratégies journalistiques*, 11–12.

66 Bots, *De Republiek der Letteren*, 138.

67 Voltaire, *Siècle de Louis XIV* 6, 43–44, lines 194–208.
68 Fumaroli, *République des lettres*, 294–297.
69 Henrick Bruno (The Hague) to Constantijn Huygens (Philippine), 11 July 1639 (Huygens, *OC* 1, 542–543, no. 1c *ePistolarium* huyg003/0001c): 'Prosodiae nuper supremum vale diximus, quod expeditos satis in recitandis regulis, ac usu caetera jugique exercitatione comparanda, cum omni, nî fallor, republica litteraria, existumarem'.
70 Ismaël Boulliau (Paris) to Leopoldo de Medici (Firenze), 19 December 1659 (Huygens, *OC* 2, no. 697; *ePistolarium* huyg003/0697):

> Quoniam iniecta mihi est a Serenissima Celsitudine Tua mentio de nuper defuncto in Poloniae Regis Aula Paulo de Bono, luctum de illo amisso comprimere meum hic nequeo. Ingenio enim in mathematicis, ac praecipue in mechanicis valebat, moribusque probis ac honestis praeditus erat; sique diutius in vivis egisset, plura proculdubio praestiturus. De Republica litteraria, ac philosophica, quam animo conceperat, quamque statuere cogitabat, aliquid intellexi. Excelsae quidem mentis, & ad magna viri nati propositum erat; sed hisce temporibus sedes inter Europaeos quaerere non debebat, cum omnibus in regnis & rebuspublicis orbis nostri nulla societas iniri queat, quae suspecta dominantibus non sit.

71 Stanislaus Lubienietzki (Hamburg) to Christiaan Huygens (The Hague), 30 October 1665 (Lubienietzki, *Theatri Cometici pars prior*, 931 Huygens, *OC* 5, no. 1490 *ePistolarium* huyg003/1490):

> Postquam multos Praestantissimos omni eruditione et laudis genere Viros, Rautensteinium, Brussellum, Guerichios, Hevelium, Bullialdum, Bartholinos, Kircherum, Ricciolum, Curtium, Schottum, aliosque, quos enumerare longum foret, sed & Tuum juxtaque meum Heinsium, scripto conveni, Te quoque convento opus fuit. Non sunt mihi, puto, hujus facinoris operose apud Te quaerenda praesidia, qui quibus legibus in Republica literaria vivatur, optime, si quisquam alius, nosti. Senatum voco Philosophicum, nullo meo merito, a sola Regina bonarum mentium Libertate Reipublicae literariae Studiosissima, Consul creatus.

72 I thank Manuel Llano Martínez for his reflections on the notion of a 'theatre'.
73 Decembrio, *De politia litteraria*; Erasmus, *Antibarbarorum liber*.
Donatus's *Pro impetrando ad rempub[licam] litterariam aditu* gave grammatical lessons, not reflections on conduct or the scholarly community's history.
74 Damian Çavall, *Oratio parenetica de optimo statu reipublicae constituendo*, translated by Helena Raussell Guillot as *Discurso exhortativo sobre la consecución del mejor estado de la República Literaria*. Note that the original title speaks of 'Respublica' only. See also Rausell Guillot, 'Oratoria y clasicismo'.
75 Schellhammer, *Threni cum Epitaphio super Obitum ... Pauli Sperlingii ... de ... universa Republica literaria meritissimi*.
76 Zschoche, *Memoriae semper-vivae viri incomparibilis deque Republica Literaria immortaliter meriti ... Iacobi Thomasii*; Hoffman, *Honori et memoriae ... viri, de Ecclesia Christi et Republica Literaria universa immortaliter meriti ... Valentini Alberti*.
77 Heideggerus, *De ratione studiorum opuscula aurea virorum de Ecclesia Christiana & Republica literaria meritissimorum, Henrici Bullingeri, Desid. Erasmi, Lud. Vivis, Jac. Breitingeri, Fr. Junii*.
78 Hannemannus, *Quatuor epistolarum fasciculus ad quatuor perillustres, excellentissimos et amplissimos in Republica Literaria primates*.
79 Hannemannus, *Sciagraphia*, sig. A2v: 'Vivimus enim iam tali seculo, quo Respublica Literaria maximum incrementum capit. Coeunt enim iam laudabili instituto ad agendam rem literariam integrae gentes, et Collegia Societasque erigunt, quae naturam hominemque summo scrutantur studio'.
80 See the delightful monograph by Kivistö, *The Vices of Learning*.
81 Romanus, *Dissertatio academica de republica litteraria*.

82 Muratori, *Primi disegni della republica letteraria d'Italia*, 178–179. For the broader context of Muratori's project to create an Italian republic of letters, see Generali, 'Repubblica delle lettere fra censura e libero pensiero'.
83 Heumannus, *Conspectus reipublicae literariae*, Hannover: N. Foerster, 1718; 2nd. ed. ibid., N. Foerster et fil., 1726; 3rd ed. ibid., J.J. Foerster, 1733; 4th ed. ibid., Heredes N. Foerster et filii, 1735; 5th ed., item, 1740; and again 1746; 6th ed., item, 1753; 7th Ed., item, 1763; 8th ed. by J.N. Eyring, Hanover, Fratres Helweghi, 1791. Note that the fifth edition appeared twice, in 1740 and 1746. I have used the third edition of 1733.
84 Siraisi and Pomata, *Historia: Empiricism and Erudition in Early Modern Europe*; Van Miert, *Communicating Observations*.
85 Schneiderus, *Oratio solemnis de forma reipublicae litterariae. Von der besten Art zu regieren in der Republic der Gelehrten.*

References

Austin, J.L. *How to Do Things with Words. The William James Lectures Delivered at Harvard University in 1955.* Ed. Urmson. Oxford: The Clarendon Press, 1962.
Barlaeus, Caspar. *Epistolarum liber. Pars prior et pars posterior.* Amsterdam: Joannes Blaeu, 1667.
Bots, Hans. *De Republiek der Letteren. De Europese intellectuele wereld, 1500–1670.* Nijmegen: Vantilt, 2016.
Bots, Hans; Vet, Jan. *Stratégies journalistiques de l'ancien régime.* Amsterdam and Utrecht: APA-Holland University Press, 2002.
Dalenpatius, Franciscus [François de Plantade]. 'Article V, Extrait d'une Lettre.' *Nouvelles de la République des Lettres* (Mai 1699): 552–555.
Damian Çavall, Cosme. *Oratio parenetica de optimo statu reipublicae constituendo.* Valencia: Francisco Díaz Romano, 1531. Translated as: *Discurso exhortativo sobre la consecución del mejor estado de la República Literaria.* Translated by Helena Rausell Guillot. Orihuela: Ayuntamiento de Orihuela, Concejalía de Cultura, 2013.
Decembrio, Angelo. *De politia litteraria.* Augsburg: Henricus Steynerus, 1540.
Donatus, Aelius. *Pro impetrando ad rempub. litterariam aditu: novitijs adolescentibus grammatices rudimenta quam aptissime dedicate.* Venice: per Theodorum de Ragazonibus, 1489.
ePistolarium. 'Corpus Metadata.' At: http://ckcc.huygens.knaw.nl/?page_id=43.
Erasmus, Desiderius. *Antibarbarorum liber unus, quem iuvenis adhuc lusit.* Basel: Ioannes Frobenius, 1520.
Fumaroli, Marc. *La République des Lettres.* Paris: Gallimard, 2015.
Generali, Dario. 'Repubblica delle lettere fra censura e libero pensiero. La communicazione epistolare filosofica-scientifica nell'Italia fra Sei e Settecento.' *Intersezioni* 6 (1983): 73–94.
Grotius, Hugo. *Briefwisseling van Hugo Grotius.* 17 vols. Eds. Molhuysen, P.C.; Meulenbroek, B.L.; Witkam, Paula P.; Nellen, Henk J.M.; Ridderikhoff, Cornelia M. The Hague: Martinus Nijhoff & Instituut voor Nederlandse Geschiedenis, 1928–2001.
Hannemannus, Johannes Ludovicus. *Quatuor epistolarum fasciculus ad quatuor perillustres, excellentissimos et amplissimos in Republica Literaria primates.* Hamburg: Köning, 1694.
Hannemannus, Johannes Ludovicus. *Sciagraphia, Thaumatographiae curiosae microcosmi physico-medico-theologico-historicae.* Ed. Hannemann, J.C.F.R. 1694.
Hardy, Nicholas. *Criticism and Confession. The Bible in the Seventeenth-Century Republic of Letters.* Oxford: Oxford University Press, 2017.

Heideggerus, Johannes Henricus ed. *De ratione studiorum opuscula aurea virorum de Ecclesia Christiana & Republica literaria meritissimorum, Henrici Bullingeri, Desid. Erasmi, Lud. Vivis, Jac. Breitingeri, Fr. Junii.* Zurich: Schaufelbergius, 1670.

Heumann, Christophorus Augustus. *Conspectus reipublicae literariae sive Via ad Historiam literariam iuventuti studiosae aperta.* Hannover: N. Foerster, 1718.

Hoffman, Gottfried. *Honori et memoriae theologi et philosophi consummatissimi viri, de Ecclesia Christi et Republica Literaria universa immortaliter meriti D[omi[n[i] D. Valentini Alberti, professoris apud Lipsienses publici et per orbem celeberrimi, paulo post obitum eius anno MDCXCVII, d[ie] 7 Novembr[is] ultimum debiti cultus officium in actu parentali, multorum de se meritorum memor praestabit Lyceum Laubanense.* Lauban, [1697].

Horst, Daniel ter. *Daniel Heinsius.* Utrecht: Hoeijenbos & Co N. V., 1934.

Huygens, Christiaan. *Oeuvres complètes de Christiaan Huygens.* 22 vols. Eds. Bierens de Haan, D.; Bosscha jr, Johannes; Korteweg, D.J.; Nijland, A.A.; Vollgraff, J.A. The Hague: Martinus Nijhoff, 1888–1950.

Huygens, Constantijn. *De briefwisseling van Constantijn Huygens.* 6 vols. Ed. Worp, J.A. The Hague: Martinus Nijhoff, 1911–1917.

Jorink, Eric. *Reading the Book of Nature in the Dutch Golden Age, 1575–1715.* Leiden and Boston, MA: Brill, 2010.

Kivistö, Sari. *The Vices of Learning. Morality and Learning at Early Modern Universities.* Leiden and Boston, MA: Brill, 2014.

Leeuwenhoek, Antonie van. *Alle de brieven van Antoni Leeuwenhoek.* Vol. 1–13. Edited, illustrated and annotated by a committee of Dutch scientists (C.G. Heringa, A. Schierbeek, J.J. Swart, J. Heniger, Gérard van Rijnberk and Lodewijk Palm). Amsterdam: Swets & Zeitlinger, 1939–1994.

Lubienietzki, Stanislaus. *Theatri Cometici pars prior. Communicationes de cometis 1664 et 1665 cum viris per Europam cl[arissimis] habitas, eorum observationes easque accuratissimis tabulis aeneis expressas continens.* Amsterdam: Franciscus Cuyperus, 1667.

Miert, Dirk van ed. *Communicating Observations in Early Modern Letters (1500–1675): Epistolography and Epistemology in the Age of the Scientific Revolution.* London and Turin: The Warburg Institute/Nino Aragno Editore, 2013.

Miert, Dirk van; Hotson, Howard; Wallnig, Thomas. 'What Was the Republic of Letters?' In Hotson, Howard; Wallnig, Thomas eds. *Reassembling the Republic of Letters: Systems, Standards, Scholarship.* Göttingen: Göttingen University Press, 2019, pp. 23–40.

More, Henry. 'Epistolae quatuor ad Renatum Des-Cartes.' In Id. *Opera omnia, 2 (Scriptorum philosophicorum tomus alter, qui suam variorum scriptorum philosophicorum collectionem primitus dictam complectitur.* London: typis R. Norton, impensis J. Martyn & Gualt. Kettilby, 1679, pp. 227–271.

Muratori, Ludovico (as Lamindo Pritanio). *Primi disegni della republica letteraria d'Italia.* Naples, 1703 [actually Venice, 1704]). In Muratori, Ludovico. *Opere.* Ed. Falco, Giorgio; Forti, Fiorenzo. Milan: Ricciardi, 1964.

Nellen, Henk. *Hugo Grotius. A Lifelong Struggle for Peace in Church and State, 1583–1645.* Leiden and Boston, MA: Brill, 2015.

Peeters, Carel. 'De Republiek der Letteren is van iedereen die denkt, leest en schrijft', review of Bots, *De republiek der Letteren* in *Vrij Nederland*, 6 March 2018. https://www.vn.nl/republiek-der-letteren/.

Rausell Guillot, Helen. 'Oratoria y clasicismo: un discurso valenciano del siglo XVI en sus fuentes clásicas.' *Revista de Historia Moderna* 24 (2006): 439–458.

Romanus, Carolus Fridericus. *Dissertatio academica de republica litteraria: quam indultu amplissimae facultatis philosophicae in Academia Philuraea sub praesidio Jo. Georgiii Pritii ... publice defensurus est.* Leipzig: Typis Gözianis, 1698.

Scaliger, Joseph. *The Correspondence of Joseph Justus Scaliger.* 8 vols. Ed. Botley, Paul; van Miert, Dirk. Geneva: Droz, 2012.

Schellhammer, Christopher. *Threni cum Epitaphio super Obitum Clarissimi Viri, Dn. M. Pauli Sperlingii, Senioris. Senis septuagenarii honoratissimi, Rectoris de Schola Hamburgensi adeoq[ue] universa Republica literaria meritissimi.* Hamburg: Venus, 1633.

Schneiderus, Ioannes Fridemannus. *Oratio solemnis de forma reipublicae litterariae. Von der besten Art zu regieren in der Republic der Gelehrten, illo tempore quo pro-rectoris munere altera vice exantlato, se abdicavit in Regia Academia Fridericiana.* Halle: sumtu Hendeliano, 1727.

Scholten, Koen; Pelgrom, Asker. 'Scholarly Identity and Memory on a Grand Tour: The Travels of Joannes Kool and His Travel Journal (1698–1699) to Italy.' *Lias* 46, no. 1 (2019): 93–136.

Siraisi, Nancy G.; Pomata, Gianni eds. *Historia: Empiricism and Erudition in Early Modern Europe.* Cambridge: MIT Press, 2005.

Trivellato, Francesca. 'A Republic of Merchants?' In Molho, Anthony; Ramada Curto, Diogo; Koniordos, Niki eds. *Finding Europe: Discourses on Margins, Communities, Images, ca. 13th – ca. 18th Centuries.* Oxford: Berghahn Books, 2007, pp. 133–158.

Voltaire. *Siècle de Louis XIV.* Tome 6. Ed. Venturino, Diego, with Cronk, Nicholas (*Les Oeuvres complètes de Voltaire*, 13D). Oxford: Voltaire Foundation, 2016.

Zschoche, Christian. *Memoriae semper-vivae viri incomparibilis deque Republica Literaria immortaliter meriti ... Iacobi Thomasii, ... solenni exequiarum die XIIX. Cal. Octob. A[nno] ae[tatis]. Dionys[iacae] M.DCLXXXIV exiguum hoc monumentum erigit ex iure pristini sodalitii moerentibus commoerens Collegium Concionatorium Magnum.* Leipzig: typis Christophori Fleischeri, 1684.

INDEX

acceptable knowledge 9, 31, 32–34, 44, 150–151, 180–185
accuracy 7, 9–10, 46, 47, 51, 75–76, 79–83, 97, 101–102, 140, 169–170, 175–177, 180–185

censorship 82–83, 193–195, 203–204
censura 6–7, 11, 24–28, 34–35, 45–46, 59–60, 78–79
circulation of knowledge 3–5, 74–75, 193–194; *see also* transfer of knowledge
codification of knowledge 2, 8–10, 24, 47–49, 71–72, 81–84, 99–102, 108–112, 152–156, 211–212, 223–227

dangerous knowledge 7, 9, 31–32, 44–60, 194–196
disciplining 8–10, 26, 34, 49–52, 73–75, 134, 152–153, 194–197, 220–223

emotion 46, 47–48, 59–60
expedition *see* travel

Holy Office 6, 9–12, 23–24, 32–34, 78–79, 81–84, 194–196, 202–204

imagination 52, 60, 169–170
Index 7, 12, 23–24, 27–28, 32–34, 78–79, 194–196, 198–199, 203–204
Inquisition *see* Holy Office
institution 5–6, 9, 10–12, 84, 152, 160–161, 193–194, 212–213, 223

instructing 8–10, 48–49, 72–73, 109–112, 129–132, 133–137, 137–140, 155–158, 195–196

journey *see* travel

labelling 4, 7–9, 33, 48–50, 196–198, 220–223
letters 10–11, 27–28, 46, 53–55, 57–58, 94–95, 97–99, 113–115, 134, 136–137, 149–151, 154–156, 197–198, 211–212, 214–216
linguistic knowledge 4, 7, 10, 71–84, 94–95, 99–100, 175, 211, 214

manual 8–10, 28–31, 74–75, 107–120, 200
Morgan, Mary 4–5, 129–130

news 1, 10, 48–49, 92–103, 108–109, 150–151, 219, 223–225

public sphere 10, 25, 94, 99, 180–185, 196, 212–213

regulating 5–6, 7–10, 34–35, 59–60, 75–78, 95–96, 99, 109–111, 129–131, 150–151, 156–158, 161, 193–194, 227
reliable knowledge 4–6, 33, 46, 72–73, 82, 94, 98, 113–115, 180–181
religious knowledge 1, 23–24, 32–33, 46, 47–48, 53–59, 71–74, 75–77, 140, 194–196, 211

Renswoude, Irene van 6, 48
Republic of Letters 9–12, 34–35, 45–46, 169–170, 185–186, 193–194, 204, 211–227
rule *see* regulating

secret knowledge 8–9, 33–34, 130–132, 138–141, 149–161
standardization 10, 27–28, 76–77, 92–93, 99–100, 119–120, 135–137, 152–153

transfer of knowledge 3–5, 7–10, 74–77, 119–120, 129–134, 137–138, 150–151, 156–158, 158–160

translation 4, 7, 46, 51–52, 56–57, 73–74, 76–77, 82–83, 111–112, 112–115, 171–73, 223–224
travel 3–4, 46–47, 59–60, 98–99, 129–131, 149–151, 170–176

unreliable knowledge *see* reliable knowledge
useful knowledge 6, 28–31, 75–79, 107–108, 117–119, 131–133

validating 7–9, 71–72, 79–83, 94–95, 113, 139–140, 154–156, 180–184, 196–198

Printed in the USA
CPSIA information can be obtained
at www.ICGtesting.com
LVHW021959130124
768851LV00005B/533